PUSHING THE MARGINS

This book is number three in the Series on Critical Race Studies and Multiculturalism in LIS, Rose L. Chou and Annie Pho, series editors.

PUSHING THE MARGINS: WOMEN OF COLOR AND INTERSECTIONALITY IN LIS

Rose L. Chou and Annie Pho
Editors

LIBRARY JUICE PRESS
SACRAMENTO, CA

Published in 2018 by Library Juice Press

Library Juice Press
PO Box 188784
Sacramento, CA 95822

http://libraryjuicepress.com/

Front cover design by Grace Danico.

Library of Congress Cataloging-in-Publication Data

Names: Chou, Rose L., editor. | Pho, Annie, editor.
Title: Pushing the margins : women of color and intersectionality in LIS / Rose L. Chou and Annie Pho, editors.
Description: Sacramento, CA : Library Juice Press, [2018] | Series: Series on critical race studies and multiculturalism in LIS ; no. 3 | Includes bibliographical references and index.
Identifiers: LCCN 2018027564 | ISBN 9781634000529 (alk. paper)
Subjects: LCSH: Minority women librarians--United States. | Minorities in library science--United States. | Women in library science--United States. | Intersectionality (Sociology)
Classification: LCC Z682.4.M56 P87 2018 | DDC 020.820973--dc23
LC record available at

Contents

Acknowledgements - *Rose L. Chou and Annie Pho* ix

Foreword - *Fobazi Ettarh* xiii

Introduction - *Rose L. Chou and Annie Pho* 1

Chapter 1. "When I Enter": Black Women and Disruption of the White, Heteronormative Narrative of Librarianship - *Caitlin M. J. Pollock and Shelley P. Haley* 15

Chapter 2. Sisters of the Stacks - *Alexsandra Mitchell* 61

Chapter 3. I Am a Muslim, a Woman, a Librarian: Muslim Women and Public Libraries - *Negeen Aghassibake* 77

Chapter 4. The Other Asian: Reflections of South Asian Americans in Libraryland - *Nisha Mody, Lalitha Nataraj, Gayatri Singh, and Aditi Worcester* 93

Chapter 5. I AM My Hair, and My Hair Is Me: #BlackGirlMagic in LIS - *Teresa Y. Neely* 121

Chapter 6. The Voice of a Black Woman in Libraryland: A Theoretical Narrative - *LaVerne Gray* 147

Chapter 7. A Woman of Color's Work Is Never Done: Intersectionality, Emotional, and Invisible Labor in Reference and Information Work - *Kawanna Bright* 163

Chapter 8. "Sister, You've Been on My Mind": Experiences of Women of Color in the Library and Information Science Profession - *Alyse Minter and Genevia M. Chamblee-Smith* 197

Chapter 9. Small Brown Faces in Large White Spaces - *Rosalinda Hernandez Linares and Sojourna J. Cunningham* 253

Chapter 10. I, Too: Unmasking Emotional Labor of Women of Color Community College Librarians - Alyssa Jocson Porter, Sharon Spence-Wilcox, and Kimberly Tate-Malone 273

Chapter 11. The Burden of Care: Cultural Taxation of Women of Color Librarians on the Tenure-Track - *Tarida Anantachai and Camille Chesley* 301

Chapter 12. Authenticity vs. Professionalism: Being True to Ourselves at Work - *Jennifer Brown and Sofia Leung* 329

Chapter 13. Identity, Activism, Self-Care, and Women of Color Librarians - *Alanna Aiko Moore and Jan E. Estrellado* 349

Chapter 14. When Will My Reflection Show?: Women of Color in the Kennesaw State University Archives - *JoyEllen Freeman* 391

Chapter 15. Selection and Self-Identity - *Robin Bradford and Stephanie Sendaula* 415

Chapter 16. Reflections on the Intersection of Publishing and Librarianship: The Experiences of Women of Color - *Charlotte Roh* 427

Chapter 17. Positionality, Epistemology, and New Paradigms for LIS: A Critical Dialogue with Clara M. Chu - *Todd Honma and Clara M. Chu* 447

About the Contributors 467

Index 481

Acknowledgements

Rose L. Chou and Annie Pho

Without our community, this book would not exist, and we want to acknowledge the many people who have helped us get here. We pursued this project in order to give back to them, because this book is for our communities.

Our peer communities in LIS have truly helped sustain and support us throughout graduate school and our careers. Not only have they provided us with professional guidance, but we have formed genuine friendships outside of LIS work as well. For all the Hackers in Hack Library School, thank you for trying to improve an education system that is hard to change. For the LIS Microaggressions collective, thank you for providing a space for library and information workers to vent and share the egregious microaggressions that they face in the workplace, and for creating a community so that people know that they aren't alone in their experiences. For the Minnesota Institute for Early Career Librarians 2014 cohort, we're grateful for the real talk about our jobs and careers, learning about navigating predominantly white spaces in libraries, and the many happy hours at Applebee's. We'll forever be grateful for our friendships that were forged over that week in Minneapolis.

The idea for this book was rooted in our initial research project, *Intersectionality at the Reference Desk: Lived Experiences of Women of Color Librarians*. We cannot thank enough the women of color who so honestly shared their stories and experiences with us. We hoped to honor and elevate their voices, and also to show that these narratives are worthy of a book and then some. Special thanks to Lucy Gonzalez and Shoma Webster for their time and patience in transcribing interviews, and to Dr. Paula Dempsey who patiently provided guidance and advice on feminist research methodologies and data collection. We are also indebted to Maria T. Accardi, who edited our book chapter and selected our project to be included in *The Feminist Reference Desk: Concepts, Critiques, and Conversations.* Her support and feedback were crucial to getting these narratives out into the world.

Pushing the Margins would not exist without all the hard work, research, and writing of all our contributors. It is really their voices and their ideas that we want to raise and center in this book. We'd like to express deep gratitude to all the individuals who reviewed chapters and provided thoughtful feedback for our authors. Thank you to Fobazi Ettarh, who has been supportive of our work since our initial research project, for giving the keynote address at our Symposium and writing our foreword.

We are also grateful to Rory Litwin and Alison Lewis of Library Juice Press for supporting not only this book, but also the Pushing the Margins Symposium that we organized in July 2017. The Symposium was made possible through funding from the UCLA Library and through collaboration with the California Academic & Research Libraries' (CARL) Diversity in Academic Libraries (DIAL) interest group. Thank you to Laura Gamez for helping with so many of the details for this event and for filming the keynote, Suzy Lee for coordinating logistics of the space, and our day-of volunteers: T-Kay Sangwand, Temo Moncada, Julia Glassman, Tamara Rhodes, and Jennifer Thompson.

We would also like to thank our work institutions—American University Library and UCLA Library—for supporting us as we spent our time and energy on this book. It's a privilege to be able to take time to read, write, and think about LIS in this space, and we are grateful to have positions that allow for us to do this kind of work.

To Casey, who has always supported these writing projects, lent an ear to ideas that were half-fleshed out, and been willing to serve as a copy-editor. Much love and gratitude to you.

To Lloyd, you have always been a true partner. Thank you for your encouragement, understanding, writing finesse, and humor--not only with this project, but throughout the past eleven years.

To our families, both of us would not be here if it were not for the courage, determination, and hope of our immigrant parents who persevered through wars and extreme hardship, and left their lives in Southeast Asia in pursuit of providing their children with a better, more stable life. Refugee trauma and cultural dissonance have not always made our relationships with our parents easy, but we can't imagine the sacrifices that they have made for us. And to them, we want to express our deep love and recognition for everything that they have given us.

Most of all, we would like to acknowledge and thank the women of color who work in libraries, and other librarians who feel like they exist in the margins. We want you to know that we see you, we hear you, and we dedicate this book to you. This book project is a step towards pushing back from the margins and into the center.

Foreword

Fobazi Ettarh

Women of color are the foundation for the concept of intersectionality. Kimberlé Crenshaw first used the term "intersectionality" in a paper to shed light on how single-axis analysis of antidiscrimination doctrine, feminist theory, and antiracist politics erase the realities of those who exist along multiple axes of identity and discrimination.[1] Since then, the concept of intersectionality has been expanded to the point of meaninglessness. White people love intersectionality ("I'm white, *but* I grew up working class," is a common refrain.). They love it because it allows them to co-opt rhetoric around marginalization. Intersectionality becomes a catch-all phrase to describe anything that makes their life uncomfortable and amplifies the discomfort to marginalization, while ignoring all of the very real social, cultural, and political systems that positively influence their life. Like conversations about anti-racism, conversations about intersectionality stop at awareness, a tactic that privileges interpersonal relationships rather than systemic power structures. When Kimberlé Crenshaw wrote "Mapping the Margins: Intersectionality, Identity Politics, and Violence against Women of Color," she defined intersectionality as "the need to account for multiple grounds of identity

1. Kimberlé Williams Crenshaw, "Demarginalizing the Intersection of Race and Sex: A Black Feminist Critique of Antidiscrimination Doctrine, Feminist Theory and Antiracist Politics," *University of Chicago Legal Forum* 1, no. 8 (1989).

when considering how the social world is constructed."[2] Intersectionality theory focuses, then, on describing phenomena such as the discrimination that women of color receive (as both women and people of color). In addition, the theory describes the inadequacy of the tools (feminist and anti-racist praxis) being used to remedy the overlapping discrimination. However, when people only use intersectionality to reach toward the highest rung of a ladder of oppression, it becomes a blunted tool. Instead, the term is flung outward as a means to deflect and silence the nuanced discussions around power and systems it was originally created for.

So, what is intersectionality? Crenshaw described it as the ways matrices of identity intersect to shape structural, political, and representational experiences of people, specifically women of color (WOC). Intersectionality, she argues, manifests in three forms: structural, political, and representational. Structural intersectionality focuses on how the societal systems in which people live or the social categories to which people belong intersect to oppress or influence experiences and discourses. As I write this, the #metoo movement is dominating the conversation. The movement was originally created by activist Tarana Burke, a Black woman, as a grassroots effort to reach sexual assault survivors in underprivileged communities. However, it took the public testimony of numerous wealthy white women with a lot of social capital for the conversation about the ubiquitousness of sexual violence against women to gain the cultural heft it now has. This is not to say the conversations occurring aren't both pertinent and empowering, but they ignore the social, cultural, and legal structures surrounding race, gender, and class.

Political intersectionality focuses on how movements working towards justice interact to exclude or marginalize the interests of some subset of the groups, or reinforces another form of injustice. For example, feminist movements and anti-racist movements throughout history have often pursued conflicting political agendas. Indeed, renowned suffragette

2. Kimberlé Williams Crenshaw, "Mapping the Margins: Intersectionality, Identity Politics, and Violence against Women of Color," *Stanford Law Review* 43, no. 6 (1991): 1241.

Susan B. Anthony declared at the Equal Rights Convention of 1866, "I will cut off this right arm of mine before I will ever work or demand the ballot for the Negro and not the woman."[3] And notably, her statement was made in response to Frederick Douglass saying that Black male suffrage was "vital," while women's suffrage merely "desirable."[4] The need to split one's political energies between two sometimes opposing groups is a prime example of intersectional disempowerment for those who exist in multiple social groups.

Finally, representational intersectionality, also known as cultural intersectionality, focuses on how images or tropes within literature and mass media are taken to be representative of the group, which then ignores or distorts the complexity of the group. For example, early representations of feminism as concerned with the exploitation and isolation of the "housewife" occluded the fact that women of color and working-class women are rarely, on the whole, solely stay-at-home wives and mothers. And the current feminist rejection of girls as princesses simultaneously ignores how rare it has been for women of color (and particularly Black women) to be represented as vulnerable and worthy of being treasured. Many cultural representations of Black women still characterize them as sexless sources of unending strength and caretaking (the Strong Black Woman, the Independent Woman, the Matriarch, the Mammy), or as irrational and angry (the Angry Black Woman). Even Tiana, the first Black Disney princess, spent most of the movie as a caretaker or someone working tirelessly. It could be argued that cultural productions of Black women as princesses (vulnerable, treasured, capable of love and romance) are needed more, not less. When the experiences of white women are taken as representative of *all* women, the complexities of those who inhabit multiple identities are ignored. This is true just as much in library and information science (LIS) as it is in a Disney cartoon.

---

3. Elizabeth Cady Stanton, Susan B. Anthony, Matilda Joslyn Gage, and Ida Husted Harper (eds.), *History of Woman Suffrage, Volume II* (1861-1876), 152-163.

4. Ibid.

It has been four years since I wrote "Black OR Queer? Life at the Intersection" for *Hack Library School*.[5] I was in the process of getting my MLIS degree at Rutgers University, and like many of the women in this book, librarianship did not encourage (or even allow) me to embrace my whole self. On a campus surrounded by people of color, my program was entrenched in overwhelming white heteronormativity. I was surrounded by those who denied my Blackness, my queerness, my entire identity, at every turn. Or, librarians accepted the parts of me with which they felt most comfortable, while denying the rest. Often this manifested as colleagues who embraced my queerness, but continually committed numerous racial microaggressions and outright discrimination. Speaking about intersectionality gave me the language to reclaim my identity and power, while also practicing self-care. And once I began, I was unable to stop. I certainly was not the first librarian to speak about how important it is to acknowledge the complex identities of librarians of color, and especially women of color, but I hadn't seen others using intersectionality as a theoretical framework in the larger library discourse. So, I spoke at conferences on the local, regional, and national scale. And the more I talked, the more librarians of color, and especially women of color, reached out and shared their stories. Like the majority of the authors in this book, and the participants in their studies, intersectionality became for me a theoretical lens to articulate the complexity of my identity, and a way to assuage racial fatigue and pain. These shared experiences created a community and a necessary force that sustained me in the profession and culminated in my first peer-reviewed article, "Making a New Table: Intersectional Librarianship."[6]

My hope is that intersectionality provides librarians and librarianship a similar sustaining and invigorating force. Equity, diversity, and inclusion

---

5. Fobazi Ettarh, "Black OR Queer? Life at the Intersection," *Hack Library School* (blog), November 19, 2013, https://hacklibraryschool.com/2013/11/19/black-or-queer-life-at-the-intersection/.

6. Fobazi Ettarh, "Making a New Table: Intersectional Librarianship," *In the Library with the Lead Pipe*, July 2, 2014, http://www.inthelibrarywiththeleadpipe.org/2014/making-a-new-table-intersectional-librarianship-3/.

(EDI) is having a big moment in librarianship. Diversity residencies are becoming more common, and it is not uncommon to have multiple presentations about EDI in one conference. Without being cognizant of structural, political, and representational intersectionality, however, these presentations, articles, programs, and initiatives will continue to fall short in their attempts to create sustainable change. Intersectionality was not meant to be used as a catchphrase for diversity. The American Library Association's literature on EDI has stretched the concept of what is considered "diverse" so far that it has become meaningless. Without nuance and care, discussions around the intersections of social groups and how they both disempower and privilege the experiences of people also risk becoming meaningless. Crenshaw herself stated that the theory of intersectionality is not meant to be used as an umbrella term to mean, "Well, it's complicated."[7] Of course it's complicated! Those in power would prefer it was not, but intersectionality provides us with an important lens through which to emphasize this complexity.

About the book

It has been almost forty years since the first edition of *This Bridge Called My Back* was published.[8] The essays in that book provided a space for radical women of color to break down barriers, see and hear each other, and build community. In a field in which white men are fast-tracked into leadership, and "nice white women"[9] act as professional

---

7. "Kimberlé Crenshaw on Intersectionality, More than Two Decades Later," *News at Columbia Law*, November 20, 2008, http://www.law.columbia.edu/news/2017/06/kimberle-crenshaw-intersectionality.

8. Cherríe Moraga and Gloria E. Anzaldúa, eds., *This Bridge Called My Back: Writings by Radical Women of Color* (Watertown, MA: Persephone Press, 1981).

9. "Nice white lady syndrome" refers to the phenomenon that often occurs at the intersection of white fragility and the weaponization of femininity. Those who exhibit it are often well intentioned, non-confrontational, female-presenting individuals who have an earnest and idealistic eagerness to help the marginalized, but only to a level with which they are comfortable. The allyship is revoked at any given time when their comfort is threatened, often with a wounded countenance that centers *them* as the victim.

gatekeepers, *Pushing the Margins* attempts to do, for librarians, what was done so many years ago: act as a safe space for women of color to break down barriers, share their stories, and come together to break bread and form community. The essays in this book present a myriad of stories, voices, experiences, and visions about what it means to be women of color within librarianship. Of course, it takes more than self-disclosure and glimpses into the lives of WOC in LIS to wrest power from those who hold it. But, it will bring into a more "legitimate" space the conversations that women of color within librarianship were already having in hallways, conference corridors, and socials, and there is a power in that. This book, in short, intends to re-center WOC in intersectionality.

Quite frankly, this book needs no foreword. It will be the afterword that will count. How are women of color within librarianship taking all of their complex identities to come together and work towards change? How are the white librarians reading this book embracing that complexity to create true partnerships with us? Intersectionality, like our lives, is unique, complex, and evolving. It is easy to shy away from engaging with things that defy simple explanation. But, let's all listen to these stories, and embark on the journey together.

Bibliography

Crenshaw, Kimberlé Williams. "Mapping the Margins: Intersectionality, Identity Politics, and Violence against Women of Color. *Stanford Law Review* 43, no. 6 (1991): 1241.

Crenshaw, Kimberlé Williams. "Demarginalizing the Intersection of Race and Sex: A Black Feminist Critique of Antidiscrimination Doctrine, Feminist Theory and Antiracist Politics." *University of Chicago Legal Forum* 1, no. 8 (1989).

"Kimberlé Crenshaw on Intersectionality, More than Two Decades Later." *News at Columbia Law*, November 20, 2008. http://www.law.columbia.edu/news/2017/06/kimberle-crenshaw-intersectionality.

Ettarh, Fobazi. "Black OR Queer? Life at the Intersection." *Hack Library School* (blog). November 19, 2013. https://hacklibraryschool.com/2013/11/19/black-or-queer-life-at-the-intersection/.

Ettarh, Fobazi. "Making a New Table: Intersectional Librarianship." *In the Library with the Lead Pipe*. July 2, 2014. http://www.inthelibrarywiththeleadpipe.org/2014/making-a-new-table-intersectional-librarianship-3/.

Moraga, Cherríe and Gloria E. Anzaldúa, eds. *This Bridge Called My Back: Writings by Radical Women of Color*. Watertown, MA: Persephone Press, 1981.

Stanton, Elizabeth Cady, Susan B. Anthony, Jocelyn Matilda Gage, and Ida Husted Harper (eds.). *History of Woman Suffrage, Volume II* (1861-1876), 152-163.

Introduction

Rose L. Chou and Annie Pho

To understand how this book came to be, you will have to understand how a friendship and professional relationship was formed between us. We first met in 2011, while we were still graduate students, at the American Library Association's Annual Conference in New Orleans. During a Hack Library School[1] meetup, someone said, "Hey, you two should be friends." And so we did.

Within a year of meeting, we became the managing editors of the Hack Library School blog, where we helped to manage the content and writers for a blog focused on trying to supplement the experiences of library school students. Our work on this project illuminated the importance of having peer spaces to support one another in the profession. Our professional relationship framed many of our conversations going forward, and our friendship allowed those conversations to occur unconstrained and without hesitation.

In 2012, we were both fortunate enough to attend the second ever Joint Conference for Librarians of Color (JCLC). This conference was the first time in our careers that we were exposed to a space dominated by librarians of color. Being surrounded by librarians of color was a

1. Hack Library School is a collaborative blog, written by and for library school students. *Hack Library School*, accessed February 15, 2018, http://www.hacklibraryschool.com.

significant and encouraging experience. Seeing librarians engaged in critical discussions about libraries and information science (LIS) was another aberration to us at the time, and further inspired us to explore what the future potential of librarianship could be—and what it might look like.

We remained good friends after we moved on from Hack Library School and got started with our first professional jobs. In 2014, we both attended the Minnesota Institute for Early Career Librarians from Traditionally Underrepresented Groups (MIECL) where, purely by chance, we were assigned to be roommates for the week. This particular experience was formative for many of the librarians who attended, and definitely was for us. What was especially valuable and important were the conversations that we had with each other after the day-long workshops. We talked about what it's like to be early-career librarians of color, the barriers that we face in the workplace, what it's like to uproot your life and move somewhere new, how to find your own community if you're the "only one" at your institution, dealing with microaggressions, and not being taken seriously as a professional and being unsure if it's racially motivated. Within intimate spaces like MIECL that are designated for librarians of color, these conversations are allowed to flow freely without fear of retaliation from administrators, and without having to explain oneself or defend one's own experience. And within these spaces, solidarity is formed and we can renew ourselves.

Designated spaces for librarians of color to gather are extremely important because people of color (POC) are truly underrepresented in the LIS field. The ALA Diversity Counts study makes a significant contribution by tracking statistics on the demographics of the profession. One of the key findings (which you will see cited often throughout the chapters in this book) is the marginal gains in recruitment of librarians of color into the profession in the last twenty years or so. The latest numbers indicate that people of color currently make up only twelve percent of the profession.[2] When we reflect on some of the shared LIS

2. American Library Association, "Table A-1: Number of Credentialed Librarians by Characteristic, 2009-2010," *Diversity Counts 2012 Tables*, accessed January 29, 2018, http://www.ala.org/aboutala/sites/ala.org.aboutala/files/content/diversity/diversitycounts/diversitycountstables2012.pdf.

spaces that are centered around POC, we know that there is much more depth and richness in experience, so in some ways it feels damaging to be reduced to a percentage. We have to pause and ask ourselves: Who are we beyond just this statistic alone?

Some writers and texts outside of LIS that have deeply influenced our selves, our practice, and our thinking are: Kimberlé Crenshaw, bell hooks, Patricia Hill Collins' *Black Feminist Thought*, Angela Davis' *Women, Race, and Class*, Audre Lorde's *Sister Outsider*, the Combahee River Collective Statement, and *This Bridge Called My Back*.[3] Upon first reading these works, we found that their words validated, confirmed, and named existing things that we already felt but didn't quite know how to express. They were able to describe and pinpoint what we live through every day as women of color. Further reading and analysis then taught and inspired us to be more critical and look deeper into systems and practices that create and perpetuate unequal power dynamics; to be more reflective about ourselves, our identities, and our roles in reproducing injustice; and also to actively seek social justice and change. Building on those foundational feminist works, our philosophy was further developed and deepened by more critical frameworks such as critical race theory, postcolonial theory, settler colonialism, and Derald Wing Sue's work on microaggressions.[4]

Crenshaw's article "Mapping the Margins: Intersectionality, Identity Politics and Violence Against Women of Color," which was described and discussed in the foreword, laid the basis for this book. At the time

---

3. Kimberlé Crenshaw, "Mapping the Margins: Intersectionality, Identity Politics, and Violence Against Women of Color," *Stanford Law Review* 43, no. 6 (1991): 1241-1299; bell hooks, *Feminist Theory: From Margin to Center* (Boston: South End Press, 1984); Patricia Hill Collins, *Black Feminist Thought: Knowledge, Consciousness, and the Politics of Empowerment* (New York: Routledge, 1990); Angela Davis, *Women, Race, and Class* (New York: Random House, 1981); Combahee River Collective, *The Combahee River Collective Statement: Black Feminist Organizing in the Seventies and Eighties* (Albany, NY: Kitchen Table: Women of Color Press, 1986); Audre Lorde, *Sister Outsider: Essays and Speeches* (Freedom, CA: Crossing Press, 1984); Cherríe Moraga and Gloria Anzaldúa (eds.), *This Bridge Called My Back: Writings by Radical Women of Color* (Watertown, MA: Persephone, 1981).

4. Derald Wing Sue, *Microaggressions in Everyday Life: Race, Gender, and Sexual Orientation* (Hoboken, NJ: Wiley, 2010).

of this writing, the term "intersectionality" has hit the mainstream, and consequently is often misused and misunderstood. When we first learned of intersectionality, it meant something very specific. To us, intersectionality isn't only about having multiple social identities—that applies to everyone. Intersectionality is also about the ways in which individuals with *multiple marginalized identities* experience oppression in more complicated ways. We want to associate ourselves with the concept expressed in Fobazi Ettarh's foreword that: "intersectionality was not meant to be used as a catchphrase for diversity." It's a heuristic, lens, and framework for women of color to understand ourselves and our experiences.

We do want to acknowledge that intersectionality isn't a perfect concept—nothing is. There are many valid critiques of intersectionality and its limits. Rita Kaur Dhamoon summarizes many of these issues in "Considerations on Mainstreaming Intersectionality."[5] Some of these critiques include the risk of essentialism—by studying identities as categories, we can end up reproducing and re-emphasizing them. Dhamoon argues instead that we must focus less on studying individual attributes or demographic categories and more on the "processes and systems that constitute, govern, and counter difference...on the techniques of power."[6] Rather than focusing on individual social categories, we need to seek and challenge the power structures that enable interlocking systems of oppression.

Within LIS, there have been some who have begun to apply this heuristic and theoretical framework to our work as librarians. In 2014, Ettarh wrote about intersectionality as a way to think about the experiences of librarians of color working in libraries and archives, making the point that even though some librarians may give advice that is supposedly feminist in nature, like "leaning in," that advice is entrenched in white feminism and does not acknowledge the complexities of social categories

---

5. Rita Kaur Dhamoon, "Considerations on Mainstreaming Intersectionality," *Political Research Quarterly* 20, no. 10 (2010): 1-14.

6. Ibid., 234.

that one may identify with, such as being black and queer.[7] She states, "By treating these issues as separate entities, we as librarians fail to fully understand how oppressions work in various contexts. Intersectionality is a tool for studying, understanding, and responding to the ways in which axes of identities intersect and how these intersections contribute to unique experiences of oppression and privilege."[8] The ability to look at the experiences of librarians with the acknowledgement that identity and social constructs are not singular, and that it can be complicated, is crucial to thinking through how we can improve our workplaces and how we can rethink diversity rhetoric. All these influences culminated in our ambition to do a research project.

In the summer of 2015, we began brainstorming ideas for a book chapter proposal that was focused on feminist librarianship practices, in response to a call for proposals for the edited monograph, *The Feminist Reference Desk: Concepts, Critiques, and Conversations.*[9] We knew that we wanted the focus of the work to be intersectional because we felt like something had been missing from LIS literature, especially with works that focused on gender and feminism. Beyond that, we specifically wanted to center women of color.

We conducted a research project in early 2016, where we interviewed women of color librarians about their experiences working in public services. Our initial findings are discussed in our book chapter, "Intersectionality at the Reference Desk: Lived Experiences of Women of Color Librarians."[10] There were many nuanced themes that we found through the research project which resonated with our own personal

7. Fobazi Ettarh, "Making a New Table: Intersectional Librarianship," *In the Library with the Lead Pipe*, July 2, 2014, http://www.inthelibrarywiththeleadpipe.org/2014/making-a-new-table-intersectional-librarianship-3/.

8. Ibid.

9. Maria T. Accardi (ed.), *The Feminist Reference Desk: Concepts, Critiques, and Conversations* (Sacramento: Library Juice Press, 2017).

10. Rose L. Chou and Annie Pho, "Intersectionality at the Reference Desk: Lived Experiences of Women of Color Librarians," in *The Feminist Reference Desk: Concepts, Critiques, and Conversations*, ed. Maria T. Accardi (Sacramento: Library Juice Press, 2017), 225-252.

experiences and discussions with other librarians of color; our research provided an opportunity to examine those experiences more closely. After finishing the book chapter, we wanted to delve further into themes such as identity, gender, sexuality, and invisible and emotional labor. We knew that there was a lot of interest in more of these discussions in LIS. We both separately had the idea that we should do a book in order to create a platform for others who were interested in researching and writing about intersectionality within LIS. In our original research project, we sought to elevate the voices of women of color who we felt were often overlooked in LIS literature. This book is an extension of that effort to signal boost the words and voices of those who want to explore other facets of what it is like to be a woman of color librarian.

Within the realm of librarianship, the influences of critical, feminist, and queer theory have shaped how those working in the profession think about and approach their work. In particular, the core tenets of critical librarianship seek to challenge systems of privilege and power, and to center marginalized and underrepresented populations in our work. Upon scanning what literature there is on the concepts of critical librarianship, we haven't seen explicit links between the work of what critical librarianship aspires to do, and the work of librarians who are writing about issues related to equity, diversity, and inclusion (EDI). As Brown, et al. succinctly point out, "Even more troubling is that the movement does not seem to want to turn a critical eye upon itself or the profession, focusing mostly on critically engaging with the work librarians do, such as instruction, reference, or cataloging. It does not, for example, question the fact that the profession is replicating structures of white supremacy in LIS curriculum, programs, recruitment, and the culture of the profession."[11] This is perhaps in response to the overwhelming whiteness of our profession, which shapes so many aspects of how librarians must operate and do their job, and adds to the disconnect between critical race and feminist theory and our everyday practice.

11. Jennifer Brown, Jennifer Ferretti, Sofia Leung, and Marisa Méndez-Brady, "We Here: Speaking Our Truth," *Library Trends,* Summer 2018.

While it's troubling that there is a gap between the practice of critical librarianship and EDI work, we have found that there is a growing body of literature that focuses on the experiences of librarians of color,[12] and more specifically on academic librarians of color.[13] Additionally, there are many scholars who have written about feminized labor and the history of librarianship in connection to gender roles and women's history.[14] But even Hildenbrand posits how a new history of librarianship might look moving forward:

> Before such a history can emerge, however, a new and better way of conceptualizing these socially constructed aspects of our identity is needed. In any given setting one may take precedence over the others, though none is ever totally submerged. And each of us must find [their] place in life, professionally and personally, in already existing, though continually evolving, social structures in which difference has traditionally resulted in dominance and subordination.[15]

What she is stating here is the gap in the literature that we have attempted to fill, first with our research study and now with this book. It's interesting that even though there are scholars who are interested in the experiences of librarians of color and interested in the role of gender and sexuality in LIS, there haven't been explicit connections made between all of these social categories using intersectionality as a lens. We must ask ourselves what it means to be in a white, *feminized* profession and

---

12. Jaena Alabi, "'This Actually Happened': An Analysis of Librarians' Responses to a Survey about Racial Microaggressions," *Journal of Library Administration* 55, no. 2 (2015): 179–191, https://doi.org/10.1080/01930826.2015.1034040.

13. Rebecca Hankins and Miguel Juárez (eds.), *Where Are All the Librarians of Color? The Experiences of People of Color in Academia* (Sacramento, CA: Library Juice Press, 2016); Isabel Gonzalez-Smith, Juleah Swanson, and Azusa Tanaka, "Unpacking Identity: Racial, Ethnic, and Professional Identity and Academic Librarians of Color," in *The Librarian Stereotype: Deconstructing Perceptions and Presentations of Information Work*, ed. Nicole Pagowsky and Miriam Rigby (Chicago: Association of College and Research Libraries, 2014), 149-173; Ione T. Damasco and Dracine Hodges, "Tenure and Promotion Experiences of Academic Librarians of Color," *College & Research Libraries* 73, no. 3 (2012): 279-301, https://doi.org/10.5860/crl-244.

14. Suzanne Hildenbrand, "Library Feminism and Library Women's History: Activism and Scholarship, Equity and Culture," *Libraries and Culture* 35, no. 1 (2000): 51-65.

15. Ibid., 61.

how we can make it a *feminist* profession—one that actively seeks to elevate women who exist in the margins specifically. Women of color have been working in libraries for a long time, but they haven't received the recognition or acknowledgement that they deserve.

David James Hudson seeks to further complicate the rhetoric surrounding current diversity discourse, stating that:

> Race remains undertheorized in the field in no small part because of the overwhelming LIS emphasis on the practical and the technical, and the attendant failure to recognize inquiry into matters of power and meaning as a worthwhile undertaking in its own right: it is difficult to undertake sustained collective discussions of theory, culture, and history when the vast majority of the intellectual output in the field collectively teaches us that research is best when it is accompanied by commodity solutions in the form of concrete policy recommendations, competencies, standards, activities, and other things that can be captured in bullet-pointed lists.[16]

As we have stated previously, race, gender, sexuality, and other social categories are complex, interwoven systems which are negotiated in an individual's experience in varying ways. Although the LIS field defaults to pragmatic approaches, there is no one practical solution that could truly address the systemic underpinnings of oppression that frame our society at large, and trickle into how libraries and archives operate. For all the efforts in scholarship about diversity, equity, and inclusion which seek to name the problems and provide strategies going forward, the reality is that they have not resulted in greater diversity in libraries and archives. Perhaps it's time to radically shift how we think about diversity. Hudson argues, "Indeed, a meaningful shift away from the diversity paradigm and its pitfalls cannot be achieved through individual writings alone; it requires the purposeful creation of spaces within which such work can be undertaken in an ongoing way."[17] This monograph creates precisely such a space: one that allows for conversations to pivot away

16. David James Hudson, "On 'Diversity' as Anti-Racism in Library and Information Studies: A Critique," *Journal of Critical Library and Information Studies* 1, no. 1 (2017): 26, https://doi.org/10.24242/jclis.v1i1.6.

17. Hudson, "On 'Diversity' as Anti-Racism in Library and Information Studies: A Critique," 26.

from the traditional diversity paradigm by applying an explicit feminist and intersectional framework. Diversity needs to be addressed from all approaches, as there is no one solution, and it must be examined through an intersectional lens.

To ensure that this book is rooted in a feminist approach, we apply the activist technique of consciousness raising. Consciousness raising is an organizing and educational tool where women gather together to try and elevate awareness of social issues that are pertinent to women. As Carol Hanisch defines it, "Consciousness raising was a way to use our own lives—our combined experiences—to understand concretely how we are oppressed and who was actually doing the oppressing. We regarded this knowledge as necessary for building such a movement."[18] Historically, this technique was done in living rooms and intimate spaces where women could gather, have discussions, and take action. The objectives of this activity were to help women educate themselves and each other by talking, venting, and organizing around issues that they faced. While there were issues with the first-wave feminist movement disregarding the experiences of black feminists and other women of color, we believe that consciousness raising is an important tool that can be used to center women of color. We can create spaces for crucial dialogue about our experiences and pinpoint issues that we want to organize around. Given the political climate in which this book is being published, it feels especially imperative to organize around focused issues that affect women of color and other marginalized populations.

Applying this approach within LIS, librarians of color—many of whom work in predominantly white spaces—see online projects like LIS Microaggressions[19] and We Here,[20] in-person gatherings at conferences, and conferences focused on EDI (e.g., JCLC and National Diversity in

---

18. Carol Hanisch, "Women's Liberation Consciousness-Raising: Then and Now," *On the Issues Magazine*, Spring 2010, http://www.ontheissuesmagazine.com/2010spring/2010spring_Hanisch.php.

19. *LIS Microaggressions*, accessed February 15, 2018, http://www.lismicroaggressions.com.

20. We Here is an online space for POC in libraries and archives. There are closed spaces designated for POC on Facebook and Slack, and open spaces on Twitter and Instagram for anyone to follow.

Libraries Conference) as ways to raise consciousness about issues they face in libraries and archives. In the summer of 2017, we organized a one-day symposium where some of the authors from this book presented on their work. The majority of the attendees were librarians of color, and we felt the importance of being able to gather in one place to learn from each other, vent, and feel validated by one another. In a predominantly white profession, these rare opportunities are cherished by librarians of color. We recognize the privilege in being able to attend conferences and other paid events, but there are other ways that organizing and community can take place, such as online and local meeting groups.

About the book

As you read through this collection, you will find that many of the same themes can be found throughout the different chapters, though to varying degrees and with different emphases. In addition to the overarching themes of racism, sexism, and feminism, repeating themes include: emotional labor, invisible labor, microaggressions, self care, support networks and community, identity, and representation. Some authors approached these topics using surveys and interviews, while others used more narrative or experiential styles. It was our intention to include a broad variety of approaches in this book, especially since traditional academic scholarship has often disregarded and invalidated the work and experiences of people of color. All of the chapters were peer-reviewed, and the majority of our peer reviewers were intentionally librarians of color. We did not conduct peer review in order to "validate" these works as traditional academia tends to use the process—our intention was to use the knowledge and expertise of others with different experiences to provide feedback and enhance our own limited perspectives. This book is not meant to be representative of all experiences of women of color in LIS. We recognize that we are missing many voices in this volume, but our hope is that this book is a beginning to many more works on examining the complexities of being a WOC working in LIS.

You will see specific vocabulary used throughout this book to refer to groups of people in the Western hemisphere who have been traditionally marginalized or underrepresented. There are many ways that disciplines like LIS refer to those who are racialized in society. Words like "diversity" are commonly thrown around as catch-alls for anyone who could be deemed as Other.[21] For the title of our book, we decided upon "women of color" because we felt that it would be the most descriptive and inclusive for the voices that we were hoping to elevate and center. Rather than use terminology like "minority" or "underrepresented" (although technically the LIS profession is predominantly white), we chose to use the designation of "women" under the framework of the term "people of color," because it "accurately designates people who belong to specific ethnic groups by focusing on a social perception of race, which is based on color."[22] We use "women" to be any persons who identify with this gender instead of "female," which suggests that there must be a biological connection to a gender identity. We recognize the limitations in the terms "people of color" and "women of color," and that some do not use these terms to describe themselves because they prefer to be more specific in how they self-identify. The shortcoming of words like "diversity" or "people of color" is that it can lump large groups of people with distinct communities and social identities into one category, and those who aren't willing to interrogate or look closer might assume that statements made by one person applies to everyone that could fit into that category. By being too vague, there is the chance that the intentions are lost and have no meaning, which is why we feel that it's important to unpack our word choices. Within the chapters, the authors have chosen to identify, name, and capitalize social identities as they saw fit, and the only time that we tried to enforce edits was to change cisnormative language. How women of color librarians approach their work varies, but what we hope is illustrated through our own research

21. Edward Said, *Orientalism* (New York: Vintage Books, 1979).

22. Yoko Takebayashi, "People of Color," in *Encyclopedia of Cross-Cultural School Psychology*, ed. Caroline S. Clauss-Ehlers (Boston, MA: Springer US, 2010), 722-723, https://doi.org/10.1007/978-0-387-71799-9_311.

and that of others in this book are the commonalities that are shared within the narratives.

When we conducted our original feminist research study on WOC librarians, one participant remarked on how, as she moved into library leadership, she wanted to begin to tackle the structures that create barriers for early-career POC librarians to join the profession. We were heartened and inspired by her words and began to think about how we could try to provide communal space for other WOC to share their own research, writing, and experiences in an effort to break down structural barriers. This book, *Pushing the Margins*, is a labor of love, and an extension of consciousness-raising in the LIS landscape. It's unapologetic in centering women of color and in making the statement that above all else, we matter, our experiences are valid, and that we will be heard.

Bibliography

Accardi, Maria T. (ed.). *The Feminist Reference Desk: Concepts, Critiques, and Conversations.* Sacramento: Library Juice Press, 2017.

Alabi, Jaena. "'This Actually Happened': An Analysis of Librarians' Responses to a Survey about Racial Microaggressions," *Journal of Library Administration* 55, no. 2 (2015): 179–191. https://doi.org/10.1080/01930826.2015.1034040.

American Library Association. "Table A-1: Number of Credentialed Librarians by Characteristic, 2009-2010." *Diversity Counts 2012 Tables.* Accessed January 29, 2018. http://www.ala.org/aboutala/sites/ala.org.aboutala/files/content/diversity/diversitycounts/diversitycountstables2012.pdf.

Brown, Jennifer, Jennifer Ferretti, Sofia Leung, and Marisa Méndez-Brady. "We Here: Speaking Our Truth." *Library Trends*, Summer 2018.

Chou, Rose L. and Annie Pho. "Intersectionality at the Reference Desk: Lived Experiences of Women of Color Librarians." In *The Feminist Reference Desk: Concepts, Critiques, and Conversations*, edited by Maria T. Accardi. Sacramento: Library Juice Press, 2017.

Collins, Patricia Hill. *Black Feminist Thought: Knowledge, Consciousness, and the Politics of Empowerment.* New York: Routledge, 1990.

Combahee River Collective. *The Combahee River Collective Statement: Black Feminist Organizing in the Seventies and Eighties.* Albany, NY: Kitchen Table: Women of Color Press, 1986.

Crenshaw, Kimberlé. "Mapping the Margins: Intersectionality, Identity Politics, and Violence Against Women of Color." *Stanford Law Review* 43, no. 6 (1991): 1241-1299.

Damasco, Ione T., and Dracine Hodges. "Tenure and Promotion Experiences of Academic Librarians of Color." *College & Research Libraries* 73, no. 3 (2012): 279-301. https://doi.org/10.5860/crl-244.

Davis, Angela. *Women, Race, and Class.* New York: Random House, 1981.

Dhamoon, Rita Kaur. "Considerations on Mainstreaming Intersectionality." *Political Research Quarterly* 20, no. 10 (2010): 1-14.

Ettarh, Fobazi. "Making a New Table: Intersectional Librarianship." *In the Library with the Lead Pipe.* July 2, 2014. http://www.inthelibrarywiththeleadpipe.org/2014/making-a-new-table-intersectional-librarianship-3/.

Gonzalez-Smith, Isabel, Juleah Swanson, and Azusa Tanaka. "Unpacking Identity: Racial, Ethnic, and Professional Identity and Academic Librarians of Color." In *The Librarian Stereotype: Deconstructing Perceptions and Presentations of Information Work*, edited by Nicole Pagowsky and Miriam Rigby. Chicago: Association of College and Research Libraries, 2014: 149-173.

Hack Library School. Accessed February 15, 2018. http://www.hacklibraryschool.com.

Hanisch, Carol. "Women's Liberation Consciousness-Raising: Then and Now." *On the Issues Magazine.* Spring 2010. http://www.ontheissuesmagazine.com/2010spring/2010spring_Hanisch.php.

Hankins, Rebecca, and Miguel Juárez (eds.). *Where Are All the Librarians of Color? The Experiences of People of Color in Academia.* Sacramento, CA: Library Juice Press, 2016.

Hildenbrand, Suzanne. "Library Feminism and Library Women's History: Activism and Scholarship, Equity and Culture." *Libraries and Culture* 35, no. 1 (2000): 51-65.

hooks, bell. *Feminist Theory: From Margin to Center.* Boston: South End Press, 1984.

Hudson, David James. "On 'Diversity' as Anti-Racism in Library and Information Studies: A Critique." *Journal of Critical Library and Information Studies* 1, no. 1 (2017): 26. https://doi.org/10.24242/jclis.v1i1.6.

LIS Microaggressions. Accessed February 15, 2018. http://www.lismicroaggressions.com.

Lorde, Audre. *Sister Outsider: Essays and Speeches.* Freedom, CA: Crossing Press, 1984.

Moraga, Cherríe, and Gloria Anzaldúa (eds.). *This Bridge Called My Back: Writings by Radical Women of Color.* Watertown, MA: Persephone, 1981.

Said, Edward. *Orientalism.* New York: Vintage Books, 1979.

Sue, Derald Wing. *Microaggressions in Everyday Life: Race, Gender, and Sexual Orientation.* Hoboken, NJ: Wiley, 2010.

Takebayashi, Yoko. "People of Color." In *Encyclopedia of Cross-Cultural School Psychology*, edited by Caroline S. Clauss-Ehlers. Boston, MA: Springer US, 2010. https://doi.org/10.1007/978-0-387-71799-9_311.

Chapter 1

"When I Enter": Black Women and Disruption of the White, Heteronormative Narrative of Librarianship

Caitlin M. J. Pollock and Shelley P. Haley

> Only the Black Woman can say "when and where I enter, in the quiet, undisputed dignity of my womanhood, without violence and without suing or special patronage, then and there the whole Negro race enters with me."—Anna Julia Cooper, *A Voice from the South*

Introduction

As we began the research for this chapter, it soon became clear that Black women have always been integral to first, literacy movements of the 1800s, and later, librarianship. It also became clear that literacy, social justice activism, and literary cultural production have always intersected for middle-class, educated Black women. As Michelle Garfield points out, "The Philadelphia women who organized the Female Literary Association...hoped to engage in activities that would expand their own mental capabilities. Yet they also used these skills to engage actively in political discussions regarding slavery and the rights of blacks."[1] Most important was the drive to satisfy both the collective needs of their people and

1. Michelle Garfield, "Literary Societies: The Work of Self-Improvement and Racial Uplift," in *Black Women's Intellectual Traditions: Speaking Their Minds*, ed. Kristin Waters and Carol B. Conaway (Burlington, VT: University of Vermont Press, 2007), 125.

their own individual needs as gifted, educated women. Garfield puts it most succinctly, "These women were not one-dimensional individuals."[2] These early literacy movements were also the beginning of the ideology of racial uplift and the obligation of the educated elite of Black America—particularly women—to improve the lot of their less fortunate sisters and brothers.[3] Even in the nineteenth and early twentieth centuries, Black women negotiated race, gender, and class. The resulting societies that brought basic educational skills to the enslaved and poor people of African descent also served as the birthing place for Black women writers. According to Garfield, "...the literary society is unique in that it brought women together with the express purpose of writing and reading their own work."[4] This history demonstrates that Black women have always operated out of a sense of communal duty and, in modern parlance, self-care. Activism, writing, and literacy have been interconnected in the history of Black women. We are attempting to place this intersectionality in the context of Black female librarianship. It should not come as a surprise that the five Black women librarians we focus on in this chapter were also authors of plays, poems, essays, children's literature, or novels.

At the same time, we would be remiss if we did not problematize and interrogate the master narrative that librarianship is a performance of white, middle-class values. That narrative comes through in now-cringe-worthy fashion in Elise Johnson McDougald's essay "The Task of Negro Womanhood," originally published in Alain Locke, *The New Negro: Voices of the Harlem Renaissance* (1925). McDougald, who was a groundbreaking educator in New York City and an activist,[5] divides

---

2. Ibid., 119.

3. These movements have been overshadowed by W.E.B. Du Bois's formulation of the "talented tenth." Clearly, the Black women's literacy movements were the precursors to that.

4. Garfield, 117.

5. Elise Johnson McDougald (1885-1971) was the first African American woman principal in New York City public schools. She was also on the supervisory committee of the North Harlem Community Forum, which took place during the 1920s. She served with Regina Anderson Andrews, one of librarians we examine in this chapter.

Black women into different "classes" which mimic white socio-economic classes. These consist of the "leisure class" (wives and daughters of men in business, professions, etc.) who suffer from the same difficulties in finding "good help" as their white counterparts. The second is women of "business and the professions"; third, "trades and industry"; and fourth, "a group weighty in numbers struggling on in domestic service."[6] McDougald reserves special praise for the second class of women, as one would expect. She describes the women in business and the professions as "a most active and progressive group."[7] She takes note of the feminization of the field of librarianship—it has not quite evolved into "library science," but endorses this new profession as ideally suited to the African American middle-class woman. "There is an ever-present hope that, once trained, the Negro woman librarian will scatter such opportunities across the country.... [Black women librarians] are thus rendering exceptional service, and additionally creating an impetus for the enlargement of this field for Negro women."[8]

These Black women were often librarians in white structures of power. They often had to struggle within those power structures that racialized and gendered them. For some of these women, they sought to contextualize their librarianship and libraries, some on a local level and some on a professional and national level. Regardless of the scope, these women had similar goals: to change, expand, and challenge libraries and librarianship. In the work of these women, we can observe the precedent and application of S.R. Ranganathan's five laws of library science, originally published in 1931. The five laws of library science are: books are for use; every reader his/her book; every book its reader; save the time of the reader; the library is a growing organism.[9] For some

---

6. Elise Johnson McDougald, "The Task of Negro Womanhood," in *The New Negro: Voices of the Harlem Renaissance,* ed. by Alain Locke, (New York: Simon & Schuster, 1992. Originally published in 1925), 370.

7. Ibid.

8. McDougald, 376.

9. S.R. Ranganathan, *The Five Laws of Library Science*, Ed. 2 reprinted, (Bangalore: Sarada Ranganathan Endowment for Library Science, 1988).

of these women, their work offered critiques of libraries that did not adhere to the ethos delineated by the laws. In their quotidian work in service to a community or the library field, the five women examined here made significant contributions to American librarianship, Black literature, and feminism.

It is important that the librarians we will examine are placed within their own historical and ideological contexts. While it would be a mistake to apply more recent advances in Black feminist thought and critical race feminist theory without this acknowledgement, our analysis has benefited greatly from the main tenets of these approaches, in particular those of social construction and intersectionality theory. For this reason, we have decided to divide the five women we consider into two groups that mirror the waves of the feminist movement in the United States. Equally important, the groupings also mirror two major waves in Black cultural and literary production: the Harlem Renaissance and the Black Arts Movement. In the first wave (1910-1930), we examine Nella Larsen, Pura Belpré, and Regina Anderson Andrews; in the second wave we consider Ann Allen Shockley and Audre Lorde. This is just a snapshot of Black female librarianship. There were, and are, many more Black female librarians whose narratives are just as insightful and fascinating as the women described in this chapter. However, for many reasons, most rooted in racialized sexism such as their absences from archives and library histories, these women do not have biographies written about them or their stories otherwise memorialized. We hope this chapter is one step in recognizing the contributions of Black women to librarianship.

The First Wave: Nella Larsen, Regina Anderson Andrews, Pura Belpré

Nella Larsen was born in Chicago, in 1891, to a father of African descent[10] and a Danish mother. She took the name Larsen from her

---

10. The race and ethnicity of Larsen's father is a Gordian knot. According to the certificate of live birth registered by the pharmacist who assisted at the birth, no race or ethnicity is listed for her father, yet she is listed as "Colored." The author's statement

mother's second husband who was also Danish. Larsen felt that her social location as a biracial person (as opposed to mixed race, as were so many of the Black bourgeoisie, especially in Harlem) whose mother was a European immigrant made her unique among the middle-class social milieu she was associated with in New York. According to her biographer, Thadious Davis, "While race and gender were the social constructions negatively affecting her youth, they recombined in New York to inspire an internal drive toward agency, visibility and voice that went beyond mere survival."[11] While Larsen attained middle-class status through her careers as a nurse, then librarian, then writer, she did not come from the middle class like so many of her friends and acquaintances in New York. She married into McDougald's leisure class of professional wives when, in 1919, she wed Elmer S. Imes, a physicist and only the second African American to earn a Ph.D. in Physics in the United States.

In June and July 1920, while still engaged in her nursing career, Larsen published pieces in the *Brownies' Book*, a magazine for African American children. In 1921, after leaving her position as a nurse with the New York City Department of Health, Larsen found herself at a professional crossroads. As Davis explains, "Nursing, though respectable and increasingly professional, was not as highly regarded as a white-collar job in a library." In 1922, after working as a volunteer, Larsen was hired as an entry-level library assistant at the 135th Street Branch of the New York Public Library (NYPL). Her supervisor was Ernestine Rose, a white librarian who worked diligently to recruit more African American women into the branch.[12] Because of Larsen's pieces in the *Brownies' Book,* Rose arranged for Larsen to be an assistant to the librarians in the children's section. She made an impression upon the young

---

for Alfred A. Knopf publishers (1926) notes, "Nella Larsen is a mulatto, the daughter of a Danish lady and a Negro from Virgin Islands, formerly the Danish West Indies."

11. Thadious M. Davis, *Nella Larsen, Novelist of the Harlem Renaissance: A Woman's Life Unveiled* (Baton Rouge, LA: Louisiana State University Press, 1994), 4-5.

12. Ernestine Rose worked closely with another member of our first wave, Regina Anderson Andrews, to increase cultural programming at the 135th Street Branch.

patrons at the branch with her well-coiffed hair and warmth.[13] In turn, Larsen seemed to thrive in this environment, and Ernestine Rose was so impressed with her aptitude and talent that she encouraged her to apply for admission to NYPL's Library School. The Library School did not have a good track record with retaining African American candidates, but Larsen succeeded and earned her certificate in 1923. She returned, certificate in hand, to a higher-grade position and more money at the 135th Street Branch. Larsen saw her position as a librarian as a step up in her individual professional status, but it was also significant in a much larger way. As Davis points out, "Whether she was conscious of it or not, Larsen was in the process of falling 'out of the marriage plot that demands not only that a woman marry but that marriage and its progeny be her life's absolute and only center.'"[14] Some scholars view Larsen's career as a librarian and a writer as a pathway to fit in with the educated, light-skinned social circle to which she was introduced by her marriage to Imes. Other scholars tend to reject the "gentility" argument and analyze Larsen's development as a librarian as an intellectual tool to broaden her critique of class and intellectual ideologies. Karin Roffman suggests, "Larsen's complicated reaction to the ideologies she was asked to absorb in library school helped her to sharpen her explorations of those critical attitudes in her fiction."[15] Roffman focuses on Helga Crane, the main character of Larsen's novel, *Quicksand,* to center her argument that the novel is a critique of the library training Larsen received at the Library School of the New York Public Library.

Quicksand tells the story of Helga Crane, a young biracial woman working as a teacher at a university in the American South. *Quicksand* follows Helga's unsuccessful search for fulfillment in both employment and romance as she travels from the South to Chicago, then to Harlem

---

13. Davis, 144.

14. Carolyn Heilbrun, *Writing a Woman's Life* (New York, 1988), 51. Quoted in Davis, *Nella Larsen: Novelist of the Harlem Renaissance*, A Woman's Life Unveiled (Baton Rouge, LA, 1994), 144.

15. Karin Roffman, "Nella Larsen, Librarian at 135th Street," *Modern Fiction Studies*, 53, no. 5 (2007): 753.

and Copenhagen. In each city, Helga finds herself confined by her race, her gender, and her penury combined with her materialism. Helga leaves higher education, where she gives "willingly and unsparingly of herself with no apparent return."[16] She finds herself constrained by the expectation of "respectable" and middle-class behavior at the university, which Helga describes as "the strenuous rigidity of conduct required in this huge educational community of which she was an insignificant part."[17] After abandoning her teaching career, Helga contemplates a career as a librarian because of her love for books. Preparing to visit the library, a structure Helga describes as an "ugly gray building where was housed much knowledge and a little wisdom, on interminable shelves,"[18] she dresses in her plainest clothing, "a suit of fine blue twill faultlessly tailored, from whose left pocket peeped a gay kerchief, an unadorned, heavy silk blouse, a small, smart, fawn-colored hat, and slim brown oxfords, and chose a brown umbrella."[19] Helga dresses in her most unassuming and respectable clothing to visit the library, her costume's plainness reflected in her muted description of the library. At the library, in a scene that hints at the discrimination against African American students which Larson experienced at the New York Public Library School, Helga encounters several gatekeepers to becoming a librarian and is dissuaded from pursuing librarianship. Helga enters a room in the library and "in less than a quarter of an hour she came out, in surprised disappointment. 'Library training' — 'civil service' — 'library school' — 'classification' —— 'cataloguing' — 'probation period' — flitted through her mind. 'How erudite they must be!' she remarked sarcastically to herself..."[20] Helga finds herself bereft of another career path and stymied by the numerous obstacles placed in front of her pursuit of librarianship.

---

16. Nella Larsen, *Quicksand and Passing*, ed. Deborah E. McDowell (New Brunswick, NJ: Rutgers University Press, 1986), 1.

17. Ibid.

18. Ibid, 31.

19. Ibid.

20. Ibid, 31-32.

The role of Larsen's librarianship in shaping her fiction still resonates today. In her article, "Librarian as Poet/Poet as Librarian," Erin Dorney interviews several poet-librarians while reflecting on her own experience as a poet and librarian. Just as Larsen's librarianship contributed to her writing, Dorney remarks, "... my librarian training has impacted my life as a poet."[21] Even as a writer, Larsen was unable to completely leave librarianship. In her writing, she was still addressing the flaws of the field. In *Quicksand*, she castigates libraries for not being welcoming to intersectional and marginalized identities. Her critique arguably had a greater goal than reforming librarianship. Claudia Tate contends that *Quicksand* goes even further and represents an attempt to explore the intersection of race and gender in a subversive and even revolutionary way.[22]

Larsen demonstrates the danger of fragmenting a complex intersectional identity into competing schools of interpretation, especially for Black women. In the early twentieth century, Black women activists tended to combine the politics of respectability[23] and revolution. Because we as Black women view ourselves as racialized, gendered beings, we cannot draw a boundary between the personal and the political. Both operated in the life of Nella Larsen; the common thread between them is Larsen's position as a librarian. Larsen resigned from her position at the 135th Street Branch to devote herself to writing full time. She would never return to Harlem. When she gave up writing, she returned, not

21. Erin Dorney, "Librarian as Poet / Poet as Librarian," *In the Library with the Lead Pipe* (February 12, 2014).

22. Claudia Tate, "Desire and Death in Quicksand, by Nella Larsen," *American Literary History* 7 (1995): 234-60.

23. The concept of respectability politics for Black women comes, in part, from the idea of the "cult of true womanhood" and chivalry. In order to be treated with dignity, Black women were expected to adhere to white and Eurocentric ideals of beauty, decorum, and feminine activities. Often, attainment of these ideals proved difficult for Black women due to systemic racialized sexism. To learn more about respectability politics, see Barbara Welter, *Dimity Convictions* (Athens, OH: Ohio University Press, 1976), Roger D. Abrahams, "Negotiating Respect: Patterns among Black Women," *Journal of American Folklore*, 88, no. 347 (1975); 58-80, and E. Frances White, *Dark Continent of Our Bodies: Black Feminism and the Politics of Respectability* (Philadelphia: Temple University, 2001.)

to librarianship, but to nursing, her first career. This may have occurred because of increased credentialing standards for librarians or because of Larsen's desire to disassociate from the memories of Harlem. Nevertheless, she died a librarian's death: in 1964, she succumbed to congestive heart failure while reading in bed.

Regina Anderson Andrews is the epitome of the social class to which Larsen wanted to belong. Born in Chicago in 1901, Andrews was the daughter of William Grant Anderson and his wife, Margaret Simons Anderson. William G. Anderson grew to prominence as a defense lawyer and "race man" who was associated with Ida B. Wells and her activism against lynching. Wells became a firm family friend and in 1940, her granddaughter, Lucille Duster, was a boarder in the Anderson homestead.[24] Andrews's mother, Margaret, also set an example by becoming involved with social justice activism and racial uplift as a Black clubwoman. Every indication, then, is that Andrews was her parents' daughter. Her artistic accomplishments as a playwright and erstwhile actress undoubtedly flowed from the influence of her mother, who was a celebrated artisan of china painting. We can say with the same certainty that Andrews learned the value of fighting injustice at her father's knee and through her acquaintance with Ida B. Wells. We cannot overstate Wells's influence: *Climbing Jacob's Ladder*, one of Andrews's most celebrated plays, was about lynching. Indeed, Andrews herself said, "Before coming to New York, I had been very much influenced by Ida B. Wells Barnett....When I was a child in Chicago and first heard of lynchings, they were incomprehensible. It's understandable that in my twenties I would have to write a play about lynching."[25] For Andrews, her literary accomplishments deeply intersected with her library activism, thus carrying on the tradition of Black women literacy activists of the nineteenth century.

---

24. Ethelene Whitmire, *Regina Anderson Andrews: Harlem Renaissance Librarian*, (Springfield, IL: University of Illinois Press, 2014), 101.

25. Lofton Mitchell, *Voices of Black Theatre*, 78. Quoted in Whitmire, *Regina Anderson Andrews: Harlem Renaissance Librarian*, 71.

Unlike Larsen, who viewed a career in librarianship as a step up from and out of the working class into the middle class, Andrews was solidly positioned in the Black bourgeoisie. Andrews's biographer, Ethelene Whitmire, claims that Andrews never gave a reason for entering librarianship,[26] but Andrews did acknowledge a "patient understanding librarian in the grammar school in Normal, Ill" as an early influence on her intellectual development.[27] In addition, Andrews was undoubtedly attracted by the opportunities for groundbreaking advancements for Black people, and Black women in particular, in a field that was becoming feminized as well as racially and ethnically diverse.

Andrews's career as a librarian most likely began as a student volunteer in the library of her high school, Hyde Park High School; she then worked as an assistant librarian while a student at Wilberforce University. After she returned to Chicago, she applied for a position at the Chicago Public Library. In August of 1921, she secured a position as a "Grade 2, Junior Library Assistant"[28] without having to be too concerned about racial discrimination, since the Chicago Public Library hired personnel through the city's Civil Service Commission.[29] Andrews asked for and received a leave of absence from her position at Chicago Public Library in June, 1922 and eventually resigned formally in September, 1922. Andrews's hiring experience with Chicago Public Library would stand in stark relief to her experience at New York Public Library, where as an applicant she was told, "Because of your color...we'll have to send you to Harlem to work."[30] This came as a surprise to Andrews, who prided herself on her mixed-race ancestry and her upbringing in integrated environments. She first identified herself as "American" and was then

26. Whitmire, 3

27. Consuelo C. Young, "Preface," *Chicago Defender*, October 29, 1938, 13. Quoted in Ethelene Whitmire, *Regina Anderson Andrews: Harlem Renaissance Librarian*, 23.

28. Whitmire, 29.

29. Whitmire, 28-29; The Civil Service Commission administered an exam and candidates were ranked for a position based on their grades. It was an effort to hire on merit rather than nepotism and corruption.

30. Whitmire, 32.

corrected by the interviewer as being "colored." The interviewer inadvertently revealed a well-known secret that "American" was code for "white" and that people of color had no claim to the protection offered by US citizenship. In one moment, Andrews's self-identification was cast aside and she was forced into a social category subscribed to by early twentieth-century America. Isabel Gonzalez-Smith, Juleah Swanson, and Azusa Tanaka state that the "freedom to claim one's identity, particularly racially and ethnically, can be empowering for people of color."[31] In the early twentieth century, for a woman of color to claim the identity of "American" in the face of a white person of some authority must have come with a healthy dose of self-confidence and assurance. In light of this racist interaction with her job interviewer, Andrews could have run from the "colored" label, but she chose instead to embrace it.

In 1923, Andrews accepted a position at the 135th Street Branch of the New York Public Library, which by then had become the "Black" branch of the NYPL. However, she would chafe at the notion that this was the only branch where she could work "because of her color." Nevertheless, there was a silver lining to this cloud of racism. Andrews, through her employment at 135th Street, was positioned to become one of the birth mothers of the Harlem Renaissance, and engaged in activism to improve and highlight the intellectual lives of African Americans.

While she disdained the gendered restrictions imposed on middle-class Black co-eds at Wilberforce and rebelled against the class and gender expectations of the Black bourgeoisie in general, her middle-class, mixed-race family background afforded her a privileged position in the growing intelligentsia and literati of Harlem. She embodied the intersection of the "New Negro" and "New Woman" movements. Her position as an assistant librarian at the 135th Street Branch made it possible to influence the cultural programming of her supervisor,

---

31. Isabel Gonzalez-Smith, Juleah Swanson, and Azusa Tanaka, "Unpacking Identity: Racial, Ethnic, and Professional Identity and Academic Librarians of Color," in *The Librarian Stereotype: Deconstructing Perceptions & Presentations of Information Work*, ed. Nicole Pagowsky and Miriam Rigby (Chicago: Association of College and Research Libraries, 2014), 165.

Ernestine Rose. Andrews was a driving force behind fora at 135th Street. The fora included talks by Margaret Sanger and literary discussions that covered topics such as social conditions in Latin America and India, race relations in the United States, and anti-war talks. Andrews used her connections and natural proclivity as a social butterfly to find guest speakers.[32] According to David Levering Lewis, "...considering the qualifications of her assistant, Regina Anderson [Andrews]...Miss Rose could have failed only if she had been resolutely dim."[33]

Whitmire describes how Andrews found physical space for artists to work in the library; users of the space included Eric Walrond and Claude McKay, as well as Langston Hughes.[34] Moreover, Andrews not only used the public space of the library to further the careers of the leading talents of the Harlem Renaissance, but she also used the private space of the apartment she shared with Ethel Ray Nance and Louella Tucker at 580 St. Nicholas Avenue in Harlem. Lewis describes 580 as "a sort of Renaissance USO, offering a couch, a meal, sympathy and proper introduction" for up-and-coming artists who made their way to Harlem.[35] Scholars of the Harlem Renaissance trace the inception of the movement to a Civic Club *Opportunity* dinner in 1924, organized under the auspices of Charles Johnson and planned extensively by Andrews and Nance. The guest of honor was Jessie Fauset and attendees, in addition to Andrews and Nance, included the leading talents of the Harlem Renaissance: Langston Hughes, Countee Cullen, and Jean Toomer. Andrews was able to further the careers of these and other writers because of her position at the 135th Street Branch. In this way, Andrews defined her activism as a librarian. Her mission was to transform the library from a space for the consumption of cultural production[36] into

---

32. Whitmire, 36.

33. David Levering Lewis, *When Harlem Was in Vogue* (New York: Penguin Books), 105.

34. Whitmire, 37.

35. Lewis, 127.

36. We are using "cultural production" here to describe the literary and other creative works that comprise the body of artistic endeavors attributed to a group of people.

a space for the creation of cultural production. Andrews's work with Harlem Renaissance artists demonstrates her role in the expansion of the library from a place merely to check out books to a place that supports the arts and sciences for the betterment of the public.

This would continue with her own artistic production, both as a playwright and actor. Her plays were often political and addressed the injustices of racism and segregation. Whenever possible, any plays she was associated with would be performed at a library branch. The basement of the 135th Street Branch had a tradition of holding theatrical performances that had been initiated by W.E.B. Du Bois and encouraged by Ernestine Rose. Andrews was part of Du Bois's original theater group that performed at 135th Street. After the group disbanded, Andrews created the Harlem Experimental Theatre (HET) with other actors, which continued performing in the basement until moving to a church.[37] The HET would not be the last theater company to work out of the 135th Street Branch. In the 1940s, the American Negro Theatre (ANT) was founded. It also performed out of the basement and featured actors like Ruby Dee and Ossie Davis. The space inhabited by ANT is still preserved at the Schomburg today as a performance and exhibition space.[38]

Andrews's work with plays in the Harlem libraries was a reimagining of what a library could offer to the public. It reconsiders what can be deemed knowledge; rather than limiting knowledge solely to books, Andrews's work with Harlem theatre groups recasts knowledge as drama, public performances, and a return to an oral tradition. Her combined efforts of fora, work with Harlem Renaissance writers, and playwriting represents the library as adaptable to its community's needs. Andrews and the other librarians at the 135th Street Branch grew the library to meet the needs of their community while also reconceptualizing the type of knowledge held in a library. However, this reconceptualization would

---

37. Whitmire, 61-63.

38. New York Public Library, "The 75th Anniversary of the American Negro Theatre," *NYPL.org*, accessed September 9, 2017, https://www.nypl.org/events/exhibitions/75th-anniversary-american-negro-theatre.

never have been possible without the explicit support and permission of Ernestine Rose, the white supervisor of Andrews and other librarians.

For all of her dedication to the encouragement of Black artistic endeavors, and thereby Black racial uplift, Andrews hated being pigeonholed as a "colored" librarian who, because of the racial politics of the New York Public Library, could only serve at the "colored" branch. Using strategies she may have learned from her lawyer father, she enlisted the aid of Du Bois in her fight to get promoted at the 135th Street Branch. She received her promotion in 1930 (still an assistant librarian but Grade 3, instead of Grade 2) and a transfer to the Rivington Street Branch.[39] The Rivington Branch, which is no longer open, was located downtown on the Lower East Side (LES), near Little Italy and Chinatown. By 1930, the library served mostly Jewish people from Eastern Europe. Although not a "colored" branch, this branch served mainly non-Protestant ethnic white people and did not have the prestige of other branches, such as the 42nd Street Branch.

Eight years later, Andrews became the first African American to head a branch of the NYPL when she became Acting Branch Librarian of the 115th Street Branch. In her speech, she summed up her approach to library activism: "We must be more than Librarians, bibliophiles, curators and catalogers in order to develop the kind of social philosophy necessary for the modern community library."[40] Andrews would become a Supervising Librarian at the 115th Street Branch and, in 1948, at the Washington Heights Branch. Before those promotions could occur, however, she had to write a thesis. According to Whitmire, Andrews began the process for the thesis in 1938 when she had to submit topics to the local examining board. One topic she entertained was a "study [of] library conditions and opportunities among Negroes in the rural regions of the South and also in certain Islands of the West Indies,

39. Whitmire, 65.

40. "Opening of Little Theatre and Auditorium," (Regina Andrews Papers, Schomburg Center for Research in Black Culture, November 3, 1938), as quoted in Whitmire, 92.

particularly Spanish speaking ones."[41] In the end, Andrews wrote her thesis on a topic more in line with her theory about library activism and with her own multiracial background and integrated upbringing. In 1945, she submitted her thesis, "A Public Library Assists in Improving Race Relations." She set her thesis statement as, "Can we as librarians extend the use to which books and working with books can create another road to racial understanding?"[42] For her, "the use of books [represented] our strongest means of promoting intercultural understanding."[43] The tools and materials of librarianship that could be used to maintain racism and marginalization were reimagined and repurposed to be useful and enriching to the lives of Black Americans. Andrews fervently believed that seeing a Black woman in a position of authority in all branches of any public library made it and the community it served all the stronger. Andrews practiced what she preached, both by refusing to be limited by the idea she could only serve as a librarian in Harlem, and by her choices in other civic engagements, like her membership and eventual appointment as an officer in the National Council of Women of the United States (NCWUS).

Regina Anderson Andrews was unquestionably a trailblazer on many fronts. Yet her pioneering efforts were accomplished firmly in the context of the politics of respectability. Unlike Zora Neale Hurston or A'Lelia Walker,[44] no rumors of lesbianism or bisexuality swirled around Andrews and her female circle of friends. Although some scholars, most notably Deborah McDowell,[45] have argued for a homoerotic sensibility in Larsen's *Passing*, there has not been any suggestion that Larsen

41. Whitmire, 93.

42. Regina M. Andrews, "A Public Library Assists in Improving Race Relations," (Thesis, New York Public Library—Circulation Department, 1945), 1, as quoted in Whitmire, 97.

43. Andrews, 14, as quoted in Whitmire, 97.

44. A'lelia Walker (1885-1931), the daughter of Madam C.J. Walker, also held literary salons in her Harlem home.

45. Deborah McDowell, "Introduction" in McDowell, ed., *Quicksand and Passing*, xxiii-xxx. An excerpt of the full introduction is anthologized as "Black Female Sexuality in Passing" in Carla Kaplan, ed., *Passing*, 363-379.

questioned her own sexuality. While the women of 580 St. Nicholas Avenue seemed to accept the gay members of their circle, including Langston Hughes and Countee Cullen, they do come across as judgmental of Hurston and Walker.[46] Class, color, and sexuality intersect with both Hurston and Walker, and it is important to remember that Andrews and her circle reacted to the intersection—not just one element of it. Whitmire makes a valiant attempt to render Andrews's heteronormativity as radical in the context of white female librarianship, stating on the very first page of her introduction, "[Andrews] had several paramours and at least one was possibly a secret—and unlike many of her contemporary white female librarians who were often single and childless, Regina married...."[47] Nevertheless, we must acknowledge that Andrews married a man from a similar background to her own.

Larsen and Andrews are united by the fact that they both began their library careers as entry-level assistant librarians at the 135th Street Branch. However, there were women of color librarians at the branch in 1922 when Larsen arrived and 1923 when Andrews arrived. Pura Teresa Belpré was hired at the 135th Street Branch in 1921 as the "Hispanic assistant" and so became the first Puerto Rican librarian on staff at the NYPL.[48] Ernestine Rose[49] had observed the growing Puerto Rican community in Harlem and actively searched for a Puerto Rican hire. Based on a recommendation from her friends, Rose recruited Belpré's older sister for a position at the branch.[50] However, Elisa Belpré Maduro's husband would not allow her to work outside the home, so she passed the offer along to her younger, unmarried sister, Pura Belpré. Belpré first became enamored of librarianship after her initial visit to the 135th

46. Whitmire, 42 (Hurston); 44-45 (Walker).

47. Whitmire, 1.

48. Julio L. Hernández-Delgado, "Pura Teresa Belpré, Storyteller and Pioneer Puerto Rican Librarian," *Library Quarterly: Information, Community, Policy* 62, no. 4 (1992): 428.

49. Rose was also the supervisor of Andrews and Larsen. She makes her third appearance during Belpré's employment at the 135th Street Branch.

50. Hernández-Delgado, 427.

Street Branch when she observed Catherine Allen Latimer,[51] an African American librarian, at work with students in the library: "As we entered the reading room, I noticed the librarian, Miss Allen, later Mrs. Latimer, moving slowing among the crowded room helping teenagers. … I thought, 'If I could do what this lady is doing for the rest of my life, I would be the happiest person on earth.'"[52] Belpré found her vocation when she discovered that there were no Puerto Rican folktales in the children's room at 135th Street. According to Hernández-Delgado, "... Pura Belpré made a personal commitment to preserve the rich Puerto Rican folklore for the children of the United States. ...To acquaint children with the cultural heritage of Puerto Rico became Belpré's primary mission throughout her professional career; it eventually served as the impetus for her later publications."[53] By including Spanish language materials in the library's collection, Belpré, who believed that books are for all, was making the library more accessible for the community. By serving her patrons, Belpré was essentially decolonizing the once English-only library collection.

Belpré entered the New York Public Library School in 1925, three years after Nella Larsen and the year before it merged with the Columbia University School of Library Service.[54] It was during a course on storytelling that Belpré revealed her talent for oral performance of folktales from Puerto Rican culture. Like Larsen, Belpré used childhood memories and stories told to her by her grandmother as the foundation

---

51. Catherine Allen Latimer (1896-1948) deserves her own in-depth study. She was, in fact, the first African-American librarian hired by the New York Public Library. She rose through the ranks to become the head of the 135th Street Branch's Negro Literature and History division. When the NYPL acquired the private collection of Arturo Schomburg in 1926, Schomburg was appointed head of the division and Latimer was demoted to his assistant.

52. Lillian Lopez and Pura Belpré, "Reminiscences of Two Turned-On Librarians," in *Puerto Rican Perspectives*, ed. Edward Mapp, (Metuchen, NJ: Scarecrow Press, 1974), 88, quoted in Hernández-Delgado, 428.

53. Hernández-Delgado, 428.

54. 1926 was also the year Regina Anderson Andrews enrolled in the Columbia University School of Library Service.

for her success as a children's librarian and storyteller. Belpré had found her niche as a librarian-activist. Because of her efforts, "the folklore of the Puerto Rican child made its beginning in English and Spanish, throughout the library system...."[55] With the expanding Puerto Rican population in Harlem, Belpré filled an important role in the NYPL's outreach efforts in the communities its branches served. In 1929, Belpré moved to the 115th Street Branch, a community which had become predominantly Puerto Rican. Regina Anderson Andrews would become her Branch Librarian in 1938. At the 115th Street Branch, Belpré continued her activism by instituting bilingual story hours and a juvenile puppet theatre, the precedent for Belpré's future career as a puppeteer. Primarily because of Belpré's efforts, the 115th Street Branch became the cultural center for New York's Hispanophone population. Belpré began publishing books of Puerto Rican folktales, starting with *Pérez and Martina: A Portorican Folk Tale* in 1932.

Belpré's activism was closely aligned with her community's cultural production. In this regard she differed from Andrews. While Andrews also saw cultural production as a means of racial uplift, her primary mission was to lead the charge for integration by example and to represent the abilities of Black women librarians by heading branches outside of the Black community. Belpré, on the other hand, moved with the Puerto Rican community as it moved into other neighborhoods of New York (Upper Manhattan, East Harlem and the South Bronx).[56] She transferred to the Aguilar Branch on 110th Street in 1939, where she continued the same library-activism that she had pursued at the 115th Street Branch.

In 1940, Belpré attended the American Library Association meeting in Cincinnati, Ohio, where she presented a paper on her work as a librarian in the Puerto Rican communities of New York. Her sojourn in Cincinnati cemented her status as an inspiring librarian-activist and

55. Pura Belpré, "The Folklore of the Puerto Rican Child in My Library Experience," (Pura Belpré Papers, Centro de Estudios Puertorriqueños, Hunter College Evelina Lopez Antonetty Puerto Rican Research Collection, n.d.), 2, quoted in Hernández-Delgado, 429.

56. Hernández-Delgado, 431.

had a transformative impact on her personal life. She met Clarence Cameron White, a highly acclaimed composer and concert violinist who happened also to be African American. White was in Cincinnati to conduct a music festival. They would marry in 1943 and remained married until White's death in 1960. Belpré loved and was devoted to her work as a librarian, but the pull of her creative work was just as strong. In a move similar to her forebear, Larsen, Belpré took a leave of absence from her position at the Aguilar Branch in 1944 to write. She resigned formally a year later to concentrate completely on her writing. Belpré viewed her literary production as an extension of her library activism. Hernández-Delgado quotes a letter written by Belpré to her supervisor at the Aguilar Branch: "One does not uproot the foundations solidly laid by a mere stroke of a pen. ...That is why there cannot be a resignation from children's work for me. I will still be carrying on, in efforts to contribute, through my future writings something which the children will enjoy."[57] In her publications in subsequent years, Belpré did just that. In addition to creating popular entertainment for children, Belpré "was fulfilling her mission of acquainting Puerto Rican children in particular, and the American public in general, with the existence and beauty of Puerto Rican folklore."[58]

After the death of her husband in 1960, Belpré found a ray of hope in her sadness by contemplating a return to librarianship. After making inquiries, she was hired to fill the newly created position of Spanish Children's Specialist through the Office of Children's Services. This meant that Belpré could travel throughout New York City and thus have a wider impact than would be possible if she were assigned to a single branch. She also managed to keep publishing, including a Spanish version of her first publication, *Pérez and Martina*. Belpré retired in 1968 when she reached the mandatory retirement age of sixty-five. By then she had cemented her legacy; she was instrumental in launching the groundbreaking South Bronx Library Project and created a mobile

57. Hernández-Delgado, 432.

58. Ibid.

puppet theater for it. To ensure the success of the project, she agreed to work with the Project on a per diem basis.[59] Because of her dedication to the South Bronx Library Project, "Puerto Rican residents became cognizant of library services and learned the value and importance of Puerto Rican folklore."[60] Belpré continued publishing until 1978, and in 1982 she was celebrated and honored by the New York Public Library. The day after this celebration, Pura Teresa Belpré passed away.

These librarians, while seemingly operating within the framework of whiteness, disrupted the established concepts of librarianship. Consequently, the "anti-gentility" school views the first wave of Black women librarians (as well as Ernestine Rose) not as practitioners of a respectable profession but rather as agents in a movement who were attempting to "[create] a new attitude toward the library as a political tool in twentieth century American culture."[61] Roffman notes that the Black women librarians at the 135th Street Branch, "were women who shared an attitude about the library's potential to shape ideas and policies on a national scale…[and] attempted to revolutionize both the library itself and a conception of cultural institutions and knowledge production that would give them a much more significant role in the shaping of both."[62] In so doing, these activist-librarians pushed back against the racism embedded in library training systems, collection development, and the Dewey Decimal System (the main classification system). Larsen, Andrews, and Belpré were not the only three to do so. Dorothy Porter Wesley, a researcher and librarian at the Moorland-Spingarn Research Center at Howard University, would later condemn the implicit bias and imperialism of the Dewey system that sought to further colonize African people by placing their works in either the category for "slavery," or most telling, "colonization."[63] Long before the practice became more

59. Hernández-Delgado, 434.

60. Ibid., 435.

61. Roffman, 753.

62. Ibid., 754.

63. Karin Roffman, *From the Modernist Annex: American Women Writers in Museums and Libraries*, (Tuscaloosa, AL: The University of Alabama Press, 2010), 71.

accepted, Black women were critiquing and modifying the tools of library science that were reinforcing the marginalization of Black Americans.

The Second Wave: Ann Allen Shockley and Audre Lorde

Ann Allen Shockley was born in Louisville, Kentucky, in 1927, just as Andrews and Belpré were becoming trailblazers in the field of librarianship by smashing its color and language barriers. Shockley represents the shift away from the realm of public librarianship to that of academic librarianship, as well as a geographical shift away from the East Coast and, more specifically, the New York Public Library. Nevertheless, Shockley continues the tradition of our first wave librarians by being a multifaceted professional. She was a journalist, a novelist, and a librarian. She has won awards for both her academic works on librarianship and her fiction.[64] She also shares other traits with her foremothers: as a daughter of social workers Henry and Bessie Lucas Allen, she was part of the Black middle class; she married and later divorced William Shockley and had two children.

Shockley's career as a librarian coincided with the standardization of librarianship credentialing. She received her BA from Fisk University in 1948 and her Masters of Library Science from Case Western Reserve University in 1959. Shockley held positions as Assistant Librarian at Delaware State College from 1959-1960, as Assistant Librarian at the University of Maryland, Eastern Shore from 1960-1966, and then as Associate Librarian there from1966-1969. She returned to her alma mater, Fisk University, in 1969 as an Associate Librarian and head of Special Collections and Archivist, and remained there until her retirement in 1988.

Shockley compiled a solid body of work dealing with critical librarianship while she was at Fisk, and this work came directly from her

64. Hatshepsut Award for Literature, New York, 1981; Martin Luther King Junior Black Author Award, Nashville, 1982; A Crossroad to Freedom Award in Recognition of Outstanding and Professional Librarianship, Western Branch Louisville Kentucky Library, 2005; Alice B. Readers Appreciation Award, 2006.

experience as a curator of Black literary production throughout her career. Titles such as *A Handbook for the Administration of Special Negro Collections* (1970), *History of Public Library Services to Negroes in the South, 1900-1955*, *Living Black American Authors: A Biographical Directory* (1973), and *Afro-American Women Writers, 1746-1933*, encapsulate Shockley's brand of library activism. She wanted to document the erasure of Black contributions, not only to literature, but also to librarianship. Furthermore, she wrote guides on collecting and preserving library and archival materials about, and by, African Americans. In *Special Negro Collections*, Shockley provides advice, exercises, and examples from her own work at Fisk University Library, including a guide on developing budgets, a list of required personnel, and examples of curricula to be incorporated within an African American library collection. However, *Special Negro Collections* is more than just a guide. In her introduction to the handbook, Shockley manages to provide background information about African American collections in libraries while criticizing "predominately [*sic*] white colleges and universities" for two actions: one, having minimal information on African Americans, and two, "hastily attempting" to develop African American special collections.[65] As the field of Black studies was developing in the late 1960s and early 1970s in predominantly white institutions (PWI), collections and research libraries on the African Diaspora were also developed to support the work of scholars. It was during this time that the Schomburg *Collection* became the Schomburg *Center* for Research in Black Culture, and in 1972, formally became one of the research libraries of the New York Public Library. In *Special Negro Collections*, Shockley chastises libraries at PWIs for devaluing African American material and only putting together African American special collections when, as she states, Black Americans have had a "revolutionary role in American society."[66] As to her motive for writing this guide, she criticizes library science programs for not including the administration

65.Ann Allen Shockley, *A Handbook for the Administration of Special Negro Collections*, (Nashville, TN: Fisk University, 1970), i.

66. Shockley, *Special Negro Collections*, i.

of African American special collections in their curricula and for neglecting and ignoring the growing field of Black Studies. Shockley's scathing criticism includes even the white scholars of Black studies. She explains that African American research collections are "established to coincide with black studies programs, to cool militant black students who are angrily aware that *their*[67] black writers, leaders, and scholars should too have an equally honorable place on library shelves, and to aid young white researchers who have found the black role in society a lucrative field for quick scholarly recognition." In one sentence, Shockley not only validates the anger of the Black Power movement on college campuses but also condemns white scholars who are researching the African Diaspora, not out of genuine academic interest, but rather to mine the field for promotion and tenure. Her language places Black students in the role of revolutionaries and white scholars as colonizers of the field. Her works, while providing documentation and guidance, do not forgive readers for their complicity in the need for Shockley's handbooks and bibliographies—in the 1970s and still today.

Arguably, Shockley's most important work in this regard is her volume, *Handbook of Black Librarianship* (1977), co-authored with her African-American male colleague at Fisk, E. J. Josey. In her review of this work, Virginia Lacy Jones stated, "Librarians interested in establishing or evaluating collections of Afro-American materials will find the *Black Librarianship* to be a valuable aid in that it contains a list of reference books which reflect the black experience, a list of African and Afro-American periodicals, a list of black authors whose books have become best sellers, and a list of black authors whose works are included in the ALA Notable Book List."[68] Earlier in the same review, Jones praises *Black Librarianship* for restoring the "contributions of pioneer black librarians to American library history."[69] It is deeply ironic that librar-

67. Emphasis is Shockley's, not the authors.

68. Virginia Lacy Jones, "Review of *Handbook of Black Librarianship* by E.J. Josey and Ann Allen Shockley," *Library Quarterly* 49, no. 1, (Jan. 1979): 104.

69. Ibid.

ians today do not recognize the contributions of Shockley to the field; Josey is seen as the driving force behind *Black Librarianship* and is given the most credit for it.

The movement of black librarians in the 70s and 80s has been distilled to just the work of E.J. Josey and has erased the work of Black female librarians who were also in the struggle, not unlike the essentializing of the late-nineteenth-century Black political thought movement to Du Bois. Du Bois did not do this work alone. Similarly, Josey was not the only African American advancing the roles of Black librarianship. While the library field is often characterized as "feminized," that does not mean that it is immune to misogyny and sexism.

Shockley, like her foremothers Larsen, Belpré, and Andrews, was also a literary artist, and most biographical references list her many and various occupations: librarian, journalist, teacher, bibliographer, essayist, and fiction writer. Occasionally, she is only listed as a writer but never as just a librarian. Unlike Larsen and Belpré, Shockley never resigned from her position as a librarian but did her writing whenever she had free time. In the introduction to her short story "A Birthday Remembered, 1980," Shockley remarked on her struggle to balance her careers as a librarian and a fiction writer, a struggle that will resonate with many women working in academia: "Working as an academic librarian, I write on weekends, holidays, and summer months, with my dogs, Tiffany and Bianca, watching the birthing pains. I wish it could be different."[70]

Outside of the world of academic librarianship, Shockley is best remembered for her groundbreaking novels which, for the first time, offered Black Lesbian characters as protagonists and heroes. As Alycee Jane quotes Jewelle Gomez in the foreword to the 1997 edition of Shockley's novel, *Loving Her* (1974), reading it "[f]or Black Lesbians was like reading *The Well of Loneliness* for the first time as teenagers and realizing there were 'others' out there."[71] Shockley garnered praise from many

70. Susan Koppelman, *Between Mothers and Daughters: Stories Across a Generation*, (New York: Feminist Press at CUNY, 1987), 285.

71. Alycee J. Lane, foreword to *Loving Her* (Boston: Northeastern University Press, 1997), v. *The Well of Loneliness*, a "lesbian novel," was published in 1928 by the British

Black Lesbian feminists for both her bravery and her achievement. In "Toward a Black Feminist Criticism," Barbara Smith poignantly remarks, "Yet there are a handful of Black women who have risked everything for truth. Audre Lorde, Pat Parker, and Ann Allen Shockley have at least broken ground in the vast wilderness of works that do not exist."[72] In her essay, "The Black Lesbian in American Literature: An Overview," Shockley brings together her intersectional analysis and her expertise as a librarian and writer. As she states, "It is my belief that those Black female writers who could have written well and perceptively enough to warrant publication chose instead to write about Black women from a heterosexual perspective. The preference was motivated by the fear of being labeled a Lesbian whether they were one or not."[73] This is a fear that Shockley challenged when she incorporated themes of women-loving-women, transgender and non-conforming gender identities, and homophobia in her novels and essays.[74] However, it has also led to some ambiguity about Shockley's own identification. Biographies of Shockley either omit any mention of sexual orientation identity or present problematic descriptions. For example, the website NNDB.com, a biographical dictionary, is one of the few which has a category for "sexual orientation." For Shockley, the compilers list her sexual orientation as "straight," with the following note:

> Is not known to have engaged in any lesbian relationships. See Yolanda Williams Page, *Encyclopedia of African American Women Writers* (2007), page 522, "Although a majority of Shockley's fictional characters are lesbian, she identifies as a feminist with lesbian sympathies."

---

novelist Radclyffe Hall. For many Lesbians at the time and later, *The Well* was the first time Lesbians saw themselves explicitly represented in a literary work.

72. Barbara Smith, "Towards a Black Feminist Criticism," *Radical Teacher*, no. 7 (1978): 26.

73. Ann Allen Shockley, "The Black Lesbian in American Literature: An Overview," in *Home Girls: A Black Feminist Anthology*, ed. Barbara Smith, (New York: Kitchen Table Press 983), 84.

74. Contemporary queer, gender and racial politics are important themes in Shockley's most recent novel, *Celebrating Hotchclaw* (2005).

Rita B. Dandridge, an important compiler of Shockley's work, gives a list of Shockley's personal intersecting and sometimes conflicting identities, including "straight woman and lesbian sympathizer."[75] The ambiguity around Shockley's sexuality has allowed the official historical record to "straightwash" Shockley. However, in a personal conversation with Margo Okazawa-Rey, a founding member of the Combahee River Collective who knows Shockley, Shelley Haley asked directly about Shockley's sexual orientation. Okazawa-Rey's answer was unequivocal: "Ann is in the life. She is one of our Black Lesbian heroes."[76]

With *Ann Allen Shockley: An Annotated Primary and Secondary Bibliography* (1987), Dandridge has compiled an invaluable aid for assessing Shockley's impact on library science; queer literature, especially Black Lesbian literature; racial, gender and queer politics; and journalism. Dandridge explains in her preface how she came to do this work, "The more of Shockley's writings I discovered, the more intrigued I became by the quantity and quality of her works and the relevance of these to black studies, women's literature, American history, and library resources."[77] Dandridge acknowledges that Shockley has received "some recognition"[78] for her work, but that this tends to come from scholars and is highly compartmentalized in a way that belies the intersectionality of Shockley's work. In the introduction to the compilation, Dandridge discusses the lack of national attention Shockley has received, "Shockley's talent is also relatively unknown on the national level because of the thoughtless reviews some critics have given her works."[79]

Shockley, like her Black foremothers in librarianship, accomplished a number of firsts and established herself as a librarian-activist, embodying

75. Rita B. Dandridge, *Ann Allen Shockley: An Annotated Primary and Secondary Bibliography* (New York: Greenwood Press, 1987.), xiv.

76. Shelley P. Haley (co-author of this chapter), Personal Conversation with Margo Okazawa-Rey at Hamilton College, Clinton, NY, May 1, 2017.

77. Dandridge, vi.

78. Ibid., xi.

79. Ibid., xii.

the spirit of the Ghanaian word and symbol, *sankofa*,[80] which now is translated as "one must reach back to reclaim that which is lost in order to move forward." *Sankofa* guided Shockley throughout her career as a librarian and as a novelist and essayist. She strove always to make her work accessible, even if it made her unpopular with academic critics. Shockley always considered herself a full-time librarian and a part-time writer. In "A Soul Cry for Reading," Shockley reveals herself "as an underpaid, overworked librarian or 'general factotum.'"[81] Although she may have, at times, resented librarianship, she never left. This cannot be said of our final librarian, Audre Lorde.

Along with Shockley, Lorde is often cited as the bravest of the brave: Black Lesbian writers who wrote openly Black Lesbian literature. While Shockley's lesbianism is debated, Lorde's self-description as a "Black, Lesbian, feminist, mother, poet warrior" leaves no doubt about her orientation. Librarianship was a vocation Shockley and Lorde shared, but like Larsen, Lorde left the field to devote herself fully to her writing and vision that "poetry is not a luxury." Lorde believed in the power of words—the power of poetry—to effect lasting change. As she states, "For women, then, poetry is not a luxury. It is a vital necessity of our existence. It forms the quality of the light within which we predicate our hopes and dreams toward survival and change, first made into language, then into idea, then into more tangible action."[82] Lorde's first steps in birthing this vision began with libraries.

Lorde was born in 1934 in New York City, the youngest of three daughters to Linda and Byron Lorde, who were recent immigrants to the United States from the Caribbean. Lorde's parents instilled in all their daughters a strong work ethic and the value of education, particularly a Catholic education, and a sense that the United States was not their home. Displaying bias against and superiority to African Americans

80. Many Black/Africana Studies programs also embrace *sankofa* as a guiding principle of their research and teaching practices.

81. Dandridge, 61.

82. Audre Lorde, *Sister Outsider* (Berkeley, CA.: The Crossing Press, 1984), 37.

common to many African and Caribbean immigrants, Linda Lorde would not allow her daughter to play or socialize with any African American children in Harlem where they lived. Linda Lorde, who was light enough to pass as "Spanish," also had a deep-seated prejudice against dark-skinned people of African descent. She often remarked that "you didn't trust anybody whose face is black because their heart is black."[83] This, in turn, had a serious impact on Audre Lorde's developing self-esteem, since she was the darkest of the Lorde daughters, which caused her to act out. In fact, it can be argued that her mother's colorism forged and fueled Lorde's poetic and bookish sensibilities. The parenting style of the Lordes was steeped in the politics of respectability and the belief that they were ethnically superior. Lorde's sisters, Phyllis and Helen, took piano lessons; Lorde herself preferred to memorize poetry, even as she was furtively writing her own poems.[84] Books, language, and poetry became Lorde's shelter from her strict, emotionally detached parents and the disinterest of her sisters. She first became aware of this haven in the 135th Street Branch of the New York Public Library.

Lorde was five years old when she first met Augusta Baker, the Children's Librarian at the 135th Street Branch. Baker, one of the first wave of Black female librarians, was also a trailblazer. According to her obituary in the *New York Times*, Augusta Baker was "a spellbinding storyteller, editor and former custodian of the children's section at the New York Public Library."[85] When Augusta Baker was hired as the Children's Librarian at the 135th Street Branch in 1937, she found her calling as a librarian-activist. Beginning in 1939, the same year Lorde first met her, Baker spearheaded a campaign at the branch to find and collect examples of children's literature that were positive and empowering representations of people of African descent. Throughout her thirty-seven years at the New York Public Library, she held various

83. Alexis De Veaux, *Warrior Poet: A Biography of Audre Lorde* (New York: W.W. Norton & Co., 2004), 18.

84. Ibid., 21.

85. Wolfgang Saxon, "Augusta B. Baker, 86, Storyteller, Editor and Children's Librarian," *New York Times*, March 6, 1998.

positions, including that of the first Black librarian in an administrative position as Coordinator of Children's Services in 1961. In this position, she fostered the vision of the South Bronx Library Project by inviting Pura Belpré to participate. In 1946, she compiled *Books about Negro Life for Children,* a reference work of titles related to the Black experience. This was retitled in 1971 as *The Black Experience in Children's Books* and, according to Baker's entry in *Pioneers and Leaders in Library Services to Youth: A Biographical Dictionary*, this work was instrumental in raising awareness about the negative stereotypes in Helen Bannerman's "The Story of Little Black Sambo."

This, then, is the remarkable woman who, in Lorde's own words, inspired her to read and, in turn, gave her hope. It is important to quote at length what Lorde remembers about her first meeting with Augusta Baker. She tells the story in *Zami: A Biomythography*:

> I learned how to read from Mrs. Augusta Baker, the children's librarian at the old 135th Street branch library… If that was the only good deed that lady ever did in her life, may she rest in peace. Because that deed saved my life, if not sooner, then later, when sometimes the only thing I had to hold on to was knowing I could read, and that that could get me through.

Lorde goes on to describe how her mother tried to keep her quiet by pinching her ears, which, of course, only made her scream louder. She goes on,

> Suddenly, I looked up, and there was a library lady standing over me. My mother's hands had dropped to her sides. From the floor where I was lying, Mrs. Baker seemed like yet another mile-high woman about to do me in. She had immense, light, hooded eyes and a very quiet voice that said, not damnation for my noise, but "Would you like to hear a story, little girl?"
>
> Part of my fury was because I had not been allowed to go to that secret feast called story hour since I was too young, and now here was this strange lady offering me my own story.
>
> ...Still bewildered by this sudden change of events, I climbed up upon the stool which Mrs. Baker pulled over for me, and gave her my full attention. This was a new experience for me and I was insatiably curious.

Baker reads a variety of stories to Lorde, and she reacts by saying,

> By the time she had finished that last one, I was sold on reading for the rest of my life. . . . I said, quite loudly, for whoever was listening to hear, "I want to read."[86]

Lorde's education came in the heady days of the Civil Rights Movement. Lorde graduated from Hunter College in 1959 and then entered Columbia University's School of Library Science, where she earned a Master's degree in Library Science in 1961. De Veaux describes this period of Lorde's life: "Bordered by Harlem, Columbia became yet another stage upon which she juggled carefully inhabited, intersecting worlds. She worked during the daytime, took classes at night, and was still involved with the 'gay-girls' scene in the East and West Village."[87]

Lorde would go on to become first the young adult librarian at the Mount Vernon Public Library, perhaps still honoring the influence of Augusta Baker, and then in 1966, the Head Librarian at the Town School in Manhattan. In the intervening years, she married Edward Rollins, a white, gay man and had two children, Elizabeth and Jonathan. She also became politically active and attended the March on Washington in 1963.

In 1968, she made the life-changing decision to resign from her position at the Town School and accept a Poet-in-Residence position at Tougaloo College in Tougaloo, Mississippi. Her activism pivoted from curation of the written word to production of it. She would never return to librarianship. In an interview with Adrienne Rich, her friend, collaborator, fellow Lesbian, and fellow poet, she explained the transformative effect Tougaloo had on her:

> *Audre*: I knew by the time I left Tougaloo that teaching was the work I needed to be doing, that library work—by this time I was head librarian at the Town School—was not enough. It had been very satisfying to me. And I had a kind of stature I hadn't had before in terms of working. But

---

86. Audre Lorde, *Zami: A Biomythography* (Freedom, CA: The Crossing Press, 1994), 22-23.

87. De Veaux, 62-63.

> from the time I went to Tougaloo and did that workshop, I knew: not only, yes, I am a poet but also, this is the kind of work I'm going to do.[88]

This does not mean, however, that librarianship was no longer part of her self-identity. In the same interview with Rich, Lorde explains the influence of librarianship on her development as an intellectual, while discussing Rich's need for documentation and Lorde's resistance to it:

> *Audre*: Don't forget that I'm a librarian. I became a librarian because I really believed I would gain tools for ordering and analyzing information. I couldn't know everything in the world, but I would gain tools for learning it.[89]

Still, it is striking that despite Lorde's admonition, "Don't forget that I'm a librarian," most, if not all of her biographers and compilers have forgotten it. De Veaux mentions Lorde's librarianship mainly as a fact of her career path. Passing mention of librarianship is made in the introduction and timeline of *I am Your Sister: Collected and Unpublished Writings of Audre Lorde.*[90] There is no mention of Lorde's librarianship in the most recent anthology by Gloria I. Joseph.[91] Within librarianship, Lorde's departure from the field is often held up as an example of the isolation of people of color, especially women of color, and a result of the field's ignorance about how the processes, tools, and practices that we engage with as librarians reflect and uphold whiteness.[92] However, this is complicated by Lorde's continued self-identification as a librarian.

---

88. Lorde, *Sister Outsider*, 92.

89. Ibid., 105.

90. *I am Your Sister: Collected and Unpublished Writings of Audre Lorde*, eds. Rudolph P. Byrd, Johnnetta Betsch Cole, and Beverly Guy-Sheftall. Introduction by Byrd mentions librarianship, 3; Chronology cites librarianship, 267.

91. Gloria I. Joseph, *The Wind is Spirit: The Life, Love and Legacy of Audre Lorde.* The omission of this important aspect of Lorde's career belies the cover blurb from bell hooks, "This anthology is awesome because unlike other biographical reminiscences, it offers a candid and *holistic* portrait of Audre Lorde." (emphasis ours).

92. Todd Honma, "Trippin' Over the Color Line: The Invisibility of Race in Library and Information Studies," *InterActions: UCLA Journal of Education and Information Studies* 1, no. 2 (2005): 19-20.

It is a missed opportunity that many researchers do not connect how Lorde's experience as a librarian affected her work on black feminist thought and theory.[93] Lorde made use of her training in cataloging and classification systems to discuss how knowledge and understanding are separate from one another. It is interesting that Lorde chose to use the word "tools" in the Rich interview, and we cannot help but be reminded of another essay in *Sister Outsider*, "The Master's Tools Will Never Dismantle the Master's House."[94] In the context of her quote from her conversation with Rich, one can argue that librarianship also influences "The Master's Tools." When library science is applied to that essay, we can see how classification tools continue to colonize people of color, unless critiqued and dismantled. So, while Lorde may have left the profession of librarianship, the identity of librarian never left Lorde, and as seen with the other women of this chapter, it influenced her writings.

Conclusion

These five women, while just a sample of how Black women contributed to librarianship, provide us with an understanding of the role of Black women in the history of American librarianship. Nevertheless, Audre Lorde's statement that "the master's tools will never dismantle the master's house" remains a question for Black librarians. Certainly, each of these Black women made significant changes, reimaginings, and disruption to the whiteness of libraries over the course of their careers. It also cannot be ignored that the women of the first wave of librarianship all benefited from an adherence to white, middle-class values. Furthermore, all of these women, by the chance of a genetic lottery, were on the lighter end of the color scale.

---

93. Lorde, *Sister Outsider*, 105.

94. "The Master's Tools Will Never Dismantle the Master's House" is considered one of the foundational texts of Black feminism.

In 1924, Regina Anderson Andrews, Ethel Ray Nance, and Louella Tucker hosted a soiree for Langston Hughes at their apartment on St. Nicholas Avenue. Photographs were taken to commemorate the event. As we study these photographs and others from the Harlem Renaissance, an uncomfortable and often neglected truth emerges: the intersection between class and skin color, now commonly referred to as colorism. We believe it is fair to say that the librarians we have discussed as part of the first wave, along with other members of the Harlem Renaissance, internalized and benefited from colorism. Of course, not all artists were comfortable with the tacit acceptance of colorism. For example, Zora Neale Hurston wrote a play in 1926 which she titled *Color Struck*, and although it was never produced, it is a biting testimonial to the existence of and awareness of colorism among the social circle of our first wave librarians. The very title is the phrase used colloquially to describe people of African descent who have internalized white supremacy and its concomitant concepts that light skin color equals intellectual capability and sexual desirability, and is an omen of economic success. Hurston's play tells the story of Emmaline (Emma) Beazely and John Turner, a couple who are always arguing because of John's blatant disrespect for Emma, demonstrated through his wandering "eye," which is always directed at "yellow" or "half-white girls." Zora leaves no doubt about the theme of the play. Appropriately, given the title, Hurston explicitly states the skin color of the main characters: John Turner, a light brown-skinned man; Emmaline Beazely, a black woman; Effie, a mulatto girl; Lou Lillian, Emma's daughter, a very white girl. Emma becomes overwhelmed with jealousy and mistrust, and her relationship with John disintegrates. Hurston is careful to demonstrate that the effects of colorism go beyond the dissolution of a dysfunctional relationship, as these lines from Scene 2 show:

> Emma: *(Calmly bitter)* He went and left me. If we is spatting we done had our last one. *(She stands and clenches her fists.)* Ah, mah God! He's in there with her—Oh them half whites, they gets everything, they gets everything everybody else wants! The men, the jobs—everything! The

whole world got a sign on it. Wanted: Light colored. Us blacks was made for cobble stones. (*She muffles a cry and sinks limp upon the seat.*)[95]

As a young girl learning double dutch jump rope, Haley encountered this chant that the more experienced jumpers used to keep time as they twirled the rope. It was also the source of a blues song by Big Bill Broonzy:

If you're white, you're alright
If you're brown, stick around, but
If you're black, get back, get back.

In recent times there has been much scholarly attention paid to colorism and the fissures and polarization it has always caused in communities of color.[96] Colorism was and is a tool of white supremacist patriarchy used to ensure the fracture and disunity of communities of color. While we can infer that class and colorism played a role in which Black women were placed in librarian positions, there has been no *explicit* scholarship on the topic. Nevertheless, recent scholarship reinforces our inference. Treva Lindsey writes in her conclusion, "The bodies and representations of the bodies of African American women

---

95. Zora Neale Hurston, "Colorstruck," in *Zora Neale Hurston: Collected Plays*, ed. Jean Lee Cole and Charles Mitchell.

96. A cursory literature review on the topic of colorism in general and colorism during the Harlem Renaissance reveals a plethora of articles and books. Ones which we find enlightening include: Taunya Lovell Banks, "Colorism: A Darker Shade of Pale," *UCLA Law Review* 47, no. 6 (August 2000): 1705-1746; Jacob S. Dorman, "Skin Bleach and Civilization: The Racial Formation of Blackness in 1920s Harlem," *The Journal of Pan African Studies* 4.4 (2011): 47-80; Margaret L. Hunter, "'If You're Light You're Alright': Light Skin Color as Social Capital for Women of Color," *Gender and Society* 16, no. 2 (2002): 175-193; Sharon L. Jones, *Rereading the Harlem Renaissance: Race, Class, and Gender in the Fiction of Jessie Fauset, Zora Neale Hurston, and Dorothy West*, 2002; Treva B. Lindsey, "Black No More: Skin Bleaching and the Emergence of New Negro Womanhood Beauty Culture," *The Journal of Pan African Studies* 4, no. 4 (2011): 97-116; Mahshidossadat Mirmasoumi and Farshid Nowrouzi Roshnavand, "Blackness, Colorism, and Epidermalization of Inferiority in Zora Neale Hurston's Color Struck: A Fanonian Reading of the Play," *Khazar Journal of Humanities and Social Sciences* 17, no. 4 (2014): 55-65; Leland Ware, "'Color Struck': Intragroup and Cross-Racial Color Discrimination," *Connecticut Public Interest Law Journal* 13, no.1 (Fall 2013): 75-110.

in Washington and other urban centers were a terrain in which the socio-cultural dynamics and competing notions of a New negro ethos was magnified. … African American women both implicitly and explicitly accepted white constructions of feminine beauty...and situated themselves at the center of a public discourse of political, economic, social, and cultural significance."[97] There are grounds to speculate that all the first wave librarians were complicit in perpetuating colorism (even if unwittingly) and gained social and class advantages because of their light skin, "good hair," and European facial features.

In addition, the general ethos of Du Bois's "talented tenth" and Locke's "New Negro"[98] reified the implicit superiority of light skin and its connection to the educated Black middle class. In fact, Du Bois's prejudice against dark-skinned folks exacerbated his political and intellectual feud with Marcus Garvey. In the February 1923 issue of *Century Magazine*, Du Bois, light-skinned, Harvard- and Berlin-educated, described Garvey as "a little fat black man, ugly, but with intelligent eyes and a big head."[99] Garvey countered by calling Du Bois an "unfortunate mulatto." Jacob Dorman, highlighting the connection between class and color here, states, "...Du Bois has interwoven class and color into the discourse of civilization to associate blackness and ugliness with a lack of civilization."[100]

Further support for the connection between colorism, class, and librarianship can be found in how Ethelene Whitmire introduces us to Regina Anderson Andrews. Andrews is seeking employment at the

---

97. Treva B. Lindsey, "Black No More: Skin Bleaching and the Emergence of New Negro Womanhood Beauty Culture," *The Journal of Pan African Studies* 4, no. 4 (2011), 111.

98. The "talented tenth" and the "New Negro" sought to combat dangerous stereotypes of African Americans and replaced them with images of erudite, cosmopolitan, and sophisticated Black intellectual leaders of society.

99. W.E.B. DuBois, "Back to Africa," *Century Magazine* 150.4 (1923), 539. Quoted in Jacob S. Dorman, "Skin Bleach and Civilization: the racial formation of Blackness in 1920s Harlem," *The Journal of Pan African Studies* 4.4 (2011), 62.

100. Dorman, 62.

New York Public Library. At this point (this is the first page of the first chapter) we know nothing about Andrews except that she is a librarian from Chicago who applies for a position with the NYPL and receives an interview. Here one might expect Whitmire to tell us about Andrews's credentials, but instead she gives a vivid and detailed description of her hair as she arrived for her interview: "No doubt she was impeccably clad, as usual, and her waist-length hair was most likely pinned up since Andrews 'combed it very high on her head in a Spanish fashion.'"[101] From there we get a physical description of Andrews: "Regina had been described as a 'beautiful, beautiful girl' and 'a pert olive-skinned girl.'" We learn that she was featured on the cover of *Messenger: World's Greatest Negro Monthly*, a periodical whose editorial direction included "[showing] in pictures as well as writing, Negro women who are unique, accomplished, beautiful, intelligent, industrious, talented and successful."

It should also be noted that all our first wave librarians selected marriage partners who were light-skinned members of the talented tenth. Larsen perceived both her occupation as a librarian and her marriage to noted physicist Elmer S. Imes as tickets to the middle class. Thadious Davis discusses Imes's choice of Larsen as a wife. She states, "This invidious emphasis on color as a measure of value perhaps contributed to Elmer Imes's initial attraction to the 'mulatto' Nella Larsen, who had straight, or 'good,' hair and features that were more Caucasian than Negroid."[102] Regina Anderson Andrews, whose own parents were part of the talented tenth, eventually married the son of another prominent member of that group, William Andrews, even though the love of her life may have been Arthur St. George Richardson. Andrews's parents had disapproved of Richardson and ended their engagement. Whitmire shares the speculations of Andrews's niece that her parents rejected Richardson because of his dark skin, and Whitmire herself adds the speculation that Andrews's parents may also have disapproved of

101. Whitmire, 14. For the description of Andrews' hairstyle, Whitmire cites (FN 2, 121) an interview with Ethel Ray Nance, Andrews' roommate at 580 conducted by Ann Allen Shockley, one of our second-wave librarians.

102. Davis, 130.

Richardson's Caribbean background—his father was born in Bermuda.[103] Finally, Belpré married the noted composer and violinist Clarence Cameron White, whose photograph reveals a light-skinned African American man with European features. Because of colorism these women achieved positions that allowed them to disrupt the "master's house."

While our first-wave librarians pushed boundaries, it is important to recognize the white power structures that they were still working in and upholding. Particularly for Andrews and Belpré, they were groundbreaking because they were allowed to be groundbreaking. Most of their work: the fora, plays, and Spanish-language library services, were sanctioned and approved by their white library supervisor, Ernestine Rose. During the era of Carnegie libraries, from the late nineteenth to the early twentieth century, libraries were created to uphold white middle-class Protestant values and provide reading materials to occupy blue-collar workers during off-hours.[104] In addition to the library services, the very architecture, the physical embodiment of the library, was thought to have a "civilizing" effect.[105] Historian Wayne Wiegand argues that libraries, especially in New York, which was the entry point for many European immigrants, became a place of assimilation to American values.[106] However, European immigrants were not the only new arrivals to large northern cities like New York. African American refugees[107] and migrants from the American South were arriving in waves to northern cities as part of the Great Migration. Just as the library was a place for

---

103. Whitmire, 49.

104. Wayne A. Wiegand, *"An Active Instrument for Propaganda": The American Public Library During World War I* (New York: Greenwood Press, 1989), 5; Wayne A. Wiegand, *Part of Our Lives: a People's History of the American Public Library* (New York: Oxford Press, 2015), 83.

105. Wiegand, *Part of Our Lives*, 95.

106. Ibid, 96-97.

107. Many scholars have reframed the Great Migration as a refugee movement in reaction to lynchings and Jim Crow, instead of economic flight as previously thought. See: Stewart E. Tolnay and E. M. Beck, "Racial Violence and Black Migration in the American South, 1910 to 1930," *American Sociological Review* 57, no. 1 (Feb., 1992), 103-116 and Isabel Wilkerson, *The Warmth of Other Suns* (New York: Random House, 2010).

European immigrants to assimilate, so too the library was a place for people of the Great Migration to be assimilated into the culture of the Harlem Renaissance. For example, Andrews's fora and plays sought to educate their audiences to be cosmopolitan, erudite, and socially aware. These were also the values that Harlemites wanted to project of the "Black Mecca."

On the other hand, the librarians of the second-wave pushed against the white power structures, rather than just existing and working within them. Lorde used information science in her essays on Black feminism to disrupt white hegemonic notions of knowledge and information. We see Shockley advocating for libraries at HBCUs to lead the way for African American special collections and incorporating the contributions of marginalized groups, including Black lesbians, into scholarly works and bibliographies. In the second wave, which aligns with the Black Arts and Black Power movements, these librarians subverted white-centric ideals and forged spaces for Black and queer people without the expectation of respectability.

But questions still remain for us. To what extent does the disruption of the librarian narrative exist merely because these are Black women? Is the expectation that, as Black women, we are all automatically disruptive? Is the exceptionalism of Black women (often phrased as the "strong, Black woman" stereotype) an unhealthy model to live up to? How much emotional labor do we expend on this disruption? To further investigate these questions, more work needs to be done by librarians interrogating the field's racial biases and how the structure of the library upholds whiteness and sexism. Because, even after all the work of our Black female forebears, Black librarianship today is still in peril. Andrew Jackson, in the preface to *The 21st-Century Black Librarian in America: Issues and Challenges*, states bluntly that: "All is not well in librarianship. Despite all that has been accomplished and all that black librarians have overcome, there is still work to be done, glass ceilings to be shattered, closed doors to be opened."[108] Librarianship in the United States is still

---

108. Andrew Jackson, "Preface," xix.

overwhelmingly white. In a blog post, Chris Bourg cleverly sums up the field's racial diversity problem as the "the unbearable whiteness of librarianship." In that same blog post, she lays out the racial makeup of librarianship as of 2010 from data collected by the ALA Diversity Office. Librarianship is over 87% white and African-American librarians make up just over five percent of the field.[109] One reason for the racial disparity is the continued structural whiteness and implicit racism in librarianship and libraries.

April Hathcock discusses how the failure of diversity initiatives is one consequence of the whiteness of librarianship. "The normativity of whiteness," Hathcock states, "works insidiously, invisibly to create binary categorizations of people as either acceptable to whiteness and therefore normal or different and therefore other."[110] The experience of Regina Anderson Andrews being told that she was "colored" and not "American" is still an experience being felt by Black librarians today. Black women in librarianship are still racialized and gendered, and their physical bodies are still political. Black librarians are still expected to "uplift the race" and the field of librarianship. Taneya Gethers, in her chapter in *The 21st-Century Black Librarian in America,* advocates that the "professional duty of black librarians is not separate from our cultural responsibility as people of African descent. An essential part of the mission is to help empower black people throughout the African Diaspora, and this undertaking is critical to our mission today."[111] Jackson echoes this sentiment, stating that "Today's call for action is for young and new black librarians to stand tall and firm on the shoulders of our ancestors...

109. Chris Bourg, "The Unbearable Whiteness of Librarianship," *The Feral Librarian* (blog), March 3, 2014, https://chrisbourg.wordpress.com/2014/03/03/the-unbearable-whiteness-of-librarianship.

110. April Hathcock, "White Librarianship in Blackface: Diversity Initiatives in LIS," *In the Library with the Lead Pipe*, October 7, 2015, http://www.inthelibrarywiththeleadpipe.org/2015/lis-diversity/.

111. Taneya Gethers, "The 21st-Century Black Librarian: Renewing Our Commitment to Liberation and Cultural Activism," in *The 21st-Century Black Librarian in America: Issues and Challenges*, eds. Andrew P. Jackson, Julius C. Jefferson Jr., and Akilah S. Nosakhere (Lanham, MD: Scarecrow Press, 2012), 224.

It is your time to keep pushing, to make a difference and address the challenges in the 21st century."[112] At five percent of librarianship, the heavy load of labor and activism for Black librarians is daunting. Making racial equity the responsibility of Black librarians allows white librarians to remain complicit in their whiteness and racism. White librarians should be just as responsible for addressing the lack of diversity in the field and just as expected to make changes for the better. Tracie D. Hall recommends that "... it is time that we more intentionally mine and theorize the histories of race and resistance in libraries and the promise of black librarianship in the fight for racial equity and social justice."[113]

Libraries have long been considered the symbol of civilization. Meanwhile, Black feminists have long argued that a free civilization is not truly free if Black women are not liberated. Anna Julia Cooper suggests that "Only if the black woman can say 'when and where I enter, in the quiet, undisputed dignity of my womanhood, without violence and without suing or special patronage, then and there the whole Negro race enters with me.' "[114] Reflecting Cooper nearly one hundred years later, and demonstrating the required need for each generation of Black feminists to repeat themselves, the Combahee River Collective stated that "If Black women were free, it would mean that everyone else would have to be free since our freedom would necessitate the destruction of all systems of oppression."[115] Concerns and anxieties about the presence and absence of Black women's physical bodies in libraries confirms the observation that "African American women and their bodies [are]

---

112. Jackson, xix.

113. Tracie D. Hall, "The Black Body at the Reference Desk: Critical Race Theory and Black Librarianship," in *The 21st-Century Black Librarian in America: Issues and Challenges*, eds. Andrew P. Jackson, Julius C. Jefferson Jr., and Akilah S. Nosakhere (Lanham, MD: Scarecrow Press, 2010), 202.

114. Anna Julia Cooper, *A Voice from the South* (Xenia, OH: Aldine Printing House, 1892), *Nineteenth Century Collections Online*, tinyurl.galegroup.com/tinyurl/5BXEW0, 31.

115. Combahee River Collective, "A Black Feminist Statement," in *All the Women Are White, All the Blacks are Men, But Some of Us are Brave: Black Women's Studies* (New York: The Feminist Press, 1982), 18.

central to discussions of civilization and its meanings."[116] When the experiences, contributions, and voices of Black women are ignored and deflected in discussions of diversity and equity in libraries, the fruit of those discussions will never develop and advance. We believe this chapter is progress in this mission to better understand how libraries, race, and gender have become inextricably intertwined into the fabric of American society.

Bibliography

Banks, Taunya Lovell. "Colorism: A Darker Shade of Pale." *UCLA Law Review* 47, no. 6 (August 2000): 1705-1746.

Bourg, Chris. "The Unbearable Whiteness of Librarianship." *Feral Librarian*, (blog). March 3, 2014. https://chrisbourg.wordpress.com/2014/03/03/the-unbearable-whiteness-of-librarianship.

Cooper, Anna Julia Haywood. *A Voice from the South*. Aldine Printing House, 1892. Nineteenth Century Collections Online, tinyurl.galegroup.com/tinyurl/5BXEW0.

Dandridge, Rita B. *Ann Allen Shockley: An Annotated Primary and Secondary Bibliography*. New York: Greenwood Press, 1987.

De Veaux, Alexis. *Warrior Poet: A Biography of Audre Lorde*. New York: W.W. Norton & Co., 2004.

Davis, Thadious M. *Nella Larsen, Novelist of the Harlem Renaissance: A Woman's Life Unveiled*. Baton Rouge, LA: Louisiana State University Press, 1994.

Dawson, Alma. "Celebrating African-American Librarians and Librarianship." *Library Trends* 49, no. 1 (2000): 49-87.

Dorman, Jacob S. "Skin Bleach and Civilization: The Racial Formation of Blackness in 1920s Harlem." *The Journal of Pan African Studies* 4, no. 4 (2011): 47-80.

116. Dorman, 55.

Dorney, Erin. "Librarian as Poet / Poet as Librarian." *In the Library with the Lead Pipe*. February 12, 2014. http://www.inthelibrarywiththelead-pipe.org/2014/librarian-as-poet-poet-as-librarian.

Garfield, Michelle N. "Literary Societies: The Work of Self-Improvement and Racial Uplift." In *Black Women's Intellectual Traditions: Speaking Their Minds*, edited by Kristin Waters and Carol B. Conaway, 113-128. Burlington, VT: University of Vermont Press, 2007.

Gethers, Taneya, D. "The 21st-Century Black Librarian: Renewing Our Commitment to Liberation and Cultural Activism." In *The 21st-Century Black Librarian in America: Issues and Challenges*, edited by Andrew P. Jackson, Julius C. Jefferson Jr., and Akilah S. Nosakhere, 223-227. Lanham, MD: Scarecrow Press, 2012.

Gonzalez-Smith, Isabel, Juleah Swanson, and Azusa Tanaka. "Unpacking Identity: Racial, Ethnic, and Professional Identity and Academic Librarians of Color." In *The Librarian Stereotype: Deconstructing Perceptions & Presentations of Information Work*, edited by Nicole Pagowsky & Miriam Rigby, 149-173. Chicago: Association of College and Research Libraries, 2014.

Hall, Tracie, D. "The Black Body at the Reference Desk: Critical Race Theory and Black Librarianship." In *The 21st-Century Black Librarian in America: Issues and Challenges*, edited by Andrew P. Jackson, Julius C. Jefferson Jr., and Akilah S. Nosakhere, 197-202. Lanham, MD: Scarecrow Press, 2012.

Hathcock, April. "White Librarianship in Blackface: Diversity Initiatives in LIS." *In the Library with the Lead Pipe*. October 7, 2015. http://www.inthelibrarywiththeleadpipe.org/2015/lis-diversity.

Hernández-Delgado, J.L. "Pura Teresa Belpré, Storyteller and Pioneer Puerto Rican Librarian." *Library Quarterly: Information, Community, Policy* 62, no. 4 (1992): 425-40.

Honma, Todd. "Trippin' Over the Color Line: The Invisibility of Race in Library and Information Studies." *InterActions: UCLA Journal of Education and Information Studies* 1, no. 2 (2005): 1-26.

Hunter, Margaret L. "'If You're Light You're Alright': Light Skin Color as Social Capital for Women of Color." *Gender and Society* 16, no. 2 (2002): 175-193.

Hurston, Zora Neale. "Colorstruck." In Zora Neale Hurston: Collected Plays, edited by Jean Lee Cole and Charles Mitchell, 33-50. New Brunswick, NJ: Rutgers University Press, 2008.

Jackson, Andrew P. (Sekou Molefi Baako). Preface: The Need for Continued Activism in Black Librarianship." In *The 21st-Century Black Librarian in America: Issues and Challenges*, edited by Andrew P. Jackson, Julius C. Jefferson Jr., and Akilah S. Nosakhere, xvii-xx. Lanham, MD: Scarecrow Press, 2012.

Jones, Sharon L. *Rereading the Harlem Renaissance: Race, Class, and Gender in the Fiction of Jessie Fauset, Zora Neale Hurston, and Dorothy West.* Westport, CT: Greenwood Press, 2002.

Jones, Virginia Lacy. "Review of *Handbook of Black Librarianship by E.J. Josey and Ann Allen Shockley*." *Library Quarterly* 49, no. 1 (Jan. 1979): 103-104.

Joseph, Gloria I. *The Wind is Spirit: The Life, Love and Legacy of Audre Lorde.* New York: Villarosa Media, 2016.

Josey, E.J. and Ann Allen Shockley. *Handbook of Black Librarianship*. Littleton, CO: Libraries Unlimited, 1977.

Koppelman, Susan. *Between Mothers and Daughters: Stories Across a Generation.* New York: Feminist Press at CUNY, 1987.

Lane, Alycee J. Preface to *Loving Her*, by Ann Allen Shockley. Boston: Northeastern University Press, 1997.

Larsen, Nella. *Quicksand and Passing.* Edited by Deborah E. McDowell. New Brunswick, NJ: Rutgers University Press, 1986.

Lindsey, Treva B. "Black No More: Skin Bleaching and the Emergence of New Negro Womanhood Beauty Culture." *Journal of Pan African Studies* 4, no. 4 (2011): 97-116.

Lewis, David Levering. *When Harlem Was in Vogue.* New York: Penguin Books, 1997.

Lorde, Audre. *I Am Your Sister: Collected and Unpublished Writings of Audre Lorde.* Edited by Rudolph P. Byrd, Johnnetta Betsch Cole, Beverly Guy-Sheftall. New York: Oxford University Press, 2009.

———. *Sister Outsider: Essays and Speeches.* Berkeley, CA: The Crossing Press, 1984.

———. *Zami: A Biomythography.* Freedom, CA: The Crossing Press, 1994, (first printing 1982).

McDougald, Elise Johnson. "The Task of Negro Womanhood." In *The New Negro: Voices of the Harlem Renaissance,* edited by Alain Locke, 369-382. New York: Simon & Schuster, 1992. Originally published in 1925.

McDowell, Deborah. "Black Female Sexuality in Passing." In *Passing: Authoritative Text, Backgrounds and Contexts, Criticism,* edited by Carla Kaplan, 363-379. New York: W.W. Norton and Company, 2007.

———. Introduction to *Quicksand and Passing,* edited by Deborah McDowell. New Brunswick, NJ: Rutgers University Press, 1986.

Mirmasoumi, Mahshidossadat and Farshid Nowrouzi Roshnavand. "Blackness, Colorism, and Epidermalization of Inferiority in Zora Neale Hurston's Color Struck: A Fanonian Reading of the Play." *Khazar Journal of Humanities and Social Sciences* 17, no. 4 (2014): 55-65.

Mitchell, Lofton. *Voices of the Black Theatre.* Clifton, NJ: J.T. White, 1975.

New York Public Library. "The 75th Anniversary of the American Negro Theatre." *NYPL.org.* Accessed September 9, 2017. https://www.nypl.org/events/exhibitions/75th-anniversary-american-negro-theatre.

Ranganathan, S. R. *The Five Laws of Library Science.* Ed. 2, reprinted. Bangalore: Sarada Ranganathan Endowment for Library Science, 1988.

Roffman, Karin. *From the Modernist Annex: American Women Writers in Museums and Libraries.* Tuscaloosa, AL: University of Alabama Press, 2010.

———. "Nella Larsen, Librarian at 135th Street." *Modern Fiction Studies* 53, no 4 (2007): 752-787.

Rubin, Richard, *Foundations of Library and Information Science.* 2nd ed. New York: Neal-Schuman Publishers, 2004.

Saxon, Wolfgang. "Augusta B. Baker, 86, Storyteller, Editor and Children's Librarian." *New York Times*, March 6, 1998.

Shockley, Ann Allen. *Afro-American Women Writers, 1746-1933: An Anthology and Critical Guide.* Boston: G.K. Hall and Co., 1988.

———. "The Black Lesbian in American Literature: An Overview." In *Home Girls: A Black Feminist Anthology*, edited by Barbara Smith, 83-93. New York: Kitchen Table Press, 1983. Reprinted from *Conditions: Five: The Black Women's Issue*, co-edited by Lorraine Bethel and Barbara Smith, 1979.

———. *A Handbook for the Administration of Special Negro Collections.* Nashville, TN: Fisk University, 1970.

———. *A History of Public Library Services to Negroes in the South, 1900-1955.* Dover, DE: Delaware State College, 1960.

Smith, Barbara. "Toward a Black Feminist Criticism." *Radical Teacher*, no. 7 (1978): 20-27.

Tate, Claudia. "Desire and Death in Quicksand by Nella Larsen." *American Literary History* 7 (1995): 234-260.

Ware, Leland. "'Color Struck': Intragroup and Cross-Racial Color Discrimination." *Connecticut Public Interest Law Journal* 13, no. 1 (Fall 2013): 75-110.

Wiegand, Wayne A. *"An Active Instrument for Propaganda": The American Public Library During World War I.* New York: Greenwood Press, 1989.

———. *Part of Our Lives: A People's History of the American Public Library.* New York: Oxford University Press, 2015.

Whitmire, E. *Regina Anderson Andrews: Harlem Renaissance Librarian.* Springfield, IL: University of Illinois Press, 2014.

Chapter 2

Sisters of the Stacks

Alexsandra Mitchell

Suzanne Hildenbrand's 1996 text, *Reclaiming the American Library Past: Writing the Women In*, offers a gendered history of library 'herstories': narratives of our library and archival foremothers that are often left untold within the contemporary discourse of the field. Chapter 2 of the text, "African-American Historical Continuity: Jean Blackwell Hutson and the Schomburg Center for Research in Black Culture," focuses on the work of Jean Blackwell Hutson (1914-1998), pioneering 20th century black librarian, curator, and later director of the Schomburg Center for Research in Black Culture. This overview of Jean Blackwell Hutson's rise in the world of libraries and archives, coupled with conversations I have had with Diana Lachatanere, former curator of the Manuscripts, Archives, and Rare Books Division at the Schomburg, inspired me to explore the impact of mentorship, growth, and development of black librarians and archivists. Additionally, I began to think deeply about the bonds between black women in the field of library and information science that have positively impacted successful black librarians and archivists, namely through the experiences of the intergenerational transference of knowledge. Here, I utilize, "African-American Historical Continuity: Jean Blackwell Hutson and the Schomburg Center for Research in Black Culture," as a framework for my interest in documenting Black women librarians and archivists' experiences for the purposes of supporting the current generation, while inspiring and sustaining the next generation. In this chapter, "Sisters of the Stacks," Black women librarians and archivists with whom I have fostered relationships, be it through friendship, mentorship, and/or sisterhood, discuss their experiences, which ultimately fostered the development of leading Black librarians and archivists within this country. I argue that these interpersonal relationships are an imperative part of the success of many of these women. Here, Dr. Angel Batiste, Joellen El-Bashir, Diana Lachatanere, and Megan Goins-Diouf discuss what made them want to become librarians, archivists and curators; the women who have supported them; how they sustain themselves; and their careers more generally.

Furthermore, the chapter discusses the ways in which contemporary Black women librarians and archivists support one another, often offering peer mentorship to carry on the tradition of our library and archival foremothers. I also inquired about the ways in which they have been supported spiritually by colleagues, as spiritual support and/or advice that I have received has allowed me to grow and to sustain myself during difficult periods. This dynamic group of librarians, archivists, and curators, both actively practicing and retired, represent some of the nation's finest institutions related to the study of the global Black experience. These institutions include: The Schomburg Center for Research in Black Culture, New York Public Library (Diana Lachatanere), Library of Congress's African and Middle Eastern Division (Dr. Angel Batiste), and Howard University's Moorland-Spingarn Research Center (Joellen El-Bashir). These three women, in addition to Megan Goin-Diouf (Bowling Green State University), have all experienced different paths towards a career in library and information science. These paths have included avid supporters, changes, and setbacks that led them to their rightful place within the field.

Each of the women highlighted within this chapter have influenced my life and career. I began my career in the field of libraries and archives while an undergraduate student at "The Mecca" of higher education in the contemporary Black world, Howard University. As a student worker with the South African Research and Archival Project, I began conducting research for the creation of an online finding aid about the work and legacy of former South African Missionary, Max Yeargen, in his papers at the Moorland-Spingarn Research Center, located in Founders Library at Howard University. It was there that I first encountered Joellen El Bashir, curator of the collection, and her brilliant archivist colleagues, Donna Wells and Ida Jones. These women patiently worked with me on this project and provided me with informal mentoring by way of sharing their work, studies, and experiences with me.

I first met Diana Lachatanere while a scholar in the Schomburg Summer Humanities Institute at the Schomburg Center for Research in Black Culture. Ms. Lachatenere, then curator of the Manuscripts, Archives and Rare Books Division, took the time to sit with me and provide career and educational advice as I explored my options for graduate study. The following year I met Dr. Angel Batiste by way of my Howard University sister and colleague, Lanisa Kitchner. Ms. Kitchner, whom I had studied with during a summer study abroad program in South Africa at the University of Cape Town, inquired about my developing intellectual and professional interests and plans post my return to campus from the Schomburg Center. Upon learning that my career interests had expanded towards working in libraries and archives, Ms. Kitchner suggested that she introduce me to her friend and colleague, Dr. Batiste, Area Specialist for West Africa in the African and Middle Eastern Division of the Library of Congress. Dr. Batiste graciously hired me as her intern during the spring semester of my senior year at Howard University.

Megan Goins-Diouf and I attended Howard University as undergraduate students but became close post-graduation during our time in New York City. Kindred spirits in many ways, Mrs. Goins-Diouf and I have traversed many of the same library and archival haunts during our studies and professional careers. We both completed the same dual master's degree program in library science and Africana studies at LIU Post and NYU, respectively, in addition to both having worked at the West African Research Center in Dakar, Senegal; Weeksville Heritage Center in Brooklyn, New York; and Schomburg Center for Research in Black Culture. Now, as co-authors of *Research Strategies and Techniques for the Study of Black Writings,* we are able to bring our expertise to provide a seminal text for study within both the fields of Africana studies and library and information science. As a black woman in a field where upwards of ninety percent of the demographic is made up of non-people-of-color, fostering relationships with these women has been crucial to learning of career opportunities, navigating difficult times within my career, and building a future that I desire for myself and my peers.

Whether they know it or not, each of these women has supported me, not only in my career, but emotionally as I made tough choices about my life and work that were not always readily supported by those around me. Looking to them, their work, and their careers provided me with the inspiration and grit to continue on when things became emotionally, and sometimes spiritually, taxing; thus, my selection of their voices for this chapter. The formal and informal networks built provided and continue to provide me with opportunities of a lifetime.

What follows is a series of transcribed interview questions with each of the aforementioned women that were conducted via email, for logistical purposes, and can also serve as a form of oral history. Each question was selected to inspire the future generation of black librarians, archivists, and curators, and to sustain current professionals during their day to day trials and tribulations. The words of the courageous interviewees provide an intimate view into their professional careers and will now live on for posterity.

AM: What made you want to become a librarian, archivist, and/or curator?

Dr. Angel Batiste: Financing my graduate studies, I began working in the African and Middle Eastern Division of the Library of Congress and developed a progressive interest in the field of Africana librarianship. Upon completing my doctoral studies at Howard University, I received a library and information science degree from the Catholic University of America.

Joellen El-Bashir: I became an avid reader as a child and remember well my days in the Children's Room in Hollis Burke Frissell Library on the campus of Tuskegee Institute (now University). In high school, I worked in the school library and was fascinated by the organization of the books on the shelves and the cards in the catalog. Many years later, I processed my first manuscript collection—supervised by an experienced archivist, Sara Jackson, at the National Archives. I was hooked and became determined to earn the M.L.S., which I did in one year and a summer at the University of Maryland, College Park.

Megan Goins-Diouf: I attended one Catholic school for grades K-8, and our coy school librarian—Ms. Romig, dazzled me for all of those years. In her I recognized that it is possible to be excited about books! I didn't realize how, early on, my interactions with her empowered me. She had the librarian role down—really delicate and deliberate voice; particularly creative when it came down to book displays. I always found her to be extremely elegant and her practice was inclusive; I always admired her and observed her carefully.

A 2008 summer study abroad trip to Ancient Egypt (KMT) further solidified my interest in wanting to attend library school. I spent time with the elders on that trip, including Queen Nzinga, President of the Association for the Study of Classical African Civilizations. She would challenge me at every temple that we would visit. I stayed close to her for most of the tour because she knew Seshat appeared. She would challenge me (and others) to do so. I always found her. I always found Seshat. Tempestuous in leopard—the Dean of the Library. So, I adhered to both Queen Nzinga and to Seshat.

I deputized myself as one of her own (I'm certain that on that tour, we all did), and when it came time for me to apply to graduate schools a year later, Ionnie, my classmate and tour shadow, shared with me an announcement for the IMLS/Laura Bush scholarship so that I could pursue graduate studies in Africana studies and library and information science in tandem. I received the fellowship! And the rest is the prologue: I went on to pursue my studies at New York University and Long Island University's Palmer School of Library and Information Science. Dr. Williams aided me in my admissions letter and helped me to amplify this voice that I had discovered.

Diana Lachatanere: This was not my first career choice; however, a move to San Francisco in 1976 led to my taking a gamble with the California Historical Society as a place where I could enter the museum field, which is what I thought I wanted to do. The staff steered me to the Society's library instead, and within a short period of time I realized that I loved and had aptitude for archival work, and within a year or two I was accepted in library school. By then it had become clear to me that I wanted to be a part of a profession whose goal is to identify and preserve the documentation that informs the historical narrative about African descended people.

AM: Did any colleagues assist you in finding a job within the field?

AB: No.

JE: As a graduate student in history at Howard University, I practically lived in the Moorland-Spingarn Reading Room and came to know some of the professionals on staff. When one librarian was leaving her position, she notified me and recommended that I apply for the job of manuscript librarian. That was 36 years ago.

MGD: At the time of graduation, it was Dr. Deborah Willis[1] (not a colleague, but an instructor) who helped me to secure a position in

1. Former curator of the Photographs and Prints Division, Schomburg Center for Research in Black Culture, NYPL and current Chair of the Photography and Imaging Department, New York University.

the manuscripts and rare books divisions at the Schomburg/New York Public Library. I trained there for a year (for a semester on my own) with a cohort of doctoral students at NYU. I worked to process two collections: the Association for Black Women in Higher Education collection, and Joel Carson/South Africa Legal Defense collection (a white South African lawyer who served Namibians in S. Africa secretly detained and tortured under the Terrorism Act of 1967—which was used to silence dissension to apartheid, among others).

DL: Stanton Biddle, who had worked at the Center in the 1960s and early 70s, was attending the University of California, Berkeley Library School during the same time I was at the school. We became friendly and when I was ready to graduate, I spoke to him about the Center and he wrote a reference letter on my behalf to the Center and to the head of personnel at NYPL, who was a black woman.

AM: What made you choose to work for your particular institution?

AB: The African Section in the Library of Congress is a major research center, and its Africana collections are the most comprehensive in the world.

JE: Even though I am a Tuskegee girl through and through, I came to love Howard and the Moorland-Spingarn Research Center, and vowed that I would work there someday.

DL: While in graduate library school I determined that I wanted to work primarily, if not exclusively, with African-American collections. I became aware at that time that few repositories were collecting in this field, which was resulting in the loss of critical documentation. As I wanted to become part of the solution, I began looking for a position with an institution, such as the Schomburg Center for Research in Black Culture, whose focus was primarily, if not solely, focused on African

American history and culture. Fortunately, a position was open at the Center when I began interviewing and I was hired as the Assistant Archivist in the Manuscripts, Archives and Rare Books Division. I was very lucky that, despite a bad patch in the early 80s, I was able to advance to Curator and then Assistant Director for Collections and Services, sealing my fate forever with the Center.

AM: Who are the women that keep you fed (sustained) and able to do your work?

AB: My greatest motivator was my Mother and Black women generally.

JE: My mother, maternal grandmother, and maternal great-aunt kept me fed, nutritionally and spiritually.

MGD: Right now, I'm obsessing over Kaitlyn Greenidge; she served as the Research Assistant at Weeksville prior to my service there. I met her while manning the welcome table at an Angela Davis event at the Institute of African American Affairs (NYU). She is a historical fiction writer, and she writes from a voiceless area of my mind. She does it, and I'm inspired by her.

On the reverse side of that coin, I'm truly inspired by the work of Leslie Hewitt, a visual artist. Her work does not compromise that space where literature, home, and interiority meet.

I also am overindulging (in moderation) in the work of Toni Cade Bambara—I read *The Salt Eaters* for the first time last year, and I really enjoy the visual taxonomies that reading her work provides me.

DL: My mother, Sara Lachatanere Guzman, and my best friend Sheryll White have been my constant and consistent supporters. During my working years, my colleagues at the various jobs I have held, as well as good friends, allowed me to grow and flourish in my career through their advice, support, and encouragement. In professional organizations it was primarily my African-American colleagues who sustained me and gave me the strength and courage to pursue an activist stance within those organizations. At the Schomburg Center, where I spent the bulk of my career, some of my female peers and staff were also extremely supportive and caring as I followed my career path.

AM: Who were your women mentors in and outside of the field?

AB: I have had notable African American librarians who made significant contributions to librarianship in America as role models, such as Dr. Dorothy Porter Wesley[2] and Virginia Lacy Jones,[3] but no formal mentors.

JE: My first mentor was Sara D. Jackson, who worked at the National Historical Publications and Records Commission of the National Archives and Records Administration. I was hired there temporarily after earning the M.L.S. and was supervised by Sara. We also carpooled together. My second and most significant mentor was my supervisor at Moorland-Spingarn, Karen L. Jefferson, who is now Archivist at the AU Center in Atlanta. Frankly, Karen taught me most of what I know about the organization and description of manuscript collections. She was intense and thorough.

MGD: I've been mentored by my peers—women whom I've studied with at Howard and NYU/LIU: Anoa Gibson-Hunter, LaShaya Howie, Jaïra Placide (who became my supervisor at the Institute of African American Affairs); as well as my instructors: Dr. Jennifer Morgan, and women that I've met as my professional self: Jennifer Scott, Elissa Blount-Moorhead, and Tia Powell Harris. Women that I've encountered at the Institute—Iris Cofield, Rashidah Ismaili, Lydia Diakhaté and

2. Pioneering curator of the Moorland Spingarn Research Center, Howard University.

3. Librarian and educator, former Dean of the Atlanta University Library School.

Margaret Porter Troupe, all gave me very vivid experiences of the gaps that our work can fill.

I've listed many others that I encountered at Howard, but I'm especially grateful for the women that created a space for me at the Moorland-Spingarn Research Center: Rosa Anthony, Amber Junipher, and Jean Currie Church, a fellow Detroiter. Ms. Church gave me my first writing assignment as a library intern. Ms. Paris and Donna Hubbard at the Flatbush Branch of the Brooklyn Public Library promoted my work as a young adult specialist. I've also held three other women dear to my librarian-center: Brittney Johnson, Ionnie McNeill, and Haven Elise Polk—three non-librarians, but literary women whom I've known for many years. These three constitute merely who I am.

DL: My first mentor in the archival profession was Lynn Bonfield, the Manuscripts Curator at the California Historical Society in the 70s. She took me on as a volunteer (in this very white organization), trained me, and encouraged my interest in pursuing a career in archives. Most significantly, when she went on her summer vacation my first year there she recommended that I be hired to provide reference and continue with the processing projects I was working on. Through this gesture on her part, I was able to "see" myself pursuing a career in the archival profession.

Although I have never formally thought of Jean Blackwell Hutson as a mentor, during her last few years with the NYPL (she had already been removed as Chief of the Schomburg Center), she took me on acquisition trips, introducing me to potential donors who were the movers and shakers of her generation. While never being didactic she was able to inform and improve my skills in this area.

My best friend (mentioned above) has also served as a mentor throughout my working life. I also consider Dr. Jualynne Dodson (sociologist) as a mentor in that she was the one who gave me the final talk that pushed me to pursue an archival career and apply for library school at UC, Berkeley.

AM: In what ways have they helped you in your career?

AB: My role models inspired my interest in the field of librarianship.

JE: Because of the training Karen Jefferson bestowed upon me, she felt confident to leave Moorland in my hands while she took a job at NEH. It was to be a temporary position, but she never returned to Moorland, so I inherited the position of Curator by default.

MGD: There are many more women who, in my family, are perpetual reminders that nothing has abandoned me. I usually turn to my sister, Mia, to help me sort through ambiguities, but all of these women have nurtured me when I've reached unusual vantage points. The great thing about women is that we can communicate through mutable gazes; and I try to reflect these movements in my work as an archivist.

DL: (see previous response for how they helped me)

AM: Is/was there a time that a colleague of yours supported you emotionally in your work? If so, please share an example.

AB: Several librarian colleagues have inspired my work at the Library of Congress and supported me during my tenure as Chair of the American Librarian Association Africa Subcommittee.

JE: Actually, I did most of the supporting and counseling for some of the staff—men and women.

MGD: I worked for the longest amount of time with Jaïra Placide, Associate Director of the Institute of African American Affairs at NYU (IAAA). My relationship with the IAAA is a hard-won one, and Jaïra is a kind mentor who helped me balance the difficulties of competing loyalties as I experienced them as a super-part time worker, mother, and wife in New York City. Jaïra taught me how to distort time and to order dessert. She taught me that complicated relationships between "sisters" are usually just a matter of fiction. I also really admire a colleague that I shared so many laughs with at BPL, Valerie Livingston.

DL: Several people in the profession and at the Schomburg Center gave critical emotional support during the period when I decided to pursue a grievance against the Library for not seriously considering my application to be head archivist in the mid-80s. Deborah Willis, who was my co-worker at the time, was especially supportive. I would also have to say that Mary Yearwood and Genette McLaurin, my colleagues at The Center, were very supportive during my years as Assistant Director for Collections and Services.

AM: What, if any, were some of the special opportunities you've had in your life because of your women colleagues?

AB: Working with women colleagues from Africa, I have been able to gain an intimate knowledge of library issues in an African context.

JE: I don't know about special opportunities, but my women colleagues have always been supportive, and never tried to hold me back.

MGD: It was from Jaïra Placide that I could experience New York with truly romantic eyes, while juggling careers. The opportunities and the space that the Institute provided are the peak aspects of my {black} imagination—with all of its contradictions, tolerances, and joys. While working with Jaïra at the institute, my husband and I met Maya Angelou on his first week here in the United States, together with Jayne Cortez and Mel Edwards at an Organization of Women Writers of Africa (OWWA) celebration.

DL: Volunteer and paid opportunity to work at the California Historical Society, which opened the door to the archival profession; Employment at the Schomburg Center for Research in Black Culture;

Helping to form the then-titled Archives and Archivists of Color Roundtable of the Society of American Archivists; Participation in exhibition planning, programming and catalog publication; National and international travel.

AM: Have you received spiritual support from women in the field? If so, please share an example.

AB: As Chair of the American Librarian Association Africa Subcommittee, spiritual support came from women colleagues in Africa who relied upon me to voice international library issues.

JE: I've never sought spiritual support from women librarians/archivists.

MGD: As such it was Jaïra who reintroduced me to the "Prayer of Serenity"—but she changed the shape of it a bit: she allowed me to access the prayer in isolated parts, and taught me that each aspect—"serenity," "courage," "wisdom"—are not iterative, and can perceived even when of the aspects is hidden.

DL: In all honesty, I don't think that I have, but I'm also not clear on what is meant by "spiritual."

AM: Please share a story that has helped you get through/make it through your current or past job as a result of the women helping you.

AB: An award as a Library of Congress Leadership Development Program Fellow was influenced by a woman colleague.

JE: Looking back, I've had a relatively easy time as I advanced in my career, and I attribute that to the great upbringing I had, with two well-educated and loving parents.

MGD: To be loved by your Professors is perhaps the greatest gift, and I'm so grateful that I've encountered women mentors who are so overwhelmingly encouraging. It is a privilege to be able to (re)visit their scholarship, and to (try to) increase their imprint, as diligently as they've pressed on us. We're (you, and I) beginning that journey together, with thanks to Dr. Dana Williams at Howard, in the book that we're writing together, *Resources and Techniques for the Study of Black Writings*; in black and white, we're creating a space for our scholarly and artistic communities to (re)visit the pluralisms that define our writings. What's better than that?

DL: The most difficult experience at the Center involved the incident previously mentioned regarding my not being hired as the head archivist in the early 80s. The incident got blown out of proportion because a white archivist was hired and community activists began criticizing the director for that hire. Although this was not a protest in support of my candidacy, it was often misinterpreted that way, and I became a focal point internally as the one who was causing and feeding the protest. Several women (and men) on staff and in the community supported me, not necessarily because I was the best candidate but simply because I was black. Deborah Willis and I were good friends at the time, and she was extremely supportive. Between her and my friend Sheryll, I was able to get through what was a very difficult and emotional period.

Conclusion

Each of these women, Sisters of the Stacks, has experienced the joys and challenges that many of us face within our career span in the field. For many, the support, guidance, ideals, and mentorship of fellow Black women librarians, as well as Black women professors within the academy, have provided job opportunities for career growth, advice that helped sustain them during tough times, and prayers that carried them forward to success. Additionally, mothers, sisters, and dear friends all provided wings of support for these "sisters" to move forward in their careers beyond perceived bounds, both locally and internationally, and in return, many of them continue in the tradition that they received of emotional laboring by mentoring and supporting colleagues. Having been inspired through their studies, whether in elementary or graduate school, their innate curiosity, and those they encountered led them down their career paths. The world-renowned institutions that these women serve and/or have served in are better due to their direct efforts, drive, vision, and pioneering work. May the next generation of librarians, archivists, scholars, and visionaries look to the stories of these women as models upon which they can ground their dreams, and as sources of inspiration in the face of adversity.

Bibliography

Hildenbrand, Suzanne. *Reclaiming the American Library Past: Writing the Women In*. Norwood, NJ: Ablex, 1996.

Mitchell, Alexsandra. "Live From the Reading Room: The Early Life of Jean Blackwell Hutson." *The New York Public Library*, The New York Public Library, September 7, 2017. www.nypl.org/blog/2017/09/07/birthday-jean-blackwell-hutson.

Sims-Wood, Janet L. *Dorothy Porter Wesley at Howard University: Building a Legacy of Black History*. The History Press, 2014.

Sinnette, Elinor Des Verney. *Arthur Alfonso Schomburg, Black Bibliophile & Collector: a Biography*. New York Public Library, 1989.

Chapter 3

I am a Muslim, a Woman, a Librarian: Muslim Women and Public Libraries

Negeen Aghassibake

In this chapter, I will argue that the growth of Islamophobia in the United States has made it imperative for libraries to provide images of Muslims that counteract stereotypes perpetuated by the media and American society. This issue is particularly important to Muslim women and girls who possess multiple intersectional identities based on religion, gender, race, socioeconomic status, and orientation. The tragic events of September 11, 2001, in which the United States suffered a major terrorist attack, put Muslims in the spotlight and often on the defensive against racist abuse and prejudice. The rapid proliferation of Islamophobia after September 11 has resulted in hate crimes against Muslims, and especially Muslim women, ranging from verbal slurs to the forceful removal of their hijabs, and even murder.[1]

A focus on Muslim women, particularly those who wear the veil, is especially important because their identities are often visible. Muslim women are frequently targeted because of their appearance and dress. Unfortunately, hate crimes against Muslims, or what should be labeled as hate crimes, are often unacknowledged by the very institutions that

1. Rachel Flint, "Self-Defence Class Over Islamophobia 'Normalisation' Fear," *BBC News*, April 19, 2017, accessed April 19, 2017, http://www.bbc.com/news/uk-wales-38981436.

are meant to protect them. As Jonathan Blitzer says of the murders of Muslims in northern Virginia and Chapel Hill, which were ultimately not deemed to meet the legal definition of hate crimes, "If law enforcement fails to call something a hate crime in the face of striking evidence, as many say was the case in Chapel Hill, a community can be left feeling unprotected."[2]

Although the term "Islamophobia" is vague and cannot address all aspects of bigotry against Muslims (or those who "appear Muslim"), it will be used in this paper to refer to deliberate and widespread anti-Muslim sentiment in the United States. While combating Islamophobia will require significant social and political change at many levels, I argue that one of the most important venues for initiating this change is America's public libraries. Public libraries, due to their prominence and accessibility, are well situated to reach an audience beyond the Muslim community. Furthermore, because of their status as providers of information, they are uniquely positioned in American society to educate and provide a voice for Muslim women. This chapter will discuss Muslim women who work as librarians and how the Muslim experience can be represented in public library collections.

The Voices of Muslim Women Librarians

Muslim women librarians can face hurtful, discriminatory, and even dangerous treatment in their positions. They are subject to microaggressions as well as more overt forms of discrimination. Tina Mat and Ayan Adem, two Muslim public librarians in Seattle who choose to wear the veil, note that they have "experienced a fair share of racists [*sic*] and discriminative remarks."[3] Some of the experiences they shared include:

---

2. Jonathan Blitzer, "A Muslim Community Responds to a Murder, Hate Crime or Not," *New Yorker*, June 23, 2017, accessed August 17, 2017, http://www.newyorker.com/news/news-desk/a-muslim-community-responds-to-a-murder-hate-crime-or-not.

3. Tina Mat and Ayan Adem, "What Is It Like to Be a Muslim Librarian in Seattle?" *Alki: The Washington Library Association Journal* 33, no. 2 (July 2017): 6.

> . . . anything from denying our credibility as librarians with comments like, "Oh, where's the librarian at? Or "Are you a real librarian?" to being more focused on our physical appearances, "How long have you been in the states?" "Your English is good." "What happened to your accent?" Yes, people [really have] these questions and it can be very emotionally draining.[4]

These experiences illustrate the effects that Islamophobia has on Muslim women librarians. Since librarians are often the public faces of the institutions where they work, they are most likely to face racist and discriminatory remarks directly from community members. Rosalie Amer, a librarian at Cosumnes River College, notes that one of the impacts of September 11 is that it has been "a challenge to educate the public about Islam."[5] Prejudice and a lack of understanding of Islam have a significant effect on the daily lives of Muslim women librarians, and this must be addressed by the public, library organizations, and individual libraries themselves.

As Ghada Elturk, a public librarian in Boulder, Colorado, puts it, "[b]eing a Muslim-American librarian is like being a librarian from any other minority except that Muslims are less understood and very much stereotyped."[6]

The Role of Public Libraries

Historically, public libraries have been perceived as free from specific political, religious, or cultural beliefs. While the perception is that "library literature abounds with expression of the centrality of intellectual freedom to the mission of libraries,"[7] this is not always reflected in reality. In practice, "a government structure such as the public library

---

4. Ibid.

5. Ron Chepesiuk, "Muslim-American Librarians Reflect: September 11 and Its Aftermath," *American Libraries* 33, no. 1 (January 2002): 40.

6. Ibid., 41.

7. Susan K. Burke, "Social Tolerance and Racist Materials in Public Libraries," *Reference & User Services Quarterly* 49, no. 4 (2010): 370.

can never be neutral."[8] Even though public libraries seek to be impartial and apolitical, they are not neutral, nor should they attempt to be. David McMenemy argues that passivity on the part of public libraries is harmful to the patrons they serve and, ultimately, the value and power of the public library is "wasted" if they do not act as advocates for their communities.[9] With proper training and an active role in the dissemination of information, public libraries are well situated in American society to provide accurate information about Muslims and Muslim-Americans. While certain anti-Muslim members of the communities they serve may be resistant to the dissemination of information that they perceive to be threatening or against their personal or political beliefs, libraries must recognize that the needs of marginalized groups take precedence over these fears and demands.

Public librarians are at the forefront of their communities and understand their unique needs. They can recognize gaps in knowledge that can be filled by different collections and programs. Just as importantly, public librarians are able to understand their community's responses to Muslims and Muslim-Americans and can thus be a valuable resource in combating discrimination. As Leonard Kniffel explains, "[O]ne of the most effective ways of fighting for free speech is to practice it, and defending open access to information means supplying it."[10] After September 11, Muslim-American librarians recognized that Muslims in the United States would suffer backlash from the attack and that librarians were in a good position to educate and share information about Muslims, Islam, and the wars in the Middle East to counter this backlash.[11]

---

8. David Shavit, *The Politics of Public Librarianship* (New York: Greenwood, 1986), 3.

9. David McMenemy, "Librarians and Ethical Neutrality: Revisiting the Creed of a Librarian," *Library Review* 56, no. 3 (2007): 180.

10. Leonard Kniffel, "Getting to Know Islam," *American Libraries* 33, no. 1 (January 2002): 48.

11 . Chepesiuk, "Muslim-American Librarians Reflect," 41.

Diverse Recruitment in Public Libraries

The field of public librarianship remains predominantly white and female,[12] so to diversify the field and represent changing American demographics, libraries need to employ greater numbers of people of color and people from diverse backgrounds. As information providers, public librarians have a key role in society. However, librarians are not merely gatekeepers of information. They also serve as human guides in an increasingly information-based world.[13] Thus, it is imperative that the services they provide reflect the needs of their patrons and also the need of the greater community to have access to information about Muslims and Islam.

However, there is a documented pattern of hostility toward Muslim patrons in public libraries, as reflected in a study by Leigh Estabrook conducted after 9/11.[14] When public librarians were asked, "'Since September 11th, would you say staff members have changed, in any way, their attitude toward or treatment of library patrons?' Almost 20% (19.9%) answered yes."[15] Muslim women who wear a veil are particularly at risk for experiencing prejudice and racism in public spaces due to their distinctive clothing, which many view as a threat to Western society.[16]

Recruiting Muslim women librarians would help to facilitate representation of Muslim women in public libraries. Patrons who belong to marginalized groups that regularly encounter prejudice and racism could

---

12. "Recruiting for Diversity," Advocacy, Legislation & Issues, February 1, 2017, accessed March 19, 2017, http://www.ala.org/advocacy/diversity/workforcedevelopment/recruitmentfordiversity.

13. Ghada Kanafani Elturk, "Cultural Collisions and Bridging the Gap between 'Don't Stare' and Care," *New Library World* 109, no. 11/12 (November 21, 2008): 579.

14. Leigh Estabrook, "Coping, View 2: Response Disappointing," *American Libraries* 33, no. 8 (September 2002): 38.

15. Ibid.

16. Danielle Dunand Zimmerman, "Young Arab Muslim Women's Agency Challenging Western Feminism," *Affilia* 30, no. 2 (May 2015): 146.

benefit from the services of librarians who represent their beliefs and backgrounds and can empathize with the impact of Islamophobia on their everyday lives. It is particularly important that libraries protect the rights of Muslim librarians who choose to wear the veil and support them when they face harassment from patrons or coworkers. Nicole Pagowsky and Miriam Rigby write,

> In thinking about who is and is not considered a "librarian," a lack of privilege conflicts with choice regarding one's ability to ignore stereotypes and others' perceptions. Numerous bloggers have taken on these issues, and considering dress as being one avenue in which we write our identities and they are read by others, these examples look to clothing.[17]

That is to say, clothing serves as both an expression of identity and a way in which we judge others. Muslim librarians who choose to wear the veil do not have the privilege of escaping the scrutiny and discrimination of others (whether coworker or patron), whereas librarians who dress in Westernized clothing do not have that concern.

Furthermore, ensuring job satisfaction and the security of librarians of color would further support the goals of community outreach and patron representation in public libraries, because it would encourage librarians to develop programming that encompasses different perspectives.[18] Coworkers and administrators should support Muslim women librarians in order to promote a sense of acceptance, inclusion, and community in the workplace and in the wider community.

---

17. Nicole Pagowsky and Miriam Rigby, "Contextualizing Ourselves: The Identity Politics of the Librarian Stereotype," in *The Librarian Stereotype: Deconstructing Perceptions and Presentations of Information Work* (Chicago: Association of College and Research Libraries, a Division of the American Library Association, 2014), 14.

18. Rebecca Hankins and Miguel Juárez, eds., *Where Are All the Librarians of Color? The Experiences of People of Color in Academia* (Sacramento, CA: Library Juice Press, 2015), 3.

Race, Ethnicity, and Religion

In order to understand the experiences of librarians who identify as Muslim women, we must also discuss race and ethnicity. Race, ethnicity, and religion are often conflated to yield a particular stereotype of Muslims in the United States. This is particularly the case in post-September 11 America, where people who say "Muslim" often mean "Arab" or "Middle Eastern." Heidi Safia Mirza discusses the intersection of race, religion, and gender and the notion of the "raced and gendered female Muslim body."[19] Through her interviews, she discovers that skin color and wearing the veil are markers of "otherness" that are used to discriminate and isolate.[20] While Islam is not tied to any particular race or ethnicity, race, ethnicity, and religion are often conflated for the purpose of discrimination and prejudice.

Non-Muslims who "look Muslim" are also victims of anti-Muslim sentiment in the United States. As Khyati Joshi explains, "Racialization results in essentialism; it reduces people to one aspect of their identity and thereby presents a homogeneous, undifferentiated, and static view of an ethnoreligious community."[21] The practice of racialization thus results in people of other religions enduring bigotry and racism because of their skin color. While Islamophobia more strictly refers to discrimination and hatred based on religion, the interconnection between race, ethnicity, and religion in America expands the scope of Islamophobia to encompass skin color and clothing.[22] Therefore, in order to understand the experiences of Muslim women who are librarians, we must also

19. Heidi Safia Mirza, "'A Second Skin': Embodied Intersectionality, Transnationalism and Narratives of Identity and Belonging among Muslim Women in Britain," *Women's Studies International Forum* 36 (January 2013): 13.

20. Ibid., 10.

21. Khyati Y. Joshi, "The Racialization of Hinduism, Islam, and Sikhism in the United States," *Equity & Excellence in Education* 39, no. 3 (September 2006): 212.

22. Steve Garner and Saher Selod, "The Racialization of Muslims: Empirical Studies of Islamophobia," *Critical Sociology* 41, no. 1 (2015): 11.

assess how physical appearance—in terms of the racialized body and women's bodies—are significant factors in developing those experiences. To do this within the library setting, librarians must be recruited from outside the pool of heteronormative, primarily white, and able-bodied potential employees.[23]

Veiling and Discrimination

The bodies and appearances of Muslim women have become a common topic of discussion in news media, politics, and other venues. Most notably, arguments over the hijab (head covering), niqab (head covering with small opening for the eyes), and burqa (full head and face covering) have called into question the agency of Muslim women and attempted to diminish their voices by implying that they are passive victims who are forced to wear the coverings.[24] According to Dolores Morando Taramundi, women who wear the veil are often "portrayed both as a *victim* (passive) of her oppressive patriarchal culture/religion and male kin, and as a *threat* (active) to Western modernity and culture of freedoms . . ."[25] The assumptions and generalizations about women who choose to wear a veil or other form of head covering diminish their agency and fail to recognize them as decision-making individuals who hold power over their own bodies. This extends into the world of public librarianship, where librarians who choose to wear the veil experience similar discrimination.

It is important to recognize that veiled Muslim women often use the veil to feel empowered and free, and the choice to wear the veil reflects the agency of Muslim women. The veil is not only a form of religious devotion, but also a visible expression of cultural and religious identity.

---

23. "Recruiting for Diversity." According to the 2012 ALA "Diversity Counts" report, ethnic minorities make up just over 12% of credentialed librarians.

24. Dolores Morondo Taramundi, "Between Islamophobia and Post-Feminist Agency: Intersectional Trouble in the European Face-Veil Bans," *Feminist Review* 110, no. 1 (2015): 56.

25. Sirma Bilge, "Beyond Subordination vs. Resistance: An Intersectional Approach to the Agency of Veiled Muslim Women," *Journal of Intercultural Studies* 31, no. 1 (February 2010): 10.

This is in direct contrast to notions that veiling is a tool of oppression.[26] Some Muslim women wear the veil to assert their own agency and choose how they communicate their Muslim identities, which is of particular importance in the post-September 11 environment that is rife with anti-Muslim stereotypes.[27]

Muslim-American women librarians, therefore, are at risk of hostile treatment from patrons, staff, and other librarians. This is particularly true for women who choose to wear the veil and are often seen as "other."[28] While Muslim women librarians are vulnerable to another layer of discrimination and stereotyping, they are also in a unique position to lead community outreach and educational programs that can inform the public about the lives of Muslims and Muslim-Americans. Authentic representations of Muslim and Muslim-American women in the United States are lacking in mainstream media, literature, and pop culture. The result, according to Laila Alawa, is that "the often one-sided, negative portrayal of Muslims in the media creates a dichotomy.... Many school children grow up exposed only to extreme representations of being Muslim in America and don't have the chance to humanize the experiences of their Muslim classmates."[29] Thus, because Muslim women librarians may experience elevated levels of discrimination because of their multidimensional identities, it is critical to focus on and evaluate representations of the Muslim-American experience in libraries, which includes both collections and librarians.

---

26. Rachel Anderson Droogsma, "Redefining Hijab: American Muslim Women's Standpoints on Veiling," *Journal of Applied Communication Research* 35, no. 3 (July 2007): 311.

27. Ibid., 313.

28. The term "other" in this instance refers to the exclusion and alienation of certain individuals or groups of people by dominant members of society based on fear and ignorance.

29. Laila Alawa, "Representing the Muslim American Experience," *School Library Journal,* May 2014, http://www.slj.com/2014/05/diversity/why-we-need-muslim-american-kidlit/.

Bridging Cultures: Muslim Journeys

Public libraries across the United States have made efforts to represent the Muslim-American experience. The National Endowment for the Humanities (NEH), along with the American Library Association (ALA), initiated and carried out the Bridging Cultures: Muslim Journeys project. This project consists of the Muslim Journeys Bookshelf, a collection of recommended books relating to the Muslim-American experience. The program has shared their collection with over 950 libraries and state humanities councils and is playing an active role in providing information about Islam, Muslims, and Muslim-Americans.[30] Due to the growing influence of the Bookshelf, it is critical that the collection is compiled by representatives of the Muslim community and that it represents intersectional identities. It is a good foundation, but there are areas of improvement that would allow further insight into different intersectional identities.

Review of the Muslim Journeys Bookshelf

The Muslim Journeys Bookshelf is a valuable resource for public libraries and humanities organizations that are interested in presenting programming about Islam and Muslims. Seven National Project Scholars have contributed to the Bookshelf, three of whom identify as women. However, there is a noticeable lack of women (or people) of color in the group of scholars as a whole; thus, there is room for more diversity overall. The Bookshelf is intended to represent Islam and the Muslim-American experience, but its primary contributors at the moment are still providing only a limited range of perspectives due to a lack of diversity.

Due to the wide availability of the Bookshelf program and its implementation in hundreds of public libraries and humanities organizations,

30. "Muslim Journeys Bookshelf," *Muslim Journeys*, accessed January 12, 2017, http://www.programminglibrarian.org/muslimjourneys/bookshelf/mj-bookshelf.html.

its lack of perspective about intersectional identities is problematic and a key area for improvement. If the Bookshelf had more and better information about intersectional identities, it could deliver a more accurate understanding of a wider range of experiences and understandings. Rather than focusing on the breadth of the program, the depth of the collection itself should be the primary concern of the Bookshelf. While it is important to share the program in libraries across the country, it is also necessary to incorporate more books written by Muslims who belong to multiple identities. There are already a number of books in the collection that discuss the history of Islam, but there are only a handful of novels that specifically explore the identities of Muslim and Muslim-American women.

One solution to the lack of information about intersectional identities would be to recruit more Muslim librarians to further develop the Bookshelf collection. Muslim librarians have a clearer understanding of the needs of their patrons and can better spot the information gaps that exist in their communities. Through their experience as Muslims, they have gleaned valuable insight into the stereotyping and discrimination that members of their community endure and what resources might be useful to combat prejudice. Hiring practices should focus on the intersectional identities of librarians (e.g., Muslims and women of color). Libraries that do not actively encourage diverse hiring practices should develop statements of inclusion for future and current employees that emphasize their commitment to welcoming intersectional identities.

Avenues for Further Research

In examining the role of the public library in American society and the potential of libraries to disseminate more accurate information about Muslims, it would be useful to have further research on perceptions of the veil and how race, ethnicity, and religion are intertwined. This could include studies on current and former programs in public libraries that are aimed at providing more information about Muslims and Islam.

Another area of study is the possibility of creating a new race/ethnicity category in the United States census form. There is a current proposal to include a category for those who identify as being from the Middle East or North Africa (MENA).[31] Despite the potential benefits that could arise from such a step, the new category could also be used to target people of color who identify as part of that group.

In addition, further research is needed about how to create the most effective staff training programs for libraries in order to ensure that librarians know how to create a welcoming and inclusive environment for all intersectional identities. Mat and Adem discuss a training session they held for library staff on Muslim-American identity, which included a panel discussion and sharing stories about their own experiences as Muslim-American women.[32] It is important to measure the impacts of such training and identify areas for further improvement.

Conclusion and Directions

The experiences of Muslim women who work as librarians have changed in post-September 11 America. The current political climate and attempts by the new president to initiate a Muslim ban[33] will continue to affect the experiences of American Muslims and influence the attitudes of librarians and program directors. Libraries must continue to be providers of information and aim to develop programs that support marginalized communities. This can be done through purchasing books by and about Muslims, developing programs that teach people about other religions and cultures, hiring Muslim women and women of color as librarians, and engaging with the Muslim communities in

31. Hansi Lo Wang, "How the U.S. Defines Race and Ethnicity May Change Under Trump," *NPR*, Novemer 23, 2017, accessed November 25, 2017, https://www.npr.org/2017/11/22/564426420/how-the-u-s-defines-race-and-ethnicity-may-change-under-trump

32. Mat and Adem, "What Is It Like to Be a Muslim librarian in Seattle?", 7.

33. James J. Zogby, "It's Not Just a Muslim Ban, It's Much Worse," *The Washington Report on Middle East Affairs* 36, no. 2 (April 2017): 11.

their area. Public libraries can partner with Islamic community centers and interfaith organizations to help create programs and receive recommendations from members who are active in those communities. Public libraries are only limited by their own passivity; if they decide to take a more active role, they can help educate and inform citizens about the importance of inclusiveness and combating Islamophobia.

I ask that public librarians recognize that neutrality in public libraries only translates into passivity by allowing stereotypes, prejudice, hate crimes, and Islamophobia to proliferate unchecked. More importantly, I ask that public librarians use their unique place in the fabric of American society to actively help fight Islamophobia.

Bibliography

Alawa, Laila. "Representing the Muslim American Experience." *School Library Journal*, May 2014. http://www.slj.com/2014/05/diversity/why-we-need-muslim-american-kidlit/.

Bilge, Sirma. "Beyond Subordination vs. Resistance: An Intersectional Approach to the Agency of Veiled Muslim Women." *Journal of Intercultural Studies* 31, no. 1 (February 2010): 9–28. doi:10.1080/07256860903477662.

Blitzer, Jonathan. "A Muslim Community Responds to a Murder, Hate Crime or Not." *New Yorker*, June 23, 2017. Accessed August 17, 2017. http://www.newyorker.com/news/news-desk/a-muslim-community-responds-to-a-murder-hate-crime-or-not/.

Burke, Susan K. "Social Tolerance and Racist Materials in Public Libraries." *Reference & User Services Quarterly* 49, no. 4 (2010): 369–379.

Chepesiuk, Ron. "Muslim-American Librarians Reflect: September 11 and Its Aftermath." *American Libraries* 33, no. 1 (January 2002): 40-42.

Droogsma, Rachel Anderson. "Redefining Hijab: American Muslim Women's Standpoints on Veiling." *Journal of Applied Communication Research* 35, no. 3 (July 2007): 294-319. doi:10.1080/00909880701434299.

Elturk, Ghada Kanafani. "Cultural Collisions and Bridging the Gap between 'Don't Stare' and Care." *New Library World* 109, no. 11/12 (November 21, 2008): 574–83. doi:10.1108/03074800810921377.

Estabrook, Leigh. "Coping, View 2: Response Disappointing." *American Libraries* 33, no. 8 (September 2002): 37–38.

Flint, Rachel. "Self-Defence Class Over Islamophobia 'Normalisation' Fear." *BBC News*, April 19, 2017. Accessed April 19, 2017. http://www.bbc.com/news/uk-wales-38981436.

Garner, Steve, and Saher Selod. "The Racialization of Muslims: Empirical Studies of Islamophobia." *Critical Sociology* 41, no. 1 (2015): 9–19.

Hankins, Rebecca, and Miguel Juárez, eds. *Where Are All the Librarians of Color? The Experiences of People of Color in Academia.* Sacramento, CA: Library Juice Press, 2015.

Joshi, Khyati Y. "The Racialization of Hinduism, Islam, and Sikhism in the United States." *Equity & Excellence in Education* 39, no. 3 (September 2006): 211–26. doi:10.1080/10665680600790327.

Kniffel, Leonard. "Getting to Know Islam." *American Libraries* 33, no. 1 (January 2002): 48.

Mat, Tina and Ayan Adem. "What Is It Like To Be a Muslim Librarian in Seattle?" *Alki: The Washington Library Association Journal* 33, no. 2 (July 2017): 6-7.

McMenemy, David. "Librarians and Ethical Neutrality: Revisiting the Creed of a Librarian." *Library Review* 56, no. 3 (2007): 177-81. doi:10.1108/00242530710735948.

Mirza, Heidi Safia. "'A Second Skin': Embodied Intersectionality, Transnationalism and Narratives of Identity and Belonging among Muslim Women in Britain." *Women's Studies International Forum* 36 (January 2013): 5–15. doi:10.1016/j.wsif.2012.10.012.

"Muslim Journeys Bookshelf." *Muslim Journeys*. Accessed January 12, 2017. http://www.programminglibrarian.org/muslimjourneys/bookshelf/mj-bookshelf.html.

Pagowsky, Nicole, and Miriam Rigby. "Contextualizing Ourselves: The Identity Politics of the Librarian Stereotype." In *The Librarian Stereotype: Deconstructing Perceptions and Presentations of Information Work.* Chicago: Association of College and Research Libraries, a Division of the American Library Association, 2014.

"Recruiting for Diversity." *Advocacy, Legislation & Issues.* February 01, 2017. Accessed March 19, 2017. http://www.ala.org/advocacy/diversity/workforcedevelopment/recruitmentfordiversity.

Shavit, David. *The Politics of Public Librarianship.* New York: Greenwood, 1986.

Taramundi, Dolores Morondo. "Between Islamophobia and Post-Feminist Agency: Intersectional Trouble in the European Face-Veil Bans." *Feminist Review* 110, no. 1 (2015): 55–67.

Wang, Hansi Lo. "How the U.S. Defines Race and Ethnicity May Change Under Trump." *NPR*, Novemer 23, 2017. Accessed November 25, 2017. https://www.npr.org/2017/11/22/564426420/how-the-u-s-defines-race-and-ethnicity-may-change-under-trump/.

Zimmerman, Danielle Dunand. "Young Arab Muslim Women's Agency Challenging Western Feminism." *Affilia* 30, no. 2 (May 2015): 145–57. doi:10.1177/0886109914546126.

Zogby, James J. "It's Not Just a Muslim Ban, It's Much Worse." *The Washington Report on Middle East Affairs* 36, no. 2 (April 2017): 11, 24.

Chapter 4

The Other Asian: Reflections of South Asian Americans in Libraryland

Nisha Mody, Lalitha Nataraj, Gayatri Singh, and Aditi Worcester

Introduction

In 2016, the Association for Research Libraries and the University of California, Los Angeles (UCLA) Library hosted the National Diversity in Libraries Conference at UCLA. The conference brought together librarians interested in diversity and social justice issues from around the country, including many librarians of color. At this conference Nisha Mody (NM), a health sciences librarian, met Gayatri Singh (GS), a fellow academic librarian. They kept in touch and sought each other out when the call for proposals was announced for this book. Nisha and Gayatri were particularly interested in exploring the professional and personal experiences central to South Asian American librarians that they felt were not adequately documented in official literature. In turn, they reached out to Lalitha Nataraj (LN), a librarian with experience in public and community college libraries, and Aditi Worcester (AW), an archivist who has worked in community and academic special collections and archives. This is how four women of color—four South Asian American librarians—four *desis* came together to invite you to peek into our insights based upon our individual professional experiences at academic libraries, public libraries, and archives. One would assume the unifying theme is the commonality of our experiences, yet it took us a while to agree upon a vocabulary that held the same meanings for each of us. For instance, are we Asian or South Asian? South Asian or South Asian American? Does a cultural grouping called *South Asian American* exist in reality, or is it a convenient way of categorizing people from a geographical region who otherwise have little in common?

Because aggregate classifications can be problematic, providing context may help explain why we found these questions particularly complicated to answer. The Asian population in the United States was estimated to be approximately twenty-one million in 2015.[1] Stated differently, over twenty-one million people in the country have "origins in any of the original peoples of the East, Southeast Asia, or the Indian subcontinent, including, for example, Cambodia, China, India, Japan, Korea, Malaysia, Pakistan, the Philippine Islands, Thailand, and Vietnam."[2] Essentially, "Asian American" is an all-encompassing category applied to people with vast ethnic, linguistic, and cultural differences. A 2014 Center for American Progress (CAP) report pointed out that the inherently diverse "Asian" grouping was created by the U.S. Census Bureau in 1990 and has no scientific basis[3] (as is also the case for other racial classifications that have typically been political constructs in the service of racism).[4] Rather, it is a result of the "interplay between Census categorization and the ways that various groups and institutions adopt,

---

1. U.S. Department of Commerce, Bureau of the Census, *Annual Estimates of the Resident Population by Sex, Race Alone or in Combination, and Hispanic Origin for the UnitedStates, States, and Counties: April 1, 2010 to July 1, 2015*, https://factfinder.census.gov/.

2. U.S. Department of Commerce, Bureau of the Census, *American FactFinder Help: Asian*, https://factfinder.census.gov/help/en/asian.htm.

3. Karthik Ramakrishnan and Farah Z. Ahmad, *State of Asian Americans and Pacific Islander Series. A Multifaceted Portrait of a Growing Population* (Washington D.C.: Center for American Progress, 2014), 12, https://cdn.americanprogress.org/wp-content/uploads/2014/04/AAPIReport-comp.pdf.

4. Geoffrey C. Bowker and Susan Leigh Star, *Sorting Things Out: Classification and ItsConsequences* (Cambridge, MA: MIT Press, 1999), 197.

or seek changes to, those categories given historical legacies and new social and political developments."[5] Takaki highlights the centrality of racial classification in serving the economics of White Supremacy in his discussion about how South Asians were historically viewed as distinct from the other Asians (the Chinese and Japanese) by white Americans:

> While white Americans wondered what should be done about the Japanese, they suddenly noticed another group of "strangers"—the "Hindus." "Tall of stature, straight of feature, swarthy of color," they were unlike the Chinese and Japanese in an important way; they were "brothers" of "our own race," "full-blooded Aryans," "men of like progenitors with us." But like the Chinese and Japanese, the "Hindus" were willing to work for "cheap" wages and able to "subsist on incomes that would be prohibitive to the white man."[6]

Racial brotherhood notwithstanding, all the members of the "Asian" category were originally excluded from entering the country, starting with the Chinese in 1882 and continuing to the point at which Congress created the "Asiatic Barred Zone" with the Immigration Act of 1917.[7] So if one were looking for a unifying thread, this would probably be it. Our discussion, however, is devoted to a small sliver of this pie—South Asian Americans. According to a 2015 demographic snapshot of South Asians in the U.S.,[8] there are nearly 4.3 million South Asians tracing their roots to Bangladesh, Bhutan, India, Nepal, Pakistan, Sri Lanka, the Maldives, and the diaspora, including but not limited to Trinidad and Tobago, Guyana, Fiji, Tanzania, and Kenya. The Pew Research Center

5. Ramakrishnan and Ahmad, *State of Asian Americans and Pacific Islander Series. AMultifaceted Portrait of a Growing Population*, 12.

6. Ronald Takaki, *Strangers from a Different Shore: A History of Asian Americans* (Boston: Little, Brown and Company, 1998), 296.

7. Gerald L. Neuman, "Immigration," *The Oxford International Encyclopedia of Legal History*, ed. Stanley N. Katz (New York, NY: Oxford University Press, 2009).

8. South Asian Americans Leading Together, "A Demographic Snapshot of South Asians in the United States," *SAALT*, 2015, http://saalt.org/wp-content/uploads/2016/01/Demographic-Snapshot-updated_Dec-2015.pdf.

Asian American Fact Sheets (2010-2015)[9] estimate that there are four million Indian-origin persons in America, making this the single largest South Asian-origin group.

Each of us has roots in India and appreciates the complexity of language, food, clothing, religion, traditions, and rituals within the country. We're also keenly aware that this internal diversity results in narrower affiliations—including regional identities (e.g., Punjabi, Tamil, and Gujarati) intersecting with religious ones (Hinduism, Sikhism, Jainism, Islam, and Christianity, among others)—that take precedence over a national identity. Per Hall's definition of "cultural identity," our diasporic Indianness can be perceived as a collective representation among people with shared history or ancestry in common.[10] Within "the terms of this definition, our cultural identities reflect the common historical experiences and shared cultural codes which provide us, as 'one people,' with stable, unchanging and continuous frames of reference and meaning."[11] Three of us identify as second-generation South Asian Americans, and growing up, our conception of cultural identity was largely informed by our immigrant parents' static, nostalgic memories of India. But we are not our parents and therefore do not have the same first-hand experiences; our Indian identities are complicated by our negotiation of American ones. Those granular categories related to geographic region, language, and even religion lack context when it comes to perceptions of Indians within the mainstream (read: white) cultural hegemony. When it comes to defining South Asians in the United States, this group transcends formal racial categorization.[12] "For several reasons, South Asians in the United States present an ideal group to examine the dynamics of racial

9. "Fact Sheets on Asians in the U.S.," *Pew Research Center*, 2015 http://www.pewresearch.org/topics/asian-americans/.

10. Hall, Stuart, "Cultural Identity and Diaspora," in *Identity: Community, Culture, Difference,* ed. Jonathan Rutherford (London: Lawrence & Wishart, 1990): 223.

11. Ibid.

12. Vinay Harpalani, "DesiCrit: Theorizing the Racial Ambiguity of South Asian Americans," *NYU Annual Survey of American Law* 69, no. 1 (2013): 137, https://papers.ssrn.com/sol3/papers.cfm?abstract_id=2308892.

ambiguity…[in spite of their] increasing visibility and prominence in American society...there is no dominant theme to South Asian American media presentation...Additionally, South Asian Americans' diverse physical features and their variety of cultural and religion practices contribute to their racial ambiguity…"[13] Brettell and Nibbs note that second-generation South Asian Americans formulate identity by

> selectively choos[ing] defining characteristics from social domains in which they operate—their families, social networks, school environments, media images, popular culture, and the broader dominant culture. These new and varied spheres of action and collaboration have led some scholars to predict the emergence of pan-ethnic identities. Thus, second-generation regionally grouped children of immigrants, such as "Asians," would be expected to develop a pan Asian-American identity.[14]

Reducing identity to "a simple sameness, in a postcolonial and transnational context, functions as a result of European colonialism,"[15] but one might argue that the conflation of disparate groups under the panethnic category of *South Asian American* can facilitate broader political representation and mobilization of resources.[16]

It is critical to note that the South Asian American librarians in this roundtable do not share identities with all regions, languages, dialects, and religions represented in South Asia. We are also aware that our group does not include Muslim perspectives, which have been historically underrepresented and continue to be marginalized through global Islamophobia. Post 9/11, Arab and Middle Eastern Americans have become conflated with religious extremism and terrorist activity, and South Asian Americans (Muslim or not) have become racialized and

13. Harpalani, "DesiCrit," 104.

14. Caroline B. Brettell and Faith Nibbs, "Lived Hybridity: Second-Generation Identity Construction Through College Festival," *Identities: Global Studies in Culture and Power* 16, no. 6 (2009): 679, doi: 10.1080/10702890903307142.

15. Chih-Yun Chiang, "Diasporic Theorizing Paradigm on Cultural Identity," *Intercultural Communication Studies* 19, no. 1 (2010): 31, https://web.uri.edu/iaics/files/03Chih-YunChiang.pdf.

16. Yen Le Espiritu, *Asian American Panethnicity: Bridging Institutions and Identities* (Philadelphia, PA: Temple University Press, 1993): 162.

ordered "by categories of national belonging into a type of apolitical, ahistorical, and racially ambiguous citizenship."[17] As Deepa Iyer explains about Islamophobia, "It targets Muslims and anyone thought to be Muslim, including Sikhs, Arabs, Hindus, and South Asians."[18] Racialization on the basis of physical features has the harmful effect of reducing group(s)[19] where brownness becomes a visible marker against which Islamophobia and hate crimes are perpetrated. Furthermore, brownness takes on a whole new dimension when it is "constructed in the context of specific issues such as war, terrorism, Islamophobia, and, notably, immigration."[20] Though none of us are members of the South Asian Muslim American community—and therefore unable to offer any authentic perspectives pertaining to this group—we stand in solidarity with them as South Asian Americans because of shared experiences of marginalization and discrimination grounded in xenophobia.

Further complicating our identities is the fact that South Asian Americans are not always considered Asian American. The 2016 National Asian American Survey took a systematic approach to answering the question "Who is Asian American?" and their data revealed "that Americans—including Asian Americans—draw a sharp boundary between Asian and non-Asian that separates East Asians (Chinese, Korean, and Japanese) from South Asians (Indians, Pakistanis, and Bangladeshis) and, to a lesser extent, Southeast Asians like Filipinos."[21] The South Asians who

---

17. Sue Brennan, "Time, Space, and National Belonging in *The Namesake*: Redrawing South Asian American Citizenship in the Shadow of 9/11," *Journal of Transnational American Studies* 3, no. 1 (2011): 3, https://escholarship.org/uc/item/6cm9z5hd.

18. Deepa Iyer, "Standing Up to Islamophobia," *School Library Journal*, October 10, 2017, http://www.slj.com/2017/10/industry-news/standing-up-to-islamophobia#.

19. Linda Martin Alcoff, *Visible Identities: Race, Gender, and the Self* (New York: Oxford University Press, 2006): 261.

20. Anjana Mudambi, "The Construction of Brownness: Latino/a and South Asian Bloggers' Responses to SB 1070," *Journal of International and Intercultural Communication* 8, no. 1 (2015): 47, doi: 10.1080/17513057.2015.991079.

21. Jennifer Lee and Karthick Ramakrishnan, "Opinion: In the Outrage Over Discrimination, How Do We Define 'Asian American'?" *NBC News*, May 16, 2017, https://www.nbcnews.com/think/news/opinion-outrage-over-discrimination-how-do-we-define-asian-american-ncna757586.

were surveyed included themselves in the Asian American category.[22] Therefore, how does falling into the "other Asian" category impact South Asian Americans in libraryland? This, among many other questions, was discussed in our roundtable conversation, which was informed by our self-described personal, and multiple social and cultural identities. According to South Asian Americans Leading Together (SAALT), a nonprofit national advocacy organization for South Asian Americans, our demographic is the "fastest growing population (10%), among all major ethnic groups, in the country."[23] However, little statistical data exists for the number of employed South Asian American librarians from this group (the Bureau of Labor Statistics estimates that 5.4% of employed librarians identify as Asian American).[24] By drawing on and documenting our experiences as often the sole South Asian American librarian at an institution, we explore what that label means. We also examine how our individual experiences can encourage other South Asian Americans to join and contribute to the profession.

Q&A Section:

Q. What made you choose to be a librarian/archivist?

NM: While I certainly have my elevator speech about why I came into librarianship, it doesn't include a narrative relating to my South Asian identity. However, I often wonder if my experiences as a daughter of Indian immigrants influenced why I did *not* become a librarian sooner. This is my third career after working in the IT world and speech-language pathology. Both of these careers had certain desired features of being a

22. Karthick Ramakrishnan, "Are Indians also Asian American? Q&A thanks to Judge Srinivasan," *Data Bits - A Blog for AAPI Data,* http://aapidata.com/blog/indian-ams-asian/.

23. South Asian Americans Leading Together, "A Demographic Snapshot of South Asians in the United States," *SAALT.*

24. U.S. Department of Labor, Bureau of Labor Statistics, "*2016 Household Data Annual Averages: Employed Persons by Detailed Industry, Sex, Race, and Hispanic or Latino Ethnicity,*" http://www.bls.gov/cps/cpsaat18.htm.

successful South Asian American: technology and healthcare. I distinctly remember feeling safe telling my own parents and others within my community that I was considering (and later, ended up choosing) these professions. However, I did not feel this way when I decided to return to receive my MLIS. I think this is partially because of the stereotypes many people had about librarians. However, I also feel that it is not viewed as a profession that our parents worked hard for us to achieve or, frankly, that they even knew existed. Speech-language pathology is also a predominantly white and feminized profession, similar to librarianship. However, the health aspect, along with the earning potential and flexibility afforded to women who wanted to raise families, contributed to a higher perceived respect within the community. Other South Asians have asked in disbelief why I no longer wanted to be a speech-language pathologist. I highly doubt I would have received such a question if I were a librarian transitioning to become a medical professional. Because of this expectation and a lack of role models within the profession, I didn't even consider it to be a future profession.

AW: I never considered a career in libraries/archives until *after* I moved to the U.S. from India in 2007. It wasn't as if I actively disregarded a career in this field. I just didn't know a single person who was a librarian in New Delhi. Unlike media or journalism, it's not a popular career choice for a young, educated, middle-class woman interested in the humanities. So, like Nisha, I had different careers (print media and television production) well into my 30s before discovering the world of archives.

I spent a lot of time at the library after moving here, both as a user and a volunteer. It was a place where I could see other people like me, who were new to the culture and figuring their way around. As a volunteer, it also offered an opportunity to contribute so that, in a way, I felt as if I did indeed belong. Once I was able to work, I produced video biographies for families who wished to preserve their unique history for future generations. This particularly appealed to first- and second-generation Americans and members of different communities who wanted to document stories and memories for their children and grandchildren. But a fee-based business model is exclusionary, because only those who could afford it had their stories heard and recorded. I returned to school to get my Master's in Information Studies with the idea of creating or managing a community archive, because I just didn't find enough mention of members of my community in official versions of history or beyond the broad stereotypes of gas-station owners, techies, doctors, etc. It's hard to address issues of visibility (or invisibility, for that matter), identity, and belonging in isolation from events of the past. And when that "past" renders entire communities mute and relegates them to the sidelines, then it's time to look beyond what already exists in cultural memory and make space for new vantage points to history. That's what drew me to archives—the platform it can provide for cultural representation.

I hadn't thought of this before, but my decision to specialize in archives coincided with my move from being in the majority (in India) to suddenly finding myself a member of an underrepresented group in the minority (in the U.S.), trying to make sense of why people were now commenting on how good my English was. I think that just as I was trying to fit in, others were trying to accommodate me within their narratives about how someone from India should look or sound. There was a disconnect on both sides, and the social justice aspect of archives started to look particularly appealing at that point.

GS: I am one of many academic librarians who had to figure out what to do with a history degree. People in my life questioned that decision more than the one to become a librarian. Unlike Aditi, I had family friends who had worked in libraries, so it was a known career path. After completing my undergraduate studies, I was working as a temp in an office. The decision to go to graduate school for a degree in library science was acceptable because it was practical in a way that my history degree was not. It was easy to envision what type of job I would be able to get.

In thinking about recruiting South Asians into the field, just as with other underrepresented groups, we have to consider that many of us have never thought about librarianship as a career due to lack of awareness. Recruitment outreach needs to be targeted toward South Asian communities. But also, as the other authors have mentioned, parental expectations (both actual and perceived) must be taken into account. How much do South Asians police their own behavior to fit these expectations? My uncle wanted to be an English major, which freaked my grandfather out, so of course he got a degree in the sciences. Even after I was working as a librarian, I had family friends tell me I should apply for jobs at Google, because libraries won't exist in the near future. I don't think that the lack of faith in libraries as a viable career path is particular to South Asian people.

All the same, because I had worked as a page in my high school library, I knew there was something about librarianship that appealed to me, but I never considered it a viable career path until after college. In high school, I remember going to the career center for an assignment, and when I explored librarianship, the staff told me, "Libraries are dying." If we want to get more South Asians into the field, I think we have to counter that myth, and also find a way to demonstrate that a library career has the traits they're looking for in a successful profession.

LN: As part of the typical South Asian immigrant narrative, there was definitely an unspoken requirement that my sister and I had to pursue white-collar professions in health- or science-related fields. Our parents expected us to follow through on these filial expectations without necessarily fostering our potential for success in those fields. But both my sister and I benefited from early literacy storytimes and programming at the local library. We became strong readers and writers and also felt welcomed in the library, a sentiment that endures. I specifically mention these educational tools because, as a public librarian, I view the library as a critical space to nurture and develop its community's knowledge. However, in my family—and, I would argue, within the broader South Asian community—there was this insular, static perception that success comes from within. That is, we essentially know what we have to do and we don't rely on others to help us. Yet being a librarian/archivist means emphasizing a collective responsibility, whether it's raising readers or preserving the heritage of marginalized groups.

I started in the profession as a student assistant at my college library; after graduation, I accepted a paraprofessional position at another academic library. I looked at the job as a temporary situation because I planned on eventually going to law school. That first post-undergrad year was eye-opening; I learned that a career in librarianship/archives was varied and complex. I was also fascinated by my colleagues' involvement in teaching, scholarly communication, budgeting and infrastructure, and campus governance. The social-justice aspect of librarianship especially appealed to me. But most importantly, I was inspired by having an Asian American female supervisor who happened to hold a high position in the library's administration. This gave me hope for what I could achieve in the field. I applied to graduate school the following year, fully intending to pursue a career as an academic librarian.

Despite the prestige attached to being a lawyer, I think my parents preferred my shift to librarianship because they appreciated the stereotypes attached to this career—quiet, meek, unassuming, stable, etc.—and felt that a good Indian daughter should embody those qualities. They also viewed the academic library as a sterile, elevated employer. But when I became a public librarian, they expressed reservations related to my personal safety and the potential obsolescence of the profession. While I doubt they gave it much thought, my parents' sentiments echo the desire for upward mobility that pervades the South Asian American community. Working as a public servant isn't considered financially lucrative.

Q. What is it like to be a female librarian or archivist who also happens to be South Asian American? From this intersectional perspective, do you believe that your professional experience is distinct?

NM: When an individual looks at me, they are fairly confident that I am Indian. The reason I know is because I am told or asked by patrons and colleagues within libraries. While the assumption is accurate, I often wonder how someone from another South Asian country or a non–South Asian country would feel if they were assumed to be Indian. What does this mean for other South Asian countries that are less recognized? They should not be othered or considered any less, which ultimately occurs through these generalizations. Also, some people who may appear to be from a South Asian country are not. This not only puts a patron or colleague in a communication quandary, but it also requires a response from said librarian. Often, my default is to make that person feel better. However, in doing so, I question if I am doing this for self-preservation, to protect their feelings, or to remain "professional."

Would I be asked about where I was "really" from or about my ethnicity if I was a man? A patron assuming something in their head and voicing it are two different things. Also, many South Asian men in the information sciences are often working in corporate jobs with more income potential and financial stability, in information technology or the like. I don't think it's a secret that there is rampant sexism within the IT and science-related fields.

GS: With my name, I've seen everything from emails that are addressed to Gary (I'm assuming autocorrect was involved) to questions like: "Where is it from? How do you spell it? What does it mean? Is it your surname? Did you name yourself?" Twice, when I was wearing a nametag, people just started reciting the Gayatri Mantra! Once I answer some of their questions, I usually receive a response along the lines of how pretty or exotic my name is, and some folks feel compelled to share some information they know about India or an Indian they know. Over time, I've become less patient. At times, I experience tension when I'm wearing my librarian hat. I feel like I censor myself or let these interactions go on longer than they need to if I'm at a service desk, in a classroom, or doing outreach. Do I do this because I'm in a service profession, because I'm a woman, or because I'm South Asian American? It's hard for me to separate my identities to answer that. I know that my "difference" is visible and people are making assumptions about me before we even have an interaction. I'm not opposed to having conversations about my culture or background, but that isn't necessarily a conversation I expect to have at work while interacting with our users.

AW: My background is a little different from Nisha, Gayatri, and Lalitha's; the three of them grew up here in America and this is where home is. And I totally get how frustrating it is for people to assume otherwise just because of the color of their skin or that they somehow look different from what a typical American "should" look like.

I, on the other hand, was born and raised in New Delhi, India, and moved here when I was twenty-six. This is home *now* but India will always be a part of who I am. So my response to "Where are you from?" is something I struggle with personally. I have felt like a poser when I say I am American because ten years after moving here, I am still learning new things, new words, new -isms that my three-year-old takes for granted. And yet, paradoxically, America *is* where I "grew" up in terms of finding myself and coming into my own. To my parents, who live in India, I am American now. I align with their version of American, even if I am not 100% clear on mine. That's the thing, isn't it? There are so many versions of identity and nationhood. What does it mean to be American? Or Indian? Does it have to be one or the other? Who decides? And then who decides which version trumps another?

It's an engaging discussion, one that I reserve for my personal life. I don't expect it at work. Work is about professionalism, competence, and carrying out the responsibilities that I have been trained and hired to do. So when a patron interrupts me during a reference question to inquire where I am from (and it happens often), it is a constant reminder that I am a distraction to their worldview—an anomaly. Not necessarily in a hostile or mean way, but when they walked into the archive to learn more about a particular subject, they did not expect a South Asian American woman archivist to be the one helping out. So yes, my appearance and cultural background do influence the way people perceive me as a professional. And so does my gender. Like Nisha, I can't help but question if someone would feel as comfortable asking a man about his cultural heritage in the workplace. Come to think of it, I would be so curious to hear about the male perspective in this profession, which is traditionally perceived as female-dominated.

But it's not all negative! I have received a lot of opportunities, too, for these same reasons. I received multiple graduate scholarships to encourage members from underrepresented communities in the profession and was also offered the opportunity to be a library residency fellow as part of diversity recruitment. So there's that.

LN: As a public librarian who works face-to-face daily with our patrons, I have a professional responsibility to provide outstanding customer service. Often, that means handling microaggressions with a smile on my face. Most public librarians will say that no matter how many times a question is asked, you must answer it as though it's the first time you're hearing it. But when it comes to responding to "Where are you *really* from?" or "What is your nationality?" over and over again, I struggle. Once, a white patron tried to engage me in a conversation about Indian politics and was surprised to hear that I had little knowledge and opinion on the matter. The confusion over ethnicity vs. nationality isn't just limited to white Americans; immigrant communities perpetuate it by conflating Americanness with race. My own parents would tell people that their daughter was married to an American (read: white dude), disregarding the fact that I identify as one, too!

I think many tend to view librarians as meek and passive, making it easy to lob offensive remarks with little fear of repercussions. And being an ethnic minority further underscores the insensitivity of people's comments. It's a double bind for sure, because my sense of professionalism precludes me from speaking my mind—and as a person of color, I feel silenced. As wonderfully supportive as my non-Asian colleagues are, I don't think they fully understand the emotional labor that goes into having to constantly justify your American identity.

Q. How can we be critical in our work as South Asian American librarians/archivists and also be allies for other marginalized groups?

NM: The model-minority rhetoric is rampant among members of the South Asian culture and outside of it. "If we can achieve success, why can't 'they' [African Americans, Latinos]?" It really hurts me to hear this type of language from other South Asians. South Asians have, and continue to be, on the receiving end of ignorance and discrimination. However, I think it is important that our histories of acceptance into this country be recognized. Ultimately, South Asians were not brought into this country on slave ships. The majority of South Asians were not sought for low-wage labor. The 1965 Immigration Act[25] allowed an influx of South Asian immigrants (and other nationalities) into the United States for specialized skills. My father was an engineer, and he came to the United States to study engineering. We were given opportunities during a time of extreme civil unrest for African Americans in this country. I think this also demonstrates how classism contributes to the idea of the model minority. When certain groups of people are sought for certain skills, they are perceived as "better" than laborers, when in fact, this was a targeted strategy by the United States.

What does this mean? While this can be an extended political discussion, I think that South Asians were given opportunities that, unfortunately, were not available to African Americans and Latinos who already lived in the United States (which is often still the case). It is our duty to recognize these histories and be allies for these marginalized groups. We cannot clump all minorities together when there are varied sociopolitical motivations for our arrival/recruitment (forced or policy-driven) into this country. That means we need to advocate for

25. Erika Lee, "Legacies of the 1965 Immigration Act," *SAADA*, October 1, 2015, https://www.saada.org/tides/article/20151001-4458.

the representation of these voices within collections, archives, reference services, programming, and outreach. Additionally, we need these perspectives to be represented as the face of libraries through hiring initiatives.

LN: I agree with Nisha. Many South Asians have a problematic pride in the model-minority label. This categorization has reinforced institutionalized racism and has historically been seen as a device to divide and conquer minority groups.[26] This type of stratification isn't new to South Asians when you consider India's caste system, which was reified and exploited by the British to maintain colonial power. Many South Asians, including my engineer father, were well educated and afforded access to special programs that allowed them to seamlessly immigrate to the U.S. These opportunities were not widely available to all immigrants, or even minority groups already in this country for generations. When South Asian community members position themselves as so-called exemplars compared to other marginalized and disenfranchised groups in the U.S., we're not doing ourselves any favors. Espousing the model-minority title means willingly accepting a second-class status; it's also done on the backs of others.

Before South Asians can properly ally ourselves with other people of color, we have to acknowledge our own oppressed status and willing acceptance of a social system that ultimately privileges the dominant white culture. As a public librarian, I am focused on making sure our collections are balanced, providing a mirror in which everyone sees themselves. As a professional reviewer for middle-grade and young-adult literature, I rely on my expertise and, frankly, my own Person of Color (POC) experience to critique titles that fall short of accurately representing cultures outside the mainstream.

---

26. Nicholas D. Hartlep, "Reconsidering the Model Minority and Black Mormon Discourses," *Northeastern Educational Research Association Conference Proceedings*, (Rocky Hill, CT: NERA, 2012), https://opencommons.uconn.edu/nera_2012/8.

GS: Learning about South Asian American history and experiences that Nisha and Lalitha refer to are topics that I think many of us had to learn on our own. So, part of my activism is ongoing education: through reading, watching films, attending lectures, etc. When I work as a South Asian American librarian, my South Asian identity helps me be aware of my privilege, even though I am part of an underrepresented group. And as much as I try to bring that into my professional work, I think we also need to have these conversations within our own community. By sharing information and engaging in difficult conversations with other South Asian Americans, I feel like I can almost be a more effective ally for other marginalized groups than in libraryland.

AW: You know, the one question I was always asked during trips back to India was whether I had ever experienced racism in the U.S. My answer was always no. Did my husband's childhood friend make an Apu joke (from *The Simpsons*) at our first meeting? Yes. Did someone in my writer's club ask if my dark Indian hair ever turned white? Yes. Did a friend and colleague at work mention how she doesn't like the smell of curry in the lunchroom? Yes. All of those moments made me cringe—then and now. And I'm sure there's an argument for all of those interactions to be considered racist. I interpret them as coming from a place of ignorance and awkwardness, rather than as acts of discrimination or assertions of racial superiority. I may be wrong, but that has been my perspective.

However, recent events have compelled me to think about this a little deeper. Have I been complacent in my worldview simply because as a South Asian American, I have been accorded a certain (dubious) privilege? The South Asian community has traditionally been a fairly non-threatening, financially prosperous immigrant group that has been slow to express political opinion or action. In return for being a "model minority," we have been "bestowed" a protection of sorts against the overt racism that members of the Hispanic or Black population may experience.[27] This precarious veneer slipped (for me) in February 2017

27. Anuhya Bobba, "The Murder of Srinivas Kuchibhotla: Beyond the Model

when an Indian engineer, Srinivas Kuchibhotla, was murdered in a Kansas bar by a white man in what was termed a "hate crime." Suddenly "racism" was now something I needed to be vigilant about, and it drove home the point that this is how most marginalized groups must feel on a daily basis. As an individual, I am becoming more sensitive to this reality, and as a professional, I hope that this sensitivity will inform decisions about collection development, representation, and balance. Not just in terms of white and non-white, but more about the plurality of existence.

Q. Is the South Asian American experience adequately represented in libraries and archives?

GS: Wearing my public-services hat, I'm impressed by the programming and outreach activities related to South Asia that I've seen. Public and academic libraries are hosting programs related to Diwali, Eid, and more. Growing up in Southern California, where there was a sizeable South Asian community, I didn't notice any of that. The community definitely came together to fill in the gap, but I never saw anything in public institutions to assist that endeavor.

Working on a campus, there is a little bit of *it's your month* programming. Black Americans get February. Women get March. Latinx get April for Cesar Chavez. And then, when May rolls around, it's time for Asians and Pacific Islanders. This is where the label of Asian American can be problematic. There is power in numbers and solidarity, but there are drawbacks as well. There have been Mays with an entire month of campus-wide programming that doesn't include any events related to South Asia. It might be because my campus doesn't have a South Asian Studies program, but there is a South Asian student population. Groups on campus, from student organizations to faculty initiatives, are trying to fill the need for representation. My experience with the library has

---

Minority Label of the Indian American Community," *Feminism in India*, March 2, 2017, https://feminisminindia.com/2017/03/02/model-minority/.

been that, if you initiate a project, they seem to be open to it. I was able to host an exhibit and event related to Indian cinema. That's the "other duties as needed" part of the job description for every librarian from an underrepresented group; you are expected to be the expert and advocate for your people and culture. Oftentimes underrepresented librarians take on this work in addition to their jobs, and don't get compensated for it.

AW: From an archival perspective, there's still a lot to be done to include and showcase historical narratives from a non-white perspective. When I worked at the state archives in Texas, I learned a lot about the history of the state and the events and people who contributed to the shaping of its personality, but information about minority communities was sparse. This is not to say that there was an active effort to exclude that perspective. But there just wasn't much about Asian or South Asian communities, even though members of these communities have been around for a while.

In California, the South Asian community has historically played an integral role in the development of the state—contributing to road, irrigation, and railroad construction; the sawmills of the Pacific Northwest; peach farms; vineyards; and sharecropping. But we don't learn about any of this in school. Smaller community archives attempt to address this gap and present a more balanced representation of history (for instance, the Austin History Center appoints community liaison officers to reach out to the African American, Mexican American, and Asian American communities for collection development), but they inevitably tend to be separate and distinct from the official archives.

The South Asian American Digital Archive (SAADA) is another independent organization trying to demonstrate that South Asian American history is not different from or contrary to American history. It is creating a dialogue and a historical narrative with pictures, stories, personal experiences, and anecdotes from real, everyday South Asian Americans—presenting an additional vantage point to official versions of history. There's an unspoken understanding that it is up to the members of underrepresented communities to document their own histories, and that's why it is so crucial to have role models from these communities—our own communities—in the profession.

NM: Representation of South Asian Americans is quite precarious. As Gayatri mentions, there are more celebrations for holidays in public library spaces. However, I feel that while this is considered inclusive, it can also be a way of tokenizing South Asian culture. I would love to imagine alternative programming that highlights the diverse historical contexts, similar to what Aditi discusses, in which many of us arrived here, as opposed to being defined solely by a holiday or a costume. I definitely agree that it can be dangerous to clump Asian Americans together. It is such a varied population with so many different histories. This truly speaks to how race is socially constructed and how this classification itself can be problematic.

I was rummaging through some of my parents' things shortly after my father passed away, and I found letters from one of my father's friends who had immigrated to the U.S. before my family. He was telling my father about how there are so many opportunities for a better life in America, and he was encouraging my father to come. It really struck me, and it made me realize how that letter was, in fact, a part of *my* story and *my* existence. These are the missing non-white narratives that can be represented in libraries.

LN: I understand Nisha's point about tokenization. It's a fine line because, on one hand, we desire inclusiveness, but on the other, the representation isn't always accurate and can be insensitive. In planning events at public libraries, I've noted that programming tends to favor mainstream cultural traditions; libraries are more likely to highlight Christmas rather than Eid, Navaratri, or Rosh Hashanah. I recall one library planning a Diwali *diya* craft in July; this Hindu observance is typically celebrated in mid-autumn.

Despite an ethical charge to maintain balanced collections, public librarians face budget constraints and, as a result, prioritize purchases of mainstream, popular titles (most of which are predominantly white, with few POC characters). I can't tell you how disheartening it is to read professional children's book reviews praising characterization, plotting, and artwork, but because the book is about South Asian culture, it might need additional handselling in order to circulate. Why invest that extra time in a non-mainstream title when there are dozens of others that will check out like hot cakes with little to no promotion? Librarians are not only stewards of the collections; we also help to shape the reading tastes of our service populations. I approach my work critically and with intentionality; when I buy books about the South Asian experience, I commit to promoting these titles through readers' advisory and programming.

Q. How can we encourage other members of the South Asian American community to consider entering this field?

NM: For me, the biggest deterrent to becoming a librarian was that I didn't realize the profession existed. Yes, I knew that librarians worked in libraries, but unfortunately, it wasn't something that felt professionalized. I think this goes back to the idea of having a strong work ethic to be what is deemed as "professional" and "profitable" within the South Asian culture. Had I known the strategy, service, and opportunities within the profession, I would have jumped at the chance right after college. I think the hardest thing is explaining to others what librarians do. It is our duty to educate those within our culture about the value of our work. Perhaps we can associate it with the work that other South Asians are more inclined to choose, such as other helping professions like medicine, advocacy in law, or information provision, organization, and access in the information technology arena. Most of us can agree that the South Asian experience, with respect to immigration and being first- or second-generation, has shared struggles and nuances. I can see librarians building upon these commonalities through work we have done in librarianship and archives.

GS: I'm of two minds about this. We can look at the professions South Asians are drawn to, as well as their motivation for selecting those fields. Making very broad generalizations, the following factors might be considered: status, income potential, stability, and flexible work schedule. We won't attract anyone with our salaries! But I think we can make a case for the other factors (perhaps academic libraries more so than the other types since income tends to be higher). At the same time, I wonder if this is the right approach. Are we falling into the stereotype of acceptable professions? Will everyone who isn't a doctor, engineer, lawyer, or computer-science major be considered a failure? I think the major hurdle is to get South Asians to realize that librarianship/archives present a viable career option. If the profession is serious about recruiting from underrepresented groups, they also need to utilize current South Asian librarians/archivists in their efforts.

AW: We need to demystify the profession in order to encourage members from underrepresented communities to consider it. I agree with Nisha that it can be quite a challenge to try and explain what it is that we do in a manner that adequately represents the excitement, potential, importance, and relevance of our work. When I tell people about my work, it's not uncommon for them to adopt a concerned look and ask (with good intentions), "But do you enjoy it?" and then look suitably confused when I nod excitedly!

It's not just about books, or paper, or cataloging. It's about critical thinking, life skills, data sets, information literacy, technology, and understanding who we are and how we got here. Had I known this, I would have opted in much earlier. Scholarships, internships, and diversity recruitments are useful and important ways to assist people already interested in the profession. But we need to do more to make the profession mainstream. Perhaps we need a leading lady or man from the profession on a TV show or as the protagonist of a popular book. If we can demystify the world of archaeology, medicine, and the justice system with high ratings, there's hope for libraries and archives. This might be an oversimplification of the problem, but we're going to have to get creative in our approach.

On a less romantic note, money is an important consideration. If this profession were to suddenly become as financially lucrative as going into medicine or law, it would be a more attractive career choice.

LN: It's ironic how one of the most notable figures in our profession, S. R. Ranganathan, is Indian, and yet librarianship/archives is rarely acknowledged as a viable career option for South Asians. But, to be fair, LIS has a perception problem in mainstream America and once that's resolved, I believe we'll make serious headway with demystifying and promoting the profession to the South Asian community. Additionally, we need to consider the roles and influence of South Asians currently engaged in the profession. The onus is really on us to raise our voices and demand representation. This means building strong networks, critiquing programming ideas around South Asian culture to ensure accuracy, and emphasizing balance in our programs, services, and library/archival collections.

Conclusion

As we wind down our conversation, we attempt to take stock of the questions that originally prompted it—questions about individual, community, and racial identities intersecting with gender and professional identities. Did we find commonalities in our daily lives working behind the reference desk or in the archives that could be attributed to a shared ethnicity? Dare we speak for all South Asian American information professionals when, by sheer coincidence, all four of us happen to have cultural roots in India and do not really reflect the diversity of religion, gender, or even sexuality that a more representative roundtable would have?

While we feel solidarity as South Asian American librarians, the nuances in our individual experiences, perceptions, and histories provide only a sample of what it is like to be women who also identify as South Asian Americans and librarians. For some of us, this profession was accepted by our families and questions, no questions asked, while for others, that wasn't the case. So, for us, the big takeaway was to acknowledge that our individual experiences have something to add to the conversation about representation in libraries and archives—expanding the scope beyond books and collections to include representation in programming, outreach, advocacy, and recruitment initiatives. We hope that this discussion, which originally arose from a need to explore *why* there is a dearth of literature on the experiences of South Asian Americans in the field of libraries and archives, can evolve into *how* we can amplify our collective voices and perspectives. This can only happen when enough members of our community articulate and share stories with the confidence that they are being heard.

As our dialogue demonstrates, our individual and collective identities are often at odds in various contexts. Additionally, this is a subset of the myriad of identities in South Asia. We are eager to continue this dialogue and include other voices that we do not represent. We hope that including more of these stories will help address the lack of commonality and cohesion that inherently exists when you're tagged Asian—and in our case, the "other" Asian—without due consultation.

Bibliography

Alcoff, Linda Martin. *Visible Identities: Race, Gender, and the Self.* New York: Oxford University Press, 2006.

Bobba, Anuhya. "The Murder of Srinivas Kuchibhotla: Beyond the Model Minority Label of the Indian American Community." *Feminism in India*, March 2, 2017. https://feminisminindia.com/2017/03/02/model-minority/.

Bowker, Geoffrey C., and Susan Leigh Star. *Sorting Things Out: Classification and Its Consequences.* Cambridge, MA: MIT Press, 1999.

Brennan, Sue. "Time, Space, and National Belonging in *The Namesake*: Redrawing South Asian American Citizenship in the Shadow of 9/11." *Journal of Transnational American Studies* 3, no. 1 (2011): 1-23. Accessed December 20, 2017. https://escholarship.org/uc/item/6cm9z5hd.

Brettell, Caroline B., and Faith Nibbs, "Lived Hybridity: Second-Generation Identity Construction through College Festival," *Identities: Global Studies in Culture and Power* 16, no. 6 (2009): 678-699. doi: 10.1080/10702890903307142.

Chiang, Chih-Yun. "Diasporic Theorizing Paradigm on Cultural Identity." *Intercultural Communication Studies* 19, no. 1 (2010): 29-46.https://web.uri.edu/iaics/files/03Chih-YunChiang.pdf.

Espiritu, Yen Le. *Asian American Panethnicity: Bridging Institutions and Identities.* Philadelphia, PA: Temple University Press, 1993."Fact Sheets on Asians in the U.S." *Pew Research Center.* 2015. http://www.pewresearch.org/topics/asian-americans/.

Hall, Stuart. "Cultural Identity and Diaspora." In *Identity: Community, Culture, Difference,* edited by Jonathan Rutherford, 222-237. London: Lawrence & Wishart, 1990.

Harpalani, Vinay. "DesiCrit: Theorizing the Racial Ambiguity of South Asian Americans." *NYU Annual Survey of American Law* 69, no. 1 (2013): 77-184. https://papers.ssrn.com/sol3/papers.cfm?abstract_id=2308892.

Hartlep, Nicholas D. "Reconsidering the Model Minority and Black Mormon Discourses." *Northeastern Educational Research Association Conference Proceedings.* Rocky Hill, CT: NERA, 2012).

Iyer, Deepa. "Standing Up to Islamophobia." *School Library Journal.* October 10, 2017. http://www.slj.com/2017/10/industry-news/standing-up-to-islamophobia#.

Lee, Erika. "Legacies of the 1965 Immigration Act." *SAADA.* October 1, 2015. https://www.saada.org/tides/article/20151001-4458.

Lee, Jennifer, and Karthick Ramakrishnan, "Opinion: In the Outrage Over Discrimination, How Do We Define 'Asian American'?" *NBC News*. May 16, 2017. https://www.nbcnews.com/think/news/opinion-outrage-over-discrimination-how-do-we-define-asian-american-ncna757586.

Mudambi, Anjana. "The Construction of Brownness: Latino/a and South Asian Bloggers' Responses to SB 1070." *Journal of International and Intercultural Communication* 8, no. 1 (2015): 44-62. doi: 10.1080/17513057.2015.991079.

Neuman, Gerald L. "Immigration." *The Oxford International Encyclopedia of Legal History*, edited by Stanley N. Katz. New York: Oxford University Press, 2009.

Ramakrishnan, Karthick. "Are Indians also Asian American? Q&A thanks to Judge Srinivasan." *Data Bits - A Blog for AAPI Data*. http://aapidata.com/blog/indian-ams-asian/.

Ramakrishnan, Karthick, and Farah Z. Ahmad. *State of Asian Americans and Pacific Islander Series. A Multifaceted Portrait of a Growing Population.* Washington, D.C.: Center for American Progress, 2014. https://cdn.americanprogress.org/wp-content/uploads/2014/04/AAPIReport-comp.pdf.

South Asian Americans Leading Together. "A Demographic Snapshot of South Asians in the United States." *SAALT*, 2015. http://saalt.org/wp-content/uploads/2016/01/Demographic-Snapshot-updated_Dec-2015.pdf.

Takaki, Ronald. *Strangers from a Different Shore: A History of Asian Americans.* Boston: Little, Brown and Company, 1998.

U.S. Department of Commerce, Bureau of the Census. *American FactFinder Help: Asian.* 2017. https://factfinder.census.gov/help/en/asian.htm.

U.S. Department of Commerce, Bureau of the Census. *Annual Estimates of the Resident Population by Sex, Race Alone or in Combination, and Hispanic Origin for the United States, States, and Counties: April 1, 2010 to July 1, 2015.* https://factfinder.census.gov/.

U.S. Department of Labor, Bureau of Labor Statistics. "*2016 Household Data Annual Averages: Employed Persons by Detailed Industry, Sex, Race, and Hispanic or Latino Ethnicity.*" http://www.bls.gov/cps/cpsaat18.htm.

Suggested Reading

Bhattacharya, Piyali, ed. *Good Girls Marry Doctors: South Asian American Daughters on Obedience and Rebellion.* San Francisco, CA: Aunt Lute Books, 2016.

Black Desi Secret History. Accessed December 15, 2017. http://blackdesisecrethistory.org/.

Iyer, Deepa. *We Too Sing America: South Asian, Arab, Muslim, and Sikh Immigrants Shape Our Multiracial Future.* New York: The New Press, 2015.

Lee, Erika. *The Making of Asian America: A History.* New York: Simon & Schuster, 2015.

Prashad, Vijay. *Everybody was Kung Fu Fighting: Afro-Asian Connections and the Myth of Cultural Purity.* Boston: Beacon Press, 2001.

Sangay K. Mishra. *Desis Divided: The Political Lives of South Asian Americans.* Minneapolis, MN: University of Minnesota Press, 2016.

Sohi, Seema. *Echoes of Mutiny: Race, Surveillance, and Indian Anticolonialism in North America.* New York: Oxford University Press, 2014.

South Asian American Digital Archive. Accessed December 15, 2017. https://www.saada.org/.

Chapter 5

I AM My Hair, and My Hair Is Me: #BlackGirlMagic in LIS

Teresa Y. Neely

> No matter who you are, no matter where you come from, you are beautiful, you are powerful, you are brilliant, you are funny… I know that's not always the message that you get from the world. I know there are voices that tell you that you're not good enough. That you have to look a certain way, act a certain way. That if you speak up, you're too loud. If you step up to lead, you're being bossy—Michelle Obama[1]

In her 2015 Black Girls Rock (BGR) awards speech, Michelle Obama spoke directly to women and girls who look like me. She acknowledged us, enumerated the criticism we get all too often, and let Black women everywhere know that she was with us, and that she was one of us. We don't usually hear words like that coming from someone who looks like her, who lived where she lived, and was married to whom she was married.

On February 12, 2017, in her acceptance speech for winning best contemporary album for *Lemonade*,[2] global icon and superstar Beyoncé

1. Office of the First Lady, "Remarks by the First Lady at BET's 'Black Girls Rock!' Event," (speech, New Jersey Performing Arts Center, Newark, NJ, March 28, 2015), https://obamawhitehouse.archives.gov/the-press-office/2015/03/28/remarks-first-lady-bets-black-girls-rock-event.

2. Beyoncé, *Lemonade* (New York, NY: Parkwood Entertainment, 2016).

Giselle Knowles-Carter (Beyoncé), heavily pregnant with twins, read a powerful statement about the beauty in Black lives. Resplendent in a Peter Dundas[3] designed, intricately beaded and embroidered gold gown with an image of her [Black] face and the lyrics to her song "Love Drought," which she had performed earlier that evening, she thanked the Grammy voters for the award, and then read, in part,

> "It's important to me to show images to my children that reflect their beauty so they can grow up in a world where they look in the mirror—first through their own families, as well as the news, the Super Bowl, the Olympics, the White House and the Grammys—and see themselves. And have no doubt that they're beautiful, intelligent, and capable. This is something I want for every child of every race, and I feel it's vital that we learn from the past and recognize our tendencies to repeat our mistakes."[4]

In these speeches, Michelle Obama and Beyoncé were speaking to global audiences about Black lives and Black people. Their words are critically important to the mental health of those of us whose career aspirations have led us to work at institutions and live in states, cities, and neighborhoods where there are few people who look like us. As Black women, their international personas on very public stages go a long way towards dispelling myths and misconceptions based on limited interactions with Black people in the aggregate, and Black women specifically. These misconceptions are keenly felt in higher education, where there are far fewer Black women in the professoriate at any given predominantly white institution (PWI). As a Black woman who has worked in academic libraries in higher education for nearly twenty-five years, I have never worked at an institution where there was another

---

3. Nicole Phelps, "Exclusive: Peter Dundas Dresses Beyoncé at the Grammys, Launches Solo Label," *Vogue.com,* February 12, 2017, http://www.vogue.com/article/beyonce-grammys-peter-dundas-dress.

4. Giovanni Russeonello, "Beyonce's and Adele's Grammy Speeches: Transcripts," *New York Times.com,* February 12, 2017, https://www.nytimes.com/2017/02/12/arts/music/beyonce-speech-grammys-trump.html.

credentialed Black librarian, female or otherwise, on the faculty. This is true for many Black women faculty in academic disciplines as well.[5]

In a study commissioned by the National Postsecondary Education Cooperative, less than five percent of tenured, and less than seven percent of tenure-track faculty surveyed identified as Black.[6] Overall, people of color (POC) represented less than twenty percent of the tenured, and less than a quarter of those in tenure-track positions in PWI's in 2013. Specific numbers for Black women were not available in that survey. Three years later, three percent of college and university faculty were Black women, compared to White women who made up thirty-five percent of the total group. Additionally, twenty-seven percent of White women were full professors, compared to only two percent of Black women.[7] The picture for women who look like me in my profession, in higher education, is quite bleak, so we need to see Mrs. Obama and Beyoncé's faces and hear their words when they speak to these large international audiences about us. And so, too, do many of our colleagues. Most days, our sanity depends on it.

Living and working in White spaces is spiritually and emotionally exhausting. In order to cope, you need to develop multiple personalities, clinically known as dissociative identity disorder,[8] and basically

---

5. Debra A. Harley, "Maids of Academe: African American Women Faculty at Predominantly White Institutions," *Journal of African American Studies* 12, no. 1 (2008): 19-36.

6. Corbin M. Campbell, Carolyn Sloane Mata, and Fred Galloway, "Meeting Today's Higher Education Goals via the National Center for Education Statistics' Postsecondary Sample Surveys," August 2017, https://nces.ed.gov/npec/pdf/MeetingTodaysHigherEd.pdf. See also Valerie Strauss, "It's 2015. Where Are All the Black College Faculty?" *Washington Post*, November 12, 2015, https://www.washingtonpost.com/news/answer-sheet/wp/2015/11/12/its-2015 -where-are-all-the-black-college-faculty/?utm_term=.03eae652f323 and "Black Faculty in Higher Education: Still Only a Drop in the Bucket," *Journal of Blacks in Higher Education*, 2006, http://www.jbhe.com/features/55_blackfaculty.html.

7. U.S. Department of Education, National Center for Education Statistics, "Characteristics of Postsecondary Faculty," *The Condition of Education 2017* (NCES 2017-144), 254, https://nces.ed.gov/pubs2017/2017144.pdf.

8. Dissociative Identity Disorder is defined as "a severe condition in which two or

live multiple lives, sometimes from meeting to meeting. You have to constantly watch your mouth and what comes out of it, and mind your countenance when you hear what comes out of the mouths of everyone else, no matter their hue. Every day is a struggle to appear neutral, to be the opposite of angry, because we all know the caricature of the "angry Black woman,"[9] and no one wants to be labeled that. Even if we are, justifiably, angry. All the damn time.

Until relatively recently, words to describe the experiences of Black women were not prevalent in the library and information science literature. Even today, we rely heavily on the research and theoretical frameworks from Education literature and other disciplines to provide the context for framing our experiences. Patricia Hill Collins[10] and CaShawn Thompson[11] have provided the context for Black women to view their experiences from what Collins calls "a special standpoint on self, family and society."[12] Thompson wanted to find a way to "describe all the greatness [she] was seeing from Black women, despite the deluge of negativity [that's] put out in media about us."[13]

Building on Patricia Hill Collins' seminal essay, "Learning from the Outsider Within," Wilder, Jones, and Osborne-Lampkin found that Black women face obstacles to achievement and success as students, faculty, and administrators in higher education. Their review of the literature identifies and documents issues that Black women face in the academy such as "invisibility, exclusion, tokenism, poor mentoring and academic

---

more distinct identities, or personality states, are present in—and alternately take control of—an individual." "Dissociative Identity Disorder (Multiple Personality Disorder)," *PsychologyToday.com*, last modified February 24, 2017, https://www.psychologytoday.com/conditions/dissociative-identity-disorder-multiple-personality-disorder.

9. Wendy Ashley, "The Angry Black Woman: The Impact of Pejorative Stereotypes on Psychotherapy with Black Women," *Social Work in Public Health* 29, no. 1 (2014): 27-34.

10. Patricia Hill Collins, "Learning from the Outsider Within: The Sociological Significance of Black Feminist Thought," *Social Problems* 33(1986): 514-32.

11. Vanessa Willoughby, "Radical Magic," *Bitch Magazine: Feminist Response to Pop Culture*, no. 71 (Summer 2016): 8-9.

12. Collins, "Learning from the Outsider Within."

13. Willoughby, "Radical Magic," 8.

support, physical and emotional burn-out, and lack of respect."[14] Howard-Baptiste notes that, although slavery and higher education are not closely related, connections can be made based on the "barriers and obstacles" Black women faculty face in the academy."[15] Additionally, she reminds us that Black women faculty have unique and dynamic experiences that "cannot be summarized as one universal experience" and provides evidence that confirms that "Black female scholars are depicted by colleagues, students, and staff in negative ways."[16] In "Maids of Academe" Harley notes that "Black women who work in PWI's are the 'recipients of deprivileged consequences'," and "subjected to 'gendered racism.'"[17] Howard-Baptiste calls these interactions "Mammy Moments," "the overt and covert ways that students, colleagues, and others communicate disrespect and distrust Black women's worth and abilities."[18]

I am an academic librarian in a profession that is getting Whiter and Whiter,[19] and by its very nature, more hostile, by the day. "Arctic space" is a term used by Howard-Baptiste's pseudo-named "Dr. Monty," who likened the experience of being a Black female professor to "being on an expedition in the Arctic." This is a space that is the opposite of warm and where you are always "trying to break through the ice."[20] The ability to survive and thrive in the kinds of spaces that we do, to not be broken by the systemic microaggressions, tokenism, ignorance,

---

14. JeffriAnne Wilder, Tamara Bertrand Jones, and La'Tara Osborne-Lampkin, "A Profile of Black Women in the 21st Century Academy: Still Learning From the 'Outsider-Within'," *Journal of Research Initiatives* 1, no. 1 (2013): 27-38.

15. Shewanee D. Howard-Baptiste, "Arctic Space, Lonely Place: 'Mammy Moments' in Higher Education," *The Urban Review* 46, no. 4 (November 2014): 767.

16. Howard-Baptiste, "Arctic Space, Lonely Place," 765.

17. Harley, "Maids of Academe," 20.

18. Howard-Baptiste, "Arctic Space, Lonely Place," 765.

19. Roger Schonfeld and Liam Sweeney, "Inclusion, Diversity, and Equity: Members of the Association of Research Libraries: Employee Demographics and Director Perspectives," *Ithaka S+R*, August 30, 2017, https://doi.org/10.18665/sr.304524.

20. Howard-Baptiste, "Arctic Space, Lonely Place," 778.

and tired, racist assumptions, scares damn near everyone. In reviewing lawsuits filed by African American faculty against PWI's, Harley found fellow faculty members, students, staff, and administrators often used the First Amendment as a defense for creating a hostile culture and work environment by "engaging in inflammatory comments and derogatory behavior" towards African American females.[21]

Howard-Baptiste's "Dr. Monty" imagined there would be few warm spaces in the Arctic and concluded that one would probably have to build a fire or make an igloo, by yourself, as in solo, in order to survive.[22] This metaphor clearly reveals the magical ability of Black women to rise above, to go high when they go low, and to persevere in the face of adversity at its worst. As iconic actor Samuel L. Jackson explained, "People know about the Klan and the overt racism, but the killing of one's soul little by little, day after day, is a lot worse than someone coming in your house and lynching you."[23] #BlackGirlMagic enables me and my fellow sisters-in-the-struggle to rise above the fray, fashion a make-shift shield and coat of armor, and rise up to face another day. In her 2016 dissertation, Allison Michelle Smith invoked Beyoncé's 2016 visual album *Lemonade* to describe how the Black women in her study succeeded against all of the obstacles placed in their paths. "It is the resolve of 'making lemonade' out of all that they face[d] that has pushed them to exceed expectations, excel at their jobs, and encourage students to realize their full potential."[24] Serena Williams' open letter in *Porter Magazine's* "Incredible Women of 2016" issue on her struggle to be acknowledged for her career success in the same way as men in her sport, echoes this resolve. "What others marked as flaws or disadvantages

21. Harley, "Maids of Academe, 30.

22. Howard-Baptiste, "Arctic Space, Lonely Place," 778.

23. David A. Keeps, "Tell It on the Mountain," *New York Guides*, August 21, 2011, http://nymag.com/guides/fallpreview/2011/theater/samuel-l-jackson/.

24. Allison Michelle Smith, "Black Girl Magic: How Black Women Administrators Navigate the Intersection of Race and Gender in Workspace Silos at Predominantly White Institutions," Ph.D. diss., Louisiana State University and Agricultural and Mechanical College, 2016, 61, https://digitalcommons.lsu.edu/gradschool_dissertations/3470/.

about myself—my race, my gender—I embraced as fuel for my success. I never let anything or anyone define me or my potential. I controlled my future."[25]

#BlackGirlMagic

CaShawn Thompson first used the BlackGirlMagic hashtag in 2013 to describe Black women who persevere in the face of adversity and inspire her with their positive achievements, which she says are like "magic."[26] "Sometimes our accomplishments might seem to come out of thin air, because a lot of times, the only people supporting us are other black women."[27]

Some days, most days, it is a real struggle to just get out of bed in the morning, knowing that a hostile workplace is waiting for you to arrive—a workplace that is hostile because you are the only Black faculty librarian who ever worked there, and your colleagues have no idea what it is like to be you.[28] As much as the United States is believed to be a big melting pot, and contrary to popular belief, most White people do not have Black friends, which presents a problem. In "Self-Segregation: Why It's So Hard for Whites to Understand Ferguson," Robert P. Jones reported that respondents to the Public Religion Research Institute (PRRI) 2013 American Values Survey revealed "the social networks of whites are a remarkable 91 percent white, one percent black," and one

---

25. Chelsea Stone, "Serena Williams' Open Letter on Gender Inequality," *Allure.com*, December 1, 2016, https://www.allure.com/story/serena -williams-open-letter-gender-inequality.

26. Dexter Thomas, "Why Everyone's Saying Black Girls are Magic," *Los Angeles Times*, September 9, 2015, http://www.latimes.com/nation/nationnow/la-na-nn-everyones-saying-black-girls-are-magic-20150909-htmlstory.html. See also *Wikipedia*, "Black Girl Magic," https://en.wikipedia.org/wiki/Black_Girl_Magic.

27. Thomas, "Why Everyone's Saying Black Girls are Magic."

28. Smith, "Black Girl Magic"; Ebony E. White, "Exceptional but Not an Exception: Understanding How African American Women Make Their Way," Ph.D. diss., Montclair State University, 2017.

percent of all other races and combinations of races.[29] Given this, the dynamics of my predominantly White workplace kind of makes sense. If you don't have Black friends or people of color in your core social networks, then you get a workplace where sometimes they say the most insensitive things,[30] but, because it happens so often, you don't even bother to call them on it—no one would ever admit that they said or did something that could be construed as racist. In a 2014 monologue on *The Daily Show*, Jon Stewart said, "...we have made enormous progress in teaching everyone that racism is bad. Where we seem to have dropped the ball... is in teaching people what racism actually is...which allows people to say incredibly racist things while insisting they would never."[31] Bonilla-Silva and Forman summarize the literature on these "discursive maneuvers" where the phrase, "I am not a racist, but..." is used as a shield "to avoid being labeled as racist when expressing racial ideas."[32]

---

29. Robert P. Jones, "Self-Segregation: Why It's So Hard for Whites to Understand Ferguson," *The Atlantic*, August 21, 2014, https://www.theatlantic.com/national/archive/2014/08/self-segregation-why-its-hard-for-whites-to-understand-ferguson/378928/. See also Robert P. Jones, Daniel Cox, Juhem Navarro-Rivera, "In Search of Libertarians in America," *PRRI.org*, October 29, 2013, https://www.prri.org/research/2013-american-values-survey/ and Daniel Cox, Juhem Navarro-Rivera, and Robert P. Jones, "Race, Religion, and Political Affiliation of Americans' Core Social Networks," *PRRI.org*, August 3, 2016, https://www.prri.org/research/poll-race-religion-politics-americans-social-networks/.

30. Eduardo Bonilla-Silva and Tyrone A. Forman, "'I Am Not A Racist But.. . ': Mapping White College Students' Racial Ideology in the USA," Discourse & Society 11, no. 1 (2000): 50-85; Karen W. Tao, Jesse Owen, and Joanna M. Drinane, "Was That Racist? An Experimental Study of Microaggresson Ambiguity and Emotional Reactions for Racial-Ethnic Minority and White Individuals," *Race and Social Problems* 9 (2017): 262-71; Jonathan W. Kanter, Monnica T. Williams, Adam M. Kuczynski, Katherine E. Manbeck, Marlena Debreaux, and Daniel C. Rosen, "A Preliminary Report on the Relationship Between Microaggressions Against Black People and Racism Among White College Students," *Race and Social Problems* 9 (2017): 291-99.

31. A. Moore, "10 Quotes That Perfectly Explain Racism to People Who Claim They're Colorblind," *Atlanta Black Star*, July 20, 2014, http://atlantablackstar.com/2014/07/20/10-quotes-perfectly-explain-racism-people-claim-theyre-colorblind/2/.

32. Bonilla-Silva and Forman, "I Am Not A Racist But. . .". See also Teum A. Van Dijk, *Prejudice in Discourse: An Analysis of Ethnic Prejudice in Cognition and Conversation* (Amsterdam and Philadelphia, PA: John Benjamins Publishing Co., 1984).

CNN's Doug Criss hails the video for Joyner Lucas' "I'm Not Racist" as "the brutal race conversation nobody wants to have."[33] The video for the song begins with a White man wearing a red "Make America Great Again" hat spewing the N-word freely and frequently and engaging in a diatribe containing every racist stereotype about Black men that you can dream up, aimed at a young Black man sitting across the table from him. After nearly four minutes, the White man sits down, winded and emotional from his efforts, and then the Black man stands up and begins his response. It is then that you realize both men are lip-syncing Lucas' verses—each interspersed and punctuated with the phrase, "I'm not racist." The video ends with the two men embracing, seemingly understanding each other's point of view. At nearly seven minutes long, if you can't make it through the first verse, you're missing half the story. Lucas explained to CNN, "It was an average white man speaking his mind on how he actually feels about black people, and it was an average black guy talking about his interactions with white people. These are suppressed feelings that both parties have but are afraid to express."[34] I include this here as evidence of at least one situation that shows both sides of the issue at the core of White and non-White relations in this country. While I think Lucas might be a bit naïve about the "suppressed feelings" on both sides,[35] the message is still clear. There is more than one side to a story, and what my colleagues and other White people who live predominantly White lives often miss is that the story for people of color, in my case Black women, rarely gets told. In part this is because

33. Doug Criss, "'I'm Not Racist' is the Brutal Race Conversation Nobody Wants to Have," *CNN.com*, November 30 2017, http://www.cnn.com/2017/11/29/entertainment/joyner-lucas-not-racist-video-trnd/index.html.

34. Criss, "I'm Not Racist."

35. Maggie Astor, Christina Caron, and Daniel Victor, "A Guide to the Charlottesville Aftermath," *New York Times,* August 13, 2017, https://www.nytimes.com/2017/08/13/us/charlottesville-virginia-overview.html; Carl Skutsch, "The History of White Supremacy in America," *Rolling Stone,* August 18, 2017, https://www.rollingstone.com/politics/features/the-history-of-white-supremacy-in-america-w498334; Kenneth P. Vogel, "White Nationalist Claims Trump Directed Rally Violence," *Politico.com,* April 17, 2017, https://www.politico.com/story/2017/04/donald-trump-rally-violence-237302.

of our numbers within the profession, and in part it is because our voices are rarely heard when nearly everyone else in the room is White, and privileged, and acknowledged.

In my experience in conversations with my White colleagues, when I describe the environment as hostile, they immediately flinch or recoil and try to figure out what they, personally, may have said or done. In reality, it may not be the fault of any one individual at all. The institutionalization of racism and racist practices within the systems and organizations that govern where we live and work are the real culprits; higher education and academic libraries have yet to figure out how to combat them. In her research, Natasha N. Croom found three central themes that emerged from her data, including *racialized and gendered microaggressions* (all participants in the study reported this theme had been present throughout their academic careers).[36] Kelli Johnson's 2016 dissertation found that "microaggressions showed the prevalence of the daily injustices that minority librarians in higher education often experience."[37] Alabi's research on racial microaggressions confirms that, although librarians of color continue to be subjected to this treatment from their colleagues, White librarians "are unlikely to recognize these disparaging exchanges."[38]

In a recent library faculty meeting, we were discussing the response of the campus and the library to the August, 2017 protests in Charlottesville, VA and their aftermath. A French-born female colleague, who is a full professor and known amongst her colleagues for her inappropriate and racist comments, began to explain how badly she felt for a

36. Natasha N. Croom, "Promotion Beyond Tenure: Unpacking Racism and Sexism in the Experiences of Black Womyn Professors," *The Review of Higher Education* 40, no. 4 (2017): 573.

37. Kelli Johnson, "Minority Librarians in Higher Education: A Critical Race Theory Analysis," PhD diss., Marshall University, 2016, iv.

38. Jaena Alabi, "Racial Microaggressions in Academic Libraries: Results of a Survey of Minority and Non-Minority Librarians," *Journal of Academic Librarianship* 41, no. 1 (2015): 47–53. doi:10.1016/j.acalib.2014.10.008; Jaena Alabi, "This Actually Happened: An Analysis of Librarians' Responses to a Survey about Racial Microaggressions," *Journal of Library Administration* 55, no. 3 (2014): 179-91.

student who found herself one of a few in the minority opinion at an open-forum discussion about the Seal at my University, which has been called offensive by student groups, as well as some faculty and staff.[39] Throughout the discussion, this colleague repeatedly commented on how ugly the atmosphere became for the student, whom she saw as "brave and courageous," in her support of the current Seal. The few faculty of color in the room were flabbergasted. She could clearly see the plight of this lone student pleading her case, but could not make the connection to the plight of the people of color with whom she works on a daily basis, even after several faculty members reminded her that that is exactly what faculty of color face within the College of the University Libraries and Learning Sciences (CUL&LS) on a daily basis. She just didn't get it—and she is not alone.

Twenty years ago, when Evan St. Lifer and Corinne Nelson[40] surveyed 400 librarians—100 each: White, Black, Latinx, and Asian (but no Native American or Indigenous)—on the state of race in the profession, eighty-four percent of the White librarians surveyed reported "awareness of racism in the library profession had improved, twenty-one percent reported awareness had stayed the same, and seven percent reported it had gotten worse."[41] Three hundred librarians of color were also surveyed. Fifty-four percent of Latinx librarians, forty-one percent of Asian librarians, and forty percent of Black librarians believed that "awareness of racism in the profession had improved." Even more telling, only seven percent of White librarians reported awareness had gotten worse, compared to nine percent of Latinx librarians, six percent of Asian librarians and nineteen percent of Black librarians. "Four of ten blacks, one-third of Asians, and one-quarter of Latinos" reported they were discriminated against in their libraries.[42]

39. "University Seal Remains the Same," *UNM Newsroom*, November 15, 2016, http://news.unm.edu/news/university-seal-remains-the-same.

40. Evan St. Lifer and Corinne Nelson, "Unequal Opportunities: Race Does Matter." *Library Journal* 122, no. 18 (1997): 42-46.

41. Ibid., 44.

42. Ibid., 44.

In the same article, Barbara Ford, then president of the American Library Association, said of the professions' progress in diversifying its ranks, "it's human nature for people to choose other people like them." She continued by noting that there is "probably unconscious racism in all of us."[43] The late Dr. E. J. Josey was also quoted in the article saying, "The old-fashioned racism, that's over...However, residual effects of the institutionalized racism, the covert racism, is just as bad."[44] From Josey to Jackson to Stewart, racism and discrimination are alive and well in the profession and continue to impact us in the workplace. St. Lifer and Nelson's survey was released shortly after *In Our Own Voices: The Changing Face of Librarianship* (*IOOV*, 1996)[45] because the authors wanted to "explore the depiction [for] themselves."[46] The thirty-one authors who have contributed to the twenty-year follow-up to *IOOV* 1996 provide a wealth of evidence to show that the landscape is virtually the same in most cases, and in some, extremely worse.[47]

I don't know how my library faculty colleagues would react and/or adapt if they worked in spaces that were overwhelmingly non-White, but fortunately for them, they will never have to. They will never have to weigh every single comment and conversation, trying desperately to mentally check the "not racist comment" box because, surely, my colleague could not have said what they just said, or meant it that way. A White woman I supervised once gave me a birthday card with a monkey on it. She said it immediately reminded her of me when she saw it. [*I had to fix my damn face with a quickness*]. Of *course* she didn't mean that it reminded her that I *looked* like a monkey, did it? Even if she truly meant well, couldn't she have given it half a second's thought before she bought

43. Ibid., 42.

44. Ibid., 42.

45. Teresa Y. Neely and Khafre K. Abif, *In Our Own Voices: The Changing Face of Librarianship* (Lanham, MD: Scarecrow Press, 1996).

46. St. Lifer and Nelson, "Unequal Opportunities," 42.

47. Teresa Y. Neely and Jorge R. López-McKnight, *In Our Own Voices, Redux: The Faces of Librarianship Today* (Lanham, MD: Rowman & Littlefield, 2018).

it, wrote my name on it, signed it, and gave it to me with a smile, all the while letting that trifling mess spew from her lips?

While employed at that same institution, I went out to lunch to my favorite Vietnamese restaurant with another White non-faculty female colleague who reported to me. When we walked in she said, "We're the only White people in here." The only other people in the establishment when we arrived were of Asian descent. I had to remind her that I was not White. That was not the first time my dark skin, my proudest and most prominent feature, had somehow been disconnected from me with surgical precision. I am not sure what kind of psychological compartmentalizing it takes in order to accomplish this, but it rolled right off her tongue as accepted truth so naturally that I immediately looked around as if to confirm her observation. This type of mental agility and acuity must be the work of the same people who say they do not see color, a feat that is so hilariously ridiculous it would be laughable if it weren't so terrifying. In a 2014 *Atlanta Black Star* article, Scott Woods (a White male) described the difference between how White people think of racism, and how non-White people actually experience it.

> The problem is that white people see racism as conscious hate, when racism is bigger than that. Racism is a complex system of social and political levers and pulleys set up generations ago to continue working on the behalf of whites at other people's expense, whether whites know/like it or not. Racism is an insidious cultural disease. It is so insidious that it doesn't care if you are a white person who likes Black people; it's still going to find a way to infect how you deal with people who don't look like you.[48]

White people don't have to watch what they say and they often don't. I currently work with a White male colleague who uses the word diversity so much that it no longer has any meaning for me in the workplace. It has to be one of his favorite words because he uses it so often. He

48. A. Moore, "10 Quotes That Perfectly Explain Racism to People Who Claim They're Colorblind," *Atlanta Black Star*, July 20, 2014, http://atlantablackstar.com/2014/07/20/10-quotes-perfectly-explain-racism-people-claim-theyre-colorblind/2/.

is usually the first to use the word "diverse" to describe our faculty make-up, particularly when we are interviewing candidates (who are usually *not* people of color) for faculty positions. Once, with a faculty candidate present, he talked at length about how great it was to work with a group of people who were so diverse and who had such a wide diversity of ideas and job responsibilities. Because I haven't really found a delicate way to say, "that's not what diversity is, stop saying that right now," I sat in silence, assimilated, alone in my Blackness, and angry as hell. Once, during an interview with a White female candidate and the college faculty, in an effort to illustrate the freedom that we as faculty in CUL&LS have to publish in peer-reviewed journals in any discipline, various colleagues began explaining their research areas. When I began to talk about my research, another White male colleague dismissed it with a wave of his hand before I could finish speaking. He pointed out to the candidate that my research areas were unique and that the majority of the faculty published on topics more closely related to their job duties. Silenced.

The Thing About Natural [Black] Hair

Natural Black hair,[49] not to be confused with natural hair as defined by women who are not of African descent, is another framework with which to view the racist, sexist, and discriminatory mistreatment of women of African descent in schools, higher education, society, the media, and all walks of life. As Lurie Daniel Favors reminds us:

> Black hair is not the same as White hair. It doesn't act the same, grow the same or look the same. And it is not supposed to. Black hair is nappy. Nappy hair has its own standard. That standard is not a brown version of the standard for Caucasian hair. Nappy hair has its own rules. Those rules are not a darker version of Caucasian hair rules. Nappy hair has its own needs. Those needs are not a negrofied version of Caucasian hair needs.[50]

49. Ayana D. Byrd and Lori Tharps, *Hair Story: Untangling the Roots of Black Hair in America* (New York: St. Martin's Press, 2001).

50. Lurie Daniel Favors, "Sarah, Your Natural Hair Ain't Like Mine. And That's OK,"

As the most prominent, visible representation of our African-ness, with the exception of our skin, our hair is often the target of colonized macro- and micro-aggression and oppressive behavior.[51]

For all the good that Beyoncé, Michelle Obama, and organizations like Black Girls Rock![52] have done for Black women by dispelling deep-seated myths and long-held assumptions and caricatures over the years, the movement to tear Black women down, at our core, is alive and thriving. The international, domestic, regional, inter-family, and intra-spective war on Black hair[53] has raged in this country, and others in North America and on the African continent, long before Spike Lee introduced us to 'Wannabees' and 'Jigaboos' in 1988's *School Daze*.[54] The all-out assault on the scalps of Black women (Gabrielle "Gabby" Douglas)[55] and Black girl children (Blue Ivy Carter)[56] continues with secondary school dress

---

Afro State of Mind, accessed December 27, 2017, http://www.afrostateofmind.com/sarah-your-natural-hair-aint-like-mine-and-thats-ok/.

51. Tabora A. Johnson and Teiahsha Bankhead, "Hair It Is. Examining the Experiences of Black Women with Natural Hair," *Open Journal of Social Sciences* 2, no. 1 (2014): 86-100; D. Wendy Greene, "Black Women Can't Have Blonde Hair...in the Workplace," *Journal of Gender, Race and Justice* 14 (2011): 405-30; Ashleigh Shelby Rosette and Tracy L. Dumas, "The Hair Dilemma: Conform to Mainstream Expectations or Emphasize Racial Identity," *Duke Journal of Gender Law & Policy* 14 (2007): 407-21; Cheryl Thompson, "Black Women, Beauty, and Hair as a Matter of Being," *Women's Studies* 38, no. 8 (2009): 831-56; Nsenga K. Burton, "Let Go of Our Hair and Let Our Girls Learn," *The Root*, May 20, 2017. http://www.theroot.com/let-go-of-our-hair-and-let-our-girls-learn-1795349148.

52. Organizations with missions like BGR! are few and far between. Since its inception in 2006, its mission has been "to change the world" by building "the self-esteem and self-worth of young women of color by changing their outlook on life, broadening their horizons and providing tools for self-empowerment and efficacy." http://www.blackgirlsrockinc.com/about-us/#.WzUXU9VKhhE.

53. D. Wendy Green, "Splitting Hairs: The Eleventh Circuit's Take on Workplace Bans Against Black Women's Natural Hair in *EEOC v. Catastrophe Management Solutions*," *University of Miami Law Review* 71 (2017): 987-1036.

54. Spike Lee, *School Daze* (Culver City, CA: Columbia Pictures, 1988).

55. Julee Wilson, "Haters Attack Gabby Douglas' Hair Again and Twitter Promptly Claps Back," *Essence.com*, August 8, 2016, http://www.essence.com/2016/08/08/gabby-douglas-hair-haters-twitter-claps-back; "Gabby Douglas Bows to Pressure Over Hair Controversy and Books Top Celebrity Stylist," *Daily Mail*, August 16, 2012, http://www.dailymail.co.uk/femail/article-2189317/Gabby-Douglas-bows-pressure-books-celebrity-hair-stylist.html.

56. April Taylor, "Are We At The Point At Which Black People No Longer Have Any

code policies,[57] federal court rulings,[58] and historical norms dictating racist and sexist practices and expectations for how Black women look and what we do with our hair.[59] Black girls, their parents, and others in South Africa protested when a thirteen-year-old girl who wanted to wear an afro had to change schools three times due to dress code restrictions.[60] After protests at that school, another school in Johannesburg amended a similar policy in a proactive "move to avoid 'subtle or structural racism.'"[61] In the same article, the author reports the outrage

---

Serious Topics to Come Together About??: Petition Launched Calling For Blue Ivy Carter's Hair To Be 'Properly Cared For'," *AfricanAmerica.org*, June 11, 2014, http://www.africanamerica.org/topic/are-we-at-the-point-at-which-black-people-no-longer-have-any-serious-topics-to-come-together-about?reply=395505057904186255; Reniqua Allen and Quartz, "Why Blue Ivy's Hair Matters," *The Atlantic*, June 19, 2004, http://www.theatlantic.com/entertainment/archive/2014/06/stop-protesting-blue-ivys-hairstyle-and-celebrate-what-it-really-means/373060/; JT, "Comb Her Hair: Petitioning Blue Ivy," *Change.org*, 2014, https://www.change.org/p/blue-ivy-comb-her-hair. A Change.org petition opened in 2014 petitioning Blue Ivy Carter (then 2 years old), to 'Comb her hair' received 5,739 supporters of the 7,500 needed before it was closed.

57. Bossip Staff, "War on Black Hair: Baton Rouge Principal Urges Parents to Cut Their Children's 'Nappy, Uncombed Hair,'" *Bossip.com*, February 26, 2016, http://bossip.com/1286890/war-on-black-hair-baton-rouge-principal-urges-parents-to-cut-their-childrens-nappy-uncombed-hair/; Erin White, "WTF: This Teen was Called into the Asst. Principal's Office Because her Afro was Too 'Extreme'," *Afropunk*, May 22, 2017, http://afropunk.com/2017/05/wtf-this-teen-was-called-into-asst-principals-office-because-her-afro-was-too-extreme/.

58. Victoria M. Massie, "Federal Appeals Court Rules It's Okay to Discriminate against Black Hairstyles like Dreadlocks," *Vox.com*, September 19, 2016, http://www.vox.com/2016/9/19/12971790/court-discriminate-dreadlocks.

59. A. Moore, "11 Examples Highlighting the War Against Natural Black Hair," *Atlanta Black Star*, December 11, 2013, http://atlantablackstar.com/2013/12/11/11-examples-highlighting-the-war-against-natural-black-hair/; Taylor, "Are We at The Point at Which Black People No Longer Have Any Serious Topics to Come Together About??"; Allen, "Why Blue Ivy's Hair Matters"; JT, "Comb Her Hair."

60. Lynsey Chutel, "Hair is Political: It Took a 13-Year Old Girl with an Afro to Make South Africans Notice their Racist School Dress Codes," *Quartz Africa*, April 31, 2016, https://qz.com/770696/it-took-a-13-year-old-girl-with-an-afro-to-make-south-africans-notice-their-racist-school-dress-codes.

61. Chutel, "Hair is Political"; Greg Nicholson, "South African Students Speak Out Against 'Aggressive' Ban on Afro Hair," *The Guardian*, August 31, 2016, https://www.theguardian.com/world/2016/aug/31/south-african-students-speak-out-ban-afro-hair-pretoria-school; "Pretoria High School for Girls Faces Fury after Black Pupils told to 'Straighten Hair,' August 29, 2016, https://www.sowetanlive.co.za/

that followed when a parent posted a picture of Black girls queuing up to be subjected to a test for neatness. Their hair had to fit into a swimming cap or a school cap to ensure they were in compliance with the school dress code.[62] In a country where White people make up less than ten percent of the population,[63] they are still enforcing rules and regulations that oppress the majority, including demoralizing attempts to destroy Black girls' heritage and sense of self-worth, while forcing them to assimilate and conform to European beauty standards.

Beyoncé directly countered the attacks on her daughter, Blue Ivy, in her 2016 platinum single, *Formation*, singing, "I like my baby hair with baby hair and afros," while simultaneously celebrating her husband Jay-Z's African features, "I like my Negro nose with Jackson 5 nostrils."[64] Again, having someone so prominent and influential reframe the definition of Black beauty is affirming and noteworthy.

In 1993, shortly after my career got underway at Colorado State University (CSU), I decided I wanted to grow my hair into dreadlocks (locs). I was 28-years old (the youngest librarian on staff there), a single, childless, Black woman beginning her first professional job in an academic library where there had never been another Black librarian, and where the demographic makeup of the school and library was overwhelmingly White.[65] In 1996, I wrote about my decision to grow my hair into locs,

---

news/2016-08-29-pretoria-girls-high-faces-fury-after-black-pupils-told-to-straighten-hair/.

62. Jeanette Chabalala, "Bloemfontein High School Re-Evaluates Hair Policy," *News24*, August 30, 2016, https://m.news24.com/SouthAfrica/News/bloemfontein-high-school-re-evaluates-hair-policy-20160830.

63. Central Intelligence Agency, "Africa: South Africa," *The World Factbook*, May 31, 2017, https://www.cia.gov/library/publications/the-world-factbook/geos/sf.html.

64. RIAA, "Gold and Platinum," http://www.riaa.com/gold-platinum/; See also Saturday Night Live, "The Day Beyoncé Turned Black," YouTube video, February 14, 2016, https://www.youtube.com/watch?v=ociMBfkDG1w.

65. Colorado State University, Institutional Research, Planning and Effectiveness, "Facts at a Glance 1998-1994," https://www.ir.colostate.edu/facts-at-a-glance-1998-1994/. In 1993, less than ten percent of the students enrolled at Colorado State University were non-White. There were 290 Black students, less than two percent of the 21,110 population, excluding international students. Statistics for faculty for fall of 1993 are not available. In fall 1994, seven percent of the faculty were minority.

the reception that decision received, and the advice I received from White women.[66] Since I had chemically straightened hair at the time, in order to achieve the style I wanted I would have to either wait until my hair had grown out so that the locs could be started with virgin (natural) hair, or shave my head and start fresh. There are some loc styles that do not require what is commonly known as "the big chop," where you cut off all chemically processed hair. I wanted to grow my own traditional locs, however, so in 1995, I shaved my head. I had no idea at the time, but that may have been the point at which I began (unconsciously or not) to use my hair as my primary mode of professional, political, social, and personal expression. It has become my armor, even though the close cut I currently wear reveals every part of my face and head. When you look at me, there is nothing to obstruct your view. You see a woman. Who is Black. And Woke. Because even at my current rank of associate professor in academe, standing at the precipice of full professorship,[67] I still sometimes feel invisible, unseen, unappreciated, and assimilated.

My Profession is Predominantly White and Female, But I Persist

I love being a library and information professional. If given a choice, however, I would seriously reconsider the route that led me away from working with and living among people who are not homogeneous. I know Black women in my profession and in other professions whose

---

There were six Black faculty (0.6%) employed with the ranks of professor, associate professor, assistant professor, instructor, and lecturer.

66. Teresa Y. Neely, "The Jackie Robinson of Library Science," in *In Our Own Voices: The Changing Face of Librarianship*, ed. Teresa Y. Neely and Khafre K. Abif (Lanham, MD: The Scarecrow Press, Inc., 1996), 183-84.

67. In the fall of 2016 I submitted my dossier to be considered for promotion to (full) Professor of Librarianship at the University of New Mexico. In the fall of 2016, the University of New Mexico reported that there were three Black full professors on main campus. In June of 2017, I learned that I had increased that number to four.

physical, emotional, and spiritual health have suffered greatly from persisting in spaces that are overwhelmingly White and combative. Some of us remain, holding out hope that it will get better or improve in some small measure—others just leave. I am conflicted about working outside of institutions with some means to support my academic pursuits; but I will be forever grateful for the opportunities I have been afforded to pursue my education and to do scholarly work with my brain, rather than work with my back.

Bibliography

Alabi, Jaena. "Racial Microaggressions in Academic Libraries: Results of a Survey of Minority and Non-Minority Librarians." *Journal of Academic Librarianship* 41, no. 1 (2015): 47–53. doi:10.1016/j.acalib.2014.10.008.

Alabi, Jaena. "This Actually Happened: An Analysis of Librarians' Responses to a Survey about Racial Microaggressions." *Journal of Library Administration* 55, no. 3 (2014): 179-91.

Allen, Reniqua, and Quartz. "Why Blue Ivy's Hair Matters." *The Atlantic.* June 19, 2004, http://www.theatlantic.com/entertainment/archive/2014/06/stop-protesting-blue-ivys-hairstyle-and-celebrate-what-it-really-means/373060/.

Ashley, Wendy. "The Angry Black Woman: The Impact of Pejorative Stereotypes on Psychotherapy with Black Women." *Social Work in Public Health* 29, no. 1 (2014): 27-34.

Astor, Maggie, Christina Caron, and Daniel Victor. "A Guide to the Charlottesville Aftermath." August 13, 2017, https://www.nytimes.com/2017/08/13/us/charlottesville-virginia-overview.html.

Beyoncé, dir. *Lemonade.* New York, NY: Parkwood Entertainment, 2016.

"Black Faculty in Higher Education: Still Only a Drop in the Bucket." *Journal of Blacks in Higher Education.* 2006, http://www.jbhe.com/features/55_blackfaculty.html.

Bonilla-Silva, Eduardo, and Tyrone A. Forman, "'I Am Not A Racist But. . .': Mapping White College Students' Racial Ideology in the USA." *Discourse & Society* 11, no. 1 (2000): 50-85.

Bossip Staff. "War on Black Hair: Baton Rouge Principal Urges Parents to Cut Their Children's 'Nappy, Uncombed Hair.'" *Bossip.com.* February 26, 2016, http://bossip.com/1286890/war-on-black-hair-baton-rouge-principal-urges-parents-to-cut-their-childrens-nappy-uncombed-hair/.

Burton, Nsenga K. "Let Go of Our Hair and Let Our Girls Learn." *The Root.* May 20, 2017, http://www.theroot.com/let-go-of-our-hair-and-let-our-girls-learn-1795349148.

Byrd, Ayana D., and Lori Tharps. *Hair Story: Untangling the Roots of Black Hair in America.* New York: St. Martin's Press, 2001.

Campbell, Corbin M., Carolyn Sloane Mata, and Fred Galloway. "Meeting Today's Higher Education Goals via the National Center for Education Statistics' Postsecondary Sample Surveys." August 2017. https://nces.ed.gov/npec/pdf/MeetingTodaysHigherEd.pdf.

Central Intelligence Agency. "Africa: South Africa." *The World Factbook.* May 31, 2017. https://www.cia.gov/library/publications/the-world-factbook/geos/sf.html.

Chabalala, Jeanette. "Bloemfontein High School Re-Evaluates Hair Policy." *News24.* August 30, 2016. https://m.news24.com/SouthAfrica/News/bloemfontein-high-school-re-evaluates-hair-policy-20160830.

Chutel, Lynsey. "Hair is Political: It Took a 13-Year Old Girl with an Afro to Make South Africans Notice their Racist School Dress Codes." *Quartz.* April 31, 2016. https://qz.com/770696/it-took-a-13-year-old-girl-with-an-afro-to-make-south-africans-notice-their-racist-school-dress-codes.

Collins, Patricia Hill. "Learning from the Outsider Within: The Sociological Significance of Black Feminist Thought." *Social Problems* 33 (1986): 514-32.

Cox, Daniel, Juhem Navarro-Rivera, and Robert P. Jones. "Race, Religion, and Political Affiliation of Americans' Core Social Networks." *PRRI.org.* August 3, 2016. https://www.prri.org/research/poll-race-religion-politics-americans-social-networks/.

Criss, Doug. "'I'm Not Racist' is the Brutal Race Conversation Nobody Wants to Have." *CNN.com.* November 30 2017. http://www.cnn.com/2017/11/29/entertainment/joyner-lucas-not-racist-video-trnd/index.html.

Croom, Natasha N. "Promotion Beyond Tenure: Unpacking Racism and Sexism in the Experiences of Black Womyn Professors." *The Review of Higher Education* 40, no. 4 (2017): 573.

Favors, Lurie Daniel. "Sarah, Your Natural Hair Ain't Like Mine. And That's OK." *Afro State of Mind.* Accessed December 27, 2017. http://www.afrostateofmind.com/sarah-your-natural-hair-aint-like-mine-and-thats-ok/.

"Gabby Douglas Bows to Pressure Over Hair Controversy and Books Top Celebrity Stylist." *Daily Mail.* August 16, 2012. http://www.dailymail.co.uk/femail/article-2189317/Gabby-Douglas-bows-pressure-books-celebrity-hair-stylist.html.

Greene, D. Wendy. "Black Women Can't Have Blonde Hair . . . in the Workplace." *Duke Journal of Gender Law & Policy* 14 (2011): 405-30.

Greene, D. Wendy. "Splitting Hairs: The Eleventh Circuit's Take on Workplace Bans Against Black Women's Natural Hair in EEOC v. Catastrophe Management Solutions." *University of Miami Law Review* 71 (2017): 987-1036.

Harley, Debra A. "Maids of Academe: African American Women Faculty at Predominantly White Institutions." *Journal of African American Studies* 12, no. 1 (2008): 19-36.

Howard-Baptiste, Shewanee D. "Arctic Space, Lonely Place: 'Mammy Moments' in Higher Education." *The Urban Review* 46, no. 4 (November 2014): 765.

Johnson, Kelli. "Minority Librarians in Higher Education: A Critical Race Theory Analysis." PhD diss. Marshall University, 2016.

Johnson, Tabora A., and Teiahsha Bankhead. "Hair It Is. Examining the Experiences of Black Women with Natural Hair." *Open Journal of Social Sciences* 2 (2014): 86-100.

Jones, Robert P. "Self-Segregation: Why It's So Hard for Whites to Understand Ferguson." *The Atlantic*. August 21, 2014. https://www.theatlantic.com/national/archive/2014/08/self-segregation-why-its-hard-for-whites-to-understand-ferguson/378928/.

Jones, Robert P., Daniel Cox, Juhem Navarro-Rivera. "In Search of Libertarians in America." *PRRI.org*. October 29, 2013. https://www.prri.org/research/2013-american-values-survey/.

Kanter, Jonathan W., Monnica T. Williams, Adam M. Kuczynski, Katherine E. Manbeck, Marlena Debreaux, and Daniel C. Rosen. "A Preliminary Report on the Relationship Between Microagressions Against Black People and Racism Among White College Students." *Race and Social Problems* 9, no. 4 (2017): 291-99.

Keeps, David A. "Tell It on the Mountain." *New York Guides*. August 21, 2011. http://nymag.com/guides/fallpreview/2011/theater/samuel-l-jackson/.

Massie, Victoria M. "Federal Appeals Court Rules It's Okay to Discriminate against Black Hairstyles like Dreadlocks." *Vox.com*. September 19, 2016. http://www.vox.com/2016/9/19/12971790/court-discriminate-dreadlocks.

Moore, A. "10 Quotes That Perfectly Explain Racism to People Who Claim They're Colorblind." Atlanta Black Star, July 20, 2014. http://atlantablackstar.com/2014/07/20/10-quotes-perfectly-explain-racism-people-claim-theyre-colorblind/2/.

Moore, A. "11 Examples Highlighting the War Against Natural Black Hair." *Atlanta Black Star*. December 11, 2013. http://atlantablackstar.com/2013/12/11/11-examples-highlighting-the-war-against-natural-black-hair/.

Neely, Teresa Y. "The Jackie Robinson of Library Science." In *In Our Own Voices: The Changing Face of Librarianship*, edited by Teresa Y. Neely and Khafre K. Abif, 183-89. Lanham, MD: The Scarecrow Press, Inc., 1996.

Neely, Teresa Y., and Khafre K. Abif, eds. *In Our Own Voices: The Changing Face of Librarianship*. Lanham, MD: Scarecrow Press, Inc., 1996.

Neely, Teresa Y., and Jorge R. López-McKnight, eds. *In Our Own Voices, Redux: The Faces of Librarianship Today*. Lanham, MD: Rowman & Littlefield, 2018.

Nicholson, Greg. "South African Students Speak Out Against 'Aggressive' Ban on Afro Hair." *The Guardian*. August 31, 2016. https://www.theguardian.com/world/2016/aug/31/south-african-students-speak-out-ban-afro-hair-pretoria-school.

Office of the First Lady. "Remarks by the First Lady at BET's 'Black Girls Rock!' Event." March 28, 2015. https://obamawhitehouse.archives.gov/the-press-office/2015/03/28/remarks-first-lady-bets-black-girls-rock-event.

"Pretoria High School for Girls Faces Fury after Black Pupils Told to 'Straighten Hair.'" August 29, 2016. http://www.heraldlive.co.za/news/2016/08/29/pretoria-girls-high-faces-fury-black-pupils-told-straighten-hair/.

Phelps, Nicole. "Exclusive: Peter Dundas Dresses Beyoncé at the Grammys, Launches Solo Label." *Vogue.com*. February 12, 2017. http://www.vogue.com/article/beyonce-grammys-peter-dundas-dress.

RIAA. "Gold and Platinum." http://www.riaa.com/gold-platinum/.

Rosette, Ashleigh Shelby, and Tracy L. Dumas. "The Hair Dilemma: Conform to Mainstream Expectations or Emphasize Racial Identity." *Duke Journal of Gender Law & Policy* 14 (2007): 407-21.

Russonello, Giovanni. "Beyoncé's and Adele's Grammy Speeches: Transcripts." *New York Times*. February 12, 2017. https://www.nytimes.com/2017/02/12/arts/music/beyonce-speech-grammys-trump.html.

Saturday Night Live. "The Day Beyoncé Turned Black." *YouTube* video. February 14, 2016. https://www.youtube.com/watch?v=ociMBfkDG1w.

Schonfeld, Roger, and Liam Sweeney. "Inclusion, Diversity, and Equity: Members of the Association of Research Libraries: Employee Demographics and Director Perspectives." *Ithaka S+R*. August 30, 2017. https://doi.org/10.18665/sr.304524.

Skutsch, Carl. "The History of White Supremacy in America." *Rolling Stone*. August 18, 2017. https://www.rollingstone.com/politics/features/the-history-of-white-supremacy-in-america-w498334.

Smith, Allison Michelle. "Black Girl Magic: How Black Women Administrators Navigate the Intersection of Race and Gender in Workspace Silos at Predominantly White Institutions." Ph.D. diss., Louisiana State University and Agricultural and Mechanical College, 2016. https://digitalcommons.lsu.edu/gradschool_dissertations/3470/.

Spike Lee, dir. *School Daze*. Culver City, CA: Columbia Pictures, 1988.

St. Lifer, Evan, and Corinne Nelson. "Unequal Opportunities: Race Does Matter." *Library Journal* 122, no. 18 (1997): 42-6.

Stone, Chelsea. "Serena Williams' Open Letter on Gender Inequality." *Allure.com*. December 1, 2016. https://www.allure.com/story/serena-williams-open-letter-gender-inequality.

Strauss, Valerie. "It's 2015. Where Are All the Black College Faculty?" *The Washington Post*. November 12, 2015. https://www.washingtonpost.com/news/answer-sheet/wp/2015/11/12/its-2015-where-are-all-the-black-college-faculty/?utm_term=.03eae652f323.

T, J. "Comb Her Hair: Petitioning Blue Ivy." *Change.org*. 2014. https://www.change.org/p/blue-ivy-comb-her-hair.

Taylor, April. "Are We at The Point at Which Black People No Longer Have Any Serious Topics to Come Together About??: Petition Launched Calling For Blue Ivy Carter's Hair To Be 'Properly Cared For.'" *AfricanAmerica.org*. June 11, 2014. http://www.africanamerica.org/topic/are-we-at-the-point-at-which-black-people-no-longer-have-any-serious-topics-to-come-together-about?reply=395505057904186255.

Tao, Karen W., Jesse Owen, and Joanna M. Drinane. "Was *That* Racist? An Experimental Study of Microaggression Ambiguity and Emotional Reactions for Racial-Ethnic Minority and White Individuals." *Race and Social Problems* 9, no. 4 (2017): 262-71.

Thomas, Dexter. "Why Everyone's Saying Black Girls are Magic." *Los Angeles Times*. September 9, 2015. http://www.latimes.com/nation/nationnow/la-na-nn-everyones-saying-black-girls-are-magic-20150909-htmlstory.html.

Thompson, Cheryl. "Black Women, Beauty, and Hair as a Matter of Being." *Women's Studies* 38, no. 8 (2009): 831-56.

"University Seal Remains the Same." *UNM Newsroom*. November 15, 2016. http://news.unm.edu/news/university-seal-remains-the-same.

U.S. Department of Education. "Characteristics of Postsecondary Faculty, 2017." *The Condition of Education 2017* (NCES 2017-144), 254-258. https://nces.ed.gov/pubs2017/2017144.pdf.

Van Dijk, Teum A. *Prejudice in Discourse: An Analysis of Ethnic Prejudice in Cognition and Conversation*. Amsterdam and Philadelphia, PA: John Benjamins Publishing Co., 1984.

Vogel, Kenneth P. "White Nationalist Claims Trump Directed Rally Violence." *Politico.com*. April 17, 2017. https://www.politico.com/story/2017/04/donald-trump-rally-violence-237302.

White, Ebony E. "Exceptional but Not an Exception: Understanding How African American Women Make Their Way." Ph.D. diss., Montclair State University, 2017.

White, Erin. "WTF: This Teen was Called into the Asst. Principal's Office Because her Afro was Too 'Extreme.'" *Afropunk*. May 22, 2017. http://afropunk.com/2017/05/wtf-this-teen-was-called-into-asst-principals-office-because-her-afro-was-too-extreme/.

Wikipedia. "Black Girl Magic." https://en.wikipedia.org/wiki/Black_Girl_Magic.

Wilder, JeffriAnne, Tamara Bertrand Jones, and La'Tara Osborne-Lampkin. "A Profile of Black Women in the 21st Century Academy: Still Learning From the 'Outsider-Within'." *Journal of Research Initiatives* 1, no. 1 (2013): 27-38.

Wilson, Julee. "Haters Attack Gabby Douglas' Hair Again and Twitter Promptly Claps Back." *Essence.com.* August 8, 2016. http://www.essence.com/2016/08/08/gabby-douglas-hair-haters-twitter-claps-back.

Willoughby, Vanessa. "Radical Magic." *Bitch Magazine: Feminist Response to Pop Culture*, no. 71 (Summer 2016): 8-9.

Chapter 6

The Voice of a Black Woman in Libraryland: A Theoretical Narrative

LaVerne Gray

The concept of voice is a cognitive practice whereby women come to knowledge through silence and speaking.[1] In the Black feminist tradition, voice is transformed from silence into language and action. This metaphorical turn of voice relies on the active transference of what it means to come to knowledge of self while embracing a language of resistance. Feminist poet and writer Audre Lorde explores the emotional and liberating embrace of voice and silence as a feminist of color. She equates silence, or the dis-utilization of voice, as fear of being seen. Black women, visibly present, are "rendered invisible" through racism.[2] Using language and words to uncover truths, the Black feminist voice becomes an act of resistance, enabling visibility and defying marginality. bell hooks reaffirms marginality as a "space of resistance;" the use of voice in those spaces ignites a profound opposition to everyday oppressive experiences.[3] This text illuminates voice in the experiences

1. Mary Field Belenky et al., *Women's Ways of Knowing: The Development of Self, Voice, and Mind* (New York: BasicBooks, 1998); Patricia Hill Collins, *Fighting Words: Black Women and the Search for Justice* (Minneapolis: University of Minnesota Press, 1998); Audre Lorde, *Sister Outsider: Essays and Speeches* (New York: Random House, 2007); bell hooks, *Yearning: Race, Gender, and Cultural Politics* (Boston: South End Press, 1990).

2. Lorde, *Sister Outsider*, 42.

3. hooks, *Yearning: Race, Gender, and Cultural Politics*, 149.

of a Black woman librarian through the theoretical exploration of personal narrative.

The purpose of the chapter is to locate the experiences of a Black woman librarian in an intersectional context. Personal narrative is used to theoretically contextualize experience by exploring how voice is relinquished and suppressed. Narrative as an approach provides researchers the opportunity to examine life experiences through storytelling.[4] It is a process whereby, as bell hooks states, "oppressed people resist by identifying themselves as subjects, by defining their reality, shaping their new identity, naming their history, telling their story."[5] The following text utilizes theoretical storytelling of experiences in support of framing the metaphor of voice through a Black woman's professional journey. The text will not lay blame on the numerically dominant White professionals or assume support networks for Black and women of color librarians. However, the text seeks to reveal how macro-discriminatory and oppressive systems reinforce marginality and limit the use of *voice*. This writing endeavors to break silence[6] through an exploration of experiences in the intersectional spaces Black women inhabit in the academic library workplace.

The chapter begins with a tale of silencing and external suppression of voice. Next, using theoretical literature, I explore the importance of Black feminist voice and solidarity.[7] Third, the chapter explores the status of Blacks in the library profession and how intersectionality plays a role in utilizing *voice* in academic library spaces. Finally, I examine

---

4. D. Jean Clandinin and F. Michael Connelly (eds.), *Narrative Inquiry : Experience and Story in Qualitative Research* (San Francisco: Jossey-Bass Publishers, 2000), 20.

5. bell hooks, *Talking Back: Thinking Feminist, Thinking Black* (Boston: South End Press, 1989), 43.

6. Patricia Hill Collins, *Black Feminist Thought: Knowledge, Consciousness, and the Politics of Empowerment* (New York: Routledge, 2002), 119.

7. Nancy Rule Goldberger, "Looking Backward, Looking Forward," in *Knowledge, Difference, and Power: Essays Inspired by Women's Ways of Knowing*, ed. Nancy Rule Tarule Goldberger, Jill, Blithe Clinchy, and Mary Belenky (New York: BasicBooks, 1996); Collins, *Fighting Words : Black Women and the Search for Justice.*

professional experiences through storytelling in the context of voice restraint and collective support.

Silencing

During my second year of study in a Master's program of Library and Information Science, I was tasked with interviewing a manager or leader in an academic library. A mentor suggested I speak to someone with many years of experience in an area I wanted to pursue. My interests were in public service in an academic library. I met with a woman who was head of the reference department in a large urban academic library. After what I considered a very smooth and structured interview, the conversation shifted to my interest in the profession. The department head informed me that she often provides opportunities for students to gain practical experience by working in her department. Student duties included performing reference work, which was essential for building experience and ensuring future placement. I didn't expect an invitation, but nevertheless viewed this as an opportunity. I was poised to respond and make the case for my need to gain such experience, as this was the very opportunity many students seek who have little to no practical experience. As I motioned to speak, the department head interrupted with a series of statements about why I would not be a good fit.

This incident occurred over ten years ago, but the clarity of each expression uttered lingers to this day. Her first statement was, "I usually have students work in the department, but I have no openings now," as if to deter me from asking if there were any current opportunities for students like me hoping to begin a career in academic libraries. Then, to make sure her point came across firmly, she said: "If you want to work in an academic library, you should have a second master's degree," further indicating, her assumption that I didn't have what was required. I responded, "I have a master's degree in Educational Psychology." To validate the fact that I was on the wrong path she said, "Students who graduate from your program are not prepared to work in academic libraries. They usually work in public and school libraries." I had no response but could tell that the manager was trying to dissuade me from pursuing an academic library career. To solidify her point she said, "Well I don't hire people who consider libraries as a second career." That last statement was to let me know that I did not have a chance in her department. I put on a smile and proceeded to thank her for her time and let her know that she was helpful.

That one-sided dialogue or attack represented the first of many battle wounds inflicted during my career in academic research libraries. But this initial encounter filled me with doubt and apprehension about proceeding with my career plans. In one hour, I discovered that I was entering a world where my visible identity as a Black woman could repel future colleagues and result in assumptions about whether I belonged. Similar narratives from Black women teaching faculty,[8] students,[9] and librarians[10] demonstrate the reality of battles in academic spaces. Their stories, like my own, created the impetus to utilize voice, silence, and outspokenness, and seek solace with other Black women librarians to survive.

Muted Voices

In the groundbreaking text *Women's Ways of Knowing,* the authors reveal a counter-epistemological perspective on the ways in which women

8. Nicole A. Cooke, "Pushing Back from the Table: Fighting to Maintain My Voice as a Pre-Tenure Minority Female in the White Academy," *Polymath: An Interdisciplinary Arts & Sciences Journal* 4, no. 2 (2014); Sheree Wilson, "They Forgot Mammy Had a Brain," in *Presumed Incompetent: The Intersections of Race and Class for Women in Academia*, eds. Gabriella Gutierrez y Muhs, Yolanda Flores Niemann, Carmen G. Gonzalez, and Angela P. Harris (Boulder, Co: University Press of Colorado, 2012), 65-77.

9. Serena Easton, "On Being Special," in *Presumed Incompetent: The Intersections of Race and Class for Women in Academia*, eds. Gabriella Gutierrez y Muhs, Yolanda Flores Niemann, Carmen G. Gonzalez, and Angela P. Harris (Boulder, CO: University Press of Colorado, 2012); Ryan Evely Gildersleeve, Natasha N. Croom, and Philip L. Vasquez, "Am I Going Crazy?: A Critical Race Analysis of Doctoral Education," *Equity & Excellence in Education* 44, no. 1 (2011).

10. Sharon K. Epps, "African American Women Leaders in Academic Research Libraries," *portal: Libraries and the Academy* 8, no. 3 (2008); Joyce K. Thornton, "African American Female Librarians: A Study of Job Satisfaction," *Journal of Library Administration* 33, no. 1-2 (2001).

understand and perceive the world.[11] Up until that point, research that focused primarily on men claimed a similar knowledge for all genders. The authors interviewed 135 women and uncovered five categories of knowledge:

1. *Silence*—women experiencing themselves as mindless and voiceless and subject to the whims of external authority

2. *Received knowledge*—women conceive of themselves receiving, even reproducing, knowledge from the all-knowing external authorities, but incapable of creating knowledge on their own

3. *Subjective knowledge*—truth and knowledge are conceived of as personal, private, and subjectively known or intuited

4. *Procedural knowledge*—invested in learning and applying objective procedures for obtaining and communicating knowledge

5. *Constructed knowledge*—view all knowledge as contextual; experience themselves as creators of knowledge and value both subjective and objective strategies for knowing.[12]

The five categories are not developmentally or mutually exclusive. They can manifest in different situations and at different times in a women's life. The connecting thread throughout the categories was the utilization of the female voice. They found that "women repeatedly used the metaphor of voice to depict their intellectual and ethical development; and that the development of a sense of voice, mind, and self were intricately intertwined."[13] The theory presents a new way of envisioning knowledge for all women. One controversy resulting from the creation of a feminist theory of knowledge is that it may come at the cost of excluding narratives based on culture and race.[14] How does the intersection of race and gender affect the voice in the five categories?

To answer this question, Hurtado offers a re-examination of the voice as it pertains to women of color in ways that overlap with *Women's Ways*

---

11. Belenky, et. al, *Women's Ways of Knowing.*

12. Ibid, 15.

13. Ibid, 18.

14. Goldberger, *Looking Backward, Looking Forward.*

of Knowing. She brings to light the multiple identities shared by women of color and how they impact voice. She states that, "many women of color struggle to develop a voice that is representative of the complexity of all the groups they belong to because, unlike many middle-class white feminists, they do not wish to reject their communities of origin. Their struggle is to make congruent all those 'voices' while being true to themselves."[15] The development of voice for women of color is as multi-layered as their identities. The use of voice for women of color varies by circumstance and manifests in different ways and different settings for specific purposes. She highlights the use of *silence* and *outspokenness* as strategies employed by women of color. Silence refers to strategic non-expression of voice in order to gain knowledge of power structures. Outspokenness is the strategic use of voice at unexpected times.[16] The voice becomes a weapon for women of color and is necessary for survival in oppressive spaces.

Strategically, Black women have used voice to speak up and mediate silences. It was Sojourner Truth, for example, who proclaimed, "Ain't I Woman," to counter the perception of Black women's experiences as separate. Using scholarship, Anna Julia Cooper penned *A Voice from the South by a Black Woman from the South*[17] to give credence to the participation of Black women in the uplift of the race. Patricia Hill Collins offers a contemporary view of Black women's voice as breaking silence whereby "individuals not only reclaim their humanity, they simultaneously empower themselves by giving new meaning to their own particular experiences."[18] This action gives Black women authority over their own experiences. When Black women break silences, they

15. Aida Hurtado, "Strategic Suspensions: Feminists of Color Theorize the Production of Knowledge," in *Knowledge, Difference, and Power*, eds. Nancy Goldberger, Jill Tarule, Blythe Clinchy, and Mary Belenky (New York: Basic Books, 1998).

16. Ibid.

17. Anna Julia Cooper, *A Voice from the South by a Black Woman from the South* (Xenia, OH: Aldine Printing House, 1892), http://docsouth.unc.edu/church/cooper/menu.html.

18. Collins, *Fighting Words*, 48.

voice publicly what is known privately within their own community and collective spaces. Through speech and collectivism Black women recover voice.

In academic libraries, voices of Black women are silenced through lack of access to opportunity, systemic discriminatory practices, isolation, and marginalization. It is a constant battle that impairs growth and sometimes leads to co-opted behaviors from Black women, such as when they borrow the posture of the oppressor to inflict wounds on the silenced. In every situation, the focus is on survival—no matter how the battle is fought.

All the Women are White

White women make up 73% of all credentialed librarians. The latest available gender statistics for credentialed *higher education librarians* indicate that 70% are women. Ethnic and racial divisions are: 60% White, 4.7% Asian Pacific Islander, 4% African American, 1.1% Latina, and 0.3% Native American/Alaskan. The numbers show a profession dominated by White women.[19] Previous research on Black women in academic libraries shows experiences of isolation, competition with white female counterparts, lack of respect, and racial discrimination.[20] These women experience what Patricia Hill Collins refers to as the *outsider-within*, in which Black women are present to do the necessary work, but do not always have a place at the table.[21]

To combat this, the library profession instituted various diversity recruitment and retention programs to increase ethnic and diversity

---

19. American Library Association, "Diversity Counts 2012 Tables. Raw Data," http://www.ala.org/aboutala/sites/ala.org.aboutala/files/content/diversity/diversitycounts/diversitycountstables2012.pdf.

20. Deborah A. Curry, "Your Worries Ain't Like Mine: African American Librarians and the Pervasiveness of Racism, Prejudice and Discrimination in Academe," *The Reference Librarian* 21, no. 45-46 (1994); Epps, "African American Women Leaders in Academic Research Libraries"; Thornton, "African American Female Librarians: A Study of Job Satisfaction."

21. Collins, *Black Feminist Thought: Knowledge, Consciousness, and the Politics of Empowerment.*

representation. In the 1990s, the Association of Research Libraries (ARL) created a diversity task force to address representational diversity by hiring a dues-supported consultant to institute diversity programs.[22] To date, ARL has instituted diversity recruitment and retention programs with various funding models in association with other library organizations. These programs include the *Initiative to Recruit a Diverse Workforce* fellowship for library students, *Leadership Career Development Program* for mid-career professionals, and *Career Enhancement Program* for library students. Other programs included partnerships with the Society of American Archivists (SAA) *Mosaic Program* and the Institute of Museum and Library Services (IMLS) supported *Fellowship for Digital and Inclusive Excellence.*[23] As of 2009, 232 individuals have benefited from the programs. Although these programs have been in existence for over eighteen years, statistically there has been little change in the retention of librarians of color. The programs prepare the individual rather than the organization, and the individual must thrive within these organizations.[24]

Many of the librarians that have participated in these programs continue to work in academic library organizations. Although the programs succeed at recruitment, everyday experiences in perceived hostile work climates are veiled. In most academic library institutions, there are very few librarians of color, and often they are relegated to frontline and mid-level management positions.[25] This dynamic creates a space where power within organizations doesn't recognize the severity of isolation and discriminatory behaviors.

The statistics uncover a reality where multiplicities of oppression can inhabit the library workplace. Perceived and realized structural

---

22. Barbara I. Dewey, "The Imperative for Diversity: ARL's Progress and Role," *portal: Libraries and the Academy* 9, no. 3 (2009), 355-361.

23. Association of Research Libraries, "Diversity and Inclusion," http://www.arl.org/focus-areas/diversity-and-inclusion#.WcDEYBPytTZ.

24. Dewey, *The Imperative for Diversity.*

25. Eric Kofi Acree et al., "Using Professional Development as a Retention Tool for Underrepresented Academic Librarians," *Journal of Library Administration* 33, no. 1-2 (2001).

discriminatory forces within the academic library terrain for women of color is framed by *intersectionality*. Intersectionality is "shaped not by a single axis of social division, be it race or gender or class, but by many axes that work together and influence each other."[26] The social divisions present within society and micro-discriminatory environments inform the lived experiences of individuals through power structures. As a twenty-first century concept, intersectionality explores the mutual forces of domination, oppression, and subjugation for those at the margins of society.

Intersectionality extends precursor language used in Black feminist writings, which recognized the dual burden of being both Black and female where white feminism fell short,[27] and the *matrix of domination* by which oppression is constituted through race, class, and gender.[28] Black women have long recognized how the combination of race, gender, and social class influence oppression and subjugation. In academic libraries, professional violence through micro-aggressive discriminatory behaviors render Black Women invisible through exclusion and silencing.

Battle Weary

The narrative presented at the beginning of the chapter illustrates how my voice was silenced as a student seeking guidance and communication from a library manager. My expectation of the interaction was one of information gathering about the profession and a search for clarity concerning the functions of a public service librarian leader. Perhaps it may be somewhat presumptuous to assume that the reason for her silencing me was that I visibly identified as a Black woman. Four

---

26. Patricia Hill Collins and Sirma Bilge, *Intersectionality (Key Concepts)*, (Malden, MA: Polity Press, 2016).

27. The Combahee River Collective, "A Black Feminist Statement," in *All the Women Are White, All the Black Are Men, but Some of Us Are Brave: Black Women's Studies*, eds. Akasha Gloria Hull, Patricia Bell-Scott, and Barbara Smith (New York: Feminist Press, 2015).

28. Collins, *Black Feminist Thought: Knowledge, Consciousness, and the Politics of Empowerment.*

years later, I met a young woman who carried out the same exact function and was rewarded with an internship and professional placement. Throughout my eight-year journey, I found that similar instances affected my voice, but I could find solidarity in a community of librarians whom I met along the way. We share battle stories and display our wounds whenever we can meet. We create our kitchen tables on the exhibit floor at conferences, social media messages, telephone calls, emails, offices, long lunches, and coffee breaks. We share our private voices and the meaning behind our silences. The next discussion offers a continuation of the narrative to demonstrate ways in which strategic voice, solidarity, and breaking silence is used in a variety of situations.

Voice Suppression

As a newly-minted professional, I found myriad opportunities to connect with librarians of color. In a professional development session of one of these programs, there was a discussion about workplace meetings. Someone used as an illustrative example the case of a Black woman who spoke her mind and was subsequently marginalized by her colleagues in the workplace. It was a warning for us not to bring our own voice to meetings. My response to the scenario was, "Why can't I bring my Southside of Chicago self, my Peace Corps self, my educated self, and my Black self to the table?" The response was that if I did, I would get a reputation as an angry black woman and face retaliation within the organization. The facilitator then offered alternative ways to effect change.

What the session lacked was strategic silence, as described by Hurtado, where I would consume the information I heard without speaking. Silence used strategically "allows the employee to learn about power without the employer's ever suspecting that he or she is being studied."[29] The facilitator offered a forced silence, where internalized suppression occurs and there is no outlet. Black women librarians must choose

29. Hurtado, 382.

suppression daily, and as a result experience mental and physical health problems. This struggle occurs in secret and is unknown by the oppressor, and often outspokenness results in highly charged confrontations in which the systemic oppression gets blurred.

In recounting the spaces for a multitude of languages or voices used by Black women, bell hooks states:

> Dare I speak to oppressed and oppressor in the same voice? Dare I speak to you in a language beyond the boundaries of domination – a language that will not bind you, fence you in or hold you? Language is also a place of struggle. The oppressed struggle in language to recover ourselves, to reconcile, to reunite to renew. Our words are not without meaning; they are action, a resistance. Language is also a place of struggle.[30]

The intersections of identities play a significant part in our struggle and the oppression we deal with in the academic library workplace. Combating the suppression involves strategic use of outspokenness and silence. Unfortunately, surviving the battles involves a self-imposed and damaging suppression of voice.

Support through Struggle

To combat this suppression of voice, Black women librarians find solidarity amongst each other through free expression. When perceived incidents of racial discrimination, lack of access, and exclusion occur, we tap into networks of support and enter private spaces to utilize voice. This mutual aid maintains our survival in sometimes-hostile environments. In makeshift private spaces, we share battle stories and un-reconciled issues with suppression of voice, outspokenness, and silence.

One such occurrence took place in a friend's office, when I spoke with a colleague about the uneven support provided for mentorship. I found myself without assistance in navigating promotion-related activities necessary for tenure. Feeling alone and without support impacted

30. hooks, *Yearning*, 146.

my professional identity and morale, and left me feeling extremely vulnerable. In contrast, my counterparts were provided with unspoken privileges for growth and sustenance. Although this is perceived, this story resonates with other Black women in the library profession. On one occasion, I broke my silence on the lack of organizational support, given that my scholarly and professional activities were done in forced isolation. I have persisted and continued to persevere, albeit damaged, and recognize that an outlet formed through secret collective support could help me survive.

I was fortunate in having allies throughout my professional struggles. Our solidarity could not change the power dynamics, but offered strategies for using silence and outspokenness, and support when breaking silence. This support system is akin to community and the activity of caring in the black community. It is a reminder that a "Black feminist orientation to caring does not borrow from White feminine ideals, but must be understood in relation to an overarching ethic to family, church, and community."[31] In private secret spaces within vast library organizations, women of color librarians constructed a community of caring whereby mutual experiences in isolation can build support in the struggle. These private spaces where communities of caring develop generate a wealth of secret knowledge where Black women come together to learn ways to deal with oppression and where access to knowledge of what is public and hidden based on experiences with the oppressor is revealed.[32]

Support and solidarity through struggle is necessary in helping to survive the battlefield of the workplace. Unfortunately, the continuation of secret support helps to maintain power structures and the perpetuation of voice suppression. To cope, many Black women maintain this survival posture so that they can continue to be invited in the house at the expense of not gaining a seat at the table.

---

31. Audrey Thompson, "Not the Color Purple: Black Feminist Lessons for Educational Caring," in *Education Feminism: Classic and Contemporary Readings*, eds. Barbara J. Thayer-Bacon, Lynda Stone, and Katharine M. Sprecher (Albany, NY: State University of New York Press, 2013).

32. Collins, *Fighting Words*.

Conclusion

This chapter seeks to reveal ways in which Black women librarians exercise voice in a predominantly white workplace environment. Examples reveal how voice suppression, silence, and outspokenness are utilized in the context of professional survival in elite library institutions. The experiences of Black Women librarians are rarely presented in academic library texts, and there are few texts that offer a Black feminist analysis of the issues faced in the workplace. My hope is that this chapter breaks the silences and creates a space for dialogue in the professional and scholarly literature of library and information science. Continual suppression of voice hinders the development of the profession and reinforces the power structures. Continued writing and scholarship will change the dialogue and influence writings-focused feminist issues in LIS.

Bibliography

Acree, Eric Kofi, Sharon K. Epps, Yolanda Gilmore, and Charmaine Henriques. "Using Professional Development as a Retention Tool for Underrepresented Academic Librarians." *Journal of Library Administration* 33, no. 1-2 (2001): 45-61.

American Library Association. "Diversity Counts 2012 Tables. Raw Data." http://www.ala.org/aboutala/sites/ala.org.aboutala/files/content/diversity/diversitycounts/diversitycountstables2012.pdf.

Association of Research Libraries. "Diversity and Inclusion." http://www.arl.org/focus-areas/diversity-and-inclusion#.WcDEYBPytTZ.

Belenky, Mary Field, Blythe McVicker Clinchy, Nancy Rule Goldberger, and Jill Mattuck Tarule. *Women's Ways of Knowing: The Development of Self, Voice, and Mind.* 10th anniversary ed.. New York: BasicBooks, 1998.

Clandinin, D. Jean and F. Michael Connelly (eds). *Narrative Inquiry: Experience and Story in Qualitative Research.* San Francisco: Jossey-Bass Publishers, 2000.

Collins, Patricia Hill. *Black Feminist Thought: Knowledge, Consciousness, and the Politics of Empowerment.* New York: Routledge, 2002.

———. *Fighting Words: Black Women and the Search for Justice.* Minneapolis: University of Minnesota Press, 1998.

Collins, Patricia Hill, and Sirma Bilge. *Intersectionality (Key Concepts).* Malden, MA: Polity Press, 2016.

The Combahee River Collective. "A Black Feminist Statement." In *But Some of Us are Brave: All the Women are White, All the Blacks are Men: Black Women's Studies*, edited by Akasha Gloria Hull, Patricia Bell-Scott and Barbara Smith, 13-22. New York: Feminist Press, 2015.

Cooke, Nicole A. "Pushing Back from the Table: Fighting to Maintain My Voice as a Pre-Tenure Minority Female in the White Academy." *Polymath: An Interdisciplinary Arts & Sciences Journal* 4, no. 2 (2014).

Cooper, Anna Julia. *A Voice from the South by a Black Woman from the South.* Xenia, OH: Aldine Printing House, 1892. http://docsouth.unc.edu/church/cooper/menu.html.

Curry, Deborah A. "Your Worries Ain't Like Mine: African American Librarians and the Pervasiveness of Racism, Prejudice and Discrimination in Academe." *The Reference Librarian* 21, no. 45-46 (1994): 299-311.

Dewey, Barbara I. "The Imperative for Diversity: ARL's Progress and Role." *portal: Libraries and the Academy* 9, no. 3 (2009), 355-361.

Easton, Serena. "On Being Special." In *Presumed Incompetent: The Intersections of Race and Class for Women in Academia*, edited by Gabriella Gutierrez y Muhs, Yolanda Flores Niemann, Carmen G. Gonzalez, and Angela P. Harris, 1-14. Boulder, CO: University Press of Colorado, 2012.

Epps, Sharon K. "African American Women Leaders in Academic Research Libraries." *portal: Libraries and the Academy* 8, no. 3 (2008): 255-72.

Gildersleeve, Ryan Evely, Natasha N. Croom, and Philip L. Vasquez. "Am I Going Crazy?: A Critical Race Analysis of Doctoral Education." *Equity & Excellence in Education* 44, no. 1 (2011): 93-114.

Goldberger, Nancy Rule. "Looking Backward, Looking Forward." In *Knowledge, Difference, and Power: Essays Inspired by Women's Ways of Knowing*, edited by Mary Field Belenky, Blythe McVicker Clinchy, and Jill Mattuck Tarule , 372-93. New York: BasicBooks, 1996.

hooks, bell. *Talking Back: Thinking Feminist, Thinking Black*. Boston: South End Press, 1989.

———. *Yearning: Race, Gender, and Cultural Politics*. Boston: South End Press, 1990.

Hurtado, Aida. "Strategic Suspensions: Feminists of Color Theorize the Production of Knowledge." In *Knowledge, Difference, and Power*, edited by Mary Field Belenky, Blythe McVicker Clinchy, Nancy Rule Goldberger, and Jill Mattuck Tarule, 372-91. New York: Basic Books, 1998.

Lorde, Audre. *Sister Outsider: Essays and Speeches*. New York: Random House, 2007.

Thompson, Audrey. "Not the Color Purple: Black Feminist Lessons for Educational Caring." In *Education Feminism: Classic and Contemporary Readings*, edited by Barbara J. Thayer-Bacon, Lynda Stone, and Katharine M. Sprecher, 263-92. Albany, NY: State University of New York Press, 2013.

Thornton, Joyce K. "African American Female Librarians: A Study of Job Satisfaction." *Journal of Library Administration* 33, no. 1-2 (2001): 141-64.

Wilson, Sheree. "They Forgot Mammy Had a Brain." in *Presumed Incompetent: The Intersections of Race and Class for Women in Academia*, eds. Gabriella Gutierrez y Muhs, Yolanda Flores Niemann, Carmen G. Gonzalez, and Angela P. Harris (Boulder, CO: University Press of Colorado, 2012).

Chapter 7

A Woman of Color's Work Is Never Done: Intersectionality in Reference and Information Work

Kawanna Bright

This chapter seeks to explore the impact of the intersectionality of race/ethnicity and gender on the experience of performing reference and information service (RIS) work. Specifically, this chapter looks at the intersectionality of race/ethnicity and gender through expressions of emotional and invisible labor within the narratives of four women librarians of color. Despite early domination by men, librarianship (or library and information science—LIS) is currently a career that is predominantly pursued by women. According to the Bureau of Labor Statistics (BLS), there were 190,000 librarians in 2016, of whom 83.8% were women.[1] These numbers are corroborated by the 2017 demographic study by the American Library Association (ALA) which showed that 81% of their members self-identify as women.[2] Gender is not the only demographic category that is overly homogeneous within librarianship, as the field also shows a decided lack of racial/ethnic diversity. Of the

---

1. United States Department of Labor, "Labor Force Statistics from the Current Population Survey," *Bureau of Labor Statistics*, February 8, 2017, https://www.bls.gov/cps/cpsaat11.htm.

2. Kathy Rosa and Kelsey Henke, "2017 ALA Demographic Study," *Office of Research and Statistics*, 2017, http://www.ala.org/research/sites/ala.org.research/files/content/Draft%20of%20Member%20Demographics%20Survey%2001-11-2017.pdf.

190,000 librarians recorded by the BLS in 2016, 79.6% were White, with 7.5%, 5.8%, and 7.1% identifying as African American, Asian, or Hispanic, respectively.[3] The ALA demographic study suggests the profession is even more skewed, with 86.7% of members identifying as White.[4] This has led to librarianship being viewed as feminized, with all of the associated stereotypes that accompany that designation,[5] and lacking in diversity.[6]

Both emotional and invisible labor are grounded within the stereotypes used to describe feminized professions. Emotional labor can be defined as the work that employees often do to express organizationally-expected or prescribed emotions, rather than those that may actually be felt.[7] While emotional labor can be performed by both men and women, the theoretical linking of gender and emotion has identified women as more emotionally expressive,[8] and thus more likely to be impacted by emotional labor. However, as noted by Brody, most studies that have indicated gender differences in the expression of emotions have not always considered the impact of stereotypes, context, cultures, or individuality—all factors that have been shown to impact the expression of emotion regardless of gender,[9] and which may also dictate experiences of emotional labor.[10] Whereas emotional labor focuses on the expression

---

3. United States Department of Labor, "Labor Force Statistics."

4. Rosa and Henke, "2017 ALA Demographic Study."

5. Barbara A. Ivy, "Identity, Power, and Hiring in a Feminized Profession," *Library Trends* 34, no. 2 (1985): 292.

6. Jennifer Craft Morgan, Bandy Farrar, and Irene Owens, "Document Diversity among Working LIS Graduates," *Library Trends* 58, no. 2 (2009): 193.

7. Arlie Russell Hochschild, *The Managed Heart: Commercialization of Human Feeling*, 2nd ed. (Los Angeles, CA: University of California Press, 2003); JungHoon (Jay) Lee, Chihyung "Michael" Ok, and Jinsoo Hwang, "An Emotional Labor Perspective on the Relationship Between Customer Orientation and Job Satisfaction," *International Journal of Hospitality Management* 54 (2016): 139-150.

8. Catherine Lutz, *Unnatural Emotions: Everyday Sentiments on a Micronesian Atoll & Their Challenge to Western Theory* (Chicago: University of Chicago Press, 1988), 58.

9. Leslie R. Brody, "Gender and Emotion: Beyond Stereotypes," *Journal of Social Issues* 53, no. 2 (1997): 372.

10. Patricia A. Simpson and Linda K. Stroh, "Gender Differences: Emotional

of emotions, invisible labor focuses on additional work expectations that women and people of color are often taxed with.[11] Similar to emotional labor, the idea that women are expected to be more nurturing (whether they are or not) ties directly to the invisible labor that women are expected to perform, particularly in their role as mentors.[12] Invisible labor also brings in the potential impact of race/ethnicity, as many of the additional work expectations are directly related to the racial/ethnic status of the employee.[13]

The concept of intersectionality, as defined by Patricia Hill Collins, focuses on the intersecting point of two systems of oppression—such as race and gender—and how this intersection can shape the experiences of those who exist within the intersection.[14] Looking at this intersection allows for a broader understanding of those who exist within both spaces, and whose experiences and perspectives may provide a different view of these systems of oppression.[15] Within LIS, few have attempted to explore intersectionality; Ettarh offers an introduction and broad overview of the role that intersectionality might play,[16] and Fox details the discussion of intersectionality in knowledge organization.[17] Because librarianship is a field comprised predominantly of women, but with

---

Expression and Feelings of Personal Inauthenticity," *Journal of Applied Psychology* 89, no. 4 (2004): 715-721.

11. Laura E. Hirshfield and Tiffany D. Joseph, "'We Need a Woman, We Need a Black Woman': Gender, Race, and Identity Taxation in the Academy," *Gender and Education* 24, no. 2 (2012): 214.

12. Albert Black, Jr., "Affirmative Action and the Black Academic Situation," *Western Journal of Black Studies* 5, no. 2 (1981): 90.

13. Amado M. Padilla, "Ethnic Minority, Scholars, Research, and Mentoring: Current and Future Issues," Educational Researcher 23, no. 4 (1994): 26.

14. Patricia Hill Collins, *Black Feminist Thought: Knowledge, Consciousness, and the Politics of Empowerment* (New York, NY: Routledge, 2000), 299.

15. Ibid, 12.

16. Fobazi Ettarh, "Making a New Table: Intersectional Librarianship," *In the Library with the Lead Pipe,* July 2, 2014, accessed December 15, 2017, http://www.inthelibrary-withtheleadpipe.org/2014/making-a-new-table-intersectional-librarianship-3/.

17. Melodie J. Fox, "'Priorities of Arrangement' or a 'Hierarchy of Oppressions?': Perspectives on Intersectionality in Knowledge Organization," *Knowledge Organization* 43, no. 5 (2016): 373-383.

few people of color, it is not surprising that few studies talk about the intersectionality of these two demographic areas (gender and race/ethnicity), or the impact that this intersectionality may have on the work performed by librarians of color who are also women. This lack of attention can be seen as a type of marginalization experienced by women of color, who have intersectional identities not addressed in the discourses that focus on only one or the other of their identities, and often leave them out of both.[18]

Additionally, there is no literature that explores this intersectionality within the concepts of emotional and invisible labor. This absence of coverage in the literature may be reflective of the view that race/ethnicity and gender were not relevant to the work of a librarian,[19] and those that focus on gender but ignore race/ethnicity use the excuse that diversity was not the focus of the study being undertaken.[20] Most of the literature that even includes the term "intersectionality" focuses on gender and sexual orientation; and the majority of that literature consists of book reviews or focuses on collection development,[21] not on the librarians themselves. Studies that do cover the combined impact of race/ethnicity and gender tend to be focused on librarianship as a whole[22] or library leadership,[23] but not on specific positions in libraries. This chapter will

---

18. Kimberlé Crenshaw discusses this marginalization within the discourses of feminism and anti-racism. Kimberlé Crenshaw, "Mapping the Margins: Intersectionality, Identity Politics, and Violence Against Women of Color," *Stanford Law Review* 43, no. 6 (1991): 1244.

19. Suzanne M. Stauffer, "The Intelligent, Thoughtful Personality: Librarianship as a Process of Identity Formation," *Library & Information History* 30, no. 4 (2014): 256.

20. Deborah R. Hollis, "Affirmative Action or Increased Competition," *Journal of Library Administration* 27, no. 1-2 (1999): 51.

21. Sujei Lugo, "A Latino Anti-Racist Approach to Children's Librarianship," *Teacher Librarian* 44, no. 1 (2016): 24-27.

22. Sweeper and Smith looked at the impact of gender and race on librarian salaries. Darren Sweeper and Steven A. Smith, "Assessing the Impact of Gender and Race on Earnings in the Library Science Labor Market," *College & Research Libraries* 71, no. 2 (2010): 171-183.

23. Hollis attempted to study the leadership competition for dean positions in academic libraries based on gender, race, and sexuality. Hollis, "Affirmative Action or Increased Competition," 50.

endeavor to explore the intersectionality of gender and race/ethnicity utilizing the lenses of emotional and invisible labor, and through the RIS experiences of four librarians of color who are also women.

Literature Review

This literature review will offer an overview of research on intersectionality within librarianship, emotional labor, and invisible labor. While this literature is not overly expansive, there are a few key studies that provide a basis for discussion of the topic.

Intersectionality in Librarianship

The intersectionality of race/ethnicity and gender has been studied in a number of occupations. Within the legal field, research has explored the intersectionality of race and gender on the careers of women who are lawyers, finding that study participants felt that the major issues they had to deal with were due to their gender, not their race or ethnicity.[24] It should be noted, however, that this study was working with a field dominated by men. It is possible that a field predominantly made up of women may present different views related to the impact of race/ethnicity, though studies that focus on pink-collar jobs tend to look at the impact of stereotypes on men and not women or people of color.[25] A study of Mexican worker burnout does hint at the possibility of cultural

24. Hilary Sommerlad, "'A Pit to Put Women In': Professionalism, Work Intensification, Sexualisation and Work-Life Balance in the Legal Profession in England and Wales," *International Journal of the Legal Profession* 23, no. 1 (2016): 67, doi: 10.1080/09695958.2016.1140945.

25. Research shows that men in pink collar careers do suffer from the negative impacts of stereotypes, including stereotype threats, that can impact their job satisfaction and engagement at work, but despite these feelings, men in pink-collar jobs are still more likely to become leaders and receive higher pay than women, indicating that their gender still affords them an advantage, even in a woman-dominated field. Elise K. Kalokerinos, Kathleen Kjelsaas, Steven Bennetts, and Courtney von Hippel, "Men in Pink Collars: Stereotype Threat and Disengagement Among Male Teachers and Child Protection Workers," *European Journal of Social Psychology* 47, no. 5 (2017): 553-565.

differences, as Mexican women working in blue-, white-, and pink-collar jobs showed lower levels of burnout than women in other cultures.[26] Since the focus of this study was not on the possible intersectionality of gender and culture on the burnout of women workers in different types of jobs, the results only suggest a need for additional study. This recommendation for studies that focus on the intersectionality of gender and race/ethnicity applies to LIS as well, since most studies within LIS that look at the impact of gender on the work of librarians, particularly in relation to leadership, do not address race/ethnicity.[27]

Emotional Labor

The concept of emotional labor has grown out of the work of Arlie Hochschild who introduced the concept in her exploration of how emotions were felt versus how they were expressed within both personal and professional situations.[28] Within professional situations, management often sets rules about how employees should feel and specifically about how they should express their feelings.[29] But how the employee actually feels, how they express those feelings, and the ramifications of their decisions are what make up the essence of emotional labor. Hochschild describes two possible responses to the requirement to express a certain emotion, even when someone does not feel or agree with that emotion: surface acting and deep acting.[30] With surface acting, the employee is able to disguise their true feelings and express the expected emotion.[31]

26. Ayala Pines and Sylvia Guendelman, "Exploring the Relevance of Burnout to Mexican Blue Collar Women," *Journal of Vocational Behavior* 47, no. 1 (1995), 15.

27. Ivy's 1985 study of identity and power in LIS is a prime example of a study that focused on gender but did not mention race/ethnicity at all, precluding the opportunity to look at possible intersection of these two areas. Ivy, "Identity, Power, and Hiring in a Feminized Profession," 291-308.

28. Hochschild's seminal work offers a full overview of what the terms "emotion work" mean. Hochschild, *The Managed Heart.*

29. Ibid, 89.

30. Ibid, 33.

31. Ibid.

With deep acting, the employee expresses the expected emotion rather than the felt emotion, but also convinces themselves that they *should* feel the expected emotion.[32] Hochschild likens both surface and deep acting to deception—of others through surface acting and of yourself through deep acting.[33] With either expression of emotion, employees may experience what Hochschild calls emotive dissonance—the strain of maintaining incongruent expressions and feelings of emotion.[34] The response to this strain usually entails trying to change how you feel or trying to change what you pretend to feel.[35]

Hochschild's work has been adopted and adapted into other fields, but especially within business and management. The definition of emotional labor found in the management literature, "the act of expressing organizationally desired emotions during service transactions,"[36] more directly ties emotional labor to the public services work done in LIS. Within this definition we see terminology that is familiar to LIS, particularly within reference and information services, as the reference desk is often referred to as "the service desk,"[37] and reference interactions are usually referred to as "reference transactions."[38] Others have explored

---

32. Ibid.

33. Ibid.

34. Ibid., 90.

35. Ibid.

36. J. Andrew Morris and Daniel C. Feldman, "The Dimensions, Antecedents, and Consequences of Emotional Labor," *Academy of Management Review* 21, no. 4 (1996), 987.

37. Reference desks have been referred to as "service desks" as far back as 1941 in an article by Gifford about a telephone service desk designed to handle an increasing number of telephone reference questions. Florence M. Gifford, "Telephone Service Desk," *Wilson Library Bulletin* 15 (1941), 826.

38. The Reference and User Services Association (RUSA) of the American Library Association (ALA) lists reference transactions first in their "Definitions of Reference" page and uses the term within other definitions of reference. Reference and User Services Association, "Definitions of Reference," *American Library Association*, January 14, 2008, http://www.ala.org/rusa/guidelines/definitionsreference.

emotional labor within LIS through other public service areas as well, including instructional services[39] and circulation services.[40]

In LIS, the existence of emotional labor has been explored within library work that entails interactions with customers. Nearly every study that has looked at emotional labor in LIS has referred to the Reference and User Services Association (RUSA) Professional Behavioral Guidelines as evidence that emotional labor is explicitly built into library work.[41] These guidelines directly address the expression of emotion, suggesting that the librarian use "a friendly greeting to initiate conversation," while also referring to the need to comply with "institutional and professional norms and policies,"[42] an important aspect of emotional labor.[43] Within RIS specifically, a 2013 study by VanScoy[44] explored emotional connection within RIS work, revealing "a strong affective dimension" in the accounts of the librarians' experiences. Matteson and Miller[45] utilized a large-scale study to further establish the presence of emotional labor in library work through quantitative exploration of variables related

39. Heidi Julien and Shelagh K. Genuis, "Emotional Labour in Librarians' Instructional Work," *Journal of Documentation* 65, no. 6 (2009), 926-937.

40. Chen Su-May Sheih, "A Study on University Circulation Librarian's Service Strategy to Cope with Aggressive Patron: The Perspective of Emotional Labor," Journal of Educational Media & Library Sciences 50, no. 4 (2013): 461-489.

41. Julien and Genuis, "Emotional Labour in Librarians' Instructional Work," 933; Miriam L. Matteson and Shelly S. Miller, "Emotional Labor in Librarianship: A Research Agenda," *Library & Information Science Research* 34 (2012), 177; Miriam L. Matteson and Shelly S. Miller, "A Study of Emotional Labor in Librarianship," *Library & Information Science Research* 35 (2013), 55; Miriam Matteson and Cynthia Boyden, "Old Wine in a New Bottle: Customer Orientation in Librarianship," *Reference Services Review* 42, no. 3 (2014), 433.; Sherianne Shuler and Nathan Morgan, "Emotional Labor in the Academic Library: When Being Friendly Feels Like Work," *Reference Librarian* 54 (2013), 119; Kathryn Arbuckle, "Emotion and Knowledge: Partners in Library Service?" *Feliciter* 54, no. 5 (2008), 219.

42. Reference and User Services Association, "Guidelines for Behavioral Performance of Reference and Information Service Providers," *American Library Association*, May 28, 2013, http://www.ala.org/rusa/resources/guidelines/guidelinesbehavioral/.

43. Shuler & Morgan, "Emotional Labor in the Academic Library," 119.

44. Amy VanScoy, "Fully Engaged Practice and Emotional Connection: Aspects of the Practitioner Perspective of Reference and Information Service," *Library & Information Science Research* 35 (2013), 274.

45. Matteson and Miller, "A Study of Emotional Labor in Librarianship," 54-62.

to emotional labor, including job-based interpersonal interactions and librarians' perceptions of the demands placed on them to express positive or suppress negative emotions. These results were further supported in a study by Matteson, Chittock, and Mease,[46] which utilized mixed methodology to gain a deeper understanding of what emotional labor looks like in real library work situations. Similarly, through a case study, Shuler and Morgan identified four emotions that tended to trigger issues with emotional labor for librarians: anger, boredom, fear, and frustration.[47] But emotional labor could also have positive emotions associated with it, like excitement or joy.[48]

Julien and Genuis[49] focused on emotional labor within instructional work, finding that librarians who performed instructional work often experienced both "emotional harmony" and "emotional dissonance." The finding of emotional dissonance, in particular, aligns directly with the concept of emotive dissonance outlined by Hochschild,[50] indicating the negative impact that emotional labor can have on librarians at work. A large-scale study by Matteson and Miller[51] delved further into the possible negative implications of emotional labor on the work of librarians and found that emotional labor, particularly when expressed as surface acting, was associated with emotional burnout and lower levels of job satisfaction. Another study found that surface acting reduced the levels of job satisfaction and performance of librarians, especially in situations where they felt inadequately supported by supervisors.[52] But research also shows that librarians may respond to these difficulties by employing

46. Miriam L. Matteson, Sharon Chittock, and David Mease, "In Their Own Words: Stories of Emotional Labor From the Library Workforce," *Library Quarterly: Information, Community, Policy* 85, no. 1 (2015): 85-105.

47. Shuler and Morgan, "Emotional Labor in the Academic Library," 123.

48. Ibid., 126.

49. Julien and Genuis, "Emotional Labour in Librarians' Instructional Work," 931.

50. Hochschild, *The Managed Heart*, 90.

51. Matteson and Miller, "A Study of Emotional Labor in Librarianship," 60.

52. Yu-Ping Peng, "Buffering the Negative Effects of Surface Acting: The Moderating Role of Supervisor Support in Librarianship," *Journal of Academic Librarianship* 41 (2015), 43.

different strategies that are often seen with deep acting. These strategies include reframing or excusing the behavior of the patron, empathizing, and using their authority to cope with the situation.[53]

These studies clearly show that emotional labor is embedded within LIS. However, what is not seen in these studies of emotional labor in LIS is whether gender and race/ethnicity also play a role in how emotional labor is experienced in the library workplace. Turner[54] noted that those with certain characteristics related to gender or race/ethnicity could encounter negative experiences with explicit or implicit workplace policies, and a study by Mirchandani directly connects race/ethnicity and emotional labor within call center work in India, finding that along with dealing with the emotional labor of their positions, participants also had to deal with "racialized customer abuse."[55] Though outside of LIS, the studies by Turner and Mirchandani reflect aspects of the work and workplace dynamics found within libraries, indicating a need to further investigate the concept of emotional labor through an intersectional lens.

Invisible Labor

Another type of labor that has not been explored in detail within LIS, but that directly relates to the work of women and librarians of color, is invisible labor. Invisible labor is a concept found within both management and higher education literature, though how it is defined differs slightly between the two. Within management scholarship, discussions of invisible labor focus primarily on the work of women, especially in woman-dominated positions such as secretaries and flight attendants.[56]

53. Shuler and Morgan, "Emotional Labor in the Academic Library," 128.

54. Rebecca A. Turner, "Culture Wars in the Workplace: Interpersonal Subtlety, Emotional Expression, and the Self-Concept," *Consulting Psychology Journal: Practice and Research* 59, no. 4 (2007): 244.

55. Kiran Mirchandani, "Learning Racial Hierarchies: Communication Skills Training in Transnational Customer Service Work," *Journal of Workplace Learning* 24, no. 5 (2012): 347.

56. Mary Anne Wichroski, "The Secretary: Invisible Labor in the Workworld of Women," *Human Organization* 53, no. 1 (1994): 33.

Within higher education, invisible labor primarily refers to the work of academics from underrepresented backgrounds.[57] What the two definitions have in common is that the work being explored is expected of the employee based on their gender or race/ethnicity but is often not acknowledged or rewarded.[58]

Within academia, invisible labor often takes the form of women or faculty of color being asked to dedicate more time to service commitments related to diversity than to teaching and research work needed to earn promotion and/or tenure. This service work may include being asked to serve on numerous committees,[59] acting as a mentor or adviser to minority students both within and outside of their program[60] and supporting campus diversity initiatives.[61] While these service activities are seen as necessary and important by the faculty and students of color, they do not receive the same level of reward or acknowledgement for this work. Academia often explores invisible labor from an either/or perspective: either gender[62] or race/ethnicity. Even when discussed within the same article, authors tend to discuss each issue separately.[63] One study

---

57. Invisible labor is also referred to by different terms within the literature, including identity taxation. Hirshfield and Joseph, "'We Need a Woman," 214.

58. Wichroski, "The Secretary," 34; Hirshfield and Joseph, "We Need a Woman," 214.

59. Paige P. Edley, Michele L. Hammers, and Ani N. Shabazian, "Are We Feminist Enough? Engaged Feminism and Invisible Labor Within Everyday University Politics," *Women & Language* 38, no. 1 (2015): 105-106; Padilla, "Ethnic Minority Scholars," 26.; James E. Blackwell, "Strategies for Improving the Status of Blacks in Higher Education," *Planning & Change* 14 (1983): 68.; William B. Harvey and Diane Scott-Jones," We Can't Find Any: The Elusiveness of Black Faculty Members in American Higher Education," *Issues in Education* 3, no. 1 (1985): 74.

60. Faculty of color are often hired with the expectation that they are better equipped to support students of color on their campus and that this should be a major part of their positions. Black, "Affirmative Action and the Black Academic Situation," 90; If gender-based, this responsibility may focus on mentoring other professionals as well. Edley, Hammers, and Shabazian, "Are We Feminist Enough," 106.

61. Edley, Hammers, and Shabazian, "Are We Feminist Enough," 106.; Padilla, "Ethnic Minority Scholars," 26.

62. Ibid.

63. Johnsrud and Des Jarlais looked at tenure barriers for women and minorities, but only found significant results for each group separately. Linda K. Johnsrud and

that did attempt to explore the intersection of gender, race/ethnicity, and invisible labor looked specifically at the impact of invisible labor on the success of women faculty of color, finding negative outcomes related to health, tenure and promotion, and workplace climate.[64] This study looked specifically at the idea of "'gendered' identity taxation," finding that women professors felt they were "tokens" in their departments, expected to take on a disproportionate amount of mentoring and advising of female students, and felt discriminated against by their male colleagues.[65] This study may offer insight into the work of women librarians of color working in academic settings.

While invisible labor within LIS has not been directly explored, the idea of extra work requirements or overemphasis on work that does not support promotion or advancement for librarians of color can be found in studies of recruitment, retention, and promotion of people of color in LIS. Within residency and internship programs designed to support the development of librarians of color, participants often find themselves assigned primarily to complete service desk hours and may receive few opportunities for professional development activities.[66] Some of the extra work that librarians of color take on is self-selected. In a narrative discussing how she integrated herself into her campus, Fong mentioned her efforts to mentor ethnic students, join advocacy groups, and serve on a newly created chancellor's committee on women.[67] While not required in her new job, Fong felt that these activities, along with the ethnic studies class she taught, were essential for her ability to be politically active and support diversity on campus.[68] The one study

---

Christine D. Des Jarlais, "Barriers to Tenure for Women and Minorities," *Review of Higher Education* 17, no. 4 (1994): 335-353.

64. Hirshfield and Joseph, "We Need a Woman," 224.

65. Ibid., 217.

66. "Recruitment Advancement and Retention," n.d., quoted in Lakeshia Darby, "Abolishing Stereotypes: Recruitment and Retention of Minorities in the Library Profession," *Rural Libraries* 25, no. 1 (2005): 13.

67. Yem S. Fong, "Race, Class, Gender and Librarianship: Teaching in Ethnic Studies," *Journal of Library Administration* 33, no. 3/4 (2001): 230.

68. Ibid.

that does directly refer to the idea of invisible labor in the form of hidden workloads utilized a survey of academic librarians of color to determine how these librarians experienced the tenure and promotion process.[69] While not universal, they did find that over half of their respondents felt they were more likely to be asked to serve on campus groups related to diversity than their White counterparts, which often meant additional work for the librarian of color.[70] Respondents also reported similar issues to that found in the literature on faculty of color, with a lack of acknowledgement and a devaluing of the service work they engaged in.[71] Whether this work is undertaken by the librarian of color under their own direction or at the behest of their organization, it is important to understand how this extra work impacts the overall work of the librarian.

Purpose of the Study and Research Questions

The purpose of this study was to identify instances of emotional and invisible labor by four woman librarians of color in their experience of providing reference and information services. Through the process of qualitative secondary analysis, the following questions were explored:

1. What emotions do these four women librarians of color express in their descriptions of their experience of providing RIS?
2. What instances of emotional labor can be identified in their experience of providing RIS?
3. What instances of invisible labor can be identified in their experience of providing RIS?

Two sub-questions were also explored:

---

69. Ione T. Damasco and Dracine Hodges, "Tenure and Promotion Experiences of Academic Librarians of Color," *College & Research Libraries* 73, no. 3 (2012): 295.

70. Ibid., 298.

71. Ibid., 291.

1. What role did the intersection of gender and race/ethnicity have on expressions of emotional labor in the experiences of these four women librarians of color in providing RIS?
2. What role did the intersection of gender and race/ethnicity have on descriptions of invisible labor in the experiences of these four women librarians of color in providing RIS?

Methodology

This study relied on qualitative secondary analysis of data collected for a larger research study, funded in part by an ALA Diversity Research grant, that focused on the experiences of librarians of color in providing RIS.[72] Secondary analysis is a common data analysis method in both quantitative and qualitative research,[73] and allows for the further exploration of additional information found in the data. VanScoy, Bossaller, and Burns offer an overview of the problems associated with qualitative secondary analysis, as well as the benefits of applying this methodology to LIS research.[74]

Participants

Participants in this study were four women librarians of color who were purposefully selected for inclusion in a larger study about their experiences of providing RIS as a librarian of color. In the larger study, a total of eight participants were selected for inclusion in the study based on three criteria: at least two years of RIS experience, RIS as a

---

72. Amy VanScoy and Kawanna Bright, "Including the Voices of Librarians of Color in Reference and Information Services Research," *Reference & User Services Quarterly* 57, no. 2 (2017): 104-114.

73. H. Russell Bernard and Gery W. Ryan, *Analyzing Qualitative Data: Systematic Approaches.* (Los Angeles, CA: Sage, 2009): 21.

74. Amy VanScoy, Jenny Bossaller, and C. Sean Burns, "Problems and Promise of Qualitative Secondary Analysis for Research in Information Science" (paper presentation, 45th Annual Conference of the Canadian Association of Information Science, Toronto, Canada, June 2, 2017).

significant part of their job responsibilities, and self-identification as a person of color. Of the eight participants, four identified as women and self-identified as African American, Latina, Asian, or a combination of those identities. The four participants were employed in a variety of library environments, and many had worked in more than one type of library during their career.

Data Collection

In the original study, all eight participants were interviewed twice by one of the two researchers. These interviews were conducted either in-person or via Skype, with most of the initial interviews conducted in-person and the follow up interviews conducted via Skype. Each interview was recorded and the recordings were transcribed into Word documents. This produced a total of eight transcribed interviews for inclusion in this study.

Data Analysis

For the previous study, both researchers analyzed the transcripts separately, identifying codes and themes related to the purpose of the initial study. For this study, only the author participated in the secondary analysis to identify expressions of emotional and invisible labor within the transcripts. Relying both on previous codes indicated in the transcripts and a thorough re-reading of each transcript, the author identified multiple expressions of emotional and invisible labor within the transcripts of the four women librarians of color. Each identified expression was copied to a new file and placed into one of two columns depending on whether it was related to emotional labor or invisible labor. While most identified quotes could easily be classified as either/or, a few were placed into both columns as both emotional and invisible labor concepts were found within the same expression. Once the quotes were identified, the author worked to categorize the quotes in each column into themes related to the concepts of emotional and invisible labor.

This study relied on *a priori* themes identified from the literature on emotional and invisible labor,[75] with four themes for emotional labor and three themes for invisible labor. The final step of data analysis was to review the identified quotes and determine if the expressions of either type of labor were gender based, race/ethnicity based, or both.

Results

Expressions of both emotional and invisible labor were evident in the transcripts of the four women librarians of color included in this study. Direct connections to gender, race/ethnicity, or the intersectionality of the two was also indicated, though not within every expression of emotional or invisible labor. The following section details the results of the secondary analysis of the eight transcripts of the four women librarians of color included in this study. The results related to emotional labor are discussed first, followed by a discussion of the results related to invisible labor. Within each section, interactions connected to the gender or race/ethnicity of the librarian are also discussed within the context of those two areas.

Expressions of Emotional Labor

The expressions of emotional labor in the data fit neatly into existing themes from the literature previously reviewed: general expression of emotion, surface acting, deep acting, and emotive dissonance.

General Expression of Emotion

Emotion was clearly a part of the RIS work experience of the four women librarians of color in this study, with a range of emotions

75. The use of a priori themes was borrowed from template analysis, a type of thematic analysis that allows for the use of pre-determined themes (usually from previous literature) as a guide (or template) for the analysis of the data in another study. Joanna Brooks, Serena McCluskey, Emma Turley, and Nigel King, "The Utility of Template Analysis in Qualitative Psychology Research," *Qualitative Research in Psychology* 12 (2015): 203.

experienced and expressed within their narratives. While both positive and negative emotions were identified, the majority of emotional expressions were negative. These negative emotions included shame, disappointment, rejection, embarrassment, frustration, hurt, incompetence, misery, discomfort, feelings of being unqualified, uncertainty, and emotional uneasiness—to name a few. There were fewer positive emotions identified, and many times these emotions were not always clearly positive. These emotions included excitement, happiness, relief, pride, and amusement.

One emotion that came across in a couple of the narratives was that of rejection. One African American librarian recounted a story in which a library patron did not acknowledge that the librarian was there and instead tried to request help from a White, paraprofessional colleague of the librarian. The librarian described it this way: "And the lady sort of looked at me and she never acknowledged me in the conversation and just went back to him and said 'oh, well I'm looking for this.' Like she just sort of tossed me a glance like 'okay?' **And I felt totally dismissed**..." In this interaction, the fact that the librarian was African American, while the patron and the librarian's colleague were both White, led to the negative emotions experienced during the interaction.

A Latina librarian described similar feelings of rejection when interacting with White male patrons in her job, though she expressed the emotion as hurt:

> ...especially when I'm dealing with white males, or mainly white males... I don't know if it's something that I perceive and I'm reading into things but it feels like, it feels like once this type of person realizes that I am who I am...I can't offer any more help...How can I possibly help him?... in my experience, it feels like it...does come mainly from white males... and it, it's almost like this switch. I...can almost see it in their eyes where it's a switch that kind of shuts off, and I can tell they're not listening to me anymore...**That hurts a little. It does.**

For this librarian, being Latina and a woman seemed to influence her perception of the treatment she received from the White male patrons she interacted with and the negative emotions associated with these interactions.

Frustration was another emotion that was fairly common in the narratives, though the context for this varied. One African American librarian expressed frustration with different aspects of her job, ranging from a feeling of being stymied in her ability to do the instructional work she felt she was trained to do as a librarian, to trying to work with students who sought her out for counseling rather than the services that she felt she should offer as a school librarian. For this librarian, emotional labor was clear in her expressions of frustration, which came across in the continued use of the term "struggle": "I guess **that's the struggle for me**, is what I feel what I should be doing as a professional. And what is expected of me and where that meets. And, **so for me it's a struggle** 'cause sometimes I feel like I'm not doing what I was trained or educated to do." It should be noted that the expectation that the woman librarian of color would mentor the students of color came from the students themselves, rather than her peers or supervisors—adding a different layer to the emotional labor she experienced.

Another emotion that was clearly expressed was that of disappointment. An Asian librarian described her disappointment, not only about a patron's attitude towards reference assistance, but also what she deemed to be her own seeming inability to help the patron: "And for her to be completely closed to learning something new that she was going to be using for at least four years of her college career, **that disappointment really stunk...And, I was disappointed in myself** that I couldn't get through to her." This idea of librarians describing negative emotions about their own work was also seen in a couple of the narratives around feelings of shame or embarrassment. An Asian librarian described being embarrassed by her initially flippant response to a student's question during a class:

> **I was kind of embarrassed** about, of my behavior. One student asked, "Well isn't there just one database that exists?" And I said, "no." And I stopped...I stopped there and I paused, I'm like, "let, let me add to that." It's like, "no, it doesn't, and here's why"...And I explained and apologized and, you know, I, I could see the appreciation of, of my further explanation and, and, you know, the acceptance of my apology for being a little flippant.

A Latina librarian described her embarrassment for the way she handled a situation with a difficult patron, feeling that she did not handle the situation as well as she would have liked to:

> And I tried to get him as far as I could—I knew I could get him a lot farther than we got, but his learning disability was really keeping us at a basic level. So I felt myself, **and I'm really ashamed to say this**, but I felt myself kind of throwing in the towel…Yeah, I don't have time for this. And **I'm embarrassed to say that**…. it turned out this person was, I don't want to say a problem, well yeah I guess a problem patron. He was making, especially the female workers, feel very uncomfortable…, it kind of escalated to the point where we had to call in student disabled services, we had to call in the dean of, dean of students because this person was being sexually inappropriate to us… I don't feel like I handled it very well, but again, because of my own discomfort…And it wasn't the actual disability that was making me uncomfortable it was the responses, the sexual responses. I just wanted to cut it short and get that person out and away from me.

In this particular situation, the librarian's gender clearly played a role in the interaction that took place and the subsequent negative emotions that she experienced.

While expressions of positive emotions were not as prevalent in the transcripts, the four women librarians of color did experience them as part of their RIS work. Excitement to be doing the work was the one most often expressed. A Latina librarian talked about the excitement of not knowing what question she might get: "I think the thing **I get excited about** with reference is, I don't know what I'm gonna get." She relayed these expressions of excitement even further as she spoke about learning something new from the patrons she works with:

> If somebody comes to me with a question that, on a subject that I have no clue, **I'm excited about learning about that topic**, but I know that…sometimes I'm the novice and the student is teaching me…**It's a little more intimidating**, but it's still, **there's still this element of excitement**. I'm gonna learn something. And that student's gonna teach me something, and **that's pretty exciting too.**

Surface Acting

Within the expressions of emotions found in the transcripts of the four women librarians of color, there was evidence of surface acting. As previously indicated, surface acting is the process of expressing an expected emotion rather than the emotion that is actually felt.[76] In the description of the situation where the African American librarian felt dismissed by a White woman patron, she further explained how she responded when the patron was redirected back to her by her male colleague: "...and he gave me the question back and was like 'well she's the librarian, she'll help you find that.' You know and you know **I was probably a little overly polite to say 'you know I do know what I'm doing.'"** While the librarian is obviously upset by the patron's behavior towards her, she still responds in the way that is expected of her by being polite to the patron.

An African American librarian also discussed instances of surface acting when working with patrons who had unreasonable requests or demands:

> It's the sense of you know your library, your branch, that's what you are representing to that whole community, you know what I mean? **I can't be mean even when it was called to say "I'm sorry but I can't do that for you."** But then it's like **Black librarians are mean.** You take on that whole role. You are the Black librarian and **it's not fair**—it shouldn't be that way but you feel that pressure.

Even though the librarian knows she has to say that she can't fulfill a request, she also recognizes that she cannot state her denial in a way that could be viewed by the patron as "mean." In this situation, race is clearly a factor: the librarian tempers her emotions and her responses based on a sense of needing to be a positive representative of all Black librarians—a role she finds unfair.

---

76. Hochschild, *The Managed Heart*, 33.

Deep Acting

While surface acting was more noticeable in the transcripts than deep acting, a few instances of librarians expressing their emotions through deep acting were identified. Deep acting is the process of trying to actually feel the expected emotion that is expressed.[77] One example from the narratives was a Latina librarian trying to reconcile the difference between working with patrons in an academic library setting and a public library setting:

> So that was a major shift for me because people in the public library setting, were expecting, "give me an answer," whereas in the academic library setting, even if they were expecting "give me an answer," that wasn't what I was expected to do.... It was a decision by the supervisor to give them the answer. **And, you know, I struggled with it at first, but I thought, "Okay, I'm not going to go against what they've been doing for years, and I'm only here part-time, one day a week so don't rock the boat... I feel like...like I was doing a disservice.**

While this is not an example of complete deep acting because the librarian still had negative emotions related to her approach to her work in the public library, this example does show the process of trying to rationalize the emotions that the librarian felt when told to work in a style that was the opposite of the one she was used to and preferred.

Emotive Dissonance

The previous example of deep acting also offers an example of emotive dissonance within the narratives of the four women librarians of color. Despite the librarian's rationalizing and her decision to do as she was directed when working with patrons (an action that she struggled with), she still expressed a sense of discomfort with her decision, since she felt "like I was doing a disservice." Another instance of emotive

---

77. Ibid.

dissonance identified in the narratives was seen in a statement by an Asian librarian who was told that she was too informal when speaking with students:

> My coworkers would notice when I would say, "hey, what's going on?" when a student walks up to the desk, and I was told I was being too informal and too familiar... and I don't think it's too familiar or too comfortable or unprofessional. I, I think it's, it's approachable, it's "engage with me," instead of, "how may I help you?" I, you know, **I could be emotionless but what would that, how would I break down their barriers and assumptions about me?** If I decided to be a clone of everybody else. And I'm not everybody else. I will never be everybody else.

The librarian likened the approach of the other librarians to being "emotionless," indicating that she felt her own response actually expressed emotion to the students. It should be noted that the librarian clearly connected her race/ethnicity to expressions of emotion in this case, as she felt she needed to be approachable and engaging in order to get past "barriers and assumptions" she felt students might have about her.

Invisible Labor

Just as emotional labor appeared throughout the narratives of the four librarians of color, invisible labor also surfaced during the secondary analysis of the transcripts. The three themes used to categorize instances of invisible labor were tokenism, visibility, and labor related to mentoring or advising. These themes often overlapped, since tokenism could lead to increased visibility, which could also lead to mentoring or advising opportunities.

Tokenism

Experiences of invisible labor as tokenism were found within the narratives of the four women librarians of color in this study. Often, tokenism was expressed as an expectation to represent an entire race.

An African American librarian talked about the pressure of being one of only a few librarians of color in her organization: "…you know that that's a lot to carry. Because it's like and I did feel like **if I mess up, I mess up for African American librarians everywhere.**" An Asian librarian also talked about being expected to represent all minorities: "So a lot of my experiences, is because **I was one of five out of two hundred**…And a lot of the times **I ended up representing [an] entire minority population**."

Visibility

Being more visible due to their status as librarians of color was a prevalent theme found in the narratives. The idea that this visibility itself was work was expressed clearly by an Asian librarian: "I think **there's a level of work that brown and black librarians do inherently, just by being present**, by showing up, being available…And just by simply saying hello…that the majority of librarians…because they come from a place of privilege, don't have to do those things." While this comment is fairly neutral in terms of whether the librarian felt this was a good or bad thing, most of the expressions of visibility had either positive or negative undertones. An African American librarian talked about how her colleagues viewed her since she was the only person of color in her organization: "I feel like me being Black has been the issue. They gotta see beyond that to see what type of person I am or what my personality is." This librarian talked further about how she felt the way her colleagues treated her was related to her status as an African American: "And I don't know if it's personally my personality or if it's me being Black. A lot of times I will automatically go to it me being Black. Because being Black in America you deal with that all the time. So, that is, you don't know how you're being perceived or how the way you're being treated is because of that. But I tend to say it is."

An Asian librarian also talked about her visibility to other diverse populations, particularly students: "But being a minority in academia and working with limited diverse populations, especially in majority populations, my role is very visible to students." This librarian talked about how this visibility often led to increased connection to other diverse communities as she became the go-to person: "I worked with a lot of different populations—minority populations. And I found out through an African American graduate student that she and many others at that university who were going through their grad programs would pass my name around to incoming graduate students."

Mentoring and Advising

The narratives of these four women librarians of color were full of references to serving as mentors or advisers, particularly to students who had shared backgrounds or experiences. In most cases, these librarians were being sought out by the patrons who wanted to work with them. As one African American librarian stated: "A lot of times I'll find students of color seek me out. And they told me you know 'I feel like I can talk to you.'" This librarian found that the patrons she worked with felt a connection to her: "So I've noticed that in places where I work… minority community of students of color they feel like we have this bond already." This librarian also found that these students were willing to wait for her to be available before they would ask for help: "I have had other people come and say 'I've been looking for you on the reference desk for days and I kept coming back.' And I was like 'well why didn't you ask the person?' And they were like 'well 'cause it wasn't you.'"

This sense of connectedness was found within the other narratives as well. A Latina librarian spoke of her connection to Latino students:

> [W]hen I'm dealing with other Latino students, I feel like we're at a, we come, we come, we meet at a certain place… There's this cultural understanding. We meet at a certain place and it's almost the, you know the head nod, you know what I mean? Yes, there's this, there's this cultural identification, and…a lot of my students are from Hispanic Latino backgrounds.

This librarian also discussed similar connections at another institution she worked at: "It was an HBCU and so what I would try to do was identify with the African American students, and I had that immediate comfort level with African American students." While this preference for working with a librarian of color often meant additional work for the librarian, it is also an indication of the importance of having the librarian available to support those patrons.

While most references to mentoring or advising patrons were due to shared race/ethnicity, one African American librarian also talked about being sought out due to her gender: "I have had women tell me stuff that I don't think, or they will say 'I can tell you this because you're a woman.' Or you know I usually in some way shape or form bring up that I have kids and I've had people say 'well as a mother you get, you understand.'" A Latina librarian talked about connections based on socioeconomic status: "I go to my supervisor and say, 'these are the classes that I want to teach,' knowing specifically that these are the classes that the lower socioeconomic students are being funneled into…So I want to be the librarian they see in the classroom so they know to look for me at the reference desk." Both of these comments indicate that factors other than race/ethnicity may lead to invisible labor for these librarians. It should also be noted that neither librarian who expressed gender or socioeconomic status as the driving force between their connection to patrons and the extra work they took on indicated that their race/ethnicity was also a factor.

Discussion

Analysis of the four transcripts for the women librarians of color revealed both emotional and invisible labor within their RIS work. While emotional labor was present, invisible labor seemed to be more salient.

The four women librarians of color experienced and expressed similar emotions to those found in VanScoy's[78] 2013 study, particularly their feelings of frustration. The narratives in this study included multiple references to feeling frustrated while engaged in RIS work. Examples

78. VanScoy, "Fully Engaged Practice," 274.

of emotional labor indicated that both surface and deep acting were possible expressions of emotion for these librarians. This aligns with other studies done in LIS, particularly of librarians working in public service departments, like circulation[79] and instructional services. Similar to work completed by Matteson, Chittock, and Mease,[80] these librarians experienced emotional labor through interactions with patrons, colleagues, and superiors, though the majority of the interactions were with patrons.

Invisible labor was much more obvious within the narratives of the four women librarians of color. Similar to research on invisible labor in academia, while the additional work being done by these librarians was seen as potentially burdensome and negative,[81] the librarians also felt the work was necessary. It is likely that for these librarians of color, the service work that they take on that also supports others who share their cultural identity is seen as service that is also important to the librarian's ability to give back to their culture.[82]

Regarding negative aspects, tokenism[83] was clearly identified as a common experience of invisible labor, since these librarians of color were often expected to represent all minorities within their racial or ethnic group. But it was mentoring and advising students of color that came through as the most prominent type of invisible labor identified in the narratives. Even when the work that the student needed assistance with was outside the scope or subject area of the librarian, the students still sought them out. This is one aspect of invisible labor that needs to be further explored in order to gain a better understanding of the

---

79. Chen Su-May Sheih, "A Study on University Circulation Librarian's," 486.

80. Matteson, Chittock, and Mease, "In Their Own Words," 100.

81. Padilla, "Ethnic Minority Scholars," 26.

82. Damasco and Hodges, "Tenure and Promotion Experiences," 291.

83. Karen Fraser Wyche and Sherryl Browne Graves, "Minority Women in Academia: Access and Barriers to Professional Participation," *Psychology of Women Quarterly* 16 (1992): 434.

impact that shared racial/ethnic backgrounds have on the relationship between librarians and patrons.[84]

Although gender and race/ethnicity were clear factors in some of the experiences of RIS that the four women librarians of color encountered in this study, no intersections of these two identities were found. This result coincides with results in other fields,[85] which found that it was either gender or race/ethnicity that played a role in the experiences of the participants being studied, but not both identities. It should be noted, however, that while race/ethnicity was a focus of the original study and the data collected and subsequently used within this study, gender was not. So, a lack of intersection may be due more to the structure of the original data collection methodology than a true reflection of a lack of intersection between gender and race/ethnicity in RIS work.

Limitations

This study has noted limitations that should be acknowledged. While secondary analysis of qualitative data is common and accepted, it does have its disadvantages. Concerns with the authenticity of the data is raised since the data analyzed was not expressly collected for the questions addressed in this chapter.[86] The author would like to note, however, that both emotional labor and invisible labor were identified during the analysis of the data for the original study, but were not found to be salient to the previous research question. The prevalence of these concepts within the data is what prompted the decision to perform secondary analysis on the data in order to fully explore the concepts. The narratives explored in this study only represent the experiences of four librarians of color. Even for qualitative analysis, this is a small

84. Some discussion of this can be found in VanScoy & Bright, "Including the Voices of Librarians of Color," 111.

85. Sommerlad, "'A Pit to Put Women In'", 67

86. Bernard and Ryan, *Analyzing Qualitative Data*, 21.

sample size. These topics, particularly invisible labor, would benefit from a deeper exploration, particularly with an initial intent to collect data on the phenomenon. Finally, it is again noted that the data analyzed for this study was not collected with the intent of looking at emotional or invisible labor. The fact that both phenomena appeared throughout the transcripts offered an opportunity to explore the concepts from an intersectional perspective, but an absence of evidence of intersectionality does not mean that there is no intersectional impact of gender and race/ethnicity within the experiences of RIS work. It simply means that additional studies need to be undertaken to better explore the possible intersectionality of gender, race/ethnicity, and other aspects of identity that may impact how librarians experience their work.

Conclusion

This study adds to and supports the literature that indicates the emotional aspects of library work, particularly RIS work. Women librarians of color, just like their majority counterparts, experience both negative and positive emotions in the undertaking of their work, and their experiences indicate that emotional labor is present and has an impact on the work of the librarians. While race/ethnicity at times appeared to be a precursor of these experiences, gender was rarely mentioned as an aspect of emotional labor experience. More studies need to be undertaken to gain a clearer view of the role that both gender and race/ethnicity may play in experiences of emotional labor in RIS work.

The results of this study also add to the existing literature on invisible labor and introduce the topic fully into the LIS literature. There have been few previous references to invisible labor within the LIS literature, so it is hoped that this study will serve as a jumping off point for additional studies on this phenomenon within LIS. The secondary analysis of the narratives of four women librarians of color clearly indicates that invisible labor is a common aspect of their work experiences, but what impact this work has on the job satisfaction and success of librarians of color still needs to be explored. And while gender and race/ethnicity were not found to intersect within either emotional labor or invisible labor within this study, both identities do play a role in the experiences of RIS for women librarians of color and should be considered in future studies of reference librarians.

Bibliography

Arbuckle, Kathryn. "Emotion and Knowledge: Partners in Library Service?" *Feliciter* 54, no. 5 (2008): 219-221.

Bernard, H. Russell, and Gery W. Ryan. *Analyzing Qualitative Data: Systematic Approaches.* Los Angeles, CA: Sage (2009).

Black, Albert, Jr. "Affirmative Action and the Black Academic Situation." *The Western Journal of Black Studies* 5, no. 2 (1981): 87-94.

Blackwell, James E. "Strategies for Improving the Status of Blacks in Higher Education." *Planning & Change* 14 (1983): 56-73.

Brody, Leslie R. "Gender and Emotion: Beyond Stereotypes." *Journal of Social Issues* 53, no. 2 (1997): 369-394.

Brooks, Joanna, Serena McCluskey, Emma Turley, and Nigel King. "The Utility of Template Analysis in Qualitative Psychology Research." *Qualitative Research in Psychology* 12 (2015), 202-222. doi: 10.1080/14780887.2014.955224.

Collins, Patricia Hill. *Black Feminist Thought: Knowledge, Consciousness, and the Politics of Empowerment.* 2nd Ed., Rev. 10th Anniversary ed., Perspectives on Gender. New York: Routledge, 2000.

Crenshaw, Kimberlé. "Mapping the Margins: Intersectionality, Identity Politics, and Violence Against Women of Color." *Stanford Law Review* 43, no. 6 (1991): 1241-1299.

Damasco, Ione T., and Dracine Hodges. "Tenure and Promotion Experiences of Academic Librarians of Color." *College & Research Libraries* 73, no. 3 (2012): 279-301.

Darby, Lakeshia. "Abolishing Stereotypes: Recruitment and Retention of Minorities in the Library Profession." *Rural Libraries* 25, no. 1 (2005): 7-16.

Edley, Paige P., Michele L. Hammers, and Ani N. Shabazian. "Are We Feminist Enough? Engaged Feminism and Invisible Labor Within Everyday University Politics." *Women & Language* 38, no. 1 (2015): 105-112.

Ettarh, Fobazi. "Making a New Table: Intersectional Librarianship." *In the Library with the Lead Pipe*. July 2, 2004. http://www.inthelibrarywiththeleadpipe.org/2014/making-a-new-table-intersectional-librarianship-3/.

Fong, Yem S. "Race, Class, Gender and Librarianship: Teaching in Ethnic Studies." *Journal of Library Administration* 33, no. 3/4 (2001): 229-240.

Gifford, Florence M. "Telephone Service Desk." *Wilson Library Bulletin* 15 (1941): 826-827.

Harvey, William B., and Diane Scott-Jones. "We Can't Find Any: The Elusiveness of Black Faculty Members in American Higher Education." *Issues in Education* 3, no. 1 (1985), 68-76.

Hirshfield, Laura E., and Tiffany D. Joseph. "'We Need a Woman, We Need a Black Woman': Gender, Race, and Identity Taxation in the Academy." *Gender and Education* 24, no. 2 (2012), 213-227.

Hollis, Deborah R. "Affirmative Action or Increased Competition." *Journal of Library Administration* 27, no. 1-2 (1999): 49-75. doi: 10.1300/J111v27n01_05.

Hochschild, Arlie Russell. *The Managed Heart: Commercialization of Human Feeling*, 2nd ed. Los Angeles, CA: University of California Press, 2003.

Ivy, Barbara A. "Identity, Power, and Hiring in a Feminized Profession." *Library Trends* 34, no. 2 (1985): 291-308.

Johnsrud, Linda K., and Christine D. Des Jarlais. "Barriers to Tenure for Women and Minorities." *The Review of Higher Education* 17, no. 4 (1994): 335-353.

Julien, Heidi, and Shelagh K. Genuis. "Emotional Labour in Librarians' Instructional Work." *Journal of Documentation* 65, no. 6 (2009): 926-937.

Kalokerinos, Elise K., Kathleen Kjelsaas, Steven Bennetts, and Courtney von Hippel. "Men in Pink Collars: Stereotype Threat and Disengagement Among Male Teachers and Child Protection Workers." *European Journal of Social Psychology* 47, no. 5 (2017): 553-565.

Lee, JungHoon (Jay), Chihyung "Michael" Ok, and Jinsoo Hwang. "An Emotional Labor Perspective on the Relationship Between Customer Orientation and Job Satisfaction." International Journal of Hospitality Management 54 (2016): 139-150.

Lugo, Sujei. "A Latino Anti-Racist Approach to Children's Librarianship." *Teacher Librarian* 44, no. 1 (2016): 24-27.

Lutz, Catherine. *Unnatural Emotions: Everyday Sentiments on a Micronesian Atoll & Their Challenge to Western Theory*. Chicago: University of Chicago Press, 1988.

Matteson, Miriam, and Cynthia Boyden. "Old Wine in a New Bottle: Customer Orientation in Librarianship." *Reference Services Review* 42, no. 3 (2014): 433-445.

Matteson, Miriam L., Sharon Chittock, and David Mease. "In Their Own Words: Stories of Emotional Labor from the Library Workforce." *Library Quarterly: Information, Community, Policy* 85, no. 1 (2015): 85-105.

Matteson, Miriam L., and Shelly S. Miller. "Emotional Labor in Librarianship: A Research Agenda." *Library & Information Science Research* 34 (2012): 176-183.

Matteson, Miriam L., and Shelly S. Miller. "A Study of Emotional Labor in Librarianship." *Library & Information Science Research* 35 (2013): 54-62.

Mirchandani, Kiran. "Learning Racial Hierarchies: Communication Skills Training in Transnational Customer Service Work." *Journal of Workplace Learning* 24, no. 5 (2012): 338-350.

Morgan, Jennifer Craft, Bandy Farrar, and Irene Owens. "Document Diversity among Working LIS Graduates." *Library Trends* 58, no. 2 (2009): 192-214.

Morris, J. Andrew, and Daniel C. Feldman. "The Dimensions, Antecedents, and Consequences of Emotional Labor." *Academy of Management Review* 21, no. 4 (1996): 986-1010.

Padilla, Amado M. "Ethnic Minority, Scholars, Research, and Mentoring: Current and Future Issues." *Educational Researcher* 23, no. 4 (1994): 24-27.

Peng, Yu-Ping. "Buffering the Negative Effects of Surface Acting: The Moderating Role of Supervisor Support in Librarianship." *Journal of Academic Librarianship* 41 (2015): 37-46.

Pines, Ayala, and Sylvia Guendelman. "Exploring the Relevance of Burnout to Mexican Blue Collar Women." *Journal of Vocational Behavior* 47, no. 1 (1995): 1-20.

Reference and User Services Association. "Definitions of Reference." *American Library Association.* January 14, 2008. http://www.ala.org/rusa/guidelines/definitionsreference.

Reference and User Services Association. "Guidelines for Behavioral Performance of Reference and Information Service Providers." *American Library Association.* May 28, 2013. http://www.ala.org/rusa/resources/guidelines/guidelinesbehavioral/.

Rosa, Kathy, and Kelsey Henke. "2017 ALA Demographic Study." *Office of Research and Statistics.* 2017. http://www.ala.org/research/sites/ala.org.research/files/content/Draft%20of%20Member%20Demographics%20Survey%2001-11-2017.pdf.

Sheih, Chen Su-May. "A Study on University Circulation Librarian's Service Strategy to Cope with Aggressive Patron: The Perspective of Emotional Labor." *Journal of Educational Media & Library Sciences* 50, no. 4 (2013): 461-489.

Shuler, Sherianne, and Nathan Morgan. "Emotional Labor in the Academic Library: When Being Friendly Feels Like Work." *The Reference Librarian* 54 (2013): 118-133. doi: 10.1080/02763877.2013.756684.

Sommerlad, Hilary. "'A Pit to Put Women In': Professionalism, Work Intensification, Sexualisation and Work-Life Balance in the Legal Profession in England and Wales." *International Journal of the Legal Profession* 23, no. 1 (2016): 61-82. doi: 10.1080/09695958.2016.1140945.

Stauffer, Suzanne M. "The Intelligent, Thoughtful Personality: Librarianship as a Process of Identity Formation." *Library & Information History* 30, no. 4 (2014): 254-272.

Sweeper, Darren, and Steven A. Smith. "Assessing the Impact of Gender and Race on Earnings in the Library Science Labor Market." *College & Research Libraries* 71, no. 2 (2010): 171-183.

Turner, Rebecca A. "Culture Wars in the Workplace: Interpersonal Subtlety, Emotional Expression, and the Self-Concept." *Consulting Psychology Journal: Practice and Research* 59, no. 4 (2007): 244-253.

United States Department of Labor. "Labor Force Statistics from the Current Population Survey." *Bureau of Labor Statistics*. February 8, 2017. https://www.bls.gov/cps/cpsaat11.htm.

VanScoy, Amy. "Fully Engaged Practice and Emotional Connection: Aspects of the Practitioner Perspective of Reference and Information Service." *Library & Information Science Research* 35 (2013): 272-278.

VanScoy, Amy, Jenny Bossaller, and C. Sean Burns. "Problems and Promises of Qualitative Secondary Analysis for Research in Information Science." Paper presentation at the 45th Annual Conference of the Canadian Association of Information Science, Toronto, Canada, June 1-3, 2017.

VanScoy, Amy and Kawanna Bright. "Including the Voices of Librarians of Color in Reference and Information Services Research." *Reference & User Services Quarterly* 57, no. (2017): 104-114.

Wichroski, Mary Anne. "The Secretary: Invisible Labor in the Workworld of Women." *Human Organization* 53, no. 1 (1994): 33-41.

Wyche, Karen Fraser and Sherryl Browne Graves. "Minority Women in Academia: Access and Barriers to Professional Participation." *Psychology of Women Quarterly* 16 (1992): 429-437.

Chapter 8

"Sister, You've Been on My Mind": Experiences of Women of Color in the Library and Information Science Profession

Alyse Minter and Genevia M. Chamblee-Smith

Introduction

Women of color (WOC) in the library and information science (LIS) profession exist simultaneously in different spheres. Like any other individuals, WOC are more than just the jobs they hold. The identities they possess outside of the profession and the ways that others perceive them, given these identities, affect the ways they approach and interact with the LIS profession. They affect how WOC make decisions about jobs, advancement, location of employment, and whether to stay in the field or leave. Honoring WOC as individuals and recognizing their humanity is a vital first step in discussing inclusion and equity in the workplace.

To better understand how the LIS field performs in terms of providing a welcoming, inclusive work environment for people of color (POC) and what could be improved, we sought the input of those currently employed in the field. Given that the field is predominantly female,[1] we focused on a sample population of WOC. Defining the term "women

1. American Library Association, "Member Demographics Study," *American Library Association*, last modified January 2017, http://www.ala.org/research/initiatives/membershipsurveys.

of color" is complicated.[2] Its usage often causes confusion about who is included and who gets to belong.[3] In this chapter, *women of color* will be used to refer to women who self-identify as non-White.

Identifying as WOC, and as African American women in particular, we are aware that holding dual identities as women and POC increases the risk of experiencing marginalization. We wanted to provide a forum in which WOC could share their professional experiences firsthand. Through recognizing the presence and accomplishments of WOC in the field, we also sought to bring visibility to issues of representation and intersectional identities. Library workers are often seen as change agents in their communities, but far too often, we neglect to delve into the issues that exist within our own professional communities.

Recognizing that *staff* and *faculty* are terms used in academia and to avoid confusion over word choice and meaning, we will be using *staff* to refer collectively to the personnel of any given organization. *Pre-MLIS* or *paraprofessional* will be used in relation to positions that do not require an advanced degree, while *post-MLIS* will be used to refer to positions that require librarian status or an advanced degree.

Literature Review

Intersectionality of Social Identities

The intersectionality framework examines the intersection of race and gender.[4] Originally proposed by Kimberlé Crenshaw to highlight

2. Zakiya Luna, "'Truly a Women of Color Organization': Negotiating Sameness and Difference in Pursuit of Intersectionality," *Gender and Society* 30, no. 5 (October 1, 2016): 773-774.

3. Lindsay Yoo, "Feminism and Race: Just Who Counts as a 'Woman of Color'?" *NPR Code Switch*, September 12, 2013, http://www.npr.org/sections/codeswitch/2013/09/12/221469077/feminism-and-race-just-who-counts-as-a-woman-of-color; Kai Minosh, "(Re)building the Links Between Native Women and Women of Color," *BGD Blog*, November 3, 2016, accessed May 31, 2017, https://www.bgdblog.org/2016/11/native-women-and-women-of-color/.

4. Mary Joyce D. Juan, Moin Syed, and Margarita Azmitia, "Intersectionality of Race/Ethnicity and Gender Among Women of Color and White Women," *Identity* 16, no. 4 (October 1, 2016): 226.

how African American women face discrimination both as women and as racial minorities, it is often extended to discuss how social identities intersect for those with multiple marginalized identities and the effect this has on how individuals experience the world around them.[5] Because WOC are both raced and gendered, mainstream perceptions of their identities are contextualized against the backdrop of "other." Gender is often viewed through the lens of heteronormativity, which dictates different expectations for women versus men, both within-group and outside of group.[6] From an in-group perspective, women are often seen as culture keepers, meaning that they are the nurturers and safe-keepers of cultural traditions and help to reinforce values through participation in community, social, and religious traditions.[7]

Like women in general, WOC often act as primary caregivers for children and elders, whether in partnerships or as single parents. As a result, accompanying concerns include work-life balance;[8] cost of child and elder care;[9] making strategic decisions about parenting;[10] and proximity to family and support networks.[11] WOC who parent also provide both within-group and mainstream cultural perspectives to their children and provide insights into how they should conduct themselves accordingly.[12] Employer sensitivity towards parenting and caregiving

---

5. Ibid, 227.

6. Neesha R. Patel, "The Construction of South-Asian-American Womanhood: Implications for Counseling and Psychotherapy." *Women and Therapy* 30, no. 3-4 (June 25, 2007): 53-54.

7. Ibid, 54.

8. Medina F. Hamidullah and Norma M. Riccucci, "Intersectionality and Family-Friendly Policies in the Federal Government: Perceptions of Women of Color," *Administration and Society* 49, no. 1 (January 1, 2017): 109-110.

9. Ibid, 110.

10. Riché J. Barnes, "Black Professional Women, Careers, and Family 'Choice,'" In *Raising the Race: Black Career Women Redefine Marriage, Motherhood, and Community* (New Brunswick: Rutgers University Press), 60.

11. Ibid, 62.

12. This could include equipping children with a strengths perspective of their own cultural identity, while also preparing children for how society stereotypes Asian, Latino, African American, and Indigenous peoples.

women and the accessibility of adequate benefits are considered to be significant factors in job satisfaction.[13]

Within the social sciences, discussions about communities of color are often broached from a perspective of perceived deficits.[14] These perceived deficits are born of devaluing minority cultures in favor of promoting the dominant culture as both the norm and the measure for success.[15] Through the process of socialization, members of the dominant culture have come to both impose and accept stereotypes as a true representation of minority culture, with dominant culture in America being of White or European descent and broadly Protestant Christian. Stereotypes reduce complex cultures to "single stories"[16] and assume that everyone within a given racial or ethnic group operates the same way,[17] ignoring social shaping tools such as language, national origin, ethnicity, region, class, and cultural values. These stereotypes have their roots in racism and colonization; they serve to isolate, undermine, and erase lived experiences, forcing WOC to try to remain upright in "crooked rooms."[18] Such distorted realities make it difficult to reconcile personal identities in an authentic manner. POC use strengths-based and assets-based strategies to counter dominant narratives of communities of color.[19]

---

13. Hamidullah and Riccucci, "Intersectionality and Family-Friendly Policies," 114-115.

14. Tara Yosso, "Whose Culture has Capital? A Critical Race Theory Discussion of Community Cultural Wealth." *Race, Ethnicity & Education* 8, no. 1 (March 2005): 75-76.

15. Ibid.

16. Chimamanda Ngozi Adichie, "The Danger of a Single Story," *TED Talk: TEDGlobal 2009*, https://www.ted.com/talks/chimamanda_adichie_the_danger_of_a_single_story.

17. Kevin L. Nadal, Silvia L. Mazzula, and David P. Rivera, "Microaggressions and Latino/a Americans: An Analysis of Nativity, Gender, and Ethnicity," *Journal of Latino/a Psychology* 2, No.2 (2014): 69.

18. Melissa Harris-Perry, "Crooked Room" in *Sister Citizen: Shame, Stereotypes and Black Women in America* (New Haven, CT: Yale University Press), 29.

19. Yosso, "Whose Culture has Capital?," 77-81.

Intersectional Feminism

Mainstream feminism, though it focuses on empowering and advocating for women on behalf of gender equality, has been criticized for failing to make space for WOC and to acknowledge other oppressive systems that impact women from marginalized communities.[20] Intersectional feminism includes feminist theories specific to Black, Indigenous, Latina, and Asian American women. These theories acknowledge that historical and contemporary oppressions exist, not just for communities of color as a whole, but also for women as individuals. Intersectional feminist theories provide lenses to examine the ways that WOC support, add value to, and strengthen the communities they inhabit. While not all WOC self-identify as feminists, as individuals existing in a society that was not designed to benefit them, intersectional feminist theories help to contextualize their experiences in relation to knowledge constructions about womanhood, power, and voice.

Indigenous women are often viewed as remnants of the past with a hyperfocus on the oppression and trauma they have experienced.[21] While it is important to critically examine the long-lasting impact of colonization and systemic racism, representation of voice and agency are critical. Too often, the academy co-opts the voices of Indigenous peoples.[22] Part of disrupting this practice involves being aware of knowledge production structures and recognizing structures that already exist within communities of study, rather than discounting Indigenous knowledge systems in favor of Western knowledge systems.[23] Indigenous feminism,

20. Nikita Dhawan and Maria do Mar Castro Varela, "'What Difference Does Difference Make?': Diversity, Intersectionality, and Transnational Feminist Politics," *Wagadu: A Journal of Transnational Women's & Gender Studies* 16, (December 2016): 14.

21. Shannon Speed, "Representations of Violence: (Re)telling Indigenous Women's Stories and the Politics of Knowledge Production," In *Sources and Methods in Indigenous Studies*, ed. Chris Andersen and Jean M. O'Brien (New York: Routledge, 2017), 178.

22. Ibid.

23. Ibid, 181.

also known as Idigena, rejects feminism as a Eurocentric framework, especially the idea of three waves, which centers on White femininity and ignores early assertions of humanity by Black and Native women.[24] In addition, for Indigenous women, being forced to take on citizenship in North America required renouncing Native rule and laws, which granted women ownership and decision-making. Part of Indigenous feminism involves asserting tribal sovereignty and pushing for recognition of this forced parallel existence.[25]

Black feminism recognizes that African American women experience oppression by virtue of their membership in social groups based on race, gender, class, sexuality, and national origin.[26] Being both Black and woman requires a specific awareness of being and involves different sorts of challenges than those faced by White women or Black men.[27] Factors such as social class and sexuality can drastically change personal experiences, while being a descendant of the African diaspora fundamentally colors existence.[28] Owing to diasporic experiences with slavery and racialized labor roles, Black women have been working outside the home for centuries. Continuing post-slavery out of necessity, rather than a need to support feminist agendas, the relationship of Black women to paid labor prevents such simplistic goals as earning as much as men or being allowed to work outside the home. Current work experiences for many Black women, in underpaid or servitude-reminiscent roles, echo the labor practices of slavery and Jim Crow.[29]

Though sometimes used in conjunction with Black feminism, many Black women see womanism as a separate, but parallel framework.[30]

---

24. Goeman, "Indigenous Interventions and Feminist Methods," 186.

25. Ibid, 187.

26. Patricia Hill Collins, "Distinguishing Features of Black Feminist Thought," in *Black Feminist Thought* (New York: Routledge, 2000), 26.

27. Ibid, 27.

28. Ibid, 29.

29. Patricia Hill Collins, "Work, Family, and Black Women's Oppression," in *Black Feminist Thought* (New York: Routledge, 2000), 53.

30. Patricia Hill Collins, "What's in a Name? Womanism, Black Feminism, and

Womanism, as proposed by Alice Walker, is about empowering, giving voice to, and recognizing WOC as experts on their own lived experience, confirming the validity of lived experience. It opposes the inequalities, inequities, and oppressions fostered by mainstream society and recognizes the role of Black women in advocating for the needs of other Black women, Black men, and Black youth, in the journey for collective liberation. The community orientation of womanism allows Black women to prioritize family and community, while also recognizing that gender, race, sexuality, and ethnicity are experienced simultaneously and cannot be separated.[31]

Bearing many similarities to Indigenous feminism, Latina feminism seeks to acknowledge the legacy of colonialist oppression for Latin American women and recognizes that Latinas experience dual marginalization as women and POC. Additionally, given the history of European colonization, they experienced separation from their Indigenous culture, losing language and ways of being. Rejecting colonialist narratives of race, gender, and sexuality, Latinas choose to center their own stories and those of their communities, promoting empowerment and healing.[32] The Chicana feminist movement (Xicanisma), in particular, emerged because of sexism experienced within broader Chicano civil rights efforts. [33] Engaged together with Chicano men in the struggle for racial justice and community empowerment, Chicana women felt that their desires

---

Beyond," *Black Scholar* 26, no. 1 (Winter/Spring96 1996): 11, Biography in Context.

31. Karen Wyche, "Womanist Research," In *Womanist and Mujerista Psychologies,* ed. Thelma Bryant-Davis and Lillian Comas-Diaz, (Washington, DC: American Psychological Association, 2016), 30.

32. Teresa Córdova, "Anti-Colonial Chicana Feminism," *New Political Science* 20, no. 4 (December 1998): 379.

33. Though Chicana and Latina may be used interchangeably in some parts of the United States, they are not synonymous. "Latina" refers to women of Latin American descent, which includes Mexican American women, while "Chicana" refers specifically to women of Mexican descent. We acknowledge that Latina feminism is as broad and nuanced as Latina identity (which requires understanding of positionality—"Latina" being a very American, immigration-based term). Much of the literature we found seemed to position Chicana feminism as foundational to the genealogy of Latina feminism (as recognized in scholarship) in the U.S., which is why we chose to include it as an example.

for gender equality were silenced as they were expected to conform to more traditional gender models.[34] At the same time, involvement in White feminist efforts resulted in continued oppression through racial privilege and the centering of White femininity, which led to the assertion of Chicana feminist movements. Present-day Latina feminism continues to create spaces for dialogue, activism, and resistance around critical issues relating to Latina womanhood.[35]

Mujerista (or Latina womanism) is centered on community empowerment; it recognizes the intricacies of daily life for Latinas, rather than centering solely on political movements. Examining the realities of Latina intersectionality provides context for how women exist within their homes, families, and communities.[36] Through this framework, women are empowered to act as change agents, rather than relying on academic scholars or so-called experts. Much like Indigenous feminism, there is an awareness of knowledge systems and how they are impacted by colonization and oppression. This affects ideas about contextualizing knowledge and the effect on voice. Like Chicana feminism, mujerista is also concerned with collective healing and restoration of communities.[37]

There is a significant shortage of literature relating to Asian American feminism. Existent writings emphasize that Asian American women define their personal experiences beyond and in defiance of model minority stereotypes. Like with other racial or ethnic groups, there is no one collective experience. Given that Asian American presence in the United States is a fairly recent response to reversing discriminatory legislation that severely limited immigration of those from non-European

34. Paula M.L. Moya, "Chicana Feminism and Postmodernist Theory," *Signs: Journal of Women In Culture & Society* 26, no. 2 (Winter 2001): 446.

35. Patricia Sánchez and Lucila D. Ek, "Cultivando la Siguiente Generación: Future Directions in Chicana/Latina Feminist Pedagogies," *Journal of Latino-Latin American Studies* (JOLLAS) 5, no. 3 (Winter 2013): 183-184.

36. Kysa Nygreen, Mariella Saba, and Ana Paulina Moreno, "Mujerista Research," in *Womanist and Mujerista Psychologies*, ed. Thelma Bryant-Davis and Lillian Comas-Diaz (Washington, DC: American Psychological Association, 2016), 41.

37. Ibid, 46.

countries, the pressure to measure up to mainstream ideals is strong.[38] Because of high expectations to support self, others, and to maintain cultural ties, Asian American women may also make decisions in light of how their actions will reflect on their cultural communities at large, since the role as culture keepers places more of an emphasis on women in relation to impact and cultural responsibility.[39] For women who are first- or second-generation immigrants, these cultural affiliations may factor into decision making to an even greater degree.[40]

Women of color are not a monolith. Their cultural, ethnic, and gendered identities are complex, while the meaning derived from these identities, such as race, ethnicity, gender/gender expression and, by extension, sexuality, differ on an individual basis. Viewing WOC in LIS as "diverse" additions to the field exotifies and others them. Effective recruitment strategies require going beyond simplistic definitions of diversity to engage with change making and empowerment of marginalized voices.

Recruitment

Representation of librarians of color fails to match the national statistics of the general population, motivating ongoing efforts for recruitment and retention of professionals from underrepresented communities. A January 2017 American Library Association (ALA) member demographic study, based on the responses of 37,666 individuals, revealed that 86.7% of respondents self-identified as White or European alone, while 13.4% of respondents self-identified as being from a racial group other than White/European alone. 4.4% self-reported as African American, 3.6% self-reported as Asian, 1.2% self-reported as Native American, 0.2 %

38. Ibid.

39. Patel, "The Construction of South-Asian-American Womanhood," 53-54.

40. Marissa Yenpasook, Annie Nguyen, Chia Her, and Valerie Ooka Peng, "Defiant: the Strength of Asian American and Pacific Islander Women," in *Killing the Model Minority Stereotype: Asian American Counterstories and Complicity*, ed. Nicholas Hartlep and Brad Porfilio (Charlotte: Information Age Publishing, 2015), 75.

self-reported as Hawaiian or Pacific Islander, and 4% self-reported as Other. In addition, 4.7% self-identified as Hispanic or Latino.[41]

Projected statistics for the general population estimate continued growth among communities of color, providing an impetus for the profession to reflect the population at large. LIS professionals who lack cultural sensitivity, fluency in languages other than English, and understanding of information needs, all present obstacles to providing adequate services to library users.[42] Programs such as ALA Spectrum Scholars have been implemented to encourage increased representation in the LIS field with some success, but recruitment and retention remains an active concern.[43] Little research exists to ascertain the extent and effectiveness of dedicated recruitment of professionals of color into LIS programs. Additionally, the majority of existing research on recruitment of librarians of color centers on academic librarianship. There is a need for research on recruitment and retention strategies for public and school librarians of color, as well as for archivists and those in special libraries.

Lack of funding was identified as a significant barrier to graduate education and entry into the field for communities of color, as was the lack of related experience, proximity to graduate programs, and lack of tailored recruitment and outreach efforts. The perceived diversity of graduate program attendees, based on enrollment demographics, also factored into student values.[44]

Diversity residency programs for early career librarians of color were developed to address the employment gap in academic libraries. Most residency programs are two or three years in length, with candidates being hired at the level of professional librarian. Mentors, typically fellow staff members, are assigned to work with resident librarians to acclimate

---

41. American Library Association, "Member Demographics Study."

42. Kyung-Sun Kim and Sei-Ching Joanna Sin, "Recruiting and Retaining Students of Color in LIS Programs: Perspectives of Library and Information Professionals," *Journal of Education for Library and Information Science* 47, no. 2 (2006): 82.

43. Ibid, 83.

44. Ibid, 90.

residents to academia and work environments.[45] While research regarding the presence of WOC in diversity residency positions is limited, broader studies on residencies suggest that a lack of institutional buy-in for diversity and inclusion initiatives on campus, combined with limitations in program structure and support, may affect resident librarians' ability to complete capstone projects, develop marketable skills, and create areas of specialization outside of diversity initiatives.[46]

Retention and Professional Practice

For library workers of color, finding a job is often the first of many concerns. Female library workers of color often experience dual discrimination, due to sexism and racism.[47] Inequities in the workplace affect overall organizational effectiveness, but awareness of the existence of these inequities, or perceptions that they exist, among library workers of color may affect individual performance and professional development. A study in Great Britain on meta-stereotyping suggests that employees of color who perceive employer biases tend to doubt their own employability, professional worth, and likelihood to succeed.[48] The effects of systemic racism extend beyond the physical and material; they also affect psychological well-being.

For WOC in the LIS field, experiencing microaggressions is not a rarity.[49] A 2015 study by Jaena Alabi suggests that academic librarians

45. Angela Boyd, Yolanda Blue, and Suzanne Im, "Evaluation of Academic Library Residency Programs in the United States for Librarians of Color" *College & Research Libraries*, 78, no.4 (2017): 478.

46. Ibid, 497.

47. Wendy Reynolds-Dobbs, Kecia M. Thomas, and Matthew S. Harrison, "From Mammy to Superwoman: Images that Hinder Black Women's Career Development," *Journal of Career Development* 35, no. 2 (December 1, 2008): 130.

48. Chuma Kevin Owuamalam and Hanna Zagefka, "On the Psychological Barriers to the Workplace: When and Why Metastereotyping Undermines Employability Beliefs of Women and Ethnic Minorities," *Cultural Diversity & Ethnic Minority Psychology* 20, no. 4 (October 2014): 522.

49. Microaggressions (Chester Pierce and Derald Wing Sue) involve subtle forms of isolating or discriminatory actions, behaviors, or words that serve to undermine and

of color are more likely to experience racial microaggressions in the workplace and to notice when other colleagues of color are experiencing racial microaggressions.[50] Because the effects of daily microaggressions accumulate over time, repeated exposure to them contributes negatively to the mental health and well-being of persons of color.[51] Interestingly, instances of workplace bullying occur in libraries and other educational institutions at a higher rate than the average place of employment.[52] According to a 2016 study by Freedman and Vreven, librarians of color reported higher rates of bullying and instances of incivility than their White peers. For academic librarians, the underlying structure of academia, including the tenure and promotion process, makes it easy for problematic interpersonal interactions to occur, especially during or around the initial tenure and promotion periods.[53]

Further detractions from professional success include, for example, lack of support and clarity of expectations for academic librarians of color in the tenure process.[54] Significant numbers of librarians reported feeling excluded from information networks and experiencing isolation in their workplaces.[55] With librarianship being overwhelmingly White, the stark lack of representation among library staff can signal

---

devalue the identities of those in marginalized communities. They can take the form of microassaults, microinsults, and microinvalidations.

50. Jaena Alabi, "Racial Microaggressions in Academic Libraries: Results of a Survey of Minority and Non-minority Librarians." *Journal of Library Administration* 41 (2015): 50.

51. Anthony D. Ong, Anthony L. Burrow, Thomas E. Fuller-Rowell, Nicole M. Ja, and Derald Wing Sue, "Racial Microaggressions and Daily Well-Being Among Asian Americans," *Journal of Counseling Psychology* 60, no. 2 (April 1, 2013): 196.

52. Shin Freedman and Dawn Vreven, "Workplace Incivility and Bullying in the Library: Perception or Reality?" *College & Research Libraries* 77, no. 6 (November 2016): 728-730.

53. Ibid, 729.

54. Ione.T Damasco and Dracine Hodges, "Tenure and Promotion Experiences of Academic Librarians of Color," *College & Research Libraries* 73, no. 3 (May 1, 2012): 287.

55. Jaena Alabi, "'This Actually Happened': An Analysis of Librarians' Responses to a Survey about Racial Microaggressions," *Journal of Library Administration* 55, no. 3 (April 2015): 186-187.

implicitly to POC that they do not belong.[56] Repeated presence on hiring committees,[57] expectations of diversity expertise,[58] and undervaluing of research[59] all contribute to burnout for library staff of color. The use of informal mentoring relationships can help to bridge the gap between institutions' expectations and the support provided.[60] Informal group mentoring can aid library staff of color in professional development, identity negotiation, and the formation of information networks in the face of social isolation or exclusion.[61] Retention is greatly affected by opportunities for professional development, perceived value, opportunity for advancement, respect for work-life balance, and acceptance by professional peers.[62] Constantly battling any or all of these factors contributes to lack of investment and eventual career change.[63]

Focusing on the benefits of a diverse workforce, communicating the values derived from a diverse staff, and evaluating performance systems for potential biases can assist library administration in creating workplaces that both welcome staff of color and encourage them to remain.[64] Authentic and sustainable change requires dedicated engagement by administrators to address systemic issues.[65] Recognizing stereotypes and the impact they have on workplace culture is a first step for those in

56. Ibid, 189.

57. Sheila Nair, "Women of Color Faculty and the 'Burden' of Diversity," *International Feminist Journal of Politics* 16, no. 3 (September 2014): 498.

58. Damasco and Hodges, "Tenure and Promotion Experiences," 282.

59. Ibid.

60. Peggy Johnson, "Retaining and Advancing Librarians of Color," *College & Research Libraries* 68, no. 5 (September 2007): 408.

61. Ibid, 407.

62. Teresa Y. Neely and Lorna Peterson, "Achieving Racial and Ethnic Diversity Among Academic and Research Librarians: The Recruitment, Retention, and Advancement of Librarians of Color - A White Paper," *College & Research Libraries News* 68, no. 9 (October 2007): 564.

63. Johnson, "Retaining and Advancing Librarians of Color," 407.

64. Alabi, "This Actually Happened," 189.

65. Nair, "Women of Color Faculty," 499.

leadership.[66] Other considerations include providing adequate support, empowering staff of color, creating avenues for agency in decision-making, clarifying expectations, creating mentorship opportunities, avoiding tokenism and isolation of staff of color, and maintaining information pipelines.[67] Administrators should be aware of how power structures operate within their organizations and how existing structures advantage or disadvantage staff of color, relative to the employee population at large.[68] Views towards WOC as "twofers," meaning organizations gain both a woman and a minority individual, does a disservice to staff of color by placing the burden of diversity work on a select few and relieves White staff of having to engage in diversity work, negating inclusion as a professional value.[69] Additionally, in the interest of effecting change, recognition that cultural capital is a valuable addition to the workplace is important. For many WOC in academia, there is a higher value placed on collective knowledge and collaborative opportunity, in the interest of building communities, which is not always respected by mainstream academic models that favor individual effort.[70]

Existing research on race and retention in LIS workplaces focuses on academic libraries, suggesting there is a need for research looking at the experiences of non-academic librarians as well as paraprofessionals of color from all sectors.

Advancement and Leadership

American work culture is replete with examples of glass ceilings for POC. From hiring, to retention, to representation in leadership positions,

66. Reynolds-Dobbs, Thomas, and Harrison, "From Mammy to Superwoman," 132.

67. "On the Way to Diversity: Organizational Barriers," *ASHE Higher Education Report* 33, no. 1 (May 2007): 60.

68. Ibid, 66.

69. Eric Selbin, "If You're Not Part of the Solution, You're Part of the Problem," *International Feminist Journal of Politics* 16, no. 3 (January 1, 2014): 506.

70. Edna W. Comer, Catherine K. Medina, Lirio K. Negroni and Rebecca L. Thomas, "Women Faculty of Color in a Predominantly White Institution: A Natural Support Group," *Social Work with Groups* 40, no. 1-2 (January 2, 2017): 150-151.

creating opportunities for advancement is an ongoing struggle.[71] POC who aspire to leadership eventually come to the realization that "good is not enough,"[72] and strategic planning is necessary in order to overcome setbacks, challenges, and discriminatory roadblocks. Unfortunately, even upon attaining positions of influence, discrimination and social exclusion may still persist.[73] In higher education, in particular, POC and White women are most likely to be hired for positions previously held by POC.[74] This means that without a concerted effort to disrupt the status quo, positions that have traditionally been held by non-POC are more likely to continue that way.

WOC often experience isolation as the "only one" in the workplace, leaving them without supportive communities.[75] The lack of a network and a forum for advocacy diminishes opportunities for advancement. In order to increase the number of librarians of color occupying positions of authority, current administrators need to invest in POC as viable candidates for leadership by providing mentorship, career support, and opportunities for professional development, and allow shadowing on the job to expose future leaders to the ins and outs of anticipated responsibilities.[76]

WOC who aspire to leadership positions face a complex negotiation of identity in the workplace. The typical recipe for leadership development is to "create social capital."[77] This might include strong

---

71. Eleanor Wilson, "Diversity, Culture and the Glass Ceiling," *Journal of Cultural Diversity* 21, no. 3 (Fall 2014): 87.

72. Ibid, 84.

73. Sharon K. Epps, "African American Women Leaders in Academic Research Libraries," *portal: Libraries and the Academy* no. 3 (2008): 258.

74. "Concluding Remarks Regarding the Importance of a Racially Diverse Administrative Workforce." *ASHE Higher Education Report* 35, no. 3 (September 2009): 67.

75. Kim-Yin Chan and Fritz Drasgow, "Toward a Theory of Individual Differences and Leadership: Understanding the Motivation to Lead," *Journal of Applied Psychology,* 86, no. 3 (June 2001): 496.

76. Neely and Peterson, "Achieving Racial and Ethnic Diversity," 565.

77. Janis V. Sanchez-Hucles and Donald D. Davis, "Women and Women of Color in Leadership: Complexity,Iidentity, and Intersectionality," *American Psychologist* 65, no. 3 (April 2010): 172.

interpersonal skills, establishment of a network, and mentorship. Being relegated to the social position of outsider based on membership in marginalized communities makes it harder to access information, resources, and networking.[78] WOC in library leadership positions are as capable, and often possess the same skills, as others who seek, occupy, and excel in library administrative positions. The main difference is that WOC are tasked with navigating systems that discriminate based on race and gender.[79]

Forums for fostering belonging, sharing of personal narratives, and professional encouragement are critical on the journey to administration.[80] Because social exclusion may prevent library staff of color from having access to the same communities as their White peers, creating parallel communities to provide feedback and support is valuable.

Both career-enhancing mentorship and psychosocial mentorship benefit those with leadership aspirations. Career-enhancing mentorship focuses on skills development, which is the more traditional understanding of mentoring, while psychosocial mentorship provides personal development supports, such as counseling or encouragement.[81] Group mentorship involves a small group of people who help an individual work towards a psychosocial goal—overcoming the fear of public speaking, for example. Professional development opportunities, such as the University of Minnesota Institute for Early Career Librarians from Underrepresented Groups, can provide valuable opportunities to build networks and facilitate group mentoring.[82]

Methodology

Study participants were asked to complete a survey relating to their experiences as WOC in the LIS field. For the purpose of this study, the

78. Ibid.

79. Epps, "African American Women Leaders," 258.

80. Amy F. Fyn, "Peer Group Mentoring Relationships and the Role of Narrative," *Journal of Academic Librarianship* 39, (July 1, 2013): 331.

81. Johnson, "Retaining and Advancing Librarians of Color," 405.

82. Ibid, 408.

descriptor *women of color* was used to refer to those who self-identified as women and possessed a racial or ethnic heritage other than White or European alone. Because we were seeking participants who self-identified as WOC, no specific definition for "color" was provided. We defined race, per the Office of Management and Budget, as a social classification "...and not an attempt to define race biologically, anthropologically, or genetically...[C]ategories...include racial and national origin or socio-cultural groups."[83] Defining ethnicity as having roots in a common social group based on national origin, we opted to list Hispanic/Latina identities separately from race, as one can have both a racial and ethnic identity. We also allowed study participants to further self-identify with a write-in field, in addition to the race and ethnicity identifiers provided.

The survey, comprised of open- and close-ended questions, was divided into five parts: demographic information, attitudes towards the profession, perspectives on personal and professional identity, perspectives on retention and advancement, and thoughts on self-care. This chapter will discuss the results relating to identity and professional practice only. Our hope is to publish findings on self-care in future publications. A copy of the survey in its entirety can be found in the appendix.

The survey was disseminated via social network platforms, such as librarian/archivist of color affiliated groups and pages on Facebook and personal Twitter feeds, tagging ALA ethnic affinity groups. It was also sent to ALA ethnic affinity group listservs (BCALA, Reforma, APALA, AILA) and POC-oriented professional listservs (e.g., Archives & Archivists of Color, Spectrum Scholars), relying on the professional networks of colleagues of color.

Quantitative data were analyzed in SPSS to create basic frequency tables. Qualitative data were analyzed in QDA Miner Lite. As qualitative data were being examined, they were coded into one of eight main categories based on survey questions: identity, entry into the field, LIS education, job satisfaction, career satisfaction, challenges as WOC, retention, and advancement. Within each of these categories, sub-codes

83. United States Census Bureau, "Race," *Census.gov*, last modified January 12, 2017, https://www.census.gov/topics/population/race/about.html.

were assigned based on common discussion points (e.g., career-microaggressions). The codes were then reported as emerging themes. All survey questions were classified as optional, meaning the total number of responses per question varied. All responses were anonymous.

Results

Personal Identity

There were 301 survey respondents total. Twenty-nine respondents did not select any particular racial identity.[84] Of those who responded to this question, 156 (57.8%) self-identified as Black or African American; 47 (17.4%) self-identified as Asian or Native Pacific Islander; 47 (17.4%) self-identified as Multiracial[85]; 17 (6.3%) self-identified as White or European American; and 3 (1.1%) self-identified as Native American or First Nations (see **Table 1**). From here on, Indigenous will be used to refer to those of Native American or First Nations ancestry. Of those who self-identified as White or European American, all but two also identified as Hispanic or Latina. 61 respondents (20.5%) self-identified as Hispanic or Latina altogether. Two respondents self-identified as White or European American alone.[86]

Racial and ethnic heritage were a vital part of respondents' identities. Reflections on personal identity provided insight into participation in community and family. Of those who offered additional insights into their personal identity (N = 161), the majority were Black women (N = 43), women of multiracial or multiethnic heritage (N = 40), Latinas (N =

84. Though they did not select a racial identity, these individuals did self-identify ethnically as Hispanic or Latina.

85. For the purpose of this study, multiracial identity was demonstrated by participants' selection of two or more racial identities or a write-in response of Biracial or Multiracial under "Other."

86. Both individuals indicated in their responses that they do not identify as women of color. Because the focus of the study was on those who self-identify as women of color, these participant responses were excluded from data analysis.

Racial Identity	Quantity	Percent
Black or African American	156	57.8
Multiracial	47	17.4
Asian or Native Pacific Islander	47	17.4
White or European American	17	6.3
Native American, Indigenous, or First Nations	3	1.1
Total	**270**	**100.0**
Not Answered	29	

Table 1: Racial Demographics

33), and Asian American women (N = 32). Other identities represented included Middle Eastern/North African (3) and Indigenous (2) women.

For those with multiracial or multiethnic heritage, there was some measure of negotiation with self and others. "Although I have European and Native American ancestry, I self-identify as African American for social and political reasons." Some multiracial women felt free to claim all parts of their heritage, "I am mixed; African American, White (specifically Irish) and Native American (Osage Tribe)." Other multiracial WOC felt that, regardless of their own held identities, "people [...] make their own assumptions" about race and identity.

Many of the women described their personal ethnic heritage, such as Latinas embracing more specific identities of Tejana, Chicana, or Mestiza over being generally Latina or Hispanic, because being lumped together as broadly Latina/Hispanic "disregards the differences in cultures" and glosses over the complex mix of racial heritage that is a part of Latin American ethnicities. Specificity in identity differed by situation, depending on who the "audience is and if they are willing to understand."

Racial or ethnic identities were not the only important parts of respondents' sense of self. Hidden identities, such as sexuality or socioeconomic status, also played a big role in determining personal experience. It was recognized that many "barriers to inclusion are socio-cultural which in a round-a-bout way ties back" to race. Intersectional identities, such as being "a feminine, light-skinned queer woman of color," had an impact on lived experience and interactions both in the workplace and away from work.

Professional Identity and Demographics

The majority of respondents were librarians (136), followed by library assistants, associates, or technicians (63). The remaining respondents identified themselves as archivists (15); department heads (13); directors, deans, or university librarians (13); supervisory librarians (12); branch managers (9); archives assistants, associates, or technicians (8); assistant directors, assistant university librarians, or university archivists (6); teaching faculty in LIS education programs (4); administrative assistants (4); and those employed in other roles (14).[87] (See **Table 2**).

Early career library staff, those employed in the field for five years or less, made up around 35.6% (105) of respondents. Mid-career library staff, those employed in the field for five to fifteen years, made up about 37.3% (110) of respondents. Advanced career library staff, those employed in the field for over fifteen years, accounted for approximately 27.2% (80) of respondents. Forty-two (42) of the survey respondents were current graduate students in an MLS, MLIS, or MIS degree program. Twenty-three (23) of the survey respondents were current or past diversity residents or fellows. (See **Table 3)**.

87. Primary position for those with multiple jobs was determined to be the full-time position when respondents indicated a mixture of full-time and part-time employment.

Position Title	Quantity	Percent
Librarian	136	45.8
Library Assistant, Library Associate, or Library Technician	63	21.2
Archivist	15	5.1
Department Head	13	4.4
Director, Dean, or University Librarian	13	4.4
Supervisory Librarian	12	4
Branch Manager	9	3
Archives Assistant, Archives Associate, or Archives Technician	8	2.7
Assistant Director, Assistant University Librarian, or University Archivist	6	2
Administrative Assistant	4	1.3
LIS Teaching Faculty	4	1.3
Other	14	4.7
Total	**297**	**100**
Not Answered	2	

Table 2: Primary Position Title

Years in Profession	Quantity	Percent
<1 year	16	5.4
1-3 years	48	16.3
3-5 years	41	13.9
5-10 years	65	22.0
10-15 years	45	15.3
15-20 years	27	9.2
20+ years	53	18.0
Total	**295**	**100.0**
Not Answered	4	

Table 3: Years in Profession

A large number of respondents were within the age range of twenty-six to thirty-five years of age (39.1%), followed by those aged thirty-six to forty-five years of age (24.6%). The remainder of respondents included those aged twenty-five and under (6.4%), those aged forty-six to fifty-five (14.5%), and those over the age of fifty-five (15.5%).(See **Table 4**).

Age Range	Quantity	Percent
18-25 years old	19	6.4
26-35 years old	116	39.1
36-45 years old	73	24.6
46-55 years old	43	14.5
55+ years old	46	15.5
Total	**297**	**100.0**
Not Answered	2	

Table 4: Age of Participants

The majority of respondents (231) had completed one or more Master's degrees. Other educational levels represented included high school diplomas or GEDs (2), some college (9), Associate's degrees (1), Bachelor's degrees (39), law degrees (4), and doctoral degrees (11), including two in progress.

Recruitment and Introduction to LIS Field

Some individuals (N = 22) cited exposure to libraries as a library user during childhood or teen years as their introduction to library work. Others gained an introduction through direct, sustained interactions (N = 73), such as through interacting with a library employee in the context of a personal relationship or being employed as a student worker or paraprofessional prior to transitioning to another position. This included working or volunteering in libraries as teenagers, being employed in libraries as student assistants while undergraduate or graduate students, being employed as a paraprofessional before transitioning to a degreed position, or learning about librarianship as a potential career from family or friends who were employed in the LIS field.

> I was a para-professional for about 25 years. Always loved libraries. Decided to get my MLIS almost 15 years ago, and have been a librarian for 10 years. (R235)

Some respondents specifically mentioned librarians of color who had influenced their decisions to enter the field, while others talked about librarians and library staff in general. The individuals who these respondents encountered "all seemed to love their work and spoke of all the possibilities it held."

Motivations for entering and remaining in the field included core professional beliefs (N = 76), such as "access to information is a right for all"; a "passion for literacy"; being drawn to "the intellectual nature of the work"; and "the opportunity to work with new technologies." Additionally, many respondents (N = 25) spoke of motivations related to representation and critical librarianship, such as the desire to have a "seat at the table to support and ensure the voices" of others are heard; the desire to make "an impact socially"; recognizing the "need for brown faces in the field"; the desire to dedicate a "career to providing information services to communities of color and low-income folks"; and wanting library "users to feel like their voice is heard."

Compared to personal beliefs about the importance of inclusive practice, of those who reflected on LIS graduate experiences (N =25), many (N = 12) were dissatisfied with their LIS graduate studies in this regard. The biggest reasons (N = 10) were lack of diversity among LIS faculty, feeling unwelcomed and isolated as a POC in the MLS/MLIS/MIS program, and the lack of coverage of diversity, social justice, or critical perspectives in the LIS curriculum. It was "[a]s if it had not yet occurred to anyone that it might be worthy of consideration." When they did take place, one respondent noted, "…most conversations about diversity turn into White Savior Complex, rather than thinking about community or agency for users."

Job Satisfaction

When asked to rate on a scale of one to five, 63.9% (191) of respondents indicated that they were either satisfied or highly satisfied with their current job. 26.1% (78) of respondents indicated that they were neither satisfied nor dissatisfied with their current job. 10% (30) of respondents indicated being dissatisfied or very dissatisfied with their current job. (See **Table 5**).

On a scale of one to five, how would you rate your satisfaction with your current job?		**Quantity**	**Percent**
Very Dissatisfied	1	10	3.3
	2	20	6.7
	3	78	26.1
	4	131	43.8
Very Satisfied	5	60	20.1
Total		**299**	**100.0**

Table 5: Job Satisfaction

For WOC who were employed in paraprofessional or pre-MLIS positions (N = 64), there was general job satisfaction (N = 36) due to having their ideas respected, being provided autonomy, and having positive relationships with colleagues and administration. However, even among those who enjoyed their jobs, respondents (N = 14) widely discussed a desire for more stable employment, increased salaries, and a better workplace environment.

> I like what I do, but at my place of employment, professional development is not really encouraged for me in particular. (R258)

These issues led to feeling undervalued or stunted in career development opportunities. There was a lack of recognition of expertise and potential among WOC in these positions, which left them feeling like their "skills and experience are often underestimated." This devaluing of paraprofessional labor manifested itself in compensation levels, as well as general assumptions about professional aspirations and interests.

> As a library assistant, I was not taken seriously. After many years as an assistant I was not paid and at one point did not recieve [sic] a raise for 10 years. It was only after I received a MLIS did I get a raise, doing the same job I had done for the past 19 years. (R230)

Those who felt neutrally (N = 22) and those who were not satisfied with their jobs (N = 6) attributed it to the desire to be "paid more," not being "given the opportunity to advance," irregular hours, and "no respect for those without an MLS."

> I am overlooked and not promoted to better or full-time positions over my co-workers. In fact, I often feel that my work and experience isn't respected, as the higher-ups do not care about my opinions, despite my years of experience and my ability to assist patrons of all backgrounds successfully. (R131)

Among post-MLIS professionals, job satisfaction was rated highly (N = 141) compared to neutral feelings (N = 60) and negative feelings (N = 28) about the workplace. Positive satisfaction was related to feeling "respected and appreciated," having a "supportive environment," positive relationships with colleagues and administrators, the type of work performed, user populations, and "advancement opportunities."

> My encounters with patrons are mostly positive. I have met a lot of wonderful people while working in libraries. Right now my boss is flexible, open to new ideas and willing to mentor and guide me. (R86)

Dissatisfactions tended to run along the same lines. Respondents (N = 59) indicated a wish for more challenging work, opportunities for advancement, better relationships with colleagues and administration, and a more diverse and inclusive workplace.

> I find my work challenging and exciting, but I find it difficult to be "very satisfied" because of my colleagues. (R42)

Salary was a common theme (N = 31) among those in both pre- and post-MLIS roles. Respondents expressed frustration with compensation, workload, cost of living, and budget cuts.

> I love variety in my work, which is a large part of my job, however, I'm currently doing the job sometimes of 4 people as my organization is very small. I would like to be compensated more for this situation. (R162)

Though it occurred less often (N = 11), the theme of community is noteworthy. Being part of communities that were "hostile towards differences" or "super white" was regarded as unsatisfactory, while being part of a "multicultural community" was attributed to feelings of satisfaction. In some cases, respondents with concerns about their work or home community environments were motivated to find something that was a better fit for their needs.

> Out of 530 employees, only 44 are African American. Out of those 44 African American employees there are only two in management—I am a supervisory librarian and there is an African American female Assistant Branch Manager. I've only been working with this library system for 11 months. I moved here to be with my husband but we are actively looking to move where there is more diversity. The library director is young, new, and would like to see more diversity however there is a layer

of administrators directly below him who have been in place for twenty years and they don't share the same views. (R198)

Career Satisfaction

When asked about their rate of satisfaction with the LIS field as a whole, 59.9% (178) of respondents indicated that they were either satisfied or very satisfied with the field in general. 33.7% (100) of respondents indicated being neither satisfied nor dissatisfied with the LIS field overall. 6.4% (19) of respondents reported being either dissatisfied or very dissatisfied with the field overall (see **Table 6**).

On a scale of one to five, how would you describe your satisfaction with the library and information science field?		Quantity	Percent
Very Dissatisfied	1	7	2.4
	2	12	4.0
	3	100	33.7
	4	121	40.7
Very Satisfied	5	57	19.2
Total		**297**	**100.0**
Not Answered		2	

Table 6: Career Satisfaction

The majority of library workers employed in paraprofessional or pre-MLIS roles (N = 63) were satisfied or very satisfied (N =38) with the LIS field, as compared to those who were neutral (N = 20) and those who were dissatisfied or very dissatisfied (N = 5). Positive satisfaction was attributed to being part of a "welcoming and supportive professional community," opportunities for "professional and intellectual growth," the ability to help "patrons with info needs," and focus within the "profession [...] about social justice issues." Criticisms (N = 39), including from those who indicated being satisfied with the field, were attributed largely to no "room for advancement," "lack of inclusiveness," and being "not accept[ed]...as equal" with librarian colleagues.

> I love the work, love the patrons, love the programming. I hate training a never-ending stream of young white women and seeing them get promoted before me year after year. (R59)

Individuals employed in post-MLIS positions (N = 172) were primarily satisfied or very satisfied (N = 97) with the LIS field, as compared to those who were neutral (N = 64) and those who were dissatisfied or very dissatisfied (N = 11). A significant number who described themselves as satisfied or very satisfied still had critiques of the field (N = 48). Satisfaction was attributed to "providing information and services to those in need," a field that is "vibrant and ever changing," and the ability to focus on "social justice matters." Criticisms (N = 120) included a "lack of diversity" in the field, difficulty "making a livable salary," "stagnation within the profession," and "the field as a whole [being] slow to adapt."

> I still love libraries, how they are developing and what they stand for. However, there is a lot of passivity and slow bureaucracy. I feel we encourage and support students but then after graduation it can be a different story, especially as an early career. We have such great perspective as professionals, but are often behind the curve and are not good at marketing ourselves/showcasing our value AT ALL. We are often grossly disconnected from our users. I think we focus on the wrong things a lot and it's disappointing. However, I want to be patient with the profession. I don't know what else I would do and feel passionately about libraries, especially colleagues, specific libraries and projects I do admire. (R58)

The largest emerging theme across both pre-MLIS and post-MLIS library workers was the lack of diversity and inclusion efforts (N = 61) in the field.

> Our stated values of diversity and social justice don't seem to match up to our visible values. I really dislike having to argue with my colleagues about how social justice does or doesn't fit into our work. It IS the foundation of our work, how is that still a question? (R301)

As with job-level discussions, compensation levels were discussed in relation to the LIS field (N = 21).

> Its [sic] good work if you enjoy it but sometimes its [sic] hard to make a living wage. (R205)

Other common themes were innovation and technology (N = 30) in the LIS field. This related to opportunities for individual innovation, as well as openness to change across the discipline.

> I feel that we really struggle to keep up with technological developments at alarmingly variable rates. On one side of the spectrum, there are those institutions that are on the cutting edge, are nimble enough to make the desired changes to keep up with technology, and are well-resourced; and on the other side of the spectrum, there are institutions struggling to meet basic service needs. (R93)

Some respondents mentioned the need for libraries to better market themselves (N = 8).

> I enjoy the field, but I wish it was made more accessible to those who don't understand it. Many of my friends think I sit at a desk and read all day. People have told me that in the age of the internet, library science is not important. (R239)

Challenges as Women of Color

31.2% (92) of respondents reported having experienced racial discrimination on the job. 35.6% (105) of respondents had not experienced racial discrimination on the job, while 33.2% (98) were unsure whether they had experienced racial discrimination on the job.

Respondents (N = 82) described experiencing microaggressions through interactions with library users, colleagues, and/or administrators, which led to feelings of being "marginalized and over-looked."

> A boss asked me once if I knew any other Indian who could read and would like to work in the library. I've had people insult my intelligence on numerous occasions but feel comfortable asking me very personal

> questions about what it's like to be Indian, uh I mean Native, uh I mean what do you call yourself? (R279)

Microaggressions were used by White colleagues or administrators to silence WOC when they attempted to critique "some unfairness" in libraries. Examples from Black women (N = 43) included having their abilities questioned or being perceived "as the angry black woman" when they "challenge[d] a decision or disagree[d] with something." Multiracial women (N = 13) described encounters such as "often [being] ask[ed] what my nationality is" and hearing "racial slurs" used by colleagues and library users. Latinas (N = 15) provided examples such as being "labeled pushy or too aggressive during simple interactions" or receiving "dismissive, condescending reactions" to their input. Asian (N = 9) women described being subjected to "common Asian & woman stereotypes," having their authority and contributions undermined, and being constantly asked, "what's your nationality?" among other responses. Indigenous women (N = 2) recounted being "asked a lot of uncomfortable questions" and receiving "a lot of inappropriate comments from patrons." Some respondents simply reported experiencing microaggressions, but did not detail specifics.

Many women reflected on whiteness (N = 55) and recounted stories of "White defensiveness around issues of race." Attempting to address realities, one respondent observed that "people get uncomfortable and try to push the conversation around to how they feel." Silencing was exemplified through a "white co-worker's word or a male co-worker's word" being "weighted more heavily," as ideas originally shared by WOC were co-opted and then accepted from the lips of White colleagues.

For some WOC, "trying do [sic] decipher white female code and cultural norms" was an added source of labor, causing them to feel "like I'm crashing a party that I wasn't really invited to." Exclusion from colleagues and supervisors caused individuals to feel out of place and not wanted. There was a feeling of facing an invisible "barrier" that made it "more difficult [...] to make connections." This could take the form of cliques among White professional peers or lack of information sharing, in which

WOC were not made aware of information that could be pertinent to career growth, causing them to miss out on opportunities and promotions. Additionally, it was perceived that White colleagues' "expectations were low," and WOC reported feeling the need to "redeem" themselves and "prove that I know what I am doing." Through codeswitching, WOC related having to alter their approach in order to be perceived as less threatening and going out of their way to "word something differently or speak clearly with less bass...to be non-intimidating."

A recurring theme was "feeling like the token voice having to represent all minorities," while also being the voice of reason to White colleagues and holding them accountable for the things they say and do, as well as the things they opt not to say and do.

> Furthermore, as a woman of color you are expected to be a [sic] advocate at all times. At times, you just want to be a person and attend meetings without having to raise your hand as [sic] asking why we aren't discussing certain issues that only affect minorities. When complaining in private, responses are often "how come you didn't say anything?" And I ask myself "why didn't somebody, not a POC, say anything?" (R295)

This expectation to be "the voice" detracted from time spent on other professional endeavors, which was described as being taxing to WOC.

> I often feel like I'm looked to, to bear this burden or point us in the right direction—or as a pulse check—when that kind of expectation can be stressful and tiring over time unless more and more people take up that burden. I totally get why librarians of color over time back away from participating on initiatives and conversations about social justice and diversity and inclusivity. There's too much to do and such flimsy support or perceived value. (R243)

Respondents mentioned feeling like they were pigeonholed into doing diversity work or working with populations of color and not being recognized as valuable contributors to the field in other areas.

> I love what I do, I love working with my people, however I have requested lateral transfers when positions became available at other branches in order to shorten my commute and it's always the same, "But we need

> you at that specific location because the community can identify with you…" (R21)

But at the same time, WOC recognized that they did have a connection, in many cases, with communities of color, and that they could be sought out to provide services, especially in instances where White colleagues were perceived as not understanding or not being sensitive to specific library users' needs. However, WOC felt they were "not given credit for" the added value they brought to the profession. An example of this is being called upon to use "language skills and outreach skills, without any extra compensation" and "[l]ack of incentives for being bicultural and bilingual."

> I am always looked to for the emotional labor of supporting students of color. I am always asked about diversity and inclusion initiatives even when I am not doing that work. I must know my job and the job of every other black person on a campus. (R170)

Respondents felt that there was "[u]ndervaluing of contributions" and that they "have to work twice as hard" to prove that their work was valuable, or that research interests in area studies, for academic librarians, were valid.

Some women reported working at historically minority-serving institutions, or very diverse institutions, where it was not "as challenging as it is for others" with regard to racial isolation or mistreatment.

> I think I'm more fortunate than many because my boss is a woman of color and out of 10 faculty librarians, five of us are of color. Our college president and a good deal of the top administration and faculty are also of color (as well as most of the college staff and nearly 100% of our students), so I don't face the same challenges that someone in a White-dominated institution would face. (R229)

The lack of mentoring relationships (N = 17) was another recurring theme: "[h]aving a mentor is extremely important when starting a professional position in the library." Some were more specific about not only wanting support navigating the professional world, but also wanting it from "someone who has gone through what I'm going through and can offer advice from the perspective of WOC." Other women stated that being a mentor allowed them to contribute back to the next generations of LIS professionals and "become the supportive mentor" that they "struggled to find" earlier in their careers. A few related feeling conflicted about recruiting other POC into LIS because of ongoing issues and lack of support. Many women mentioned the importance of connecting with "other women of color in the profession who have been in the field much longer [...] and who are wonderful role models and mentors."

When asked about the impact of workplace challenges related to race and gender, the two greatest responses were feeling discouraged and disengaged (N = 41) and feeling the need to work twice as hard (N = 40). Other high ranking responses included increasing the desire to effect change within the LIS profession (N = 30); increased likelihood of negative effect on workplace relationships with colleagues (N = 25); decreased feeling of belonging (N = 25); increased assertiveness (N = 23); seeking supportive communities of color in the profession (N = 23); increased desire to change jobs or careers (N = 22); feeling pigeonholed or stuck (N= 20); and feeling fatigued or stressed regarding work (N = 20).

> The levels of stress and the constant distractions, when I can no longer ignore the issues, take away from time I can use for professional development. I have spoken to both my manager and director and no resolutions are ever met so the incidents continue and interfere with how quickly projects are completed. I know how efficiently I work, so seeing a project drag on that I could have completed sooner frustrates me. The sense of being held back due to my race, gender and age are overwhelming and the effect on my emotional and mental health are beginning to show in my physical health. I have tried to view these set backs [sic] as a learning curve to reach the top the fastest. I hope this is not the norm. (R78)

Other responses of note included decreased opportunities for professional development (N = 16); feelings of anger or frustration (N = 15); and decreased productivity (N = 14).

> I am allowed to grow to a certain point that is beneficial to my supervisor, but not to me. I have to stay in my lane. Whenever I try to advance in

> the profession, I am met with resistance. That resistance takes the form of decreased professional development. (R284)

Constantly being scrutinized, excluded, and dismissed led to feelings of "overall uncertainty about my merits and qualifications, and about how I am valued and perceived by my peers." Though they possessed diverse skillsets and talents, WOC felt their institutions saw them as "only of value for a few things (like diversity work)." At the same time, WOC saw it as imperative for libraries and information institutions to do diversity work, because "if we're not here doing this hard work and challenging people and their assumptions than [sic] nothing gets done and we look less and less in touch with our patrons." Having the sole or primary responsibility for this work placed on library staff of color created expectations that "can be stressful and tiring over time."

Retention

When asked to rate intent to remain in the field for the next five years, 73.4% (218) of respondents indicated that they were either likely or very likely to remain in the field over the next five years. 14.8% (44) of respondents indicated that they were neither likely nor unlikely to remain in the field. 11.8% (35) of respondents indicated that they were either unlikely or very unlikely to remain in the field over the next five years.

Compensation (N = 48) was often discussed in relation to retention. Being underpaid led to feelings of being undervalued. Respondents related that it is "hard to make a living wage," especially for those who live in high-cost urban areas, those who do not live in dual-income households, and those who single parent. Another issue related to compensation was the trend of libraries' hiring strategies and the effect on paraprofessionals and professionals alike.

> The pay isn't that great, either. I cannot afford to support myself with just my income, and I currently work part-time at two organizations, a public library and an academic library, because, unfortunately, they don't hire many people full-time, except the ones they like or create positions for. (R131)

Many women (N = 46) mentioned wanting the "opportunity to advance" and take on more responsibilities, including those who were "doing the work on [sic] a librarian/archivist" at the pay rate and position title of a paraprofessional.

> The only thing I can imagine that could change my mind about this field is if I cannot move up. My career and title have been stagnant. I need to be at the next level of my career, as a true librarian, or at least a manager or director something-er-other. If I'm unable to break through and get a FT job with those responsibilities and a title, I may look around at where else I can use my skills. (R140)

Availability of jobs (N = 40) was a strong factor in retention for women who were seeking to transition workplaces or positions, as was continued job satisfaction (N = 20) for those who preferred to stay at their current place of employment.

Sense of belonging and proximity to community was another topic that surfaced often; LIS initiatives related to diversity and inclusion (N = 15) and more inclusive workplaces (N = 14) were particularly valued. WOC related that they often felt like they were "the only" and felt "like a speck of pepper in a sea of salt." Location (N = 9) was important to women who lived in regions of the United States where they were the "only woman of color" and felt isolated.

> It can feel a little lonely sometimes working in places where I am one of few people of color. Right now I live in the Midwest, and there are so few librarians of color, I can probably count the number on my hands. (R209)

Personal reasons related to family and health accounted for some uncertainty (N = 12), including those who had to balance a partner's career or manage work-life balance related to child-rearing. This included responses such as "i'm [sic] struggling to find a career that can be fulfilling but also gives room for me to raise my family" and "I am actively seeking to leave the field because I must stay in the area due to my husband's work."

Some women (N = 35) already had plans or were willing to consider leaving the field in the near future. Retirement (N = 27) was another reason for departure, though some indicated a desire to remain involved with the field "on a part time basis" afterwards. A significant number (N = 41) had no plans or desire to leave the field at all.

Relationship with Administration

When asked to rate the quality of their relationship with their administration, 57.4% (168) of respondents reported having a good or very good relationship with their administrators. 33.4% (98) of respondents reported that their relationship with administration was neither good nor bad. 9.2% (27) of respondents indicated their relationship with their administration was either bad or very bad.

Respondents who witnessed effective administration (N = 174) described it as open communication (N = 46), good management skills (N = 41), positive working relationships with colleagues and reporting staff (N = 38), demonstrating value for contributions of staff (N =15), accessibility by staff (N = 15), establishing trust (N = 8), transparency around actions and decision making (N = 8), and promoting inclusivity in the workplace (N = 5). Those with positive relationships with administrators ascribed it most often to mutual respect, understanding, and concerted effort on behalf of those in leadership to build relationships with staff, making it "easy for me to sit down and discuss this [sic] issues with my supervisor." Respondents also appreciated "a fair amount of flexibility to pursue projects" within interest areas.

> I report to an Asst. VP of the college. Very open door policy. Listens and allows me and the staff to do whatever we feel is best for our students and faculty. This includes securing the funding. Our college president is like that also. VERY supportive of libraries and me personally. I have a personal relationship with both and there is mutual respect. (R27)

Respondents who witnessed ineffective administration (N = 127), described it as a lack of open communication (N = 25), poor management skills (N = 25), lack of inclusivity in the workplace (N = 19), lack of accessibility by staff (N = 16), negative working relationships with colleagues or staff (N = 11), lack of transparency around actions and decision making (N = 7), demonstrating a lack of value for contributions of staff (N = 7), lack of trust (N = 6), disruption by workplace politics (N = 5), inability to address or resolve conflicts in the workplace (N = 4), and lack of respect for staff (N =2). Poor relationships with administration most often resulted from feeling undervalued, unheard, and unsupported, prompting one librarian to wish that "more people felt they could offer honest critique to administration."

> Our Dean supports diversity and inclusivity, but she's incredibly uncomfortable with conflict and often avoids it. I truly believe she appreciates when I speak up with my perspective, but she's reticent to make any meaningful change in this area. Instead, her solutions throw this work back on those who identify in marginalized groups. (R93)

Advancement

The majority, 65.1% (192), of respondents indicated they were either likely or very likely to seek a more advanced position within the next five years, while 20% (59) of respondents reported being unlikely or very unlikely to seek a more advanced position within the next five years. 14.9% (44) reported being neither likely nor unlikely to seek a more advanced position within the next five years.

When asked about desire to pursue library or archives administration, 22.1% (66) indicated that they were definitely interested. 40.1% (120) of respondents were unsure, and 24.4% (73) were not interested in pursuing administration. 12.7% (38) of respondents were already employed in administrative positions.

The majority of respondents indicated that they were either interested in pursuing administration (N = 41) or possibly open to it (N =72), as compared to those who were not interested at all (N = 34). Of women who were interested in seeking more advanced positions, one of the biggest factors was a desire to effect change in the LIS field (N = 27).

> I used to be reluctant about taking on leadership roles but I realize if I want things to change for the better I have to be willing to step up and do. To lead, essentially. (R88)

Other high-ranking factors included aptitude and fit for the job (N = 17), the availability of opportunities for employment (N = 14), and increasing the representation of POC in administration (N = 11).

> There's [sic] not many POC in administrative roles. I hear a lot of my colleagues who dislike some of the directives from their administrators. One main reason is that their administrators are not from [Location]; they do not have the cultural competency or historical understanding to work well with staff or even patrons. Not many of my colleagues want to take on such high position because of the stress involved. I see it as a necessity to have more POC in these administrative roles, especially when the staff is quite diverse. (R100)

Availability of professional development and training (N = 9), and personal and family issues (N = 5) are also worth mentioning.

For those who were interested in gaining administrative positions, the factors seen as most predictive of success were experience (N = 44), training and professional development (N = 39), networking (N = 23), mentorship (N = 22), obtaining more education (N = 20), being provided with opportunities (N = 16), and having support from colleagues and present administrators (N = 16).

> I need more experience, mostly. To get that experience, I'll need future employers to see how my skills are transferable, even if I haven't worked in the same type of library or position. I've also been working on building a network, and would like to widen and strengthen that. Then I just need to take the leap and apply for positions. (R11)

Also mentioned as significant was the ability to fine-tune communication and interpersonal skills (N = 15), self-development and personal growth (N = 10), and self-advocacy (N = 9).

> Effective communication; openness to change; commitment to the profession and valuing professional development in all areas of the library; developing positive and working relationships with colleagues; the ability to delegate and trusting others to do their job while also providing constructive feedback if needed are some of the most important in becoming an administrator. I also do feel that a good library administrator should have reasonable experience as a practitioner and should hold an MLIS/MLS. (R159)

Of interest were those (N = 4) who felt some measure of codeswitching or shrinking oneself was important to being successful in LIS administration.

> Making waves that are big enough to cause change, but not cause me to [sic] branded (again) as "sassy" or "bossy" or something else people see as negative. (R29)

This included "being able to be the right amount of white" and making attempts to appear less confrontational.

Discussion

Having a connection to the LIS field seemed to be a motivating factor for WOC to consider it as a professional career option. Even more impactful was having a prior connection to another librarian of color. Additionally, for those who recalled utilizing library services as a child or teen, they were able to draw upon models of good librarianship while envisioning their own professional practice. The potential for recruiting from undergraduate and graduate student employees may be an untapped pipeline. Not everyone is going to be interested in the LIS field as a profession, but the exposure to librarianship may serve a dual purpose of allowing students greater access to information sources and the skills to utilize them, and providing an opportunity to explore library work in a low-stakes setting.

An intrinsic motivation to improve efforts relating to diversity and inclusion creates communities of passionate professionals with vision. This vision, often combined with a desire to provide quality services for underrepresented communities, points back to multicultural feminisms and the value of community.[88] Womanism and mujerista both emphasize community uplift. WOC in LIS indicated a desire to positively impact communities by providing access to information and resources. Some

---

88. Evangelina Holvino, "Intersections: The Simultaneity of Race, Gender and Class in Organization Studies," *Gender, Work & Organization* 17, no. 3 (May 2010): 252.

spoke specifically about the desire to be present for students of color and provide emotional and academic support.[89] WOC may see themselves as community activists through an emphasis on building the community as "loving warriors."[90] Many women mentioned their passion for community and desire to create opportunities for those who resemble them or with whom they have a shared heritage.

The LIS field is sometimes described as a social justice field—one in which librarians and library staff create access to information in a variety of formats with the belief that libraries are a public good and that archives should preserve and share stories. Practices, though, do not always align well with beliefs. Fobazi Ettarh speaks of "vocational awe," which causes the LIS field to be regarded as "inherently good."[91] This type of elevated self-assessment from within the LIS field makes critique and subsequent improvement extremely difficult. There has been increased discussion in the LIS field around the lack of attention to social justice and inclusive practices. Currently, individual organizations such as the Association of College and Research Libraries (ACRL) and the Young Adult Library Services Association (YALSA) have developed resources that highlight cultural competency as a professional value, but there has been no larger adoption of these values as part of ALA-accredited graduate programs. Given that the discussion of race and systemic inequity is not a socially accepted norm, the opportunity to build cultural competency, self-awareness, and critical reflection could be invaluable for new and continuing professionals. WOC expressed concern that colleagues' lack of awareness and cultural competency within the workplace not only affected professional relationships, but also influenced the quality of information services provided, as well as outreach to library users.

---

89. Wyche, "Womanist Research," 34.

90. Thelma Bryant-Davis and Lillian Comas-Diaz, "Introduction," in *Womanist and Mujerista Psychologies*, ed. Thelma Bryant-Davis and Lillian Comas-Diaz (Washington, DC: American Psychological Association, 2016), 18.

91. Fobazi Ettarh, "Vocational Awe?" - *WTF is a Radical Librarian Anyway?*, May 30, 2017, https://fobaziettarh.wordpress.com/2017/05/30/vocational-awe/.

WOC who faced explicit and implicit discrimination reported feeling less valued and included in their workplaces, as well as in the profession as a whole. These invalidating experiences were present in interactions with peers and those in authority, leaving WOC feeling that they had no voice in their organizations. The use of stereotypes to silence and shame women echoes intersectional oppression, while expectations of "performing diversity" perpetuate racism through expectation of labor. Those from privileged identity groups have the choice to opt out of labor expectations, while those from historically oppressed groups do not. Likewise, the co-opting of ideas and lack of compensation for language skills and cultural knowledge promotes an exploitive labor model. Lack of attention from those in leadership when issues are raised by WOC communicates tacit approval of these models.

Vernā Myers says that "diversity is coming to the party, while inclusion is actually being invited to dance."[92] For too many WOC, they are allowed in the workplace—maybe even given a seat at the table — but their presence is tolerated rather than welcomed, and their voices are not respected. Relationships with professional peers are reported as not rewarding, since WOC are often kept at a distance. Many WOC reported not being offered the same sort of opportunities or even knowing that those opportunities existed. Often, they were not provided with the resources to take advantage of opportunities that would further their professional development. Again, this echoes inequitable labor practices in a subtle nod to racist ideologies that would expect POC to perform, but not provide them with the tools to do so.

There was a clear divide observed between expectations and treatment of those in pre-MLIS positions as compared to those in post-MLIS positions. While feeling undervalued was a theme among WOC in general,

92. Vernā Meyers, "Diversity is Being Invited to the Party; Inclusion is Being Asked to Dance," in *Moving Diversity Forward: How to go From Well-Meaning to Well-Doing*, ed. Verna Myers (Chicago: ABA Book Publishing, 2011), 5, retrieved from https://www.americanbar.org/groups/gpsolo/publications/gpsolo_ereport/2012/june_2012/diversity_invited_party_inclusion_asked_dance.html.

those in pre-MLIS positions struggled with advancement and lack of opportunities for professional growth.

WOC reported feeling as if they were always "on": having to maintain their own workload, ensure that communities of color were being given appropriate consideration, and provide education and feedback to White colleagues and administrators. Along with that, the pressure to constantly perform at high levels led to fatigue from trying to maintain a "two times" as hard a pace. Because communities of color have always been judged more harshly, POC in the United States have developed coping mechanisms to anticipate and strategically address discrimination. This sort of strategic action was demonstrated by respondents, but often negatively impacted administrators' perception of their value as a sustainable investment for the workplace.

In order to provide work environments that demonstrate value for all employees, a greater emphasis should be placed on awareness of the need for more diverse staff, as well as ways in which privileged identities interact with historically oppressed identities. Operating in ignorance, while comfortable for those from majority cultures, could be causing library staff and administration to unknowingly replicate relationships that cause harm and exacerbate trauma for staff of color. This creates a workplace that is not supportive and reduces the likelihood of retention.

Income disparities in the LIS field are not unique to WOC. However, because many communities of color have been prevented from accumulating wealth, hardships that arise from obtaining advanced degrees and pressure to work in under- or un-compensated jobs as new professionals have a unique impact on those from lower to low-middle income backgrounds.[93] This may lead to working multiple jobs out of necessity, which then contributes to burnout and fatigue. Part of communicating value to individuals is paying fair living wages, taking into account regional cost of living, and ensuring that pay is equitable along gender and race lines.

93. Holvino, "Intersections," 252.

Mentorship is another theme that surfaced often. Many WOC didn't just want professional support for LIS issues, they had overlapping concerns about navigating the workplace as a woman of color and dealing with the issues that accompany that existence. Positing mentoring and networking with library staff of color circles as "collectives" in which WOC "empower and strengthen themselves" and share "knowledge and wisdom" with other WOC allows for a richer understanding of the desire for mentoring relationships and in-group community building.[94] Just being present within the profession creates a protest for change.

WOC who seek to lead face the reality that they are less likely to be perceived as effective leaders because of implicit bias, which is important to keep in mind when discussing issues like mentorship, rising through the ranks, and professional experience.[95] What roadblocks exist to WOC's success and how can these roadblocks be dismantled? Individuals with an orientation to social justice and those who possess strengths-based and resiliency models[96] are well-equipped to lead and advocate for change in structures that are in need of change. The skills that are highly valued for effective leadership are ones that are born of intersectional feminist, womanist, and mujerista orientations. Additionally, lived experiences of injustice coupled with successful in-community leadership provides WOC with skillsets that are difficult to find elsewhere. It is opportunity that makes a difference. Discrimination is a big factor in this lack of opportunity.[97]

94. Bryant-Davis and Comas-Diaz, "Introduction," 13.

95. Malba J.T. Vasquez, "The Value of Promoting Womanist and Mujerista Leaders," in Womanist and Mujerista Psychologies, ed. Thelma Bryant-Davis and Lillian Comas-Diaz (Washington, DC: American Psychological Association, 2016), 265.

96. Resiliency is used here to speak of within-group cultural practices, in which members of the group recount or create narratives of overcoming as a coping or empowerment strategy.

97. Vasquez, "The Value of Promoting Womanist and Mujerista Leaders," 265.

Conclusion

Despite the challenges they face, WOC overwhelmingly remain present and invested in the LIS field. They believe in the missions and goals of the LIS profession, but believe there is potential for the profession to do so much more. Some of the most recurrent issues mentioned were the lack of diversity and feelings of isolation in their professional communities, as well as feeling silenced and undervalued. The desire for greater inclusion came not just from a personal perspective, but from a desire to better represent the communities with whom they work. These changes cannot be enacted by WOC alone and, as evidenced by the survey responses, such implicit expectations from White administrators and colleagues prove fatiguing to WOC and exacerbate the systemic issues that already exist. Meaningful engagement and willingness to go beyond surface discussions of diversity and inclusion are needed if change is to be made.

Social identities appear to have a large impact on how WOC experience the workplace and influence the decisions they make regarding job performance, professional development, advancement, and retention. More research in this area, particularly looking expressly at the experiences of WOC in pre-MLIS positions and WOC in public libraries is needed.

Our work was limited by some factors. We did not ask survey respondents to describe the type of library or institution in which they were employed (e.g., public or academic), though some respondents indicated this within the context of their answers. We also did not gather data on region, which might have been beneficial in determining whether or not job satisfaction differed based on location and type of community (e.g., urban or rural).

Because our survey questions did not specifically ask respondents to reflect on the meaning they crafted from gender and gender expression in their own lives, this chapter did not contain an in-depth analysis of gender identities in the workplace. There is an extreme shortage of research situated at the intersection of queer theory, feminist theory, and critical race theory, and how they operate within the realm of LIS professional practice. We definitely see this as an area for potential research and hope to delve more deeply into gendered existence in the workplace in future research.

Our hope is to be able to develop this project into a book based on the experiences of WOC in LIS. We have a number of interviews that we captured as part of this study, which we would like to transcribe, analyze, and share. In addition, due to time constraints and decisions we made about the scope of this chapter, we did not include survey data on self-care. We would like to analyze and share the survey results on self-care in future publications, as well as continue to explore the complexities of race, ethnicity, gender, and class in professional practice and what that means for WOC in LIS.

Bibliography

Adichie, Chimamanda Ngozi. "The Danger of a Single Story," TED Talk: TEDGlobal 2009. https://www.ted.com/talks/chimamanda_adichie_the_danger_of_a_single_story.

Alabi, Jaena. "Racial Microaggressions in Academic Libraries: Results of a Survey of Minority and Non-minority Librarians." *Journal of Library Administration* 41 (January 2015): 47-53.

Alabi, Jaena. "'This Actually Happened': An Analysis of Librarians' Responses to a Survey about Racial Microaggressions." *Journal of Library Administration* 55, no. 3 (April 2015): 179-191.

American Library Association. "Member Demographics Study." Last modified January 2017. Accessed May 15, 2017. http://www.ala.org/research/initiatives/membershipsurveys.

Barnes, Riché J. "Black Professional Women, Careers, and Family 'Choice.'" In *Raising the Race: Black Career Women Redefine Marriage, Motherhood, and Community*, 53-86. Rutgers: Rutgers University Press, 2015.

Boyd, Angela, Yolanda Blue and Suzanne Im. "Evaluation of Academic Library Residency Programs in the United States for Librarians of Color." *College & Research Libraries*, 78, no. 4 (2017): 472-511.

Bryant-Davis, Thelma, and Lillian Comas-Diaz. "Introduction." In *Womanist and Mujerista Psychologies*, edited by Thelma Bryant-Davis and Lillian Comas-Diaz, 3-25. Washington, DC: American Psychological Association, 2016.

Chan, Kim-Yin, and Fritz Drasgow. "Toward a Theory of Individual Differences and Leadership: Understanding the Motivation to Lead." *Journal of Applied Psychology*, 86, no. 3 (June 2001): 481-498.

Collins, Patricia Hill. "What's in a Name? Womanism, Black Feminism, and Beyond." *Black Scholar* 26, no. 1 (Winter/Spring, 1996): 9-17.

Collins, Patricia Hill. "The Politics of Black Feminist Thought." In *Black Feminist Thought.* New York: Routledge, 2000.

Collins, Patricia Hill. "Distinguishing Features of Black Feminist Thought." In *Black Feminist Thought*, 24-48. New York: Routledge, 2000.

Collins, Patricia Hill. "Work, Family, and Black Women's Oppression." In *Black Feminist Thought*, 51-75. New York: Routledge, 2000.

Comer, Edna W., Catherine K. Medina, Lirio K. Negroni, and Rebecca L. Thomas. "Women Faculty of Color in a Predominantly White Institution: A Natural Support Group." *Social Work with Groups* 40, no. 1-2 (January 2, 2017): 148-155.

"Concluding Remarks Regarding the Importance of a Racially Diverse Administrative Workforce." *ASHE Higher Education Report* 35, no. 3 (September 2009): 65-86.

Córdova, Teresa. "Anti-Colonial Chicana Feminism." *New Political Science* 20, no. 4 (December 1998): 379.

Damasco, Ione.T., and Dracine Hodges. "Tenure and Promotion Experiences of Academic Librarians of Color." *College & Research Libraries* 73, no. 3 (May 1, 2012): 279-301.

Dhawan, Nikita, and Maria do Mar Castro Varela. "What Difference Does Difference Make? Diversity, Intersectionality, and Transnational

Feminist Politics." *Wagadu: A Journal of Transnational Women's & Gender Studies* 16, (December 2016): 11-39.

Epps, Sharon K. "African American Women Leaders in Academic Research Libraries." *portal: Libraries and the Academy* no. 3 (2008): 255-272.

Ettarh, Fobazi. "Vocational Awe?" — *WTF is a Radical Librarian Anyway?* (blog). May 30, 2017. https://fobaziettarh.wordpress.com/2017/05/30/vocational-awe/.

Freedman, Shin, and Dawn Vreven. "Workplace Incivility and Bullying in the Library: Perception or Reality?" *College & Research Libraries* 77, no. 6 (November 2016): 727-748.

Fyn, Amy F. "Peer Group Mentoring Relationships and the Role of Narrative." *The Journal of Academic Librarianship* 39, (July 1, 2013): 330-334.

Goeman, Mishuana. "Indigenous Interventions and Feminist Methods." In *Sources and Methods in Indigenous Studies*, edited by Chris Andersen and Jean M. O'Brien, 178-184. New York: Routledge, 2017.

Hamidullah, Madinah F., and Norma M. Riccucci. "Intersectionality and Family-Friendly Policies in the Federal Government: Perceptions of Women of Color." *Administration and Society* 49, no. 1 (January 1, 2017): 105-120.

Harris-Perry, Melissa, "Crooked Room" In *Sister Citizen: Shame, Stereotypes and Black Women in America*, 28-50. New Haven, CT: Yale University Press, 2011.

Holvino, Evangelina. "Intersections: The Simultaneity of Race, Gender and Class in Organization Studies." *Gender, Work & Organization* 17, no. 3 (May 2010): 248-277.

Hughey, Matthew W., Jordan Rees, Devon R. Goss, Michael L. Rosino, and Emma Lesser. "Making Everyday Microaggressions: An Exploratory Experimental Vignette Study on the Presence and Power of Racial Microaggressions." *Sociological Inquiry* 87, no. 2 (May 2017): 303-336.

Johnson, Peggy. "Retaining and Advancing Librarians of Color." *College & Research Libraries* 68, no. 5 (September 2007): 405-417.

Juan, Mary Joyce D., Moin Syed, and Margarita Azmitia. "Intersectionality of Race/Ethnicity and Gender Among Women of Color and White Women." *Identity* 16, no. 4 (October 1, 2016): 225-238.

Minosh, Kai "(Re)building the Links Between Native Women and Women of Color." *BGD Blog*, November 3, 2016. Accessed May 31, 2017. https://www.bgdblog.org/2016/11/native-women-and-women-of-color/.

Kim, Kyung-Sun and Sei-Ching Joanna Sin. "Recruiting and Retaining Students of Color in LIS Programs: Perspectives of Library and Information Professionals." *Journal of Education for Library and Information Science* 47, no. 2 (2006): 81-95.

Lopez, Johana P. "Speaking with Them or Speaking for Them: A Conversation about the Effect of Stereotypes in the Latina/Hispanic Women's Experiences in the United States." *New Horizons in Adult Education & Human Resource Development* 25, no. 2 (Spring 2013): 99-106.

Luna, Zakiya. "Truly a Women of Color Organization": Negotiating Sameness and Difference in Pursuit of Intersectionality." *Gender and Society* 30, no. 5 (October 1, 2016): 769-790.

Meyers, Vernã. "Diversity is Being Invited to the Party; Inclusion is Being Asked to Dance." In *Moving Diversity Forward: How to go From Well-Meaning to Well-Doing* (Chicago: ABA Book Publishing, 2011), 5-13. Retrieved from https://www.americanbar.org/groups/gpsolo/publications/gpsolo_ereport/2012/june_2012/diversity_invited_party_inclusion_asked_dance.html.

Moya, Paula M.L. "Chicana Feminism and Postmodernist Theory." *Signs: Journal of Women in Culture & Society* 26, no. 2 (Winter 2001): 441-483.

Nadal, Kevin L., Silvia L. Mazzula, and David P. Rivera, "Microaggressions and Latino/a Americans: An Analysis of Nativity, Gender, and Ethnicity," *Journal of Latino/a Psychology* 2, no. 2 (2014) 67-78.

Nair, Sheila. "Women of Color Faculty and the 'Burden' of Diversity." *International Feminist Journal of Politics* 16, no. 3 (September 2014): 497-500.

Neely, Teresa Y., and Lorna Peterson. "Achieving Racial and Ethnic Diversity among Academic and Research Librarians: The Recruitment, Retention, and Advancement of Librarians of Color - A White Paper." *College & Research Libraries* News 68, no. 9 (October 2007): 562-565.

Nygreen, Kysa, Mariella Saba, and Ana Paulina Moreno. "Mujerista Research." In *Womanist and Mujerista Psychologies*, edited by Thelma Bryant-Davis and Lillian Comas-Diaz, 3-25. Washington, DC: American Psychological Association, 2016.

"On the Way to Diversity: Organizational Barriers." *ASHE Higher Education Report* 33, no. 1 (May 2007): 57-73.

Ong, Anthony D., Anthony L. Burrow, Thomas E. Fuller-Rowell, and Derald Sue. "Racial Microaggressions and Daily Well-Being among Asian Americans." *Journal of Counseling Psychology* 60, no. 2 (April 1, 2013): 188-199.

Owuamalam, Chuma Kevin, and Hanna Zagefka. "On the Psychological Barriers to the Workplace: When and Why Metastereotyping Undermines Employability Beliefs of Women and Ethnic Minorities." *Cultural Diversity & Ethnic Minority Psychology* 20, no. 4 (October 2014): 521-528.

Patel, Neesha R. "The Construction of South-Asian-American Womanhood: Implications for Counseling and Psychotherapy." *Women and Therapy* 30, no. 3-4 (June 25, 2007): 51-61.

Reynolds-Dobbs, Wendy, Kecia M. Thomas, and Matthew S. Harrison. "From Mammy to Superwoman: Images that Hinder Black Women's Career Development." *Journal of Career Development* 35, no. 2 (December 1, 2008): 129-150.

Sánchez, Patricia and Lucila D. Ek. "Cultivando la Siguiente Generación: Future Directions in Chicana/Latina Feminist Pedagogies." *Journal of Latino-Latin American Studies (JOLLAS)* 5, no. 3 (Winter 2013): 181-187.

Sanchez-Hucles, Janis V., and Donald D. Davis. "Women and Women of Color in Leadership." *American Psychologist* 65, no. 3 (April 2010): 171-181.

Selbin, Eric. "If You're Not Part of the Solution, You're Part of the Problem." *International Feminist Journal of Politics* 16, no. 3 (January 1, 2014): 505-507.

Speed, Shannon. "Representations of Violence: (Re)telling Indigenous Women's Stories and the Politics of Knowledge Production." In *Sources and Methods in Indigenous Studies*, edited by Chris Andersen and Jean M. O'Brien, 178-184. New York: Routledge, 2017.

Squire, Jan S. "Job Satisfaction and the Ethnic Minority Librarian." *Library Administration & Management* 5, no. 4 (Fall 1991): 194-203.

United States Census Bureau. "Race." Last Updated January 12, 2017. Accessed May 15, 2017. https://www.census.gov/topics/population/race/about.html.

Vasquez, Malba J.T. "The Value of Promoting Womanist and Mujerista Leaders." In *Womanist and Mujerista Psychologies*, edited by Thelma Bryant-Davis and Lillian Comas-Diaz, 3-25. Washington, DC: American Psychological Association, 2016.

Wilson, Eleanor. "Diversity, Culture and the Glass Ceiling." *Journal of Cultural Diversity* 21, no. 3 (Fall 2014): 83-89.

Wyche, Karen. "Womanist Research." In *Womanist and Mujerista Psychologies*, edited by Thelma Bryant-Davis and Lillian Comas-Diaz, 3-25. Washington, DC: American Psychological Association, 2016.

Yenpasook, Marissa, Annie Nguyen, Chia Her, and Valerie Ooka Peng. "Defiant: The Strength of Asian American and Pacific Islander Women." *In Killing the Model Minority Stereotype: Asian American Counterstories and Complicity*, edited by Nicholas Hartlep and Brad Porfilio, 61-80. Charlotte, NC: Information Age Publishing, 2015.

Yoo, Lindsay. "Feminism and Race: Just Who Counts As a 'Woman of Color'?". *NPR Code Switch.* Last updated September 12, 2013. Accessed May 31, 2017. http://www.npr.org/sections/codeswitch/2013/09/12/221469077/feminism-and-race-just-who-counts-as-a-woman-of-color.

Yosso, Tara. "Whose Culture has Capital? A Critical Race Theory Discussion of Community Cultural Wealth." *Race, Ethnicity & Education* 8, no. 1 (March 2005): 76.

Appendix: Survey Questions

Demographic Information

1. What is your racial identity? Check all that apply.
    - Asian or Native Pacific Islander
    - Black or African American
    - Native American, American Indian, or Alaska Native
    - White or European American
    - Other:
2. Do you identify as Hispanic or Latina? Mark only one oval.
    - Yes
    - No
3. Would you like to describe your racial or ethnic identity more specifically?
4. Are you currently a graduate student in an MLS/MLIS/MIS program? Mark only one oval.
    - Yes
    - No
5. Select the item(s) that most closely describe your position title. Check all that apply.
    - Library Assistant, Library Associate, or Library Technician
    - Archives Assistant, Archives Associate, or Archives Technician
    - Administrative Assistant

- Librarian
- Archivist
- Supervisory Librarian
- Department Head
- Branch Manager
- Assistant Director, Assistant University Librarian, or University Archivist
- Director, Dean, or University Librarian
- LIS Faculty
- Other:

6. Which item most closely describes your age range? Mark only one oval.

    - 18-25 years of age
    - 26-35 years of age
    - 36-45 years of age
    - 46-55 years of age
    - 55+ years of age

7. What is your highest level of education completed? Mark only one oval.

    - High school diploma or GED
    - Some college
    - Bachelor's degree
    - Master's degree
    - Doctoral degree
    - Other:

8. How many years have you worked in the LIS profession? Mark only one oval.

    - <1 year
    - 1-3 years
    - 3-5 years
    - 5-10 years
    - 10-15 years
    - 15-20 years
    - 20+ years

9. Have you ever been employed as a diversity resident or diversity fellow in a library or archives? Mark only one oval.

    - Yes
    - No

The Profession

10. What factors influenced your decision to work in the library and information science profession?

11. On a scale of one to five, how would you rate your satisfaction with your current job? Mark only one oval. (1= Very Dissatisfied; 5 = Very Satisfied)

12. Explain your rating.

13. On a scale of one to five, how would you describe your satisfaction with the library and information science field? Mark only one oval. (1= Very Dissatisfied; 5 = Very Satisfied)

14. Explain your rating.

Personal and Professional Identity

15. What specific challenges have you faced as a woman of color in the LIS profession?

16. How have these issues influenced or impacted your professional work?

17. Have you ever faced discrimination on the job on the basis of race or ethnicity? Mark only one oval.

    - Yes
    - No
    - Maybe

18. Please explain your answer.

Retention and Advancement

19. On a scale of one to five, how likely are you to remain in the field over the next five years? (1= Very Unlikely; 5 = Very Likely)

20. What factors might influence your decision on whether to remain in the field?

21. On a scale of one to five, how likely are you to seek a more advanced position within the next five years? This could include a promotion, more responsibility, or a transition from support staff to professional staff. Mark only one oval. (1 = Very Unlikely; 5 = Very Likely)

22. What factors might influence your desire to seek a more advanced position?

23. On a scale of one to five, how would you describe the quality of your relationship with your administration? For librar-

ians and library staff, this could be library administration. For teaching faculty, this could be the department chair or dean, etc. Mark only one oval. (1= Very Bad; 5 = Very Good)

24. What factors influence the quality of your relationship with your administration? For librarians and library staff, this could be library administration. For teaching faculty, this could be the department chair or dean, etc.
25. Do you desire to be employed as an administrator in the future? This could include a position in management at a library or archive, an LIS department chair or dean, etc. Mark only one oval.
    - Yes
    - No
    - Maybe
    - I'm already a library administrator
26. What factors might influence your desire to be employed in an administrative role?
27. If you are interested in administration, what factors do you think would be most important to successfully attaining this goal?

Self-Care

28. How would you define self-care?
29. How do you engage in self-care?
30. What self-care advice do you have for other women of color?

Chapter 9

Small Brown Faces in Large White Spaces

Rosalinda Hernandez Linares and Sojourna J. Cunningham

Introduction

In this chapter we will explore how multiculturalism in the field of academic librarianship is mobilized and what the shape of that mobilization can tell us about issues of identity and the body. As former resident librarians of color, we the authors felt unmoored by the expectations put upon us as diversity resident librarians for a multitude of reasons. We had to learn quickly, but not ask too many questions or else we would seem unprofessional; we had to be ambitious, but not be intimidating to our coworkers. Above all, we had to be successful, which allowed little room for error or discord. This is our attempt to pull back that narrative and use our voices to represent our full identity.

Diversity residency librarians are a product of pipeline initiatives that aim to increase the number of librarians from underrepresented racial and ethnic groups within the field of librarianship. Other pipeline initiatives include specific scholarships for librarians from underrepresented groups who are matriculating into library school, travel funds to library conferences, and residency, fellowship, and internship programs, which are pre- or post-degree professional work designed specifically for entry-level librarians.

Typically, participants in these programs represent intersections of race, ethnicity, and gender. They have struggled historically for recognition in terms of bodily presence in physical spaces and culturally distinct but overlapping identities within academia as a whole. Programs in academic librarianship that are specifically created to provide entry points into librarianship have often placed the onus of responsibility for representation of a specific racial or ethnic community upon their bodies and identities as they move through white-centered expectations of "what a librarian should be" within the academy.

In the mid 2000's, vocabularies that had been endemic in women's studies, gender and ethnic studies, and law began to enter the lexicon of library literature. As a result, terms like white supremacy, intersectionality, and microaggressions are now interrogated in relation to librarianship.[1] Throughout this work, we will apply the sociological term "person of color," which refers to racial and ethnic minority groups, to librarians who self-identify as non-white, by using the specific designation "librarians of color."[2] The usage of "librarian of color" has spread throughout the profession and is in use by the Ethnic Caucuses of the American Library Association (ALA) and affiliate groups: Asian/Pacific American Librarians Association (APALA), Black Caucus of the American Library Association (BCALA), Chinese American Librarians Association (CALA), National Association to Promote Library and Information Services to Latinos and the Spanish Speaking (REFORMA), and Progressive Librarians Guild. The usage of "librarian of color" was codified by the creation of the Joint Council of Librarians of Color (JCLC).[3]

---

1. David James Hudson, "On 'Diversity' as Anti-Racism in Library and Information Studies: A Critique," *Journal of Critical Library and Information Studies* no. 1 (2017); Jaena Alabi, "Racial Microaggressions in Academic Libraries: Results of a Survey of Minority and Non-Minority Librarians," *Journal of Academic Librarianship* 41, no. 1 (2015): 47-53; Michelle Caswell, "Teaching to Dismantle White Supremacy in Archives," *Library Quarterly* 87, no. 3 (2017): 222-235.

2. Richard T. Schaefer, *Encyclopedia of Race, Ethnicity, and Society* (Los Angeles: SAGE Publications, 2008).

3. American Library Association Executive Board, "ALA EXECUTIVE BOARD 2015 Fall Meeting Agenda," *Ebd* 9, no. 1 (2015).

In "Unpacking Identity: Racial, Ethnic and Professional Identity and Academic Librarians of Color," Gonzalez-Smith, Swanson, and Tanaka ask, "How do academic librarians of color perceive themselves in a predominantly white profession, and how can we interpret those perceptions to better understand their experiences?"[4] We intend to extend this critical and essential work with a specific, race-gendered lens on perception and identity formation that have been influenced by systemic barriers, specifically the problematic legacies of both early-career programs for librarians of color and issues of retention stemming from historic racism, sexism, and homophobia in the academy.

In this chapter, based on our exploratory research, we consider the legacy of the language and rhetoric of multiculturalism in higher education and in doing so, we interrogate the relationship between multiculturalism and pipeline programs in academic librarianship. Through this rhetoric, librarians of color act as symbolic mechanisms charged with contributing to a hegemonic institutional culture. Our goal is to provide critical insight into the lives of women of color in librarianship by narrating the collective stories we tell about our identity. As such, we approached our data collection and analysis from a grounded theory approach that allowed us to identify themes in the stories we collected and connect them to known feminist theories in an attempt to "utilize our lived relations as a basis of knowledge."[5]

Our hope is to change what is and is not allowed to be said within public and academic discourses.[6] We believe that by giving ourselves the space to tell these stories, we can begin to theorize our experiences in

---

4. Isabel Gonzalez-Smith, Juleah Swanson, and Azusa Tanaka, "Unpacking Identity: Racial, Ethnic, and Professional Identity and Academic Librarians of Color," *The Librarian Stereotype: Deconstructing Perceptions and Presentations of Information Work*, ed. Nicole Pagowsky and Miriam Rigby (Chicago: ACRL, 2014): 149-174.

5. Barney G. Glaser, Anselm L. Strauss, and Elizabeth Strutzel, "The Discovery of Grounded Theory; Strategies for Qualitative Research," *Nursing Research* 17, no. 4 (1968): 364; Chandra Talpade Mohanty, Ann Russo, and Lourdes Torres, *Third World Women and the Politics of Feminism* (Bloomington: Indiana University Press, 1991), 338.

6. Dian Million, "Felt Theory: An Indigenous Feminist Approach to Affect and History," *Wicazo Sa Review* 24, no. 2 (2009): 53-76.

"radical and innovative ways" and contribute to new veins of scholarship within our field. [7] We consider this work a preliminary step in utilizing our own tools to address issues of power and influence within the academy, and we hope to ultimately facilitate environments where the traditionally disempowered are able to claim their multitudinous identities.[8]

Multiculturalism in the Twentieth-Century Academy

In the twentieth century, the term "multiculturalism" within the sphere of education had many uses. The rhetoric of multiculturalism served as a project of "reconstruction," aimed at addressing institutional factors surrounding educational theories of cultural pluralism.[9] The academy subsumed the term multiculturalism in the 1970s and 1980s, and administrative bodies wielded the surrounding rhetoric to attack, de-radicalize, and institutionalize ethnic studies and women's studies programs whose roots go back to the second-wave feminism of the 1960s and the post-civil rights influx of racial and ethnic minority students who were entering higher education en masse.[10]

With the growth of ethnic studies programs that focused on African American, Latino, Asian American, and American Indian/Native American Studies, and as Gender and Women's Studies entered mainstream curricula, there was a tangible corrective path that contended with racial and gender inequalities on an institutional level by bolstering student retention and engaging academic discourse on minority topics.

---

7. Judith Roof and Robyn Wiegman, *Who Can Speak? Authority and Critical Identity* (Urbana, IL: University of Illinois Press, 1995), 251.

8. Audre Lorde, "The Master's Tools Will Never Dismantle the Master's House," in *Feminist Postcolonial Theory: A Reader*, ed. Reina Lewis and Sara Mills (Abingdon, UK: Routledge, 2003): 27.

9. Christopher Newfield and Avery F. Gordon, "Multiculturalism's Unfinished Business," in Mapping Multiculturalism, ed. Avery F. Gordon and Christopher Newfield (Minneapolis, MN: University of Minnesota Press, 1996), 76.

10. Ramon A. Gutierrez, "Ethnic Studies: Its Evolution in American Colleges and Universities," in Multiculturalism: A Critical Reader, ed. David Theo Goldberg (Oxford, UK: Blackwell, 1995), 158.

In the 1980s, multiculturalism was seen as a project of the humanities, with a focus on language and literature programs in a handful of elite universities.[11] Academics surveying the landscape of multiculturalism in the mid-1990s point to its many compounding contradictions in interpretation and use, both inside and outside of the academy.[12]

Multiculturalism and Pipeline Programs

In the early 1990s, pipeline programs such as residencies began functioning as a mechanism to integrate multicultural bodies and identities in an attempt to add racial and ethnic representation to academic librarianship. By doing so, these pipeline programs have been used to create a homogeneous identity, which can be simply defined as "the other" for librarians of color who inherently hold multiple identities.

There are significant disparities between the racial makeup of librarians and that of the current U.S. population. As of the 2012 update of Library Counts, "a comprehensive study of gender, race, age and disability statues in the library profession," non-white librarians made up 13.6% of credentialed librarians. That percentage is consistent among academic libraries. If libraries were reflective of the actual population of the United States, the percentage of non-white librarians should be 40.9%.[13] The major organizations of academic librarianship (i.e., the American Library Association and the Association of College and Research Libraries) prioritize "diversification" of the field through top down "inclusion and diversity" efforts and initiatives in an attempt to correct the critical imbalance between the whiteness of librarianship and the communities they serve. Significant portions of these "inclusion and diversity" efforts are embodied in the creation of diversity resident librarianship programs. These temporary one- to three-year programs,

11. Newfield and Gordon, "Unfinished Business," 77.

12. Ibid., 83.

13. Chris Bourg, "The Unbearable Whiteness of Librarianship," *Feral Librarian* (blog), March 3, 2014.

aimed at early-career librarians of color, are put in place with the goal of increasing the percentage of librarians of color within academia.

In effect, however, all of these initiatives place the burden of representation on the shoulders of librarians of color, who are often new in their career and still finding their place within the profession. Additionally, there have been no significant increases in the percentage of non-white librarians over the past two decades.[14] As a result, large public research universities, where a majority of these programs are housed, have struggled in their approach to increasing the numbers of librarians of color.[15] The legacy of these pipeline programs is that librarians of color are often subject to systems that disembody their personhood, voice, and individuality.

Methodology

In February of 2016, we sent out a call for self-identified women of color who had participated in an MLS-related internship, fellowship, or residency. We also intentionally sought out those with some kind of professional librarianship experience in both a public research institution and a small liberal arts college as a way of holding some institutional variables as constant as possible. We conducted sixty-minute interviews with our four subjects. Our interview subjects were split between those who were still in early-career programs and those who were already in

---

14. Lisa K. Hussey, "Why Librarianship? An Exploration of the Motivations of Ethnic Minorities to Choose Library and Information Science as a Career," in *Advances in Library Administration and Organization* 28 (2009), 153-217; Linda R. Musser, "Effective Retention Strategies for Diverse Employees," *Journal of Library Administration* 33, no. 1-2 (2001): 63-72; Joyce K. Thornton, "African American Female Librarians: A Study of Job Satisfaction," *Journal of Library Administration* 33, no. 1-2 (2001): 141-164; Laura Bayard and Linda Fisher, "Project to Recruit the Next Generation of Librarians: The First Year," *Indiana Libraries* 25, no. 2 (2006); Musser, *Effective Retention Strategies for Diverse Employees*, 63-72.

15. Kelly McElroy and Chris Diaz, "Residency Programs and Demonstrating Commitment to Diversity," *Faculty Publications* 46 (2015), https://digitalcommons.nl.edu/faculty_publications/46.

permanent professional positions. Some had come to librarianship as a second career or also had additional master's degrees in other disciplines.

We state unequivocally that the thoughts, feelings, and experiences narrated by the individual librarians of color that we interviewed cannot, and should not, be taken as the general experience of all librarians of color. The creation of these narratives is a form of resistance against the institutional language and rhetoric surrounding pipeline programs, which do not allow a space for women of color librarians to reflect on their own experiences. In this work we explore the effect that the legacy of pipeline programs and other systemic pressures have on how we perceive the world.

The interview questions covered topics such as identity formation, performance of identity at work, mentorship, and career drive. Organizing the narratives of these interviews through the grounded-theory model,[16] women of color can begin to tell our own stories of how our preconceived notions inform who we believe librarians are or should be, how we feel others perceive us, what our expectations are of pipeline programs, how or when we feel empowered or supported, and where we find community. Ultimately, this exploratory research is an attempt to build community knowledge we wish to share with future women of color librarians.

Librarianship as Written on the Body

"I knew during undergraduate that I wanted to become a librarian"

"I don't think I saw a librarian of color until I was in college, I'm pretty sure."

"You know I was very scared to get into the library field because first of all, I'm a librarian of color, and all the librarians I grew up with were white women, so I wasn't sure."

16. Glaser, Strauss, and Strutzel, "Grounded Theory," 364.

"I didn't see a librarian of color until college, and it was important for me to be present and visible."

Gonzalez-Smith, Swanson, and Tanaka describe the factors contributing to the dynamic nature of identity as time and context dependent. They also present identity formation as spanning local and global registers, in that the identity-creation process occurs at the individual corporeal level, the level of claimed communities, and the societal level. This reveals a complicated relationship for librarians of color between their professional, racial, and ethnic experiences and raises questions about how we might describe exactly who a librarian can and should be.[17]

On the individual level, just as pre-conceived notions of the identity of "librarian" are often reduced to a singular "white woman," the opposite, singular identity of "librarian of color" emerges as a counterpoint. Women of color claim this singular identity as indicative of commonality, distinctiveness, and community within the profession. In terms of visibility, the body of the "librarian of color" is comprised of an "amalgamation of all our identities, mixed into one self."[18] Women of color can also feel a responsibility to be present as a singular representation of their claimed communities in a professional capacity:

"So, I had decided to become a librarian, but I was alone until I met any non-white librarians. I thought that would be a pretty cool way of a) helping me become a professional librarian, b) aid in the visibility of, you know, "we are here," which I think is an important part of the profession, and helped me expand my network of other librarians who look like me."

"The reason why I went for it, is because I was coming from a totally different area, like I worked in television, so I wanted to know, this was a big risk, becoming a librarian for me, because I had spent ten years trying to get into television, getting

17. Gonzalez-Smith, Swanson, and Tanaka, "Unpacking Identity," 149-173.

18. Ibid., 165.

to the position I was in, and I definitely wanted to try it out and see how it was, you know to be a librarian, especially a librarian of color."

In the first quote above, the interviewee stating that she was "alone," makes it clear that, for her, the identity of "librarian of color" is essential and separate from "librarian." She refers to her community as a kind of physical presence where she can identify with other bodies that "look like me." The second quote above points to the overlapping aspects of community and identity, as the interviewee has a strong professional identification and affiliation with her first career, and also points to a similar distinction between "librarian" and "librarian of color." By using the phrase "especially a librarian of color," she indicates her professional identification with "librarian of color," not as an innate marker of non-white librarians, but rather as an identity to be pursued.

Bodies at Work

Gender, as well as identity, is a powerful determinant of experience in the professional, racial, and ethnic contexts of the individual.[19] Beyond any societal categorizations based solely on physiology of the body, gender affects how we interact with, and are perceived by, the communities we inhabit on a contextual basis.[20] The notion of perception, more specifically how one sees and is seen, is defined in philosophical theories of the self and of how we understand our individual identity in part as an identity with the potential to be recognized by others.[21] The absence of such recognition, or even misrecognition, is harmful to multidimensional identities and affects how women of color form

19. Michel Foucault, *The History of Sexuality*, trans. Robert Hurley (New York: Pantheon, 1978); Judith Butler, *Gender Trouble: Feminism and the Subversion of Identity*, (New York: Routledge, 1990).

20. Mary Hawkesworth, *Feminist Inquiry* (New Brunswick, NJ: Rutgers University Press, 2006).

21. Charles Taylor and Amy Gutmann, *Multiculturalism and "The Politics of Recognition": An Essay* (Princeton, NJ: Princeton University Press, 1992), 112.

identities in a professional environment, as social constructs of gender are ever present at work.[22] The hegemonic nature of higher education spaces that our black and brown bodies must negotiate compounds these issues of identity.[23]

Ford's work on bodily misrecognition enriches this feminist reading of multidimensional identities. "Bodily misrecognition," as defined by Ford, refers to the perceptions of others about the ways in which women of color faculty in the academy interact in the classroom.[24] Bodily misrecognition occurs when women of color enter hegemonic academic spaces where inaccurate perceptions about them based on racial and gendered stereotypes are prevailing and inescapable. This leads women of color faculty to manage their bodies, both physically and behaviorally, in order to come to some kind of mutual acceptance of their authority in a classroom with their students. The phenomenon of body management appears and is interrogated ubiquitously in feminist scholarship as a negotiation with the male-oriented approaches to the body that have left out the experiences of women of color in the past.[25]

As women of color librarians in academic spaces, we can feel the pressure to negotiate academic institutions as physical spaces where our non-white bodies are present amidst colleagues, faculty, and students:

"One, you know, you don't want to be viewed... especially, I mean, this is just me personally, but I don't want to be viewed as unprofessional. A lot of people think that – because, you know, I look young, so a lot of people are like, oh I thought that you were really young, and things like that, so I would try to stay serious, so that

22. Barbara J. Risman, "Gender as a Social Structure: Theory Wrestling with Activism," *Gender and Society* 18, no. 4 (2004): 429-450.

23. Roof and Wiegman, "*Who Can Speak?*", xi.

24. Kristie A. Ford, "Race, Gender, and Bodily (Mis)Recognitions: Women of Color Faculty Experiences with White Students in the College Classroom," *Journal of Higher Education* 82, no. 4 (July, 2011): 444-478.

25. Susan Bordo, *Unbearable Weight: Feminism, Western Culture, and the Body* (Berkeley, CA: University of California Press, 1993).

people think I'm, you know, a little older. Including wearing makeup, wearing... trying to make yourself look a little older, to play the role, you know of a librarian."

The interviewee worries that she will be misrecognized as "not a librarian" due to her youthful appearance, where notions of youth confer lack of "seriousness" or authority to do the work required in the workplace. In order to overcome these notions placed on her gendered body, the interviewee equates professionalism with application of makeup as a marker of femininity that legitimizes her authority as a librarian. If she is "playing the role" of librarian by upholding Western, white stereotypes around beauty standards and femininity, she is both accepting librarianship as a feminized form of labor and also one that her non-white body has to physically alter in order to be seen as worthy of that labor and the authority it confers.

Similarly, another interviewee states:

"It's hard for me because, so I'm half Japanese and I feel like I look...some people think I'm white and some people think I'm Hispanic and I don't know how faculty and students see me, if they see me as just another white librarian, and I know my supervisor she has made comments to me like you know, do you eat this type of food or like, about, does your mom speak Japanese, things like that. I think...she expects me to be a certain way that I'm not."

She is misrecognized by her physical appearance as either white or Hispanic, the former implying that her body exists as "just another" contribution to hegemony. Simultaneously, her supervisor places cultural stereotypes upon her by asking about her cultural history and gastronomic preferences once her presumed identity is "known" and expects the interviewee to manage her behavior to meet those cultural stereotypes. In this case the interviewee is compelled to collapse her intersectional identity to fit the expectations of her white supervisor.

One interviewee, who came to the library profession after a career in the military, sees both the advantages and disadvantages of the intersectionality of her professional identity as time and context dependent, and strategically reveals and manages them to gain power and retain her sense of worth in the workplace:

"I have been able to leverage my military identity in some ways because people might give me more respect than they otherwise would. But then I do also have my studious librarian identity because, you know, being a black woman I definitely, I can't always be happy and smiling because people sometimes read that as a lack of intellect or professionalism. My professional librarian self, while I might have a sense of humor, I tend to have to talk sharper and drop all my big words, despite my goofy demeanor, [to show] I actually do know what I'm talking about."

The physical and behavioral implications of bodily misrecognition in these narratives show a myriad of interactions that women of color experience on a daily basis. The identities and bodies of women of color are complicated by their historic exclusion from academic spaces.

Expectations and Belonging

Our own formations of identity, taken as time and context dependent, inform our expectations of the transparency of identity-based recruitment into pipeline programs.[26] At their best, early career programs deliver on their promise to expose librarians of color to the rigors of academic professions. As one interviewee describes her program where residents are considered non-tenure track faculty:

"We were encouraged to do the same things that would be expected of us as tenure track faculty. We were expected to teach, do service, publish, all of those things. It was sort of a slightly less stressful way of acclimating us to that environment."

But the intention behind pipeline programs is not always so transparent, nor are the objectives realized as advertised. As one interviewee relates:

26. Gonzalez-Smith, Swanson, and Tanaka, "Unpacking Identity," 149-173.

"I have a residency that is not billed as a diversity residency or anything like that. I know that a bunch of colleges and academic libraries have those kinds of residencies, and I wouldn't have applied had that been in the job description. I wouldn't want other staff and faculty to see me as an entry-level librarian who was there just because I wasn't white.

There were two people of color on my hiring committee which was awesome, and I met a few more people here and there, but then I got to the job and I realized, 'Oh, I met every single not-white person while I was interviewing.' I then realized that two of the three people of color who work at [my institution] had my position before me, then transitioned into permanent roles, which I thought was weird. It is not a "diversity" residency, but there seems to not be any other avenue for diverse people to enter the staff."

Creating pipeline programs marked with the term "diversity" initiates a pool of librarians of color in a hierarchical fashion, because residents' status are fixed as early-career and temporary. These programs breed an atmosphere that feels separate and unequal, especially when the institutions that hire these residents simply draw from the same pool to keep residents in order to fulfill staffing objectives. The interviewee above thought she had avoided such "marked" programs, but in fact chose a program whose transparency was suspect.

Once librarians of color attempt to transition from pipeline programs into a permanent position, expectations of hiring practices and how they will be perceived change yet again. Many times, this is based on who they see on prospective employers' current staff:

"And I think my library director was deliberate to try to hire people that were of color 'cause there was no one of color here. That was nerve-wracking because the position was open before and I saw it and I said, I'm interested in this position, but when I looked through the people that were in the library, I saw that no one looked like me. I was like, I don't know, I don't know if I'll get hired, you know? And I said, I'm just not going to go out for it, so they ended up hiring someone else, a white male, and they, he didn't do well, and they let him go or he left — I don't know what the circumstances were."

In this case, the interviewee passed on an opportunity to apply for a job, because she could not see herself reflected as a part of the library's personnel.

Mentoring and Community

The benefits of formal and informal mentoring in support of librarians of color are directly linked to issues of recruitment and retention.[27] Opportunities for librarians of color to be supported and mentored by fellow librarians of color can counteract the "aloneness" of perceived whiteness as noted earlier. As one interviewee relates about her experience:

"She was a big—she was of course a woman of color, and she was a big influence on me. I said, you know, I really want to do what she's doing for the library. I just felt like she had influence, people listened to her. So I was like, this was something -- she showed me something I didn't even think existed. I just didn't even think a person of color can be in that top position in the library system. I was like, wow, I want to go out for an outreach position, and she started telling me what she did, and we maintained our friendship. I'm still friends with her to this day."

The interviewee, in her first role as librarian, met a librarian of the same ethnic background and began an informal mentoring relationship that encouraged her to see herself as capable of "something I didn't even think existed." Bonnette's large-scale, U.S. Census-based statistical research shows that professional skills and competencies developed in mentoring relationships that lead to self-confidence and self-motivation in the workplace are early indicators of success and retention for librarians of color. Feelings of isolation felt by early-career librarians of color were found in Johnson's research to be mitigated by group mentoring;

27.Ashley E Bonnette, "Mentoring Minority Librarians Up the Career Ladder," *Library Administration & Management* 18, no. 3 (Jul 1, 2004): 134; Peggy Johnson, "Retaining and Advancing Librarians of Color," *College & Research Libraries* 68, no. 5 (Sep 1, 2007): 405-417.

similarly, Olivas and Ma found that mentoring led to increased job satisfaction.[28] Expectations of formal, structured mentoring do not always align between the mentee and the institution.[29] This interviewee describes a mentorship in their program as:

"There was an attempt at mentorship. It was a thing that I feel like they were trying to mentor, but I feel like a lot of the mentorship ended up being me mentoring people. It was a type of mentorship very focused on how to navigate their institution."

That mentoring, however, was very narrowly based and focused on navigating the ins and outs of their institution rather than mentoring aimed at crafting a larger career. The same interviewee describes her definition of formal mentorship, which was at odds with her experience:

"When I think of a mentor, I'm thinking of someone who is really helping you craft your career potentially even beyond wherever it is you currently are, they're giving you words of wisdom and advice and definitely it's back and forth."

Support outside of formal mentoring programs many times comes directly from supervisors:

"I think that most of the people I interact with, like my supervisors, are invested in my growth as a professional on a more personal level, because they're genuinely nice people and they would encourage me, they have encouraged me to apply for other positions, despite the fact that I've only been at [my institution] a year."

This interviewee feels that her colleagues are personally invested in her success on an individual basis. Identifying with communities

---

28. Johnson, "Retaining and Advancing Librarians of Color"; Antonia Olivas and Richard Ma, "Increasing Retention Rates in Minority Librarians through Mentoring," *Electronic Journal of Academic and Special Librarianship* 10, no. 3 (Winter 2009).

29.Angela Boyd, Yolanda Blue, and Suzanne Im, "Evaluation of Academic Library Residency Programs in the United States for Librarians of Color," *College & Research Libraries* 78, no. 4 (2017): 472.

outside of professional relationships with fellow colleagues, faculty, or librarians is also common. As one interviewee still in an early career residency reflects:

"I feel much more kinship with the students, who are very diverse. I look like them, I'm closer to them in age, and also there's more diversity in the student body than is found among my colleagues."

In addition to kinship with students, librarians of color have the opportunity to mentor student workers and affect how other students see their peers. Positive interactions with students can lead to the elevation of status for students of color library assistants. One interviewee describes the implications of such interactions:

"I've had students who say, this is awesome, I can't believe I didn't come sooner. And they're so grateful for my help that I was like, see I've changed somebody's perspective on a librarian of color. They'll never think that again. Matter of fact, sometimes people come up and ask some of the student workers, are you a librarian? And they're Black or they're Hispanic and they say, no, but I'll go get one of the librarians."

When pointedly asked about whether interviewees felt that they had found a community of peers, many replied that they had not:

"I don't know, maybe it's kind of gloomy, but I feel community-less."

"No. I do have people at my job that I can talk to about things that I'm going through, but it's not the same because they don't have the same background. It's hard. They sympathize, but they don't know, they can't empathize with you. There's no one."

Conclusion

Throughout this exploratory work, we have attempted to interrogate links between the legacies of multiculturalism as put into practice in the

1990s and residency programs instituted within academic librarianship during the same time period to recruit and retain librarians of color. Over the intervening years and up to the present, these programs have failed to increase the number of professional academic librarians of color. If we consider our current bodily presence in the field in light of these failed projects, turning towards the lived, intersectional experiences of women of color librarians can help us work through the ways in which our present is informed by our past. By deeply interrogating previous narratives and creating new descriptions of record that accurately reflect the lived experience of women of color, we hope to use these new narratives, not only to shift attitudes and open up broader conversations on identity and the body in our profession, but also to validate, empower, and ultimately support women of color within the profession.

Bibliography

American Library Association Executive Board. "ALA EXECUTIVE BOARD 2015 Fall Meeting Agenda." *Ebd* 9, no. 1 (2015).

Alabi, Jaena. "Racial Microaggressions in Academic Libraries: Results of a Survey of Minority and Non-Minority Librarians." *Journal of Academic Librarianship* 41, no. 1 (2015): 47-53.

Bayard, Laura and Linda Fisher. "Project to Recruit the Next Generation of Librarians: The First Year." *Indiana Libraries* 25, no. 2 (2006).

Bonnette, Ashley. "Mentoring Minority Librarians Up the Career Ladder." *Library Administration & Management* 18, no. 3 (Jul 1, 2004): 134.

Bordo, Susan. *Unbearable Weight: Feminism, Western Culture, and the Body.* Berkeley, CA: University of California Press, 1993.

Bourg, Chris. "The Unbearable Whiteness of Librarianship." *Feral Librarian* 3, (2014).

Boyd, Angela, Yolanda Blue, and Suzanne Im. "Evaluation of Academic Library Residency Programs in the United States for Librarians of Color." *College & Research Libraries* 78, no. 4 (2017): 472

Butler, Judith. *Gender Trouble: Feminism and the Subversion of Identity*. New York: Routledge, 1990.

Caswell, Michelle. "Teaching to Dismantle White Supremacy in Archives." *Library Quarterly* 87, no. 3 (2017): 222-235.

Ford, Kristie A. "Race, Gender, and Bodily (Mis)Recognitions: Women of Color Faculty Experiences with White Students in the College Classroom." *Journal of Higher Education* 82, no. 4 (July, 2011): 444-478.

Foucault, Michel. *The History of Sexuality*, trans. Robert Hurley. New York: Pantheon, 1978.

Glaser, Barney G., Anselm L. Strauss, and Elizabeth Strutzel. "The Discovery of Grounded Theory; Strategies for Qualitative Research." *Nursing Research* 17, no. 4 (1968): 364.

Gonzalez-Smith, Isabel, Juleah Swanson, and Azusa Tanaka. "Unpacking Identity: Racial, Ethnic, and Professional Identity and Academic Librarians of Color." In *The Librarian Stereotype: Deconstructing Perceptions and Presentations of Information Work*, edited by Nicole Pagowsky and Miriam Rigby, 149-174. Chicago: ACRL, 2014.

Gutierrez, Ramon A. "Ethnic Studies: Its Evolution in American Colleges and Universities." In *Multiculturalism: A Critical Reader*, edited by David Theo Goldberg, 157-167. Oxford, UK: Blackwell, 1995.

Hawkesworth, Mary. *Feminist Inquiry*. New Brunswick, NJ: Rutgers University Press, 2006.

Hudson, David James. "On 'Diversity' as Anti-Racism in Library and Information Studies: A Critique." *Journal of Critical Library and Information Studies* 1, no. 1 (2017).

Hussey, Lisa K. "Why Librarianship? An Exploration of the Motivations of Ethnic Minorities to Choose Library and Information Science as a Career." *Advances in Library Administration and Organization* 28 (2009): 153-217.

Johnson, Peggy. "Retaining and Advancing Librarians of Color." *College & Research Libraries* 68, no. 5 (Sep 1, 2007): 405-417.

Lorde, Audre. "The Master's Tools Will Never Dismantle the Master's House." In *Feminist Postcolonial Theory: A Reader* edited by Reina Lewis and Sara Mills, 25-28. Abingdon, UK: Routledge, 2003.

McElroy, Kelly, and Chris Diaz. "Residency Programs and Demonstrating Commitment to Diversity." *Faculty Publications* 46 (2015). https://digitalcommons.nl.edu/faculty_publications/46.

Million, Dian. "Felt Theory: An Indigenous Feminist Approach to Affect and History." *Wicazo Sa Review* 24, no. 2 (2009): 53-76.

Mohanty, Chandra Talpade, Ann Russo, and Lourdes Torres. *Third World Women and the Politics of Feminism.* Bloomington, IN: Indiana University Press, 1991.

Musser, Linda R. "Effective Retention Strategies for Diverse Employees." *Journal of Library Administration* 33, no. 1-2 (2001): 63-72.

Newfield, Christopher and Avery F. Gordon. "Multiculturalism's Unfinished Business." In *Mapping Multiculturalism*, edited by Avery F. Gordon and Christopher Newfield, 76-115. Minneapolis, MN: University of Minnesota Press, 1996.

Olivas, Antonia and Richard Ma. "Increasing Retention Rates in Minority Librarians through Mentoring." *Electronic Journal of Academic and Special Librarianship* 10, no. 3 (Winter 2009).

Risman, Barbara J. "Gender as a Social Structure: Theory Wrestling with Activism." *Gender and Society* 18, no. 4 (2004): 429-450.

Roof, Judith and Robyn Wiegman. *Who Can Speak? Authority and Critical Identity.* Urbana, IL: University of Illinois Press, 1995.

Schaefer, Richard T. *Encyclopedia of Race, Ethnicity, and Society.* Los Angeles: SAGE Publications, 2008.

Taylor, Charles and Amy Gutmann. *Multiculturalism and 'The Politics of Recognition": An Essay.* Princeton, NJ: Princeton University Press, 1992.

Thornton, Joyce K. "African American Female Librarians: A Study of Job Satisfaction." *Journal of Library Administration* 33, no. 1-2 (2001): 141-164.

Chapter 10

I, Too: Unmasking Emotional Labor of Women of Color Community College Librarians

Alyssa Jocson Porter, Sharon Spence-Wilcox, and Kimberly Tate-Malone

Who We Are

We, the authors, identify as women of color (WOC) librarians whose professional experiences are routinely impacted by our race/ethnicity and gender. We work in the library at Seattle Central College, a community college in Seattle, WA, but our experiences vary based on our differing ethnic/racial backgrounds.[1] Realizing that our daily connections with students and colleagues were draining and stressful, we joined forces to better understand and cope with this shared phenomenon of disconnect, dissatisfaction, and disillusion. The low representation of WOC in the library profession[2] and in the state of Washington's community and technical colleges (CTCs) drives us to share our perspectives and experiences navigating primarily white institutions (PWIs) while

1. When we use the term "women of color" (WOC), we are referring to those who identify as women and as a non-white race/ethnicity. Use of the word "we" refers to the authors, and the use of "WOC librarians" refers to ourselves, our survey respondents, and the documented experiences of other WOC librarians.

2. U.S. Department of Labor, Bureau of Labor Statistics, "Employed Persons by Detailed Occupation, Sex, Race, and Hispanic or Latino ethnicity," *Current Population Survey*, accessed August 22, 2017, Table 11, http://www.bls.gov/cps/cpsaat11.pdf.

managing the emotional labor that comes in this context. In this chapter, we explore stories gathered from other WOC librarians in CTCs, published literature, and personal anecdotes.

Introduction

Community colleges and their libraries have always occupied a unique space in the United States' education system. Historical economic and educational disparities along racial lines mean that CTCs frequently offer educational opportunities to students of color and those without the resources to attend a traditional four-year institution.[3] In 2016, just over 50% of all community college students in the United States were non-white.[4] At Seattle Central's location, 4,066 of 7,393 students (55%) identified themselves as people of color (POC).[5] Yet, from 2010-2014, only 112 of 443 (26%) of faculty identified as people of color, and 56% identified as "female."[6] In addition to the low number of faculty of color, "faculty work conditions at many of the colleges [have] deteriorated."[7] In 2009, only 30% of the 400,000 faculty hired at CTCs across the country were full-time.[8] In 2014, 32% of all state-supported faculty at Seattle Central were full-time.[9]

---

3. Steven Brint and Jerome Karabel, *The Diverted Dream: Community Colleges and the Promise of Educational Opportunity in America, 1900-1985* (Oxford: Oxford University Press, 1989), 10.

4. American Association of Community Colleges, "2016 Fact Sheet," February 2016, accessed August 21, 2017, http://www.aacc.nche.edu/AboutCC/Documents/AACCFactSheetsR2.pdf.

5. Seattle Central College, "Facts and Figures," accessed May 22, 2017, http://www.seattlecentral.edu/newscenter/facts-and-figures/.

6. Washington State Board for Community and Technical Colleges, "Fall Enrollment & Staffing Report 2013," accessed July 27, 2017, https://www.sbctc.edu/resources/documents/colleges-staff/research/fall-quarter-research/2014/7_FQR_Staff_2014.pdf.

7. Steven Brint, "Few Remaining Dreams: Community Colleges since 1985," *Annals of the American Academy of Political and Social Science* 586, no. 1 (2003): 16-37.

8. Center for Community College Student Engagement, "Contingent Commitments Bringing Part-Time Faculty into Focus," last modified March 21, 2014, http://www.ccsse.org/docs/PTF_Special_Report.pdf.

9. Washington State Board for Community and Technical Colleges, 75.

Although we have data for all faculty of color at Seattle Central, it is difficult to quantify the number of WOC librarians in Washington CTCs because state data does not account for intersectional[10] identities (i.e., no numbers capturing who is both a woman and a person of color). However, we do know that in 2010, only 13.9% of librarians working in higher education in the United States were people of color.[11]

Methods

We gathered stories from WOC librarians working in State of Washington CTCs by distributing a survey asking about how their WOC identity affects their workplace experience, emotional labor, and self-care practices. Our main mode of distribution was to send the survey link to the College Librarians and Media Specialists (CLAMS) list-serv. CLAMS is a non-profit association that connects library professionals in Washington CTCs. All thirty-four libraries in State of Washington CTCs are institutional members, thus we felt confident we would reach our intended survey audience. Since this listserv might not include adjunct librarians or former librarians, we also emailed invitations to individuals we knew fit our scope.

During the approximately six-week open period, twenty respondents started the survey. All responses were voluntary and anonymous. Of those twenty, three were disqualified (for not fitting our scope), and nine completed the survey, while eight did not. We imagined reasons individuals might not have completed the survey: they felt uncomfortable answering some questions, had no time to finish, or did not initially understand the scope. **Table 1** details the survey respondent demographics.

---

10. Kimberlé Crenshaw coined the term intersectionality to describe the overlap or intersection of social identities and related systems of oppression, domination, or discrimination, especially as relate to race and gender. Kimberlé Crenshaw, "Mapping the Margins: Intersectionality, Identity Politics, and Violence Against Women of Color," *Stanford Law Review* (1991): 1241-1299.

11. American Libraries Association, "Diversity Counts Report," accessed July 27, 2017, http://www.ala.org/aboutala/sites/ala.org.aboutala/files/content/diversitydiversitycounts/diversitycountstables2012.pdf

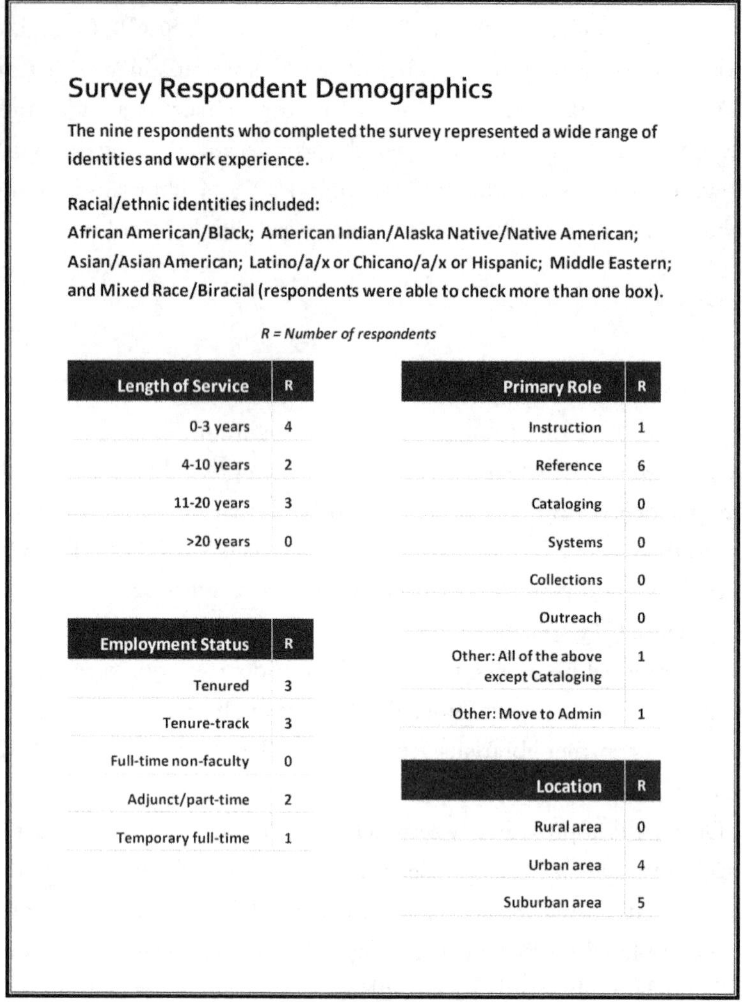

Survey Respondent Demographics

The nine respondents who completed the survey represented a wide range of identities and work experience.

Racial/ethnic identities included:
African American/Black; American Indian/Alaska Native/Native American; Asian/Asian American; Latino/a/x or Chicano/a/x or Hispanic; Middle Eastern; and Mixed Race/Biracial (respondents were able to check more than one box).

R = Number of respondents

Length of Service	R
0-3 years	4
4-10 years	2
11-20 years	3
>20 years	0

Employment Status	R
Tenured	3
Tenure-track	3
Full-time non-faculty	0
Adjunct/part-time	2
Temporary full-time	1

Primary Role	R
Instruction	1
Reference	6
Cataloging	0
Systems	0
Collections	0
Outreach	0
Other: All of the above except Cataloging	1
Other: Move to Admin	1

Location	R
Rural area	0
Urban area	4
Suburban area	5

Table 1. Survey Respondent Demographics

Emotional Labor

"Can I take off my mask at the end of the day? … I have everything. I can see, I can feel, I can breathe."—Mehnaz Hoosein[12]

12. Mehnaz Hoosein, "Everything," *Silence*, performed by Manooghi Hi, Compact Disc, Mowlawner Music, 2011.

In her seminal work, *The Managed Heart*, sociologist Arlie Russell Hochschild identifies the concept of emotional labor as something faced by employees in many service-driven jobs, in addition to physical and mental labor. "Emotional labor is the effort required to manage one's emotions to meet organizational expectations; ...it calls for a coordination of mind and feeling, and sometimes draws on a source of self that we honor as deep and integral to our individuality."[13] While Hochschild conducted research with flight attendants in the early 1980s, the experience of emotional labor has been widely evident in the rapidly growing service industry ever since, and librarianship is no exception. To illustrate the form that this labor takes in the twenty-first century library, we use personal reflections and survey responses to acknowledge and process our experience.

Many librarians are driven to wear a mask while on duty so they can regulate their emotions to fulfill workplace expectations. Matteson, Chittock, and Mease describe two levels of acting that create emotional labor.[14] The mask of surface acting simply involves faking an appropriate response. The alternative deep acting response encourages the librarian to look at the situation from a different perspective so their emotional response is more authentic.

Emotional labor is an inevitable experience for CTC reference and instruction librarians, who must regulate the complicated emotions that arise for the sake of their students, colleagues, and themselves. While professional literature offers insights into emotional labor from multiple academic disciplines, there is seldom focus on the CTC setting and the intersectionality of gender and race.

---

13. Arlie Russell Hochschild, *The Managed Heart* (Berkeley, CA: University of California Press, 2012).

14. Surface acting matches the external expression of emotion with the organization's guidelines while the underlying emotion is still present. With deep acting, there is an attempt to reframe the situation by bringing empathy and authenticity to the underlying emotion. (Miriam L. Matteson, Sharon Chittock, and David Mease, "In Their Own Words: Stories of Emotional Labor from The Library Workforce," *Library Quarterly* 85, no. 1 [2015]: 86).

Contextualizing Emotional Labor

A study conducted by Julien and Genuis on the emotional labor experienced by instructional librarians revealed "frustration due to relationships with students and other faculty; students and faculty partners who don't trust the librarian, are unresponsive, who distance themselves from the librarian."[15] These relationships often stem from ongoing general perceptions that discredit the professional worth of librarians and women in academia. As WOC librarians in a State of Washington CTC, we experience an added dimension where, despite faculty status, we are not seen or respected as equal partners working toward the educational mission of our institution. We have no perceived authority in our frequent interactions with disrespectful students. Often, we must educate other faculty about how librarians can make intellectual contributions to their courses and curriculum. We may struggle to manage our emotions in settings where accountability, consequences, follow-up, and outcomes are virtually absent. Wingfield cautions that "gender and racial inequality further reinforces emotional labor in service fields where employees are faced with varied emotional norms; certain negative feelings such as frustration, boredom, and anger are expected to be suppressed by some not all."[16] The stories we gathered begin to fill the gaping hole in the professional library literature regarding the impact of race and gender on emotional labor. These stories affirm that the invisible emotional labor experienced by librarians in the classroom, at the reference desk, and with coworkers may be compounded by these long-standing inequities and be more draining for us than for others.

In addition to interpersonal interactions, the structures of our institutions, rooted in racism, contribute to emotional labor. Higher status workers tend to control the rules about workplace behavior. Guidelines

---

15. Heidi Julien and Shelagh K. Genuis, "Emotional Labour in Librarians' Instructional Work," *Journal of Documentation* 65, no. 6 (2009): 926-937.

16. Adia Harvey Wingfield, "How 'Service with a Smile' Takes a Toll on Women," *The Atlantic*, January 26, 2016, https://www.theatlantic.com/business/archive/2016/01/gender-emotional-labor/427083/.

and expectations may be created externally and adopted internally. Examples include professional librarian standards, or employee contracts developed completely in-house. A sociology study by Froyum asserts that the ideal of color-blind "professionalism" serves as a control mechanism to suppress, rather than acknowledge and address, racially-based emotional labor for people of color.[17] Survey responses and personal experiences reveal that many WOC librarians suppress their needs and identities while we engage in emotional labor, presenting the appropriate emotional façade that allows us to be compatible with organizational norms. Constant interaction with white colleagues and POC who have internalized white supremacist ideals often leads to performance weariness and racial battle fatigue.[18]

Deconstructing Emotional Labor

"It appalls us that the West can desire, extract and claim ownership of our ways of knowing, our imagery, the things we create and produce, and then simultaneously reject the people who created and developed those ideas and seek to deny them further opportunities to be creators of their own culture and own nations."—Linda Tuhiwai Smith[19]

We recognize that the concepts of emotional labor, impostor syndrome, and racial battle fatigue are related and often used interchangeably. We developed **Figure 1**, the *Interplay of IRE*, to differentiate among these concepts, which we discuss below.

17. Carissa Froyum, "'For the Betterment of Kids Who Look Like Me': Professional Emotional Labour as a Racial Project," *Ethnic and Racial Studies* 36, no. 6 (2013): 1070-1089.

18. Racial battle fatigue is the physiological and psychological strain exacted on racially marginalized groups and the amount of energy lost dedicated to coping with racial microaggressions and racism. (Dimpal Jain, Untitled Presentation at Seattle Central College's Women of Color Employee Affinity Group, Seattle, WA. Oct 27, 2016).

19. Linda Tuhiwai Smith, Decolonizing Methodologies: *Research and Indigenous Peoples* (London: Zed Books Ltd, 2013), 1.

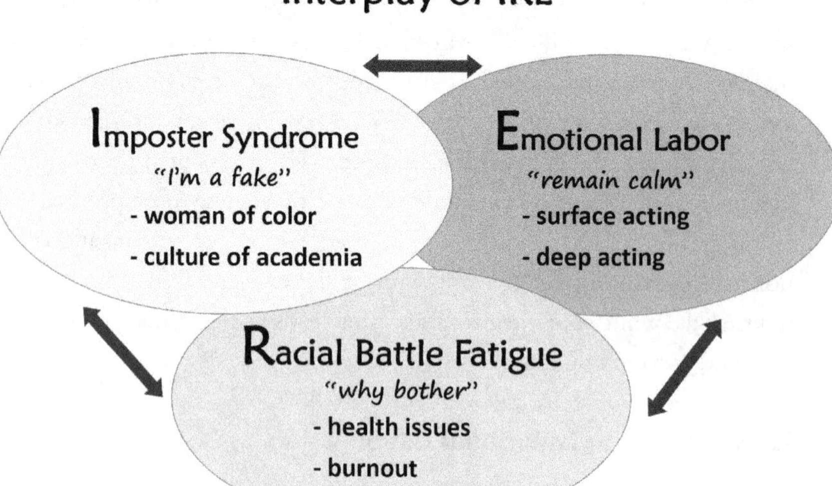

Figure 1. The Interplay of IRE

Women of color in academia often experience impostor syndrome, which occurs when individuals are unable to internalize their success. These individuals often believe that any success they achieve is not a product of their own ability and that they will eventually be exposed as frauds.[20] In our experience, these feelings of impostor syndrome are exacerbated by racial and gender microaggressions[21] from colleagues and students.

---

20. Joan C. Harvey and Cynthia Katz, *If I'm So Successful, Why Do I Feel Like a Fake? The Impostor Phenomenon* (New York: St. Martin's Press, 1985).

21. "[Microaggressions are] subtle assaults (verbal and nonverbal) directed towards people of color that are often enacted automatically or unconsciously. [These can often be] layered assaults, based on race and its intersections with gender, class, sexuality, language, immigration status, phenotype, accent, or surname. Cumulative assaults can take a psychological, physiological, and academic toll on People of color" (Jain, Untitled Presentation).

Interactions with students and coworkers cause us to question ourselves about whether and how we belong as community college librarians. Feelings of inadequacy, ignorance, and disconnection move us to put on masks that allow us to fit in according to the expectations of others. Here, the three of us share our own stories:

As a relatively young Asian American, I often feel underestimated or disrespected. People often ask me how old I am, if I am a student, if I have my degree, where I come from. I spend too much time thinking about how to present myself. To look older, I started wearing makeup, wearing my hair short, and wearing jeans less often. To hide my body, I started wearing more layers and baggier clothing.

Many students and some faculty/staff, assume I am a student. Some combination of my race, gender, and age leads folks to make assumptions about my education, expertise, and qualifications. My stress over not being seen as competent sometimes leads me to perform what I think 'professionalism' should look like. I've adopted a more conservative way of dress and speaking to be seen as a colleague to other faculty and an authority to students.

Interactions with colleagues, students, and administrators tend to focus on my identity as a Black, female, immigrant, first-generation college student who is not quite savvy about the culture of academia. To compensate for this feeling that I do not fit the librarian mold of an innovative, progressive and high profile intellectual, I work above and beyond my compensated hours into the wee hours of the night.

These experiences are painful and can have real consequences. Unfortunately, they are not isolated stories. Two respondents shared similar experiences:

Other workplace and life experiences have made me think that African-American women are not seen as feminine, so I often wear skirts or dresses at work; I never wear jeans... However, my colleagues with both more and less seniority than me do wear jeans.

Although I identify as multiracial, because I am very light-skinned and present as ethnically ambiguous, I hesitate to speak out about diversity issues or participate in initiatives for people "of color" because I question whether I will be perceived as not belonging there or not being entitled to my views.

Faced with a case of impostor syndrome, the WOC librarian engages in emotional labor to deal with the feeling of not belonging and the experience of microaggressions, and this surface and deep acting in turn brings on racial battle fatigue, which can be complicated by gender. "College and university campuses and their surrounding communities are often located in historically White environments where racial discrimination exists in both subtle and overt forms."[22]

Workplace Expectations and Experiences

"In every position that I've been in, there have been naysayers who don't believe I'm qualified or who don't believe I can do the work. And I feel a special responsibility to prove them wrong."—Sonia Sotomayor[23]

Many WOC librarians at State of Washington CTCs work in a primarily white environment where they face unfair perceptions while striving to meet expectations in their workplace. WOC in academia are often "presumed incompetent"[24] both in the classroom and while fulfilling other professional obligations. This presumption, accompanied by frequent racial microaggressions, means WOC librarians (in varied institutions) can spend a significant amount of time and effort pushing against those perceptions. Working in such an environment can require

22. Jain, Untitled Presentation.

23. Sonia Sotomayor, interview by Terry Gross, *Fresh Air,* NPR, January 13, 2014, retrieved from https://www.npr.org/2014/01/13/262067546/as-a-latina-sonia-sotomayor-says-you-have-to-work-harder.

24. Gabriella Gutiérrez y Muhs, Yolanda Flores Niemann, Carmen G. González, and Angela P. Harris. *Presumed Incompetent: The Intersections of Race and Class for Women in Academia* (Boulder, CO: Utah State University Press, 2012).

one to manage conflict, encounter mental health issues, and fend off unwanted attention, all while managing one's emotions. In our survey, 88% of respondents said that their race and/or gender influences the way they navigate their workplace. This emotional labor is often paired with added traditional labor, such as being expected to volunteer for or lead diversity-related tasks. The combination of emotional and traditional labor can result in problematic work conditions for WOC librarians.

Professional Standards for Reference and Instruction

The Association of College and Research Libraries (ACRL) has professional standards and proficiencies that guide the work of instruction librarians in academic institutions. These guidelines cover skill sets in several areas, including: assessment and evaluation, communication, information literacy integration, instructional design, and teaching.[25] Similarly, the Reference and Users Services Association (RUSA) details standards for reference librarians in any setting. Though these standards and guidelines are not always directly referred to at each institution, they do reflect the wide range of duties and expertise that librarians are expected to hold and are largely regarded as best practices. Some of these standards are listed in **Table 2**.

While these standards create a structure for reference and instruction work, each can also engender emotional labor. Librarians are expected to perform these responsibilities with alternating visible authority and empathy.

A survey respondent stated: "race, gender, and other intersections of my identity affect how others see me. Women of color are often seen as less intelligent and less capable than the whites." Such perceptions are often an expression of implicit bias, defined as the attitudes or stereotypes that affect our understanding, actions, and decisions

---

25. Since the time of writing, the ACRL professional standards were updated. This new document titled "Roles and Strengths of Teaching Librarians" still does not address the role of emotional labor in instruction librarianship. Our analysis stands.

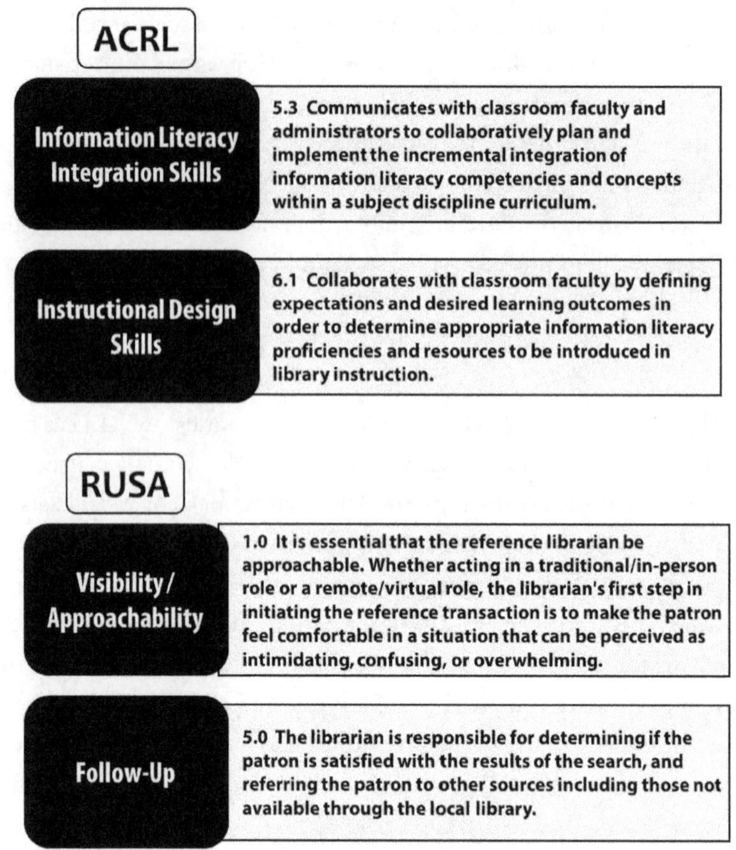

Table 2. Professional Standards.[26]

in an unconscious manner.[27] These implicit biases held by others in the academy influence how WOC librarians interact with their colleagues. One respondent stated, "I feel like I am always trying to fit

26. "Guidelines for Behavioral Performance of Reference and Information Service Providers," The Reference and User Services Association, revised May 28, 2013, http://www.ala.org/rusa/resources/guidelines/guidelinesbehavioral; "Standards for Proficiencies for Instruction Librarians and Coordinators," Association of College and Research Libraries, revised June 24, 2007, http://www.ala.org/acrl/standards/profstandards.

27. Patricia Russell, "Implicit Bias & Microaggressions: Recognizing & Rectifying" (presentation, Seattle Central College Library's Conversations on Social Issues series, Seattle, WA, Feb 25, 2016).

in, to ascertain what is expected of me and ensure that I meet those expectations." Another stated that she "also felt the need to become 'more white' (assertive, louder) in order to fit into the predominantly white faculty culture." This demonstrates that rather than the true collaboration detailed in ACRL Standards 5.3 and 6.1, WOC librarians are adapting their interactions with other faculty to accommodate the expectations of others.

When addressing these experiences, one survey respondent wrote that she "ha[s] been silenced a few times when [white] faculty don't feel comfortable talking about the issues that POC face"; another wrote, "I don't always address some disrespectful behaviors and comments because I want to keep my job." Inside the library, these same experiences can exist: the microaggressions that one respondent experienced from another library employee around her workplace autonomy and competency made her behavior more "guarded," and though the colleague later tried to be friendly, our respondent stated that "it's tough to befriend those that seem to consider you their social and professional inferior."

The RUSA Guideline 5.0 on follow-up can also create additional work when WOC librarians are at the reference desk. In Chou and Pho's work examining intersectionality at the reference desk, they found that WOC librarians felt that patrons were dissatisfied with the answers they received, and as a result, the "librarian fe[lt] as though they were not perceived as a trained professional."[28] This led to WOC librarians doing extra work with students at the reference desk to demonstrate their competency.

Similarly, our survey respondents wrote:

I am very conscious of how I "work twice as hard to be thought half as good." During my first few years in librarianship, sometimes I presented too many research sources to students when teaching, because I feared they would assume that I was not knowledgeable, well educated, or capable of doing my job.

---

28. Rose L. Chou and Annie Pho, "Intersectionality at the Reference Desk: Lived Experiences of Women of Color Librarians," in *Feminist Reference Desk*, ed. Maria T. Accardi (Sacramento, CA: Litwin Books/Library Juice Press, 2017), 237.

Often times when I'm staffing the ref desk with a white colleague—students of all colors may go to them [first].

Librarians' behavioral performance at the reference desk is complicated by frequent and varied microaggressions from students. Survey respondents described instances of receiving compliments on their English fluency (even if they are American-born), being treated disrespectfully for having a spoken accent, or having their American identity/citizenship questioned. Two respondents also described often being mistaken for other college employees of the same race/ethnicity.

The twin expectations of being in a service role and being a WOC can result in a special burden while at the reference desk. The guideline on visibility/approachability (RUSA Guideline 1.0) emphasizes the librarian's responsibility to make patrons feel comfortable. However, as WOC librarians who occupy both faculty and service space and who teach in a non-classroom setting (the reference desk), we have also experienced harassment, both verbal and sexual, based on our gender, nationality, and/or race. The desire to be seen as approachable (RUSA Guideline 5.0) can be misconstrued by patrons as an opportunity for them to display inappropriate behavior. One survey respondent wrote:

As a fifth generation [multi-ethnic] Asian American, I have been asked if I am from America a few times. Another student mentioned that being ethnically pure/racially pure is the best.

Doing reference and instruction work while feeling hyper-critiqued necessitates managing one's emotions. In the wider context, this means that the standards listed above often rely on WOC librarians remaking themselves and adjusting their emotions to fit into the college environment. In a PWI, this often means diminishing those pieces of ourselves that may not be "standard" until we are palatable to primarily white faculty and administrators. For example, one survey respondent grapples with managing workplace expectations while also being a new mother:

As a relatively new mother, the demands of motherhood have definitely impacted my work life as I have struggled to juggle work demands with domestic and childcare responsibilities and align my work schedule with my child's daycare schedule.

Currently, these standards do not refer to, or explicitly recognize, emotional labor. As Accardi proposes, the skills necessary to manage emotions should be acknowledged in professional standards, including those from the ACRL and RUSA.[29]

The intersectionality of race and gender and the emotional labor associated with having to develop coping skills for internal and external expectations seem compounded in the CTC setting, especially for librarians in an urban location with a large student population of varied backgrounds and urgent needs, and few faculty or staff of color.

Diversity Representation on Committees

In addition to the national standards for reference and instruction, there are also institutional expectations and contractual obligations at Seattle Central. Faculty members, including librarians, contribute to the institution by serving on committees[30] at the program, college, and district[31] level. We have observed that administrators and colleagues often expect WOC librarians to serve on committees related to diversity, equity, and inclusion. Consequently, we are often expected to educate white colleagues on these topics. This can increase the emotional labor our jobs require as we work to contribute to the committee's goals while also fending off possible microaggressions and ignorant comments from colleagues.

---

29. Maria Accardi, "Emotional Labor and Library Instruction," *Librarian Burnout*, April 23, 2015, https://librarianburnout.com/2015/04/23/emotional-labor-and-library-instruction/.

30. Agreement: Seattle Community College District VI Board of Trustees and American Federation of Teachers; Seattle Community Colleges 1789 (July 1, 2013–June 30, 2016).

31. The Seattle Colleges District includes North Seattle College, South Seattle College, Seattle Central College, and Seattle Vocational Institute.

For example, Seattle Central's 2016-2020 strategic plan includes "address[ing] institutional racism and achiev[ing] equity and inclusion."[32] One of the objectives for this goal includes reaching out to underrepresented student populations in order to recruit, retain, and support these students through the educational process. Another sets out to standardize an anti-racist, anti-bias search and hiring process to build a diverse workforce. Prioritizing equity is necessary to address educational disparities among our students. However, when PWIs, including community colleges, set outcomes and goals around creating an equitable and diverse campus environment without allocating additional funding or personnel, this results in "cultural taxation"[33] for faculty of color as they are asked or expected to serve on committees and lead initiatives, primarily because of their race, ethnicity, and/or gender.

One survey respondent wrote that they are "often asked to work long hours for pretty much any equity related work as well as ongoing regular work." A student population diversifying faster than the faculty population means faculty of color who work at PWIs are an "unheralded linchpin in institutional efforts to create an inclusive learning environment."[34]

Negative Impacts

The emotional labor WOC librarians face can lead to racial battle fatigue which often results in one or more of three stress response types: psychological, physiological, or behavioral. Psychological responses to racial battle fatigue include, but are not limited to, frustration, anger and

32. Seattle Central College, "Preliminary Strategic Plan 2016-2020," accessed December 11, 2017, https://www.seattlecentral.edu/pdf-library/strategic-planning/strategic-plan.pdf.

33. Amado M. Padilla, "Research News and Comment: Ethnic Minority Scholars; Research, and Mentoring: Current and Future Issues," *Educational Researcher* 23, no. 4 (1994): 24-27.

34. Audrey Williams June, "The Invisible Labor of Minority Professors," *Chronicle of Higher Education*, November 8, 2015, http://www.chronicle.com/article/The-Invisible-Labor-of/234098.

exhaustion, and physical avoidance. Traditional physiological responses include insomnia, fatigue, loss of appetite, frequent illness, anxiety, loss of self-confidence, and resentment. Behavioral responses include "keeping quiet," high effort coping, overeating, and neglect of responsibility.[35] Individually or together, these responses can negatively affect WOC librarians' personal and professional lives, as detailed in our survey responses and our own stories.

Some WOC librarians burn out[36] easily and frequently because they are driven by an unspoken obligation fueled by impostor syndrome to always be ahead of the game, to be productive and perfect. Burnout can creep up with the growing impatience and exhaustion from helping students and can manifest as withdrawal from committee work. It can also appear as a sudden, uncharacteristic exclamation of frustration or even resignation. Eighty-nine percent of survey respondents indicated that they have experienced burnout. Many spoke of feeling emotionally drained and experiencing a loss of passion for work.

Other survey respondents listed depression, stress, anxiety, insomnia, lack of exercise and proper nutrition, weight gain, and respiratory problems as work-related health concerns. Additionally, respondents mentioned that family members and close friends are also impacted, as they are often enlisted to provide counsel and support.

While none of the survey respondents mentioned experiencing sexual harassment from students (and sometimes staff), this has been a common point of discussion among several Seattle Central librarians. Such unwanted attention includes compliments on our appearance, being asked out on dates, "tactless utterances and lustful ogling," and questioning if our wedding rings are authentic. Sometimes unwanted attention comes in the form of seeing us librarians as motherly figures

35. William A. Smith, Walter R. Allen, and Lynette L. Danley, "'Assume the Position...You Fit the Description': Psychosocial Experiences and Racial Battle Fatigue among African American Male College Students," *American Behavioral Scientist* 51, no. 4 (2007): 551-578.

36. Burnout is "a chronic syndrome describing a dysfunctional relationship with work. People experiencing burnout are tired, uninvolved, and ineffective." *Corsini Encyclopedia of Psychology*, (Hoboken, NJ: Wiley, 2010), s.v. "Burnout."

(seeking hugs or other familial treatment, for example). The librarian's emotional labor is compounded when the unwanted behavior is paired with exotifying comments, such as asking where we are from or expressing a preference for WOC specifically. When trying to adhere to our professional standards for approachability, we run the risk of having our interest misinterpreted as romantic interest.

These interactions, which often happen at the reference desk, are awkward and the emotional labor involved includes managing our feelings of discomfort while being able to continue a reference interview (and ensure respectful reference interviews happen in the future). We are tasked with drawing boundaries and balancing the need to provide a service with the need to protect ourselves. Coping with unwanted attention can go beyond an interaction itself, causing us to spend time afterward thinking about how we physically present ourselves or practicing ways to stop inappropriate comments.

Positive Impacts

For WOC librarians, the examples of emotional labor examined above can be exhausting and disheartening; however, the very same intersectionality can be enriching and provide rewarding experiences, both inside and outside of the library. Some benefits include role modeling, community building, and nurturing other positive relationships through sincere, genuine interactions (Hochschild's "deep acting"). Students of color, who have lower graduation rates than white students,[37] often express comfort when asking for research help from a librarian who looks like them. It is especially heartening when a student of color shares their interest in the field of librarianship, and we can share details about our paths and the possibilities that exist.

Finding support, both in and outside of the institution, from colleagues who have had similar experiences of negotiating race/ethnicity

37. Mamie Lynch and Jennifer Engle, "Big Gaps, Small Gaps: Some Colleges and Universities Do Better than Others in Graduating African-American Students," *The Education Trust,* August 9, 2010.

and gender in the workplace can be an empowering experience. This reaffirms our experiences and allows us to share our professional frustrations and joys. We have found this support from off-campus organizations like the Asian/Pacific American Librarians Association and the Spectrum Scholars program. The many connections made with mentors, role models, and friends increased our confidence and sense of belonging. On-campus support from other WOC faculty/staff extends our professional networks and allows us to be a witness for others and to learn from them as well. When we feel supported and safe, we are able to "be real."

When this happens, our emotional labor can then take the form of deep acting, where we bring authenticity to our behavior and interaction with students, faculty, and the public. We are able to engage with another person's story, recognize its value, and build empathy through this "awareness of other." With this response, we mediate emotional labor with emotional intelligence.[38] Being self-aware, having awareness of others, and being able to manage the two different emotional responses allows us to create something positive for all involved.

Self-Care

"Caring for myself is not self-indulgence, it is self-preservation, and that is an act of political warfare."—Audre Lorde[39]

"To fly, we have to have resistance."—Maya Lin[40]

When microaggressions or unrealistic expectations are sustained for extended periods, we often begin to grasp at something or someone in

38. Emotional intelligence, at the most general level, refers to the ability to recognize and regulate emotions in ourselves and in others. Cary Cherniss and Daniel Goleman, *The Emotionally Intelligent Workplace: How to Select for, Measure, and Improve Emotional Intelligence in Individuals, Groups, and Organizations* (San Francisco, CA: Jossey-Bass, 2001), 14.

39. Audre Lorde, *A Burst of Light: Essays by Audre Lorde* (Ithaca, NY: Firebrand Books, 1988).

40. Michael Brenson, *Maya Lin* (Milano: Electa, 1998), 74.

order to survive. It is imperative that we cultivate strategies to survive and thrive in sometimes hostile environments. Below we explore how we and our survey respondents care for our emotional, mental, and physical well-being as an act of self-preservation and empowerment.

High expectations from students and colleagues often translate into extra work, both through emotional labor and traditional labor. Coping involves making sure that all the work we do is valued. "Value" might mean recognition, but ideally it also includes (monetary) compensation for our time and effort. Coping might include leaning on a support system, such as having someone who has gone through the tenure process themselves to advocate on your behalf when expectations are unreasonable. High expectations come from both external and internal sources. One survey respondent wrote, "If I ever feel burnt out it's mainly because I've done that to myself and not because my boss is throwing too much at me." Perfectionism and the tendency to over-work are a common theme in WOC librarian stories.

Several survey respondents described drawing boundaries as a strategy to avoid burnout. The same respondent who mentioned her self-inflicted burnout wrote, "I'm the type of person that likes to improve instruction, services, procedures, etc. so I can easily create more work for myself. I usually take a step back and decide on 1-2 goals I want to accomplish during the quarter or year to not feel so overwhelmed." Other strategies mentioned were: being specific about the capacity to work (or not work) on a project; repeating mantras ("one thing at a time," "I am enough"); saying "No" more often; turning off email notifications; and not checking work email at home. It is a challenge to maintain these boundaries all the time. Though we may not always be successful in keeping these boundaries, practice is progress.

The majority of survey respondents experienced burnout, microaggressions, and/or overtly racist interactions in their jobs. To manage these emotions and stressors, respondents identified the following self-care practices: reading, exercising, meditation, watching movies, cooking, and writing. They also included interacting with people of color and other support systems. One identified family as her main source of support: "they share many of the life experiences that have shaped me, and they understand my perspective." Others identified their colleagues as valuable members of their support system: "...our institution does have many allies that I have developed relationships with and seek them out if I feel the need" and "I have a circle of trusted colleagues and friends outside of work. They let me be who I am. I do not have to wear a 'mask' to see them." In addition to these practices, we personally identified singing, listening to music, attending sessions with a WOC therapist, and seeking learning opportunities that promote well-being.

Practicing self-care requires discipline and compassion. Sometimes the burden seems too much to handle. Evans and Moore state that "when incidents of microaggression occur, they require a process of emotional management that includes the decision of how and when to respond, an understanding of how one's response will be co-opted into a white frame, and a conscious decision about how one will feel about that process after responding—all before even making the decision to respond to white racism."[41] Their research suggests micro-resistance as a strategy for people of color to counter everyday microaggressions by managing our own emotions through an empowering inner dialogue.[42] They recognize the "additional labor required for people of color within systems of institutional racism, and the impossible burdens faced by people of color as they negotiate how to resist the racialized mechanisms of those systems."[43]

Conclusion

"I will not have my life narrowed down. I will not bow down to somebody else's whim or to someone else's ignorance."—Maya Angelou[44]

41. Louwanda Evans and Wendy Leo Moore, "Impossible Burdens: White Institutions, Emotional Labor, and Micro-Resistance," *Social Problems* 62, no. 3 (2015): 452.

42. Ibid., 451.

43. Ibid., 452.

44. Melvin McLeod, "There's No Place to Go but Up: A Conversation between Maya Angelou & bell hooks," *Shambhala Sun*, January 1998, 19.

We believe the institution's role in mitigating emotional labor in libraries should happen at several levels and should include colleagues, direct supervisors, human resources, and upper administration. Seventy-eight percent of survey respondents said their institutions are making efforts to create/maintain a supportive work environment. These include on-campus counseling services and regular faculty of color group meetings. While these are steps in the right direction, one respondent also mentioned that she experienced support from "other faculty more so than with the administration." Another cautioned, "sometimes these [college-led diversity events] can feel stressful and evolve instead into conversation about all the wrong or hateful things that are happening, not the positive." As mentioned earlier, WOC librarians are in a unique position: they often teach without a classroom and they are service providers. As a result, they are regularly on the front lines for hearing and meeting student needs. We believe their work life would improve if others in the college educated themselves and addressed the intersectional nature of the challenges faced by WOC librarians.

At Seattle Central College, library staff have incorporated diversity and self-care into library-wide efforts to promote an inclusive, caring environment. Examples include:

- Hosting cultural competency trainings;
- Revising job descriptions and interview questions to explicitly identify the library's values in support of diversity and social justice and its active engagement in their implementation;
- Beginning librarian meetings with a few minutes of mindfulness;
- Maintaining a quarterly library staff reading group, in which we discuss books reflecting the various perspectives and lived experiences of our student population;
- Participating in the Washington State Board for CTCs' faculty of color mentorship program, which pairs faculty of color from colleges across the state and hosts quarterly retreats.

Similar programming and tasks can be implemented at other campus libraries.

As institutions and colleagues strive toward creating an equitable environment that meets student needs, it is necessary that teaching and non-teaching faculty of color are prioritized and retained. As PWIs work to racially diversify their staff, administrators should identify successful faculty of color retention programs at other institutions and consider implementing them on their own campuses. In response to the stories of emotional labor included in this chapter, we call for institutions and individuals (men of color and white colleagues) to address the issues WOC librarians face by doing the following:

- Recognize the additional mentorship of POC students and peers at the reference desk as legitimate work;
- Advocate for compensation for the extra labor (outside of contracted hours) involved in serving on endless diversity committees;
- Respect boundaries regarding time and work, as set by individual WOC librarians;
- Strategize to bring accountability to professional development training on sexual harassment and cultural humility;[45]
- Provide a space for contemplative teaching and learning that builds self-awareness;
- Value the intellectual contribution of twenty-first century librarians in academia;
- Interrupt the oppression that librarians face when women are objectified;
- Implement equitable strategies to recruit and track retention of WOC faculty.

While we lament that we collected more negative narratives than positive, we learned that we are not alone. By gathering and sharing these stories, we hope to:

- Encourage others to share their experiences;

45. Originating from an effort to capture the experience of Peace Corps volunteers, cultural humility "refers to respecting the validity of the other person's culture and accepting the creative tension of holding two different perspectives simultaneously." Alan Guskin, *SAGE Encyclopedia of Intercultural Competence* (Los Angeles: SAGE Reference, 2015), s.v. "Cultural Humility."

- Recognize that it is our setting and not our intellect or ability that results in our exhaustion and self-doubt;
- Find strategies that help others negotiate their settings in order to maintain their work for other faculty and students of color;
- Inspire additional research to expose the emotional labor of WOC librarians in CTCs.

Though we believe that the responses and experiences we have shared provide valuable insight into the experiences of WOC librarians at State of Washington CTCs, we recognize that the sample size of our respondents limits the generalizability of their experiences. Gathering the experiences of a larger group of CTC librarians inside and outside Washington State and finding ways to include the stories of our colleagues in traditional university settings can enrich our understanding of the challenges faced by WOC librarians and their responses to these challenges. We are also interested in knowing more about how WOC librarians consider men of color colleagues as allies. In addition, we recognize that people of color are underrepresented in all library roles. Further investigation should be done to understand the experiences of WOC library employees who fill paraprofessional roles. Understanding the interplay of race, gender, and emotional labor and taking steps to address it can improve workplace morale and customer service. We are driven to continue the process of unmasking emotional labor to support and enrich the professional experiences of WOC librarians.

Bibliography

Accardi, Maria. "Emotional Labor and Library Instruction." *Librarian Burnout.* April 23, 2015. https://librarianburnout.com/2015/04/23/emotional-labor-and-library-instruction/.

Agreement: Seattle Community College District VI Board of Trustees and American Federation of Teachers Seattle Community Colleges Local 1789 (July 1, 2013–June 30, 2016).

American Association of Community Colleges. "2016 Fact Sheet." http://www.aacc.nche.edu/AboutCC/Documents/AACCFactSheetsR2.pdf.

American Libraries Association. "Diversity Counts Report." Accessed July 27, 2017. http://www.ala.org/aboutala/sites/ala.org.aboutala/files/content/diversity/diversitycounts/diversitycountstables2012.pdf.

American Library Association. "Standards for Proficiencies for Instruction Librarians and Coordinators: A Practical Guide." 2008. http://www.ala.org/acrl/sites/ala.org.acrl/files/content/standards/profstandards.pdf.

Brenson, Michael. *Maya Lin.* Milano: Electa, 1998.

Brint, Steven. "Few Remaining Dreams: Community Colleges since 1985." *The Annals of the American Academy of Political and Social Science* 586, no. 1 (2003): 16-37.

Brint, Steven, and Jerome Karabel. *The Diverted Dream: Community Colleges and the Promise of Educational Opportunity in America, 1900-1985.* Oxford: Oxford University Press, 1989.

Center for Community College Student Engagement. "Contingent Commitments Bringing Part-Time Faculty into Focus." 2014. http://www.ccsse.org/docs/PTF_Special_Report.pdf.

Cherniss, Cary, and Daniel Goleman. *The Emotionally Intelligent Workplace: How to Select for, Measure, and Improve Emotional Intelligence in Individuals, Groups, and Organizations.* San Francisco: Jossey-Bass, 2001.

Chou, Rose L., and Annie Pho. "Intersectionality at the Reference Desk: Lived Experiences of Women of Color Librarians." In *The Feminist Reference Desk*, edited by Maria T. Accardi, 225-252. Sacramento, CA: Litwin Books/Library Juice Press, 2017.

Crenshaw, Kimberlé. "Mapping the Margins: Intersectionality, Identity Politics, and Violence against Women of Color." *Stanford Law Review* (1991): 1241-1299.

Durr, Marlese, and Adia M. Harvey Wingfield. "Keep Your 'N' in Check: African American Women and the Interactive Effects of Etiquette and Emotional Labor." *Critical Sociology* 37, no. 5 (2011): 557-571.

Evans, Louwanda, and Wendy Leo Moore. "Impossible Burdens: White Institutions, Emotional Labor, and Micro-Resistance." *Social Problems* 62, no. 3 (2015): 439-454.

Froyum, Carissa. "'For the Betterment of Kids Who Look Like Me': Professional Emotional Labour as a Racial Project." *Ethnic and Racial Studies* 36, no. 6 (2013): 1070-1089.

Guskin, Alan. "Cultural Humility." In *SAGE Encyclopedia of Intercultural Competence*. 162-164. Vol. 1. Los Angeles: SAGE Reference, 2015.

Gutiérrez y Muhs, Gabriella, Yolanda Flores Niemann, Carmen G. González, and Angela P. Harris. *Presumed Incompetent: The Intersections of Race and Class for Women in Academia*. Boulder, CO: Utah State University Press, 2012.

Guy, Mary E., and Hyun Jung Lee. "How Emotional Intelligence Mediates Emotional Labor in Public Service Jobs." *Review of Public Personnel Administration* 35, no. 3 (2015): 261-277.

Harvey, Joan C., and Cynthia Katz. *If I'm So Successful, Why Do I Feel Like a Fake? The Impostor Phenomenon*. New York: St. Martin's Press, 1985.

Hochschild, Arlie Russell. *Managed Heart*. Berkeley: University of California Press, 2012.

Hoosein, Mehnaz. "Everything," *Silence,* performed by Manooghi Hi. Compact Disc. Mowlawner Music, 2011.

Jain, Dimpal. Untitled Presentation at Seattle Central College's Women of Color Employee Affinity Group, Seattle, WA. October 27, 2016.

Julien, Heidi, and Shelagh K. Genuis. "Emotional Labour in Librarians' Instructional Work." *Journal of Documentation* 65, no. 6 (2009): 926-937.

June, Audrey Williams. "The Invisible Labor of Minority Professors." *Chronicle of Higher Education*. November 8, 2015. http://www.chronicle.com/article/The-Invisible-Labor-of/234098.

Leiter, Michael P. "Burnout." In *Corsini Encyclopedia of Psychology*, 4th ed., edited by Irving B. Weiner and W. Edward Craighead, 264-266. Vol. 1. Hoboken, NJ: Wiley, 2010. *Gale Virtual Reference Library* (accessed September 5, 2017).

Lorde, Audre. *A Burst of Light: Essays by Audre Lorde.* Ithaca, New York: Firebrand Books, 1988.

Lynch, Mamie, and Jennifer Engle. "Big Gaps, Small Gaps: Some Colleges and Universities Do Better than Others in Graduating African-American Students." *The Education Trust.* August 9, 2010. https://edtrust.org/resource/big-gaps-small-gaps-in-serving-african-american-students/.

Lynch, Mamie, and Jennifer Engle. "Big Gaps, Small Gaps: Some Colleges and Universities Do Better Than Others in Graduating Hispanic Students." *The Education Trust.* August 9, 2010. https://edtrust.org/resource/big-gaps-small-gaps-in-serving-hispanic-students/.

Matteson, Miriam L., Sharon Chittock, and David Mease. "In Their Own Words: Stories of Emotional Labor from the Library Workforce." *Library Quarterly* 85, no. 1 (2015): 85-105.

McLeod, Melvin. "There's No Place to Go but Up: A Conversation between Maya Angelou & bell hooks." *Shambhala Sun*, January 1998, 16-22.

Padilla, Amado M. "Research News and Comment: Ethnic Minority Scholars; Research, and Mentoring: Current and Future Issues." *Educational Researcher* 23, no. 4 (1994): 24-27.

The Reference and User Services Association. "Guidelines for Behavioral Performance of Reference and Information Service Providers." Revised May 28, 2013. http://www.ala.org/rusa/resources/guidelines/guidelinesbehavioral.

Russell, Patricia. "Implicit Bias & Microaggressions: Recognizing & Rectifying." Presentation at Seattle Central College Library's Conversations on Social Issues series, Seattle, WA, February 25, 2016.

Seattle Central College. "Facts and Figures." Accessed May 22, 2017. http://www.seattlecentral.edu/newscenter/facts-and-figures/.

Seattle Central College. "Preliminary Strategic Plan 2016-2020." *Office of the President.* http://www.seattlecentral.edu/president/strategic-plan.pdf.

Smith, Linda Tuhiwai. *Decolonizing Methodologies: Research and Indigenous Peoples.* London: Zed Books Ltd., 2013.

Smith, William A., Walter R. Allen, and Lynette L. Danley. "'Assume the Position... You Fit the Description': Psychosocial Experiences and Racial Battle Fatigue among African American Male College Students." *American Behavioral Scientist* 51, no. 4 (2007): 551-578.

Sotomayor, Sonia. *Fresh Air.* By Terry Gross. NPR, January 13, 2014. Retrieved from https://www.npr.org/2014/01/13/262067546/as-a-latina-sonia-sotomayor-says-you-have-to-work-harder.

U.S. Department of Labor, Bureau of Labor Statistics. "Table 11: Employed Persons by Detailed Occupation, Sex, Race, and Hispanic or Latino ethnicity." *Current Population Survey. 2011.* http://www.bls.gov/cps/cpsaat11.pdf.

Washington State Board for Community and Technical Colleges. "Fall Enrollment & Staffing Report 2013." https://www.sbctc.edu/resources/documents/colleges-staff/research/fall-quarter-research/2014/7_FQR_Staff_2014.pdf.

Wingfield, Adia Harvey. "How 'Service with a Smile' Takes a Toll on Women." *The Atlantic.* January 26, 2016. https://www.theatlantic.com/business/archive/2016/01/gender-emotional-labor/427083/.

Chapter 11

The Burden of Care: Cultural Taxation of Women of Color Librarians on the Tenure-Track

Tarida Anantachai and Camille Chesley

Introduction

As a service-oriented profession, librarianship is often seen as being in the realm of care work. A charitable interpretation of this perception suggests that librarians operate in the literal service of others; however, there are also deeper, more troubling implications at play. The emotional, affective labor of care work is also largely devalued. Within higher education, for instance, academic librarians are often viewed by other faculty as support staff rather than equal scholars, even when they too hold faculty status.[1] Not only is their work perceived as requiring none of the intellectual capacities that are typically valued in academic work, but it also is largely ignored or rendered invisible.[2]

Historically, caregiving and other service-related jobs have been considered the responsibility of women. The concept of "burden of care," which arose in medical literature in the 1980-1990s, is typically used to

1. Lisa Sloniowski, "Affective Labor, Resistance, and the Academic Librarian," *Library Trends* 64, no. 4 (Spring 2016): 660.

2. Sloniowski, "Affective Labor, Resistance, and the Academic Librarian," 657.

refer to the physical, emotional, and social toll experienced by family caregivers (usually women) over an extended period of time.[3] Numerous studies have examined the gender division of household labor and found that, even when such duties are divided more equally, women continue to bear the burden of the invisible mental and emotional labor of the household (e.g., assigning tasks, researching physicians, and otherwise "noticing" and being more attentive to problems).[4] Indeed, even in higher education, a number of studies have corroborated that female faculty engage in more domestic and "institutional housekeeping" than their male colleagues, ranging from the more official (e.g., committee work and teaching) to the unofficial (e.g., mentoring students and volunteering for projects outside of their regular duties).[5] These gendered labors often go unrecognized or are undervalued during tenure and promotion reviews. They are especially significant when considering how women faculty are underrepresented in higher education. According to data from the National Center for Education Statistics, women made up 44% of total faculty in 2013, but only 37% of tenured faculty (i.e., at the associate professor or professor rank).[6]

---

3. Gail O'Neill and Margaret M. Ross, "Burden of Care: An Important Concept for Nurses," *Health Care for Women International* 12, no. 1 (1991): 111-115.

4. Suzanne M. Bianchi, et al., "Is Anyone Doing the Housework? Trends in the Gender Division of Household Labor," *Social Forces* 79, no. 1 (September 2000), 191-228; Marjorie L. DeVault, *Feeding the Family: The Social Organization of Caring as Gendered Work* (Chicago, IL: University of Chicago Press, 1991); Susan Walzer, "Thinking About the Baby: Gender and Divisions of Infant Care," *Social Problems* 43, no. 2 (May 1996): 219-234.

5. Sharon Bird, Jacquelyn S. Litt, and Yong Wang, "Creating Status of Women Reports: Institutional Housekeeping as 'Women's Work,'" *NWSA Journal* 16, no. 1 (2004): 195; Cassandra M. Guarino and Victor M. H. Borden, "Faculty Service Loads and Gender: Are Women Taking Care of the Academic Family?" *Research in Higher Education* (2017): 672, 676-677; Shelley M. Park, "Research, Teaching, and Service: Why Shouldn't Women's Work Count?" *Journal of Higher Education* 67, no. 1 (January/February 1996): 55; Kelly Ward and Lisa Wolf-Wendel, *Academic Motherhood: How Faculty Manage Work and Family* (Piscataway, NJ: Rutgers University Press, 2012), 57.

6. "Full-Time Faculty in Degree-Granting Postsecondary Institutions, By Race/Ethnicity, Sex, and Academic Rank: Fall 2009, Fall 2011, and Fall 2013," accessed July 5, 2017, https://nces.ed.gov/programs/digest/d15/tables/dt15_315.20.asp?current=yes.

Along similar lines, the concept of "cultural taxation," coined in 1994 by Amado Padilla, refers to the burden that faculty of color assume as a result of their cultural background (e.g., extra diversity-related service roles, tasks, or other responsibilities) and the resultant strain caused by these demands.[7] While these time-consuming and emotionally taxing activities are undertaken in support of their institutions and the students they serve, they are also typically overlooked or undervalued by their colleagues—again, presenting additional hurdles to achieving tenure.[8] These also have grave implications when considering the underrepresentation of faculty of color, who made up only 21% of total faculty and only 18% of tenured faculty in 2013.[9] While representation of faculty of color in academia has historically been low, the makeup of academic librarians of color is even lower. According to the 2009-2010 update to the American Library Association's "Diversity Counts" report, they made up just 15% of academic librarians.[10]

The intersections between the burden of care and cultural taxation faced by women of color in higher education are already apparent. For women of color librarians, the burdens they face as a result of their intersectional identities are further exacerbated by their professional characterization as care workers. In this chapter, we will examine how

---

7. Amado M. Padilla, "Ethnic Minority Scholars, Research, and Mentoring: Current and Future Issues," *Educational Researcher* 23, no. 4 (1994): 26.

8. Audrey Williams June, "The Invisible Labor of Minority Professors," *Chronicle of Higher Education*, November 8, 2015, accessed December 21, 2016, http://www.chronicle.com/article/The-Invisible-Labor-of/234098; Patricia Matthew, "The Invisible Labor of Faculty of Color on Campus," *The Atlantic*, November 23, 2016, accessed December 21, 2016, https://www.theatlantic.com/education/archive/2016/11/what-is-faculty-diversity-worth-to-a-university/508334.

9. "Full-Time Faculty in Degree-Granting Postsecondary Institutions, By Race/Ethnicity, Sex, and Academic Rank: Fall 2009, Fall 2011, and Fall 2013," accessed July 5, 2017, https://nces.ed.gov/programs/digest/d15/tables/dt15_315.20.asp?current=yes.

10. "Diversity Counts 2009-2010 Update," last modified September 2012, accessed April 25, 2017, http://www.ala.org/offices/diversity/diversitycounts/2009-2010update. (Note that while this report provides data on the diversity of academic librarians as a whole, it does not include data on how many of these librarians hold tenured status.).

the burden of care and cultural taxation intersect for women of color on the tenure- or promotion-track. In addition to reviewing the higher education and library literature, we will examine data and comments gathered from a survey aimed at investigating these experiences within academic librarianship. We do this in order to bring the lived experiences of women of color librarians to light and explore how they are reconciling their identities within an academic system that has historically been defined by the majority culture.

Women of Color Faculty: A Literature Review

Over the past decade, discussions of the unique challenges facing both women and faculty of color in academia have increasingly garnered attention. The recently published book *Written/Unwritten: Diversity and the Hidden Truths of Tenure* documents the discrimination and cultural barriers that directly affect faculty of color on the tenure track.[11] Inspired by her own experience being denied tenure (later overturned by appeal), Patricia Matthew and her fellow contributors offer numerous examples that speak to the burden of care and cultural taxation facing faculty of color (in particular, women of color faculty). These hurdles range from the demands of taking on extra service-oriented tasks to the penalties they face in their time, emotional well-being, and tenure reviews by doing so. Joanne Cooper and Dannelle Stevens' similar volume, *Tenure in the Sacred Grove: Issues and Strategies for Women and Minority Faculty*, also echoes these concerns, including the problematic and limited view of what traditionally counts as tenure-granting work and the bargains that women of color make in order to succeed professionally in the eyes of their white male colleagues.[12] Likewise, in *Presumed Incompetent: The Intersections of Race and Class for Women in Academia*, Gutiérrez y Muhs et

11. Patricia Matthew, ed., *Written/Unwritten: Diversity and the Hidden Truths of Tenure* (Chapel Hill, NC: University of North Carolina Press, 2016).

12. Joanne E. Cooper and Dannelle D. Stevens, eds., *Tenure in the Sacred Grove: Issues and Strategies for Women and Minority Faculty* (Albany, NY: State University of New York Press, 2002).

al. further emphasize the structural issues and problematic biases within academia that disproportionately hinder the advancement of women of color.[13] These personal stories are not merely anecdotal; rather they are emblematic of the systemic inequities within higher education and its tenure processes. Indeed, academia has seen a number of highly publicized controversies regarding the denial of tenure to faculty of color, raising, or strengthening, the institutions' supposed commitment to diversity and inclusion.[14] What these works and other similar literature suggest is that women of color faculty are uniquely positioned at the intersection of racism and sexism on their campuses—that is, doubly subject to discriminatory practices.

A common trend in the literature notes how women of color often feel pressured to contribute to service beyond what is required, both as a result of the gendered expectations to undertake such "motherwork" (i.e., burden of care), as well as the personal, political, and emotional duty to support the marginalized communities that are turning to them in greater numbers on their campuses (i.e., cultural taxation).[15] These service obligations sometimes provide a meaningful outlet for women of color to build deep, valued relationships with the communities they are serving. However, the value of such caregiving work is often not recognized by tenure review committees, which have historically been

13. Gabriella Gutiérrez y Muhs, et al., eds., *Presumed Incompetent: The Intersections of Race and Class for Women in Academia* (Boulder, CO: Colorado State University Press, 2012).

14. Colleen Flaherty, "Campus Unrest Follows Tenure Denial of Innovative, Popular Faculty Member of Color," *Inside Higher Ed*, May 17, 2016, accessed December 21, 2016, https://www.insidehighered.com/news/2016/05/17/campus-unrest-follows-tenure-denial-innovative-popular-faculty-member-color; Colleen Flaherty, "American U Scholar Says Provost Cherry-Picked Negative Ratings of Her Teaching to Deny Her a Promotion," *Inside Higher Ed*, June 29, 2017, accessed July 5, 2017, https://www.insidehighered.com/news/2017/06/29/american-u-scholar-says-provost-cherry-picked-negative-student-ratings-her-teaching; Kari Lydersen and Rachel Cromidas, "Questions of Racial Discrimination on Tenure Unsettle DePaul," *New York Times*, December 23, 2010, accessed December 21, 2016, http://www.nytimes.com/2010/12/24/us/24cncdepaul.html.

15. Kimberly A. Griffin, Jessica C. Bennett, and Jessica Harris, "Marginalizing Merit? Gender Differences in Black Faculty D/discourses on Tenure, Advancement, and Professional Success," *Review of Higher Education* 36, no. 4 (Summer 2013): 503.

governed by the majority white, male culture's view of what qualifies as quality, tenure-earning work (i.e., traditional research output). For instance, race-, gender-, and other culture-related scholarship are considered less "traditionally academic," and their applied and community-based research methods are often discredited, ignored, or viewed as inappropriate.[16] In addition to their research, women of color faculty are often judged more harshly due to gender- and race-based stereotypes about their abilities.[17]

Numerous other studies also note the predicament that many women of color face in negotiating parts of their identities, such as self-silencing, struggling to "fit in" with the dominant culture, and often losing a part of themselves in order to survive professionally. In addition to being tokenized, these negotiations create additional hardships for faculty who are already more vulnerable to isolation and marginalization on their predominantly white campuses.[18]

Historic systems of inequality also manifest within the academic library profession. As a historically feminized profession, academic librarians function in a unique place that "[straddles] both academic and nonacademic work"[19] within their institutions. Yet, despite the wide variety of titles and responsibilities they possess, the popular image of librarians focuses on their expected role as "care workers" or waged domestic laborers.[20] This problematic view renders invisible the

16. Linda S. Behar-Horenstein, et al., "Resilience Post Tenure: The Experience of an African American Woman in a PWI," *Florida Journal of Educational Administration* & Policy 5, no. 2 (Spring 2012): 71; Tammy Boyd, Rosa Cintrón, and Mia Alexander-Snow, "The Experience of Being a Junior Minority Female Faculty Member," *Forum on Public Policy* 2 (2010): 5; Cooper and Stevens, eds. *Tenure in the Sacred Grove*, 4, 6-7, 37; Griffin, Bennett, and Harris, "Marginalizing Merit," 492.

17. Behar-Horenstein, et al., "Resilience Post Tenure," 69; Boyd, Cintrón, and Alexander-Snow, "The Experience of Being a Junior Minority Female Faculty Member," 4; Griffin, Bennett, and Harris, "Marginalizing Merit," 491.

18. Behar-Horenstein, et al., "Resilience Post Tenure," 69; Boyd, Cintrón, and Alexander-Snow, "The Experience of Being a Junior Minority Female Faculty Member," 4.

19. Sloniowski, "Affective Labor, Resistance, and the Academic Librarian," 659.

20. Sloniowski, "Affective Labor, Resistance, and the Academic Librarian," 659-660.

intellectual contributions librarians make in the academy, potentially hindering their ability to earn tenure.

This inequity of expectations also extends beyond university campuses and into the home. For instance, some women faculty librarians struggle to balance their family responsibilities with the demands of tenure, especially given the social assumption that they take on the majority of familial obligations.[21] Academic librarians of color have similarly expressed the challenges of being increasingly expected to serve on diversity committees, as liaisons to cultural groups and units outside of their libraries, and as their libraries' "diversity specialist" for the spectrum of identities across all underrepresented populations.[22]

Still others note the systemic microaggressions affecting librarians of color, such as having their intelligence or ability questioned, overextending themselves in order to disprove cultural stereotypes, and being held to biased performance standards established by white, male norms.[23] Meanwhile, the systems that both perpetuate and diminish the work of women of color librarians also reward those of the majority culture, who are allowed the time to focus on research or other projects that are generally held in higher regard. In other words, the imbalanced service workloads and the devaluation of the burdens and taxations facing women of color librarians ultimately create an inequitable environment that hinders their work-life balance as well as their prospects for earning tenure and professional esteem.

---

21. Quinn Galbraith, Leanna Fry, and Melissa Garrison, "The Impact of Faculty Status and Gender on Employee Well-being in Academic Libraries," *College & Research Libraries* 77, no. 1 (January 2016): 73, 82, accessed December 21, 2016, https://doi.org/10.5860/crl.77.1.71.

22. Ione T. Damasco and Dracine Hodges, "Tenure and Promotion Experience of Academic Librarians of Color," *College & Research Libraries* 73, no. 3 (May 2012): 298, accessed December 21, 2016, https://doi.org/10.5860/crl-244.

23. Jaena Alabi, "'This Actually Happened': An Analysis of Librarians' Responses to a Survey about Racial Microaggressions," *Journal of Library Administration* 55 (2015): 181-182, 189.

Methodology

While prior studies have described the struggles of both women faculty and faculty of color, we noticed a lack of actual narratives from women of color librarians about their own experiences. We recognized a need to uncover these stories in order to amplify their lived experiences and draw attention to their significant implications. To begin this process, we designed an online questionnaire aimed at capturing how identifying as a woman of color can shape the types of responsibilities and services they assume, and the impact this may have on their overall career advancement.

After scanning the literature to identify topics to further explore, we created a series of questions organized by themes. For example, we asked participants to reflect on their general experiences navigating the tenure/promotion process, including the clarity of its requirements, the support systems in place, and the pressure to adjust various aspects of their portfolios to achieve tenure or promotion. We expanded this line of inquiry by further examining the burden of care and cultural taxation of service activities these librarians shouldered as a result of their race and/or gender identity. In another section, we queried participants on other issues related to identity and inclusion, particularly as they relate to support and professional advancement. These included questions regarding the climate of their work environments, the negotiation of their identities to conform to expectations, and the experience or observance of unjust practices due to race and/or gender identity.

In order to better parse our results, we gathered demographic data, such as the gender, racial and/or ethnic group with whom participants most identified, their rank and tenure/promotion status, and their number of years in the field. We incorporated multiple choice, Likert scale, and open-ended questions, as well as multiple opportunities for participants to further elaborate on their responses. All questions were voluntary and offered options for participants to self-describe or to withhold whatever personal information they did not wish to share.

Recognizing the need to specifically target women of color librarians, our main mode of distribution was through selected mailing lists, including ALA's ethnic affiliates (e.g., the Asian Pacific American Librarians Association), ACRL Residency Interest Group, ARL Diversity Programs, and Spectrum Scholars listservs. Additional postings were disseminated through selected social media and other online forums, such as those for the alumni of the Minnesota Institute for Early Career Librarians from Traditionally Underrepresented Groups, the ALA Diversity Member Initiative Group, and "we here" (an independently created and burgeoning community of library professionals of color). We sought to recruit women of color who were currently working or had previously worked in tenure- or promotion-track positions.

Findings and Results

We began analyzing our data by excluding responses that were incomplete, as well as those outside of our target demographic. We also broke down the data and examined them at a more granular level (e.g., by race, rank, institution type, etc.) in order to uncover any noticeable trends.

In total, 54 women completed our survey. A slight majority of the respondents (36.7%) identified as Black or African American, followed by Asian (30%), and Hispanic or Latina/Latinx (16.7%). A majority (66%) hailed from doctorate-granting institutions, with the next largest group (15.1%) working at Masters-granting institutions.

Respondents skewed heavily toward early and mid-career librarians, with 74.1% indicating that they had been employed as librarians for less than ten years. 46.3% held the rank of Assistant or Senior Assistant Librarian/Professor, while 22.2% held the rank of Associate, and 20.4% held the rank of full Professor or Librarian. When asked about their experience with the tenure/promotion process, slightly over half (55.6%) indicated that they had never gone through the process. 20.37% had been through the process and received tenure/promotion and another 20.37% indicated that they were eligible for tenure/promotion but had left their positions before completing the process. Only 3.7% reported that they had been denied tenure/promotion.

Job duties and areas of expertise varied among respondents. Unsurprisingly, most respondents selected two or more areas as part of their main job responsibilities. Reference, instruction, collection development, and subject specialization were the areas cited most often, but scholarly communications, administration, marketing, and assessment also stood out.

It is remarkable that, with the exception of a few questions related to perceptions of the tenure/promotion process, our survey revealed a unified experience across all demographic categories for women of color in librarianship. The following subsections detail just some of these shared burdens, taxations, and overall experiences.

Tenure and Promotion

We began our survey with queries about navigating the tenure/promotion process, internal and external support networks in place, and professional autonomy. As some institutions use different terminology despite similar tenure- and promotion-track processes, we use the word "tenure" to also encompass "permanent status" rankings in order to reduce confusion throughout this chapter. As it is possible to be promoted to a higher rank once tenure is awarded, we felt that this nomenclature would be less confusing. As far as we were able to determine, there are currently no data regarding the number of institutions that award librarians tenure versus other types of permanent status.

The majority of our respondents (68%) felt that the requirements for tenure and promotion were clearly communicated at their institutions; only 19.6% disagreed. While responses were generally positive regarding the clarity of their tenure expectations, many librarians expressed dissatisfaction with the support provided by their libraries. Overall, librarians felt free to pursue their own interests, but felt that they lacked internal support systems at their institutions. One respondent explained,

"I have not felt external pressure to change what I do but I also have not necessarily felt well supported in terms of advising my entire career. It was only after seeking out new mentors for myself that I felt like my support improved. I still feel like support from my supervisory line could be better."

Echoing what we found in the literature regarding what institutions traditionally "count" as tenure-earning scholarship, some librarians spoke of proactively adjusting their research agendas and hedging their bets with regards to diversity-related research. One librarian, despite describing her workplace as "generally supportive," still worried how her research would be received: "I consciously tried to beef up my promotion file with other research [agendae] (e.g., instruction) just in case my diversity work didn't end up being as heavily valued when the time came to put forward my promotion file." One librarian recounted a hair-raising story of being denied promotion due to her diversity-related research; only after stripping her dossier of her diversity work and resubmitting it did she receive promotion. Other librarians spoke about the lack of objectivity in evaluations of reappointment and tenure dossiers. For instance, one librarian described feeling as though she was "judged with a different yardstick than others in my cohort."

Departmental support networks and mentoring were two areas where there were divisions within the data that were only revealed by a more granular examination. While an overall majority (57.6%) of respondents indicated that they needed to seek support networks outside of their institution or library, a closer examination revealed that librarians at the Associate or full Librarian rank were more likely to respond affirmatively. At this rank, 70% of librarians had sought outside support networks compared to 55% of librarians at the Assistant or Senior Assistant level. Similarly, while 48.1% of respondents felt that they had received adequate internal support from their libraries, higher-ranked librarians were evenly split, lower-ranked librarians were more likely (73%) to agree that they had received adequate departmental support during the tenure and promotion process. This could be indicative of institutional policies that tend to be more supportive of newer, untenured faculty.

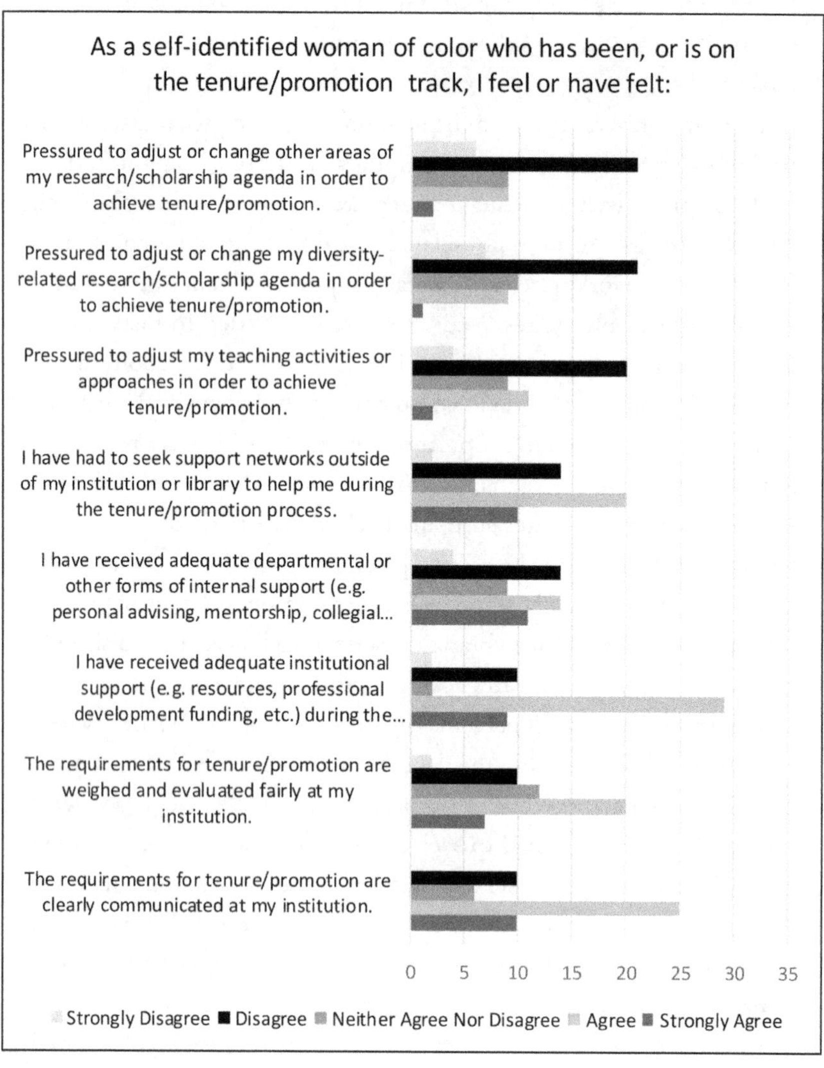

Figure 1. Perceptions of the Tenure and Promotion Process

Service

With regard to burden of care and cultural taxation, our results reflected what we found in the literature. Over half of respondents (56.6%) felt that they took on more service activities because of their racial identity. There were slight differences when respondents were broken down by race. Respondents who identified as Asian were more likely than those who identified as Black or Hispanic to agree or strongly agree that they take on more service work than their colleagues. 66% of Asian respondents agreed, versus 43% of Black respondents and 50% of Hispanic respondents. Responses were nearly inverted when the focus switched to gender identity, which may be due to the overwhelmingly female representation in the library profession. 60.4% of respondents disagreed with the statement that they took on more service activities because of their gender identity. This trend extended beyond their more formal library duties as well, since 52.9% indicated that they were involved in more "unofficial" service activities than colleagues because of their race and/or gender identity.

Some librarians echoed the literature regarding seemingly well-intentioned diversity policies and the burdens that accompany them. One librarian described her experience with the policy at her institution: "I am often the 'diversity' member appointed to committees due to my race and gender so that they can cover all of the bases." However, most librarians stated outright or strongly implied that they considered their heavier service load as part of a self-imposed burden of care, rather than an official duty. Only 35.2% admitted that they felt pressured to take on extra, uncompensated work because of their race and/or gender identity. One respondent elaborated on that, saying:

"I don't necessarily feel pressured to take on other extra work but more so a personal need to do it as a responsibility to our native/diverse students and my native community. I want the library to be involved in the work of our campus's native

student serving programs and know that we wouldn't otherwise participate - so sometimes the only way to support this work is to do it in addition to my 'normal duties.'"

Related to this, nearly two-thirds of respondents (62.3%) replied that they had been approached by students for help because of their race and/or gender identity. One librarian expressed her frustration with what she saw as a burden imposed by a systemic lack of diversity:

"I am at a [predominantly white institution], so any Muslim students or students from my cultural background seek me out for all sorts of things. So, while I can't say that I take on more service because my colleagues expect me to, or that I think I need to in order to be good enough (I don't feel that way), I do take more on because I know that no one else in my organization will offer the perspective. All my colleagues are white, except one, and it is so isolating. This whole field is isolating sometimes."

Another librarian put a positive spin on her service: "It's a bit of a catch-22: I do a lot of diversity work, so I'm asked to do more diversity work. Intersections of my identity and scholarship and work!"

Work-Life Balance

As noted earlier, the literature establishes that women often take on a disproportionate share of the emotional and physical labor inside the home. Guarino and Borden note that women often assume an imbalanced amount of this labor at work, which has the potential to disadvantage women when they seek tenure.[24] When surveyed, 56% of our respondents agreed that they take on additional household and family responsibilities outside of work. Close to half (48.9%) noted that they received adequate support from their institution to help manage their work-life balance.

Slightly less than half (45%) of respondents noted that they did not feel pressured to reduce service activities because of how such service might be weighed against other tenure-earning activities. However,

24. Guarino and Borden, "Faculty Service Loads and Gender," 690-691.

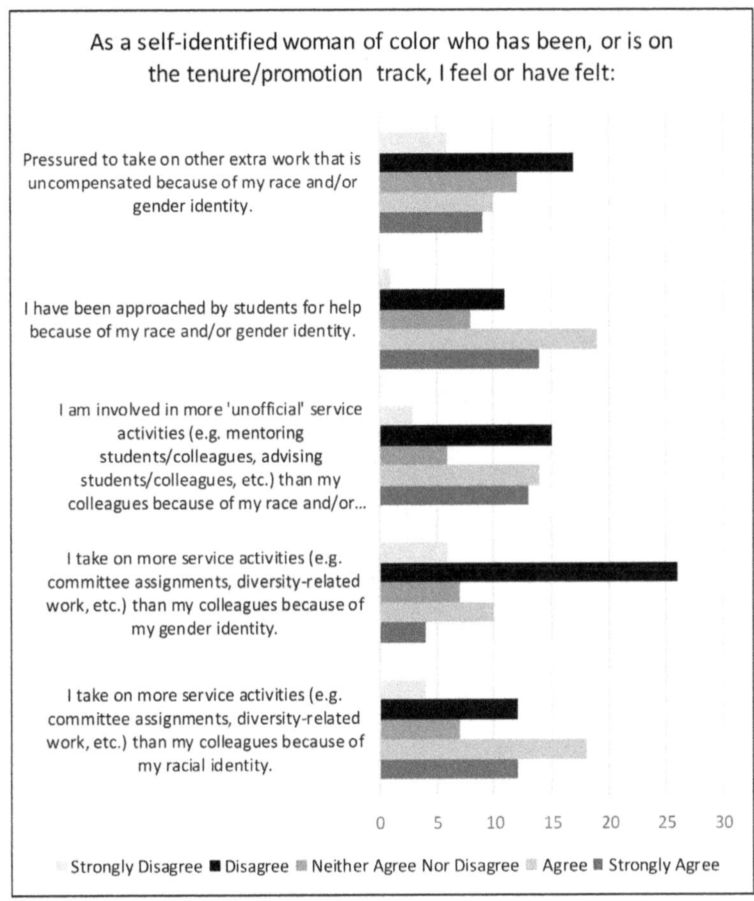

Figure 2. Perceptions of Service Loads

one quarter (27.5%) agreed with this statement. One librarian spoke of feeling pressured to hedge her bets in order to pursue her interest in diversity-related research: "I feel like I have had to take on a large amount of additional projects just in case my diversity work wouldn't be weighed as heavily. It makes for some really long hours." Respondents were split nearly evenly as to whether they felt pressured to take on extra work beyond their normally scheduled hours, with 41.5% agreeing with this statement and 43.4% disagreeing. Many librarians noted that they voluntarily took on this burden, but their reasons varied. One librarian observed, "I think I am also more involved in diversity related work

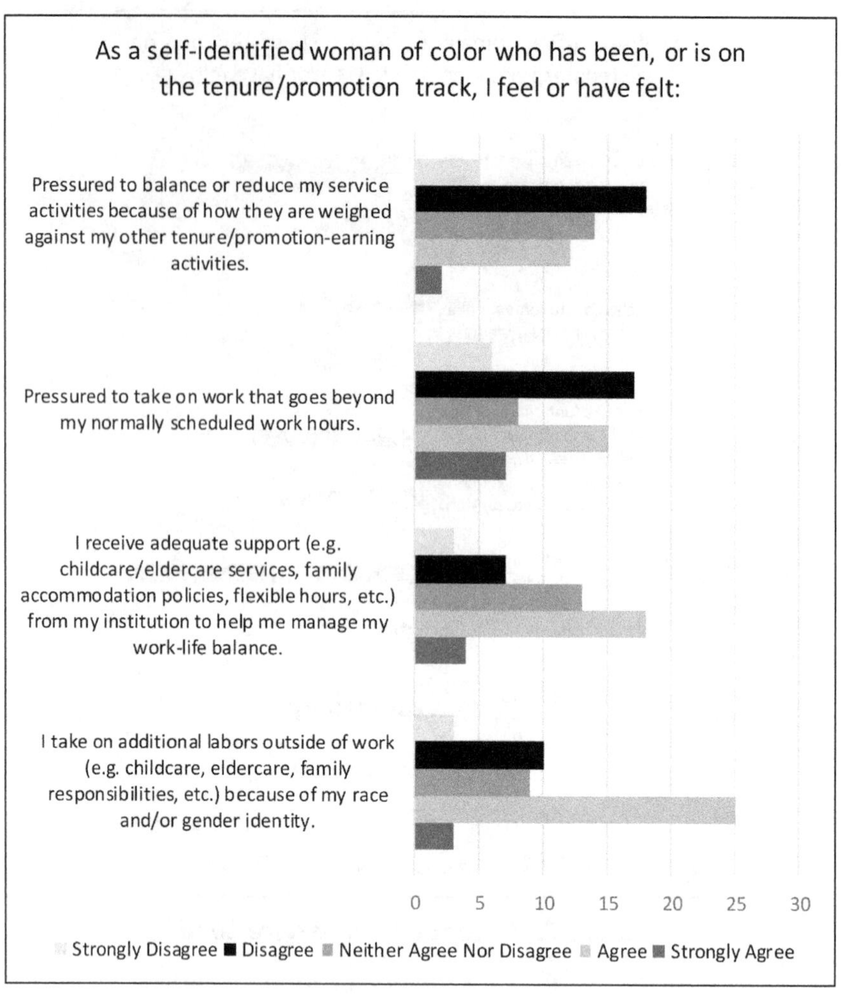

Figure 3: Perceptions of Factors Contributing to Work-Life Balance

because I am more interested in it than others (because it is something I am more aware of as a [woman] of color)."

Several librarians spoke of their experiences with imposter syndrome and how this led them to take on additional burdens or responsibilities in order to prove themselves or disprove stereotypes. One librarian explained that "as a person of color I always felt like I had to do more than anybody else to prove that Latinxs were as good or better than everyone else. As a total go-getter I never felt pressure from my institution to take on work beyond work hours. I put that pressure on myself."

Some librarians also spoke of the struggle they felt maintaining balance within their predominantly white institutions. In a profession where librarians of color are often isolated, some librarians expressed that they felt as though they could not relax. One librarian put it this way: "I also want to take care of myself and not get fatigued from always expected to be 'on' while away from a support system who share my values. Colleagues assume my needs are the same as theirs or my work style is the same or my commitments are the same."

Institutional Climate

Only 42% of respondents reported being satisfied with the overall climate of their institution, and only 46.3% were satisfied with the overall climate of their library. One consistent theme in the comments was the lack of meaningful institutional commitment to diversity and inclusion. Only 50% of respondents felt that their library valued diversity and inclusion, and a similar percentage (48.2%) felt that it was valued at the institutional level. Several librarians noted that their libraries displayed only a superficial commitment to diversity and inclusion. One librarian described her institution and library as "extremely well-versed at talking about diversity and seeming to support it, but actually on a daily basis promote actions that are diametrically opposed to furthering diversity, equity and inclusion."

Only 39% of respondents agreed that their library actively demonstrated a commitment to being a diverse and inclusive workplace. Several respondents noted that they had to constantly "self-police" to get by. One librarian stated: "I do not feel that my identity will cause problems in promotion. However, it's the work environment that feels uncomfortable. I am often invalidated or interrupted. I work with a lot

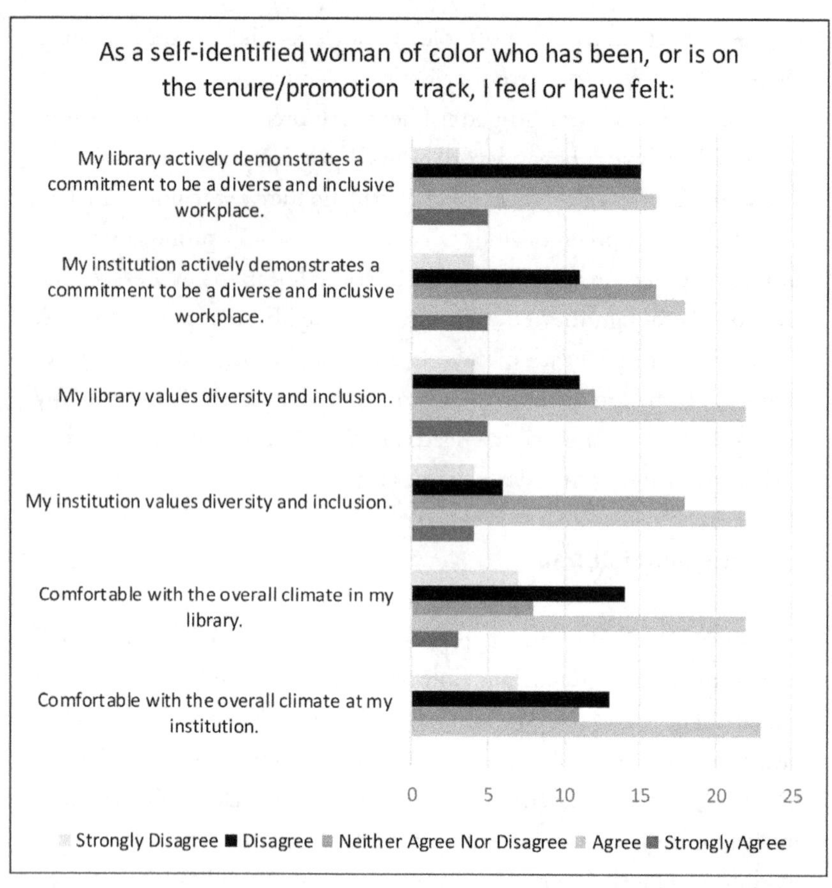

Figure 4: Perception of Institutional and Library Climate

of experienced white women, but I am an emerging Asian American librarian. Everything that comes out of my mouth has been filtered and strategized with a list of back-up remarks to defend myself. I can't just be myself or think out loud EVER."

Many respondents reported incidences of microaggressions, usually typified by "clueless" or "ignorant" comments and implicit biases, rather than overt hostility. One librarian described her colleagues as "well-intentioned," noting that they "struggle with the idea that others' gender/ethnic experiences do impact work." Another librarian described the impact of working through microaggressions: "I have experienced and observed ignorant comments and assumptions about race that have bothered me and took some emotional labor to address. But they were not hostile in nature, just ignorant." It is also worth mentioning that even in this survey, which explicitly requested respondents who identified as women of color in order to capture their specific experiences, we received a hostile response. One individual began the survey just to note their race as "American." (This respondent's submission was later filtered out of our data because they did not complete the survey.)

Negotiating Identities

Our respondents were evenly split as to whether they had experienced or observed other unjust personnel practices, such as salary inequities and reappointments due to race and/or gender identity. 42.3% agreed with this statement, and 44.2% disagreed. 35.4% noted that they had experienced or observed unjust promotion/tenure or dismissal practices due to race and/or gender identity, while 60.4% noted that they had not. Despite this, many librarians spoke of their struggles navigating their libraries at every level of the organization. One librarian in administration addressed the difficulty negotiating her identity at the management level, noting that "being the only person of color on my organization's senior management team has been a 'tightrope' situation. I have addressed diversity in hiring through my limited autonomy."

Our respondents' comments revealed the complexities and different dimensions of identity, even within their own communities, and the burden this places upon them. Several librarians spoke of experiencing pressure both from within and without while negotiating their identities in the workplace. One librarian noted that she felt pressure from other librarians of color: "I think there is a lot of pressure to give back to the community, and I want to, but I also want to do so when I am not focusing on other things and feel I have more time." Along similar lines, a more senior librarian commented that she had "a hard time understanding librarians who say they have to wait until they get tenure to become involved in controversial issues that affect communities of color on campus or in the community." While 35.9% agreed that they have had to negotiate parts of their identity in order to conform to expectations in the tenure/promotion process, a higher percentage (45.3%) admitted that they have had to negotiate parts of their identity in order to conform to their work environment.

Microaggressions emerged again and remained a common theme throughout every section of our survey. One respondent described her workplace as "[lacking] empathy and understanding of people of color, even for the students." Another librarian spoke of the direct negation of her identity by colleagues:

"Due to my ambiguous ethnic looks, my colleagues often forget I'm a [person of color] and treat me as another white person. Because of this, I often share in the white privilege that surrounds me, but I find that this situation makes it even harder to speak up when I see behaviors that conflict with their professed commitment to diversity; that and the negation of my identity (e.g., comments like 'you're not really Asian') when I do speak up."

More alarmingly, within this section of the survey, two-thirds of respondents (64.8%) remarked that they had experienced or observed hostility, harassment, exclusions, microaggressions, or other unjust practices at their institution due to race and/or gender identity. Only 20.4% noted that they had not experienced this.

Discussion and Implications

We feel that our data have already begun to uncover the intersectional narratives of women of color librarians on the tenure- and promotion-track, and the unique burdens and cultural taxations they experience. Our next steps include further unpacking these stories by re-interviewing those respondents who voluntarily agreed to be contacted for follow-up and conducting focus groups. We hope to gain more detailed insight

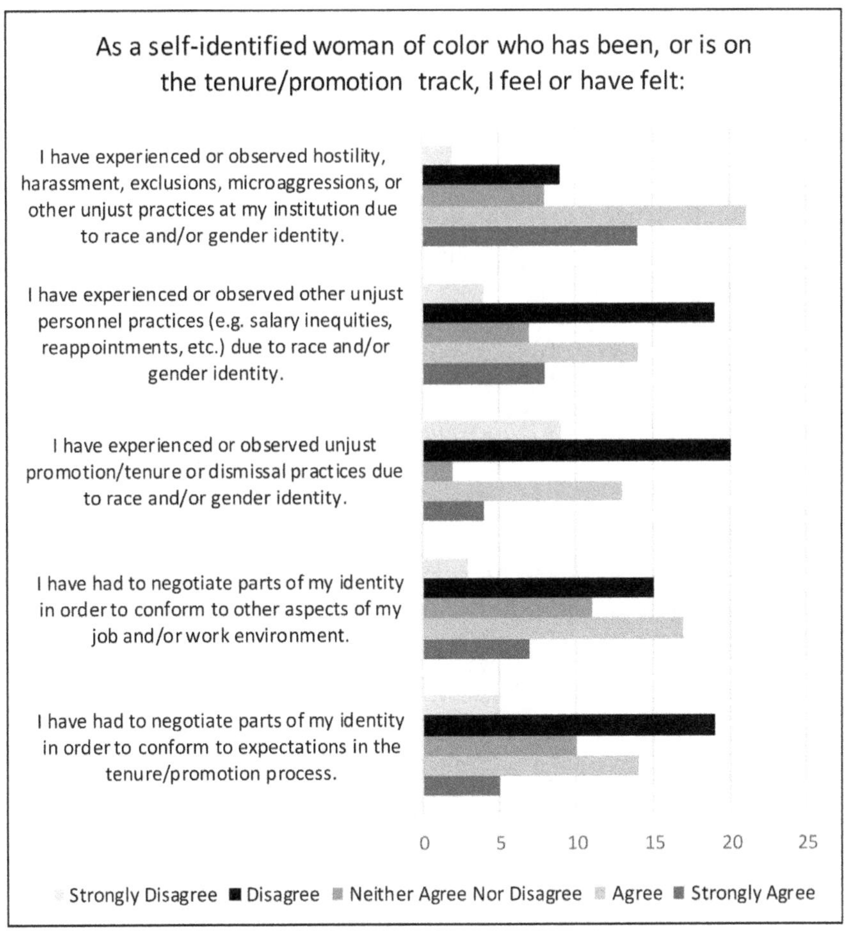

Figure 5: Perceptions of Factors Related to Negotiating Identity in the Workplace

into the trends within our data and to clarify other areas, including a few flaws in the survey. For instance, we had not asked for the marital status, age, or parental or elder care obligations of our participants in order to avoid overwhelming them with our opening demographic questions. In retrospect, this would have been useful information. For example, in response to our questions about additional labor outside of work and maintaining a work-life balance, some of our respondents mentioned that they were single and/or physically distant from family members. Data regarding marital status or other family duties might have shed more light on their responses to our questions.

Our survey clearly showed that the tenure process was not the true issue in the library profession. The majority of librarians in our study felt that their tenure requirements were fairly communicated and applied; however, they also overwhelmingly commented on professional and institutional dynamics that led to situations where external or internal pressures imposed an additional burden upon them. One librarian described her desire to help students of color succeed as an "intense obligation." As another librarian observed, "It's the way of life when one is a minority at an institution. It's tiring at times but we have to start somewhere."

Perhaps one of the most interesting takeaways from our survey was the universality of the results. As previously detailed, there were slight deviations, but our results largely remained consistent, regardless of whether the data were broken down by race, rank, length of time in the profession, or job duties. Thus, we believe our study highlighted many of the structural problems with diversity and inclusion in the library field and higher education. There was a palpable sense of frustration from respondents, and we felt that "burden of care" served as a particularly apt lens through which to view the experiences of women of color. As one librarian summarized, "My library and institution are better than others, but everyone could be doing better, which is painful because they KNOW they could be doing better."

Conclusion

There are still some major questions that remain unanswered—particularly, how can librarians and libraries better advocate for women of color librarians and better sustain them in the field? For women faculty and faculty of color, the literature provides some suggestions: broadly envision the trajectory of their careers, selectively identify the types of service activities that excite them, and opportunistically find ways to connect service work to their research agenda.[25] Seeking formal and informal mentors—including those outside of one's immediate unit—is also suggested.[26]

However, the onus cannot be solely on these librarians if libraries and institutions are truly committed to retaining diverse women faculty and easing their burden. It is clear from our study that the status quo places a heavy toll on women of color librarians, regardless of whether or not they have experienced explicit harassment, microaggressions, or other such hostilities. Indeed, the causes for these inequities are systemic and embedded, and as such, institutions and libraries must lead the charge to actively advocate for their women of color. Intentional recruitment is one starting point; in particular, those in management and hiring positions need to be proactive about their efforts, not only to recruit women of color (perhaps even taking a more targeted, hands-on approach beyond the traditional search process), but must also make clear to their units that such efforts to diversify their workforce are a priority. Similarly, cohort hires are another method that can potentially provide a valuable peer network and community of practice for incoming faculty.[27] Numerous studies underscore the need for strong mentoring and other socialization programs to encourage ongoing retention and advocacy networks for women of color faculty.[28] Such mentors must also have cultural competency training to better address the unique challenges that women of color faculty face and to act as supportive change agents for them.[29]

---

25. Eric Anthony Grollman, "Invisible Labor: Exploitation of Scholars of Color in Academia," *Conditionally Accepted*, December 15, 2015, accessed December 21, 2016, https://conditionallyaccepted.com/2015/12/15/invisible-labor.

26. Behar-Horenstein, et al., "Resilience Post Tenure," 78-79.

27. J. B. Mayo, Jr. and Vichet Chhuon, "Pathways to the Tenure Track: Reflections from Faculty of Color on Their Recruitment to a Research University," *International Journal of Educational Reform* 23, no. 3 (Summer 2014): 233.

28. Boyd, Cintrón, and Alexander-Snow, "The Experience of Being a Junior Minority Female Faculty Member," 19.

29. Behar-Horenstein, et al., "Resilience Post Tenure," 78-79.

Institutions must also be willing to purposefully self-assess in order to address the effectiveness of their policies and procedures in supporting their marginalized faculty. For instance, enhancing support for family leave or specifically allocating time meant for service commitments can better outline the need for and value of such activities.[30] Ultimately, institutions must recognize and champion (both informally and through tenure and promotion reviews) the work and perspectives of these faculty, the new forms of research scholarship they bring to their disciplines, and the meaningful engagement they are building with their increasingly diverse students bodies.[31] Until diversity, inclusion, and anti-racist work become actualized priorities for libraries, not only will women of color librarians continue to shoulder this disproportionate burden, but the institutional inequities that have historically disadvantaged them will continue to severely impede their sense of belonging and ability to advance in the profession.

Bibliography

Alabi, Jaena. "'This Actually Happened': An Analysis of Librarians' Responses to a Survey about Racial Microaggressions." *Journal of Library Administration* 55 (2015): 179-191.

American Library Association. "Diversity Counts 2009-2010 Update." Last modified September 2012. Accessed April 25, 2017. http://www.ala.org/offices/diversity/diversitycounts/2009-2010update.

Behar-Horenstein, Linda S., Cirecie A. West-Olatunji, Thomas E. More, Deidre F. Houchen, and Kellie W. Roberts. "Resilience Post Tenure: The Experience of an African American Woman in a PWI." *Florida Journal of Educational Administration & Policy* 5, no. 2 (Spring 2012): 68-84.

30. Boyd, Cintrón, and Alexander-Snow, "The Experience of Being a Junior Minority Female Faculty Member," 19; Guarino and Borden, "Faculty Service Loads and Gender," 19.

31. Damasco and Hodges, "Tenure and Promotion Experience of Academic Librarians of Color," 300; Mayo, Jr. and Chhuon, "Pathways to the Tenure Track," 223.

Bianchi, Suzanne M., Melissa A. Milkie, Liana C. Sayer, and John P. Robinson. "Is Anyone Doing the Housework? Trends in the Gender Division of Labor." *Social Forces* 79, no. 1 (September 2000): 191-228.

Bird, Sharon, Jacquelyn S. Litt, and Yong Wang. "Creating Status of Women Reports: Institutional Housekeeping as 'Women's Work.'" *NWSA Journal* 16, no. 1 (2004): 194-206.

Boyd, Tammy, Rosa Cintrón, and Mia Alexander-Snow. "The Experience of Being a Junior Minority Female Faculty Member." *Forum on Public Policy* 2 (2010): 1-23.

Cooper, Joanne E., and Dannelle D. Stevens, eds. *Tenure in the Sacred Grove: Issues and Strategies for Women and Minority Faculty*. Albany, NY: State University of New York Press, 2002.

Damasco, Ione T., and Dracine Hodges. "Tenure and Promotion Experience of Academic Librarians of Color." *College & Research Libraries* 73, no. 3 (May 2012): 279-301. Accessed December 21, 2016. https://doi.org/10.5860/crl-244.

DeVault, Marjorie L. *Feeding the Family: The Social Organization of Caring as Gendered Work*. Chicago, IL: University of Chicago Press, 1991.

Flaherty, Colleen. "Campus Unrest Follows Tenure Denial of Innovative, Popular Faculty Member of Color." *Inside Higher Ed*, May 17, 2016. Accessed December 21, 2016. https://www.insidehighered.com/news/2016/05/17/campus-unrest-follows-tenure-denial-innovative-popular-faculty-member-color.

Flaherty, Colleen. "American U Scholar Says Provost Cherry-Picked Negative Ratings of Her Teaching to Deny Her a Promotion." *Inside Higher Ed*, June 29, 2017. Accessed July 5, 2017. https://www.insidehighered.com/news/2017/06/29/american-u-scholar-says-provost-cherry-picked-negative-student-ratings-her-teaching.

Galbraith, Quinn, Leanna Fry, and Melissa Garrison. "The Impact of Faculty Status and Gender on Employee Well-being in Academic Libraries." *College & Research Libraries* 77, no. 1 (January 2016): 71-86. Accessed December 21, 2016. https://doi.org/10.5860/crl.77.1.71.

Griffin, Kimberly A., Jessica C. Bennett, and Jessica Harris. "Marginalizing Merit? Gender Differences in Black Faculty D/discourses on Tenure, Advancement, and Professional Success." *The Review of Higher Education* 36, no. 4 (Summer 2013): 489-512.

Grollman, Eric Anthony. "Invisible Labor: Exploitation of Scholars of Color in Academia." *Conditionally Accepted*, December 15, 2015. Accessed December 21, 2016. https://conditionallyaccepted.com/2015/12/15/invisible-labor.

Guarino, Cassandra M., and Victor M. H. Borden. "Faculty Service Loads and Gender: Are Women Taking Care of the Academic Family?" *Research in Higher Education* (2017): 672-694.

Gutiérrez y Muhs, Gabriella, Yolanda Flores Niemann, Carmen G. González, and Angela P. Harris, eds. *Presumed Incompetent: The Intersections of Race and Class for Women in Academia*. Boulder, CO: Colorado State University Press, 2012.

June, Audrey William. "The Invisible Labor of Minority Professors." *Chronicle of Higher Education*, November 8, 2015. Accessed December 21, 2016. http://www.chronicle.com/article/The-Invisible-Labor-of/234098.

Lydersen, Kari, and Rachel Cromidas. "Questions of Racial Discrimination on Tenure Unsettle DePaul." *New York Times*, December 23, 2010. Accessed December 21, 2016. http://www.nytimes.com/2010/12/24/us/24cncdepaul.html.

Matthew, Patricia. "The Invisible Labor of Faculty of Color on Campus." *The Atlantic*, November 23, 2016. Accessed December 21, 2016. https://www.theatlantic.com/education/archive/2016/11/what-is-faculty-diversity-worth-to-a-university/508334.

Mayo, Jr., J. B., and Vichet Chhuon. "Pathways to the Tenure Track: Reflections from Faculty of Color on Their Recruitment to a Research University." *International Journal of Educational Reform* 23, no. 3 (Summer 2014): 223-239.

National Center for Education Statistics. "Full-Time Faculty in Degree-Granting Postsecondary Institutions, By Race/Ethnicity, Sex, and Academic Rank: Fall 2009, Fall 2011, and Fall 2013." Accessed July 5, 2017. https://nces.ed.gov/programs/digest/d15/tables/dt15_315.20.asp?current=yes.

Matthew, Patricia, ed. *Written/Unwritten: Diversity and the Hidden Truths of Tenure*. Chapel Hill, NC: University of North Carolina Press, 2016.

O'Neill, Gail, and Margaret M. Ross. "Burden of Care: An Important Concept for Nurses." *Health Care for Women International* 12, no. 1 (1991): 111-121.

Padilla, Amado M. "Ethnic Minority Scholars, Research, and Mentoring: Current and Future Issues." *Educational Researcher* 23, no. 4 (1994): 24-27.

Park, Shelley M. "Research, Teaching, and Service: Why Shouldn't Women's Work Count?" *Journal of Higher Education* 67, no. 1 (January/February 1996): 46-84.

Sloniowski, Lisa. "Affective Labor, Resistance, and the Academic Librarian." *Library Trends* 64, no. 4 (Spring 2016): 645-666.

Walzer, Susan. "Thinking About the Baby: Gender and Divisions of Infant Care." *Social Problems* 43, no. 2 (May 1996): 219-234.

Chapter 12

Authenticity vs. Professionalism: Being True to Ourselves at Work

Jennifer Brown and Sofia Leung

For early-career librarians of color, academic librarianship contains a number of unspoken and unacknowledged expectations. While it is widely recognized that the majority of librarianship is white and female,[1] there is still a lack of action that directly addresses the consequences of this dearth of diversity. In fact, we have seen through personal experience that some attempts to remedy this problem have resulted in further marginalization of librarians of color in the workplace. The American Library Association (ALA), among other professional organizations, continually calls for academic and public libraries to increase the representation of marginalized professionals on library staff and to create diversity and inclusion initiatives. These efforts have put increasing expectations on libraries to also diversify programs and collections, and to become more inclusive spaces. However, carrying the burden of planning, promoting, defending, and/or assessing the work of social justice often falls to the very marginalized professionals that institutions struggle to recruit and retain. This tokenization results in the shouldering

1. Myrna Morales, Em Claire Knowles, and Chris Bourg, "Diversity, Social Justice, and the Future of Libraries," *portal: Libraries and the Academy* 14, no. 3 (2014): 439–451, https://doi.org/10.1353/pla.2014.0017.

of invisible and emotional labors that burden us further; we operate at a deficit working under these conditions, as this toll then affects the -isms we experience while embodying our intersecting identities in the workplace.

As a black, bisexual, cisgendered, able-bodied woman of color and a Chinese American, heterosexual, cisgendered, able-bodied woman of color in academic librarianship, we, the authors, want to push back against the simplistic narrative that diversity work is the work of people of color (POC). By exploring the personal and professional challenges of balancing the invisibility and hypervisibility of our labor among peers and library administrators, we want the profession to acknowledge the emotional and psychological toll that providing diversity programming, awareness, and education takes on POC, to the point that many of us leave the profession, and how the structural oppression of predominantly white institutions (PWIs) further complicates our undertaking. We want to examine the pressures we feel to perform diversity work as women of color, particularly as many non-POC librarians and staff pay lip service to diversity, but do not show up when the work needs to happen. To add to this burden, administrators often do not protect the librarians of color or others doing this social justice work, nor do they value or give credit to those who do this work. The expectation is that we, as "the experts," can do it alone, when, in reality, this work cannot be done without the committed contributions of staff and administrators at every level.

Using an intersectional lens, we consider how each author's identity shapes their perceptions and experiences, so as not to generalize or speak for other librarians with so-called marginalized identities working in the field. We hope that, by using this gaze and incorporating applicable research, our chapter will provide some insight into potential steps library organizations can take to create better work environments for staff to fully embody their identities without incurring further burden or tokenization. Through understanding how our social identities specifically intersect and interact with our work, we as a profession can realize the promise of social justice.

Diversity Work

What do we mean by "diversity work" in academic libraries? For those of us who believe in the work of libraries as the active promotion of diversity and equity, there is a sense that all library work should be diversity work. This seems particularly valid given that "Diversity" and "Social Responsibility" are stated values in the ALA "Core Values of Librarianship." Diversity is understood by the profession as the need to diversify the people who become librarians.[2] ALA defines social responsibility as:

> the contribution that librarianship can make in ameliorating or solving the critical problems of society; support for efforts to help inform and educate the people of the United States on these problems and to encourage them to examine the many views on and the facts regarding each problem; and the willingness of ALA to take a position on current critical issues with the relationship to libraries and library service set forth in the position statement.[3]

This policy statement is very close to a definition of social justice. "Diversity" can also be a code word for equity, social justice, or antiracism, but is often used instead of those terms to allow for white fragility.[4]

The very nature of diversity work also begets the idea of "performance," and we want to be clear and intentional about why we refer to it this way. Sara Ahmed weaves a narrative linking institutional documentation and diversity work to "performance culture," stating that "Institutional performance involves an increasing self-consciousness

---

2. Morales, Knowles, and Bourg, "Diversity, Social Justice, and the Future of Libraries," 439–451.

3. American Library Association, "Core Values of Librarianship,"*Advocacy, Legislation & Issues*, June 29, 2004, http://www.ala.org/advocacy/intfreedom/statementspols/corevalues.

4. "White Fragility is a state in which even a minimum amount of racial stress becomes intolerable, triggering a range of defensive moves...[including] outward display of emotions such as anger, fear, and guilt, and behaviors such as argumentation, silence, and leaving the stress-inducing situation." Robin DiAngelo, "White Fragility," *International Journal of Critical Pedagogy* 3, no. 3 (2011): 55–70.

about how to perform well in these systems, by generating the right kinds of procedures, methods, and materials, where rightness is determined as the fulfillment of the requirements of a system."[5] She links this to the notion that "doing well [within the bounds of performance culture] involves generating *the right kinds of appearance*."[6]

Librarianship has its own set of top-down, hierarchically organized documents that frame acceptable ways for diversity work to be thought of, articulated, and performed across institutions, such as ALA's "Core Values" document; another example is the Association of College and Research Libraries' (ACRL) 2012 "Diversity Standards: Cultural Competency for Academic Libraries," which seeks to "provide a framework to support libraries in engaging the complexities of providing services to diverse populations, and recruiting and maintaining a diverse library workforce."[7]

As bodies of the larger ALA, the creation of such documents smacks of "rightness" creation, aiding a systemic idea of what diversity efforts *should* look like across institutions. Now, we don't begrudge the language of these documents; it's one of the more meaningful examples of what happens when you give groups charged with this work (in the case of the latter document, the Racial and Ethnic Diversity Committee of ACRL) an opportunity to shape the larger discourse. However, these documents aren't capable of holding individual institutions accountable. We argue that, as a result, institutions will primarily use them to *appear* to perform in professionally acceptable ways. And even if an institution doesn't officially adopt documents like these, it often looks to its academic peers (who are also being informed by larger professional documents) for direction. Doing the work of diversity and inclusion within our institutions does manifest as a kind of performance, one that's

5. Sara Ahmed, *On Being Included: Racism and Diversity in Institutional Life* (Durham, NC: Duke University Press, 2012), 84.

6. Ibid., 85.

7. Association of College and Research Libraries, "Diversity Standards: Cultural Competency for Academic Libraries (2012)," *Association of College & Research Libraries* (ACRL), May 4, 2012, http://www.ala.org/acrl/standards/diversity.

arguably about performing in pre-existing ways deemed "right"; if the language of these professional statements and standards doesn't push the boundaries, then neither will our "performances" of their suggestions. If we view social justice as a foundational value of librarianship, shouldn't diversity work just be considered library work?

In practice, this has never been the case. Diversity work is the dirty work that no one wants to do, because to *do* it means that something is wrong with librarianship, a values-based profession that is meant to help others and to benefit society. How could there be something wrong with our profession? From our personal experience and those of colleagues, there is a refusal to even accept that librarianship has a social justice problem or that, as members of these institutions, we participate daily in systems of oppression.[8] So what does this mean for diversity work? It means that very few librarians understand or are even interested in dismantling institutional systems of oppression.

Hudson has characterized diversity in LIS as being preoccupied "with demographic inclusion and individual behavioral competence [which] has...left little room in the field for substantive engagement with race as a historically contingent phenomenon."[9] The lack of diversity within our profession and the fact that it is so difficult to retain librarians of color in our field (the inclusion piece) are symptoms of these systems of oppression. If white librarians cannot recognize this, the work that we as librarians of color have taken on—to dismantle these systems—will be nearly impossible.

---

8. For example, Drabinski notes that "the Library of Congress Classification (LCC) and Library of Congress Subject Headings (LCSH) fail to accurately and respectfully organize library materials about social groups and identities that lack social and political power." (Emily Drabinski, "Queering the Catalog: Queer Theory and the Politics of Correction," *Library Quarterly* 83, no. 2 [April 1, 2013]: 94–111. doi:10.1086/669547). However, many of our institutions continue to use LCC and LCSH to catalog and organize their collections without challenging these systems at an institutional level and continue to make them a core part of the education that librarians receive in Library and Information Science Master's programs.

9. David James Hudson, "On 'Diversity' as Anti-Racism in Library and Information Studies: A Critique," *Journal of Critical Library and Information Studies* 0, no. 1 (January 31, 2017), http://libraryjuicepress.com/journals/index.php/jclis/article/view/6.

Diversity work means questioning our job conditions every day. Why is this system in place? Who was originally intended to benefit from this service? Who benefits from it now? How can we dismantle these systems of oppression and create a better system—one that benefits those in the margins of our community? The answer cannot be "this is how it's always been done, so that's how we should continue to do it." For us, entering the profession as early career librarians of color, to be hit with the stark reality of academic librarianship and its whiteness was very much like thinking you were about to hug a friendly dog but it turns out to be a hungry anaconda. In a profession that claims "diversity" and "social responsibility" as its core values, it is difficult for those of us who became values-based librarians to swallow the reality of how those values do or don't show up in the field.

White librarians do not want to face the fact that there's something wrong in their own house. In this work, we actively incorporate April Hathcock's definition of "whiteness"—"I use 'whiteness' to refer not only to the socio-cultural differential of power and privilege that results from categories of race and ethnicity; it also stands as a marker for the privilege and power that acts to reinforce itself through hegemonic cultural practice that excludes all who are different."[10] In a panel presentation during the 2017 Identity, Agency, and Culture in Academic Libraries conference, Fobazi Ettarh built upon these concepts of whiteness and privilege when she coined the term "vocational awe," which is the assumption that because libraries are inherently good (and well-intentioned), there is "some core aspect of the profession [that] is beyond critique."[11] A small subset of librarians seems to be willing to engage with critical librarianship[12] to the extent that it serves their users, but

10. April Hathcock, "White Librarianship in Blackface: Diversity Initiatives in LIS," *In the Library with the Lead Pipe*, October 7, 2015, http://www.inthelibrarywiththeleadpipe.org/2015/lis-diversity/.

11. Fobazi Ettarh et al., "'I Love Being a Librarian, But...': Reconciling Vocational Awe, Emotional Labor, and Social Change in Librarianship" (presentation: Identity, Agency, and Culture in Academic Libraries Conference, Los Angeles, CA, May 22, 2017).

12. Critical librarianship is "a movement of library workers dedicated to bringing social justice principles into our work in libraries.... Recognizing that we all work under

asking them to question their own complicity in the system becomes problematic. As Ahmed writes, "statements of commitment (to equality and diversity) can be used *in* or even *as* an institutional response to racism, often taking the form of an assertion disguised as a question: 'how can we be racist if we are committed to equality and diversity?'"[13] This circular argument removes the possibility of actively engaging with what equality, diversity, and social justice mean, both systemically and individually.

In the instances where libraries do want to be seen doing diversity work, sometimes because it makes them look good to care about diversity, the work is assigned to either a position (e.g., Diversity Librarian) or a committee as though that will be enough. It's easy to point to these as clear evidence that diversity work is being done—after all, it's in the name—and that absolves anyone else in the organization from having to do diversity work. "The uneven distribution of responsibility for equality can become a mechanism for reproducing inequality."[14] We have seen this ourselves, in situations where both we the authors and colleagues of color at other institutions end up on the diversity committee or in a diversity residency. This checks many boxes for the organization; not only do they have one or two "diverse" staff members—and usually not in positions of power—but those staff are also responsible for diversity work. This box-checking means the organization doesn't have to address structural issues of inequity, such as the barriers many POC face when trying to enter the profession.[15]

Oftentimes, those of us doing the diversity work find ourselves in a position where we have to call out these uncomfortable truths, because

---

regimes of white supremacy, capitalism, and a range of structural inequalities, how can our work as librarians intervene in and disrupt those systems?" "About / Join the Discussion." Accessed August 30, 2017. http://critlib.org/about/.

13. Ahmed, *On Being Included*, 116.

14. Ibid, 91.

15. Some of the barriers to entry are low representation in the field (which means many POC can't imagine themselves as librarians or educators), the requirement of an expensive Master's degree, and sometimes a second Master's if you want to be in higher education.

"nobody else will say them."[16] This leaves it to the person of color to point out the fact that a particular policy or procedure is not equitable or that activists of color on campus do not want the university administrators to offer them workshops on self-care, as one author has done. This author explicitly stated to library administrators that these students were asking administrators to make the campus safe for black students, for queer and trans students, and for women. Instead, when this author voiced that concern and others, she was either told that these experiences cannot be true because our other colleagues can't see it for themselves or, worse, she was met with silence and ignored. In fact, some of these colleagues and administrators will read this very paragraph and scoff at these words.

"Performing" Diversity Work

What does the "performance" of diversity work look like in practice? Let's consider things like the blanket diversity or anti-discrimination statement featured on many job ads in and outside of librarianship. Institutions might be willing to admit that they should "review recruitment, hiring, and promotion policies, procedures, and practices to remedy inadvertent exclusion of or discrimination toward underrepresented, underserved, and historically oppressed groups,"[17] as the ACRL Cultural Competencies document suggests, but are they also comfortable with exchanging that boilerplate blurb for language that explicitly calls for dedication to anti-oppression frameworks? Or would a performance like that be deemed *too* radical, within the confines of "rightness" they've devised? It's also likely that institutions put this language forward to comply with federal regulations surrounding equal opportunity hiring practices, so it's unlikely that they feel a need to push the boundaries in these circumstances when standard rhetoric meets the qualifications.

16. Ahmed, *On Being Included*, 61-62.

17. Association of College and Research Libraries, "Diversity Standards."

The authors' "performance" of diversity work within institutional systems has taken many forms: serving on or chairing institutional and national diversity and inclusion committees, collaborating with colleagues and administrators on diversity and inclusion mission statements, devising programming directly serving marginalized students, and the like. But as we've come to critique these performances, we've asked ourselves whether they do what Ahmed suggests, which is to value a "community of voices"[18] we don't normally hear from? And, more importantly, are we holding our performances, and by extension ourselves, accountable? As Nicole Cooke states in her powerful autoethnographic article, "while diversity is desirable on paper, it is often resisted in practice."[19]

Emotional Burden and Authenticity in the Workplace

For some, performing diversity work is a conscious choice that is focused on understanding the ways that systemic forms of power, privilege, and oppression are reflected—both in libraries and the larger society. However, it's also a fairly personal choice, and the degree to which (or ways in which) it's performed depend on a variety of factors—the level of risk one is willing to take within their institution, the willingness to decenter one's own identit[ies] (and, in particular, one's whiteness) to amplify voices and perspectives at the margins, and others. Still, what seems to be a conscious choice for our white, able-bodied, cisgender peers looking to support diversity and anti-oppression initiatives isn't so for us. As marginalized women of color, the navigation of systemic inequalities and the overall distance from whiteness means that performing the "work" of diversity *isn't* a choice. We live its reality in our everyday lives by having to justify our mere existence in a myriad of white spaces and places. Examining our positionality and cracks within the system often comes as second nature.

---

18. Ahmed, *On Being Included*, 29.

19. Nicole A. Cooke, "Pushing Back from the Table: Fighting to Maintain My Voice as a Pre-Tenure Minority Female in the White Academy," *Polymath: An Interdisciplinary Arts and Sciences Journal* 4, no. 2 (June 28, 2014): 39.

The decision to take on diversity work at the office begets conversations about its impact on one's perceived professionalism; generally, it's fine to "do the work"[20] outside of the institution on our own time but bringing anti-oppression, anti-racist, or other frameworks into the academy is typically only sanctioned in specific ways. Thus, being authentic to the selves we embody outside the workplace becomes fraught with peril. Do we speak our minds and risk angering those who think this work doesn't pertain to them, or to the library overall? Do we risk being devalued or derailed in institutions that would rather ignore our efforts? Do we hide our frustrations and pain when we encounter microaggressions[21] or outright racism at work, not to mention sexism or ageism? And, even if the academy welcomes this work and our actions within it, are we willing to deal with the constant co-opting of our ideas and efforts by white colleagues doing the work alongside us? These questions aren't exhaustive, and they certainly don't represent the thought process or reality of *every* marginalized librarian in the profession, but they are central to the ways that we navigate diversity work within the field.

Research shows that, regardless of our choice between authenticity or professionalism, the academy tends to *expect* people of color (especially women of color) to perform diversity work in ways not required of our white colleagues. Mignon R. Moore addresses this in her piece "Women of Color in the Academy: Navigating Multiple Intersections and Multiple Hierarchies," stating "The service that women of color are consistently asked to perform, and sometimes feel a personal obligation to participate in, tends to go unreported and unacknowledged, many

20. April Hathcock, "DO THE WORK!!! #libleadgender Chat March 9," *At The Intersection* (blog), March 4, 2016, https://aprilhathcock.wordpress.com/2016/03/04/do-the-work-libleadgender-chat-march-9/.

21. "Racial microaggressions are brief and commonplace daily verbal, behavioral, or environmental indignities, whether intentional or unintentional, that communicate hostile, derogatory, or negative racial slights and insults toward people of color." Derald Wing Sue et al., "Racial Microaggressions in Everyday Life: Implications for Clinical Practice," *American Psychologist* 62, no. 4 (2007): 271–86, https://doi.org/10.1037/0003-066X.62.4.271.

times even to the individuals doing the work."[22] Moore also cites Thomas and Hollenshead,[23] who found that black women faculty experience "organizational barriers that disproportionately rely on them for student mentoring activities and other types of work that are not rewarded in department evaluations."[24] When service expectations aren't equitably distributed and women of color are implicitly (or explicitly) asked to shoulder the burden, is it any wonder that we become overwhelmed or burn out altogether? Even beyond diversity or service work, themes from an in-depth survey of the literature on experiences of faculty of color across academe highlight issues of "isolation, perceived biases in the hiring process, unrealistic expectations of doing [our] work and being representatives of [our] racial/ethnic group."[25] This suggests that we already navigate this profession feeling overtaxed and unsupported as we work to deconstruct legacies of oppression that bedrock the academy. Why should we take on diversity work when we know that those efforts won't help with tenure or promotional portfolios in the ways they should? Results from the survey also highlight that:

> Although service can be detrimental to faculty of color as they progress toward tenure and promotion, it can also be what provides inspiration and passion as they fulfill their desire to serve in response to the needs of their communities.[26]

---

22. Mignon R. Moore, "Women of Color in the Academy: Navigating Multiple Intersections and Multiple Hierarchies," *Social Problems* 64, no. 2 (May 1, 2017): 200, doi:10.1093/socpro/spx009.

23. Gloria D. Thomas and Carol Hollenshead, "Resisting from the Margins: The Coping Strategies of Black Women and Other Women of Color Faculty Members at a Research University," *Journal of Negro Education* 70, no. 3 (2001): 166–75, doi:10.2307/3211208.

24. Moore, "Women of Color in the Academy," 201.

25. Caroline Sotello Viernes Turner, Juan Carlos González, and J. Luke, "Faculty of Color in Academe: What 20 Years of Literature Tells Us," *Journal of Diversity in Higher Education* 1, no. 3 (2008): 143, doi:10.1037/a0012837.

26. Ibid.

To be authentic to our beliefs and passions is to cultivate a professional identity unique to ourselves; it's akin to making ourselves visible within a profession that often values careful neutrality, devoid of the personal.

Invisibility vs. Hypervisibility

> "It is a peculiar sensation, this double-consciousness, this sense of always looking at one's self through the eyes of others, of measuring one's soul by the tape of a world that looks on in amused contempt and pity. One ever feels his two-ness,—an American, a Negro; two souls, two thoughts, two unreconciled strivings..."[27]

The duality of invisibility and hypervisibility in the academy pervasively affects librarians who identify as multiply marginalized; it's a type of double-consciousness wherein we're acutely aware of the academy's measuring stick (proximity to whiteness) and how well we meet it. Here, invisibility refers to the unseen-ness that passing begets; it stems from trying to navigate an organization that implicitly or explicitly says you need to minimize difference: "You have to pass by passing your way through whiteness. If whiteness is what the institution is oriented around, then even bodies that do not appear white have to inhabit whiteness."[28] This is where we get into conversations about institutional "fit" and assimilation, which cross boundaries to suggest "fitting" into perceived notions of gender, sexuality, class, ability, and socially constructed identities all centered around whiteness as a primary identity marker. The closer your proximity to straight, white, cisgender, middle/upper class, able-bodiedness gets, the better you fit.

So we shrink—we stuff down the parts of ourselves deemed too far from normative identities—and we *cope*. But the reality is that no amount of pretending or silence erases who we are, and it certainly doesn't stop

27. W. E. B. DuBois, *The Souls of Black Folk* (Chicago: A.C. McClurg & Co, 1903), 3, accessed May 30, 2017, http://www.bartleby.com/114/index.html.

28. Ahmed, *On Being Included*, 41.

us from being made hypervisible at will. In this context, hypervisibility stems from being singled out *solely* on some basis (such as one's identity); it's ephemeral in nature, primarily undertaken when the majority needs its token(s) to address, act, or influence institutional or sociopolitical spheres that the majority doesn't know how to. Constantine et. al. communicate the results of a study about how black faculty in Counseling and Psychology experience these intertwined phenomena:

> Most of the Black faculty members in this study (n = 10) indicated that they had experienced alternating feelings of invisibility/marginalization and hypervisibility in their departments and institutions, depending on the situation or context. These participants generally reported feeling that many individuals on campus, especially White faculty members and administrators, often did not 'notice' their presence on campus until their expertise (particularly with regard to racial or ethnic minority issues) was needed or valued. When their expertise was needed or when they were asked to help recruit an applicant of color for an available position, many of the research participants reported feeling "hypervisible" and overexposed.[29]

There's a special kind of visibility that comes from being asked "What should we do about our institution's diversity problems?" in the middle of a meeting comprised of all-white colleagues, as one author was. One of us was invisible until it was decided that we *needed* to speak on behalf of our entire race, explicitly feeling as though we'd become "exotic spectacles" or "racial/ethnic/gender/other-category experts."[30] You might argue that this was an effort to value that "community of voices" Ahmed mentions, but it's actually a prime example of the duality between invisibility and hypervisibility. This author was expected to modulate their proximity to whiteness (and everything that is non-other-ness) *until* called upon to solve an institutional challenge.

---

29. Madonna G. Constantine et al., "Racial Microaggressions Against Black Counseling and Counseling Psychology Faculty: A Central Challenge in the Multicultural Counseling Movement," *Journal of Counseling & Development* 86, no. 3 (Summer 2008): 351.

30. Katrina Bell McDonald and Adia M. Harvey Wingfield, "(In)visibility Blues: The Paradox of Institutional Racism," *Sociological Spectrum* 29, no. 1 (December 5, 2008): 32, doi:10.1080/02732170802480501.

If you're aware that marginalized librarians already carry the emotional burden of conforming to whiteness *and* shouldering the brunt of the institution's diversity work, then you should know that dictating *when* and *where* they perform their identity (as they're tasked with solving all your institution's problems) actually devalues their work. By doing so, you essentially bind them to identity expression on your terms, positioned right alongside epicenters of power, privilege, and whiteness that your institution operates from. If you're really about encouraging communities of voices, ensure such questions are asked of *everyone*, right on up to chancellors, provosts, and university presidents.

Why Do We Still Do This Work?

If serving within these institutional structures (like diversity and equity committees) is so difficult and we suffer for it, why do we keep doing it? The simple answer is that we have to. It is essential for us to remain in the profession. For the authors, and for many librarians of color that we know, we joined this profession to help people, to make a difference for those less fortunate than us. For those of us who have made it into this profession, we know what it took to battle structural and systemic racism to get to where we are today, but what about those of us who did not make it or decided they couldn't stay once they made it? Those who either could not take the daily microaggressions, the narrow qualifications to enter the profession, the isolation of being one of the few or only people of color, or the questioning of your work ethic, your right to be in this profession, to exist in this space. We do this work for all of those who did not make it, those who did and are made small by the system, those who did and are fighting alongside us, and for those who might come after us. Our individual achievements are meaningless without our community achieving alongside us.

If we do not do this work, who else will do it? Who else is supporting and mentoring people of color in our profession? Who else is questioning these systems of oppression and the traditional ways of library work? Who else is putting themselves at risk to do any of this? The risk of taking on this work is burnout; it's having to work alongside white folks who want you to educate them constantly, so that they can do the work alongside you using only half as much effort. For one of us, that risk involved facing mockery from white colleagues who felt diversity work was unnecessary and fruitless. But not doing the work? That means enduring tasteless jokes about microaggressions and colloquial expressions like Cinco De "Drinko"; it means hearing folks extol the importance of free speech without regard to intersectional identities. Not doing the work means silence, complacency. It means *acceptance* of the status quo, which is...unacceptable.

What Can YOU Do to Make This Better for Current and Future Librarians of Color Doing Diversity Work?

We want to round out our chapter by providing potential recommendations for librarians who want to do and be better with "doing the work" (especially upper-level administrators). It's important to note that none of these should be considered exhaustive or all encompassing — each is just a small piece of the larger whole, and doing one alone won't change anything.[31]

Hiring

While the statistics from as recently as 2010 show that librarianship is still approximately 88% white,[32] the reality is that having fewer marginalized librarians within the profession means more of us have to shoulder the burden of diversity efforts within our organizations anyway. Efforts should be made to transition from talking about diversity hiring initiatives to enacting them meaningfully; to actively recruit or attract, and then put effort into maintaining POC/LGBTQ/differently-abled

31. Hudson, "On 'Diversity' as Anti-Racism in Library and Information Studies."

32. Chris Bourg, "The Unbearable Whiteness of Librarianship," *Feral Librarian*, March 4, 2014, https://chrisbourg.wordpress.com/2014/03/03/the-unbearable-whiteness-of-librarianship/.

folks, particularly in leadership roles where authority is given to make real change.

Support Programs

Given that the literature (and the authors' personal experiences) reflect feelings of isolation and ostracization, efforts should be made to create opportunities for mentorship and connection wherever possible; while such efforts benefit all librarians, particular emphasis should be placed on establishing programs that directly benefit librarians outside centers of whiteness, able-bodied-ness, neurotypical-ness, and others. If queer/trans/disabled/POC librarians are going to take this work on, they shouldn't have to do it without support networks. Particular emphasis should be put on matching staff with others who occupy similar positionalities or identities, and if the institution can't accommodate this, then prioritize funding for librarians to attend conferences, workshops, or other professional development opportunities that *do* afford such connections.

Accountability

Holding upper-level administrators accountable for moving beyond acceptable diversity performances to meaningful action is crucial; it's the difference between our work being responded to versus it being swept under the proverbial academic rug. Administrators and others who occupy positions of power should use their authority to advance this work (preferably without being prompted to do so by librarians of color). Real institutional change might be achieved if diversity efforts focused on ensuring that upper-level administrative positions are made up of diverse candidates. Don't just hire librarians of color in entry-level roles; consider us for leadership opportunities in the same way you do mediocre white folks.

Accountability should also encompass keeping white colleagues who don't traditionally do (or want to do) this work honest about their lack of effort.

Conclusion

We've attempted to lay out a meaningful roadmap for understanding diversity work and emotional burden as they relate to how two women of color have traversed such experiences. However, the core of this centers around choice—we may be subject to –isms and –aggressions while serving on these committees, speaking at national conferences, or writing about our struggles, but we've worked to *choose* how we engage within those spheres while drawing important boundaries that help us reclaim (or restructure) those performances. One of us, for example, has chosen to perform diversity work on a university-wide committee composed of students and administrators of color. It took withdrawing from the library to find a place where that author could work toward equity without the burden of invisibility or tokenization. Another of us has chosen to create informal structures of support, mentoring, and professional development for librarians of color, since there are far fewer formal opportunities available. If we put ourselves at risk, we choose to do so knowing that we are at least trying to make things better with the resources available to us and within the boundaries we set. We encourage you, reader, to draw those boundaries in ways that empower and embolden you—to decide when, where, and how your performance occurs.

Bibliography

"About / Join the Discussion." Accessed August 30, 2017. http://critlib.org/about/.

Ahmed, Sara. *On Being Included: Racism and Diversity in Institutional Life*. Durham, NC: Duke University Press, 2012.

American Library Association. "Core Values of Librarianship." *Advocacy, Legislation & Issues*, June 29, 2004. http://www.ala.org/advocacy/intfreedom/statementspols/corevalues.

Association of College and Research Libraries. "Diversity Standards: Cultural Competency for Academic Libraries (2012)." *Association of College & Research Libraries (ACRL)*. May 4, 2012. http://www.ala.org/acrl/standards/diversity.

Constantine, Madonna G., Laura Smith, Rebecca M. Redington, and Delila Owens. "Racial Microaggressions Against Black Counseling and Counseling Psychology Faculty: A Central Challenge in the Multicultural Counseling Movement." *Journal of Counseling & Development* 86, no. 3 (Summer 2008): 348–55.

Cooke, Nicole A. "Pushing Back from the Table: Fighting to Maintain My Voice as a Pre-Tenure Minority Female in the White Academy." *Polymath: An Interdisciplinary Arts and Sciences Journal* 4, no. 2 (June 28, 2014): 39–49.

DiAngelo, Robin. "White Fragility." *International Journal of Critical Pedagogy* 3, no. 3 (2011): 55–70.

Drabinski, Emily. "Queering the Catalog: Queer Theory and the Politics of Correction." *Library Quarterly* 83, no. 2 (April 1, 2013): 94–111. doi:10.1086/669547.

DuBois, W. E. B. *The Souls of Black Folk*. Chicago: A.C. McClurg & Co, 1903. Accessed May 30, 2017. http://www.bartleby.com/114/index.html.

Ettarh, Fobazi, Sveta Stoytcheva, Kelly McElroy, James Castrillo, and Charissa Powell. "'I Love Being a Librarian, but...': Reconciling Vocational Awe, Emotional Labor, and Social Change in Librarianship." Presentation at the Identity, Agency, and Culture in Academic Libraries Conference, Los Angeles, CA, May 22, 2017.

Hathcock, April. "DO THE WORK!!! #libleadgender Chat March 9." *At The Intersection* (blog), March 4, 2016. https://aprilhathcock.wordpress.com/2016/03/04/do-the-work-libleadgender-chat-march-9/.

———. "White Librarianship in Blackface: Diversity Initiatives in LIS." *In the Library with the Lead Pipe*. 2015. http://www.inthelibrarywiththeleadpipe.org/2015/lis-diversity/.

Hudson, David James. "On 'Diversity' as Anti-Racism in Library and Information Studies: A Critique." *Journal of Critical Library and Information Studies* 0, no. 1 (January 31, 2017). http://libraryjuicepress.com/journals/index.php/jclis/article/view/6.

McDonald, Katrina Bell, and Adia M. Harvey Wingfield. "(In)Visibility Blues: The Paradox of Institutional Racism." *Sociological Spectrum* 29, no. 1 (December 5, 2008): 28–50. doi:10.1080/02732170802480501.

Moore, Mignon R. "Women of Color in the Academy: Navigating Multiple Intersections and Multiple Hierarchies." *Social Problems* 64, no. 2 (May 1, 2017): 200–205. doi:10.1093/socpro/spx009.

Morales, Myrna, Em Claire Knowles, and Chris Bourg. "Diversity, Social Justice, and the Future of Libraries." *Portal: Libraries and the Academy* 14, no. 3 (2014): 439–451. https://doi.org/10.1353/pla.2014.0017.

Sue, Derald Wing, Christina M. Capodilupo, Gina C. Torino, Jennifer M. Bucceri, Aisha M. B. Holder, Kevin L. Nadal, and Marta Esquilin. "Racial Microaggressions in Everyday Life: Implications for Clinical Practice." *American Psychologist* 62, no. 4 (2007): 271–86. doi:10.1037/0003-066X.62.4.271.

Thomas, Gloria D., and Carol Hollenshead. "Resisting from the Margins: The Coping Strategies of Black Women and Other Women of Color Faculty Members at a Research University." *The Journal of Negro Education* 70, no. 3 (2001): 166–75. doi:10.2307/3211208.

Turner, Caroline Sotello Viernes, Juan Carlos González, and J. Luke. "Faculty of Color in Academe: What 20 Years of Literature Tells Us." *Journal of Diversity in Higher Education* 1, no. 3 (2008): 139–68. doi:10.1037/a0012837.

Chapter 13

Identity, Activism, Self-Care, and Women of Color Librarians

Alanna Aiko Moore and Jan Estrellado

Introduction

The aim of this paper is to report the findings of a study about women of color in the library and information science profession who self-identify as activists. The research questions explore issues of identity,[1] activism[2] and social justice,[3] and self-care affecting women of color librarians. The purpose of the current study is three-fold. First, we wished to better understand how women of color examine their identities in relation to their work as librarians. Second, we wanted to explore why activist women of color librarians believe that social justice work is necessary in the profession. Finally, we hoped to examine how commitments to activism both sustain and detract from women of color librarians' well-being.

1. For the purposes of this study, identity is defined as how an individual understands themselves and their social classification and membership.

2. We define activism as an individual or group acting to affect social change and working to identify and fight inequality and injustice in society.

3. We define social justice as a commitment to civil and human rights and equality.

To accomplish these goals, we will be centering the voices and experiences of women of color librarians. The voices of women of color activists are often unseen and unheard in the wider race and gender research in the library profession, even though activism is acknowledged as a central tenet of librarianship. Women of color librarians see and relate to the world in unique ways because of their different social locations and lived experiences.[4] Research on this topic is important because it centers the perspective of women of color, using their own voices and stories.

Literature Review

Women of Color in the Library and Information Science Profession

Librarians of color in the United States are both underrepresented and have disproportionate attrition rates relative to their white counterparts. While percentages of racial and ethnic minorities receiving MLIS degrees increased from 9% to 13% from 1990 to 2000, the same groups in the general population grew by 152% in the same time period.[5] The lack of ethnic and racial diversity in librarianship is evident from the time students enter Library and Information Science (LIS) graduate programs, due to a lack of diverse faculty and alumni.[6] From 1990 to 2000, the American Library Association's report, "Diversity Counts," documented the "dramatic rates of attrition" experienced by librarians

4. Renu Sharma, "Researching the Spiritual: Applying Soul to Research Practice," in *Critical Issues in Anti-Racist Research Methodologies*, ed. George Jerry Sefa Dei et al. (New York: Peter Lang, 2005), 152.

5. Denise M. Davis and Tracie D. Hall, "Diversity Counts," *American Library Association*, accessed May 15, 2017, http://www.ala.org/aboutala/sites/ala.org.aboutala/files/content/diversity/diversitycounts/diversitycounts_rev0.pdf.

6. Kyung-Sun Kim, Ming-Hsin Chiu, Sei-Ching Joanna Sin, and Louise Robbins, "Recruiting a Diverse Workforce for Academic/Research Librarianship: Career Decisions of Subject Specialists and Librarians of Color," *College & Research Libraries* 68, no. 6 (2007): 533-552, https://doi.org/10.5860/crl.68.6.533.

of color.[7] The American Library Association states that the attrition rates among racial and ethnic minority groups is due to limited professional mobility and lack of access to leadership positions.[8] Other factors that likely contribute to librarians of color leaving the profession include lack of effective mentorship and a dearth of available and meaningful social contexts through which librarians of color can connect with each other.[9] While librarians of color are certainly not the only professionals serving diverse communities, ethnically diverse librarians are necessary to build the most effective models for serving those communities.[10] A focus on efforts to both recruit and retain librarians of color is necessary to diversify the profession and to competently provide the range of services offered by the library profession.

Librarians of color who do remain in the profession struggle with institutional and individual biases against them. Alabi, in her study on the racial microaggression experiences of librarians of color, found that librarians of color are faced with both explicit and implicit forms of racism at interpersonal and systemic levels of their workplaces.[11] The thematic impacts of these race-based experiences on librarians of color in Alabi's study include invalidation, isolation, and a desire to leave the profession. Kumaran and Cai found similar results in their Canadian study of "visible minority librarians" (Canada's parallel terminology for "ethnic minority" in the U.S.).[12] Participants reported a lack of diversity

---

7. Davis and Hall, "Diversity Counts."

8. Davis and Hall, "Diversity Counts."

9. Peggy Johnson, "Retaining and Advancing Librarians of Color," College & Research Libraries 68, no.5 (2007): 407, https://doi.org/10.5860/crl.68.5.405.

10. Martín J. Gómez, "Who is Most Qualified to Serve Our Ethnic-Minority Communities?" American Libraries 31, no. 7 (2000): 40.

11. Jaena Alabi, "'This Actually Happened': An Analysis of Librarians' Responses to a Survey about Racial Microaggressions," Journal of Library Administration 55, no.3 (2015): 179-191, http://dx.doi.org/10.1080/01930826.2015.1034040.

12. Maha Kumaran and Heather Cai, "Identifying the Visible Minority Librarians in Canada: A National Survey," Evidence Based Library & Information Practice 10, no. 2 (2015): 108-126, https://doi.org/10.18438/b8zc88.

in their library, particularly in their organization's leadership, resulting in feelings of isolation and alienation.

Although the majority of librarians are women (making up 82% of the total),[13] gender bias remains a significant challenge for the profession. Women continue to be disproportionately underrepresented in library leadership, despite increases in the numbers of women librarians in senior non-leadership positions.[14] DeLong further states that the cohort of librarian women currently in leadership positions is nearing retirement in the next five to ten years, suggesting an even greater need to recruit women into the ranks of librarian leadership.[15] The Association of Research Libraries found that although the gender salary gap is decreasing among professional academic librarians, women have not yet achieved salary parity with men.[16]

The quality of work life in librarianship may differ across genders. A study by Galbraith, Fry, and Garrisson[17] found no statistically significant differences in job satisfaction or personal fulfillment between women and men in academic settings. Men, however, reported a better work/life balance and lower levels of stress than women, despite the fact that their gender is a minority in the profession. Simpson's study of men in women-dominated fields[18] provides a reasonable explanation for this finding. Simpson suggests that men are assumed to have more authority, are looked upon more favorably, and have increased career prospects

---

13. Davis and Hall, "Diversity Counts."

14. Kathleen DeLong, "Career Advancement and Writing about Women Librarians: A Literature Review," *Evidence Based Library & Information Practice* 8, no. 1 (2013): 59-75, https://doi.org/10.18438/b8cs4m.

15. DeLong, "Career Advancement and Writing about Women Librarians," 59-75.

16. Martha Kyrillidou and Shaneka Morris, *ARL Annual Salary Survey 2013–2014*, accessed May 28, 2017, http://publications.arl.org/ARL-Annual-Salary-Survey-2013-2014/.

17. Quinn Galbraith, Leanna Fry, and Melissa Garrison, "The Impact of Faculty Status and Gender on Employee Well-being in Academic Libraries," *College & Research Libraries* 77, no. 1 (2016): 71-86, https://doi.org/10.5860/crl.77.1.71.

18. Ruth Simpson, "Masculinity at Work," *Work, Employment and Society* 18, no. 2 (2004): 349-68, doi:10.1177/0950017200404273.

due to their minority status in women-dominated fields.[19] The results of Simpson's study found that men benefit from being a numerical minority in the profession and that the privileges associated with masculinity (assumed authority and increased career prospects, for example) carry over into the field of librarianship.[20]

The dimension of sexual orientation adds complexity to the experiences of women of color. For queer[21] women of color, there are multiple oppressions that can be experienced at any given time. Cherie Moraga suggests that queer women of color not only need to examine the ways these oppressions impact their lives, but that they can also radicalize themselves based on their multiple oppressions.[22] The "specificity" of each oppression, according to Moraga, impacts queer women of color both internally and externally.[23]

Given the biases along gender and race in the library profession, how might we better understand the racialized and gendered experiences of women of color librarians, including queer women of color librarians? The intersectionality[24] literature offers a helpful framework to better understand this question. Collins, for example, in her seminal text, *Black Feminist Thought*, suggests that black women have unique contributions to make, both to feminist and to African American movements.[25] According to Collins, because of the unique social spaces that black women inhabit, they have opportunities to define their own realities, truth,

19. Simpson, "Masculinity at Work," 357.

20. Simpson, "Masculinity at Work," 356.

21. We are using the term "queer" as a reclaimed term used to challenge the traditional fixed binaries of sexual orientation and gender. See Meg Barker, Christina Richards & Helen Bowes-Catton, 2009.

22. Cherrie Moraga, "La Güera," in *This Bridge Called My Back: Writings by Radical Women of Color*, ed. Cherrie Moraga and Gloria Anzaldúa (Albany: State University of New York [SUNY], 2015), 23.

23. Moraga, "*La Güera*."

24. See Kimberlé Crenshaw, "Mapping the Margins: Intersectionality, Identity Politics, and Violence against Women of Color," *Stanford Law Review* 43, no. 6 (1991): 1241, doi:10.2307/1229039.

25. Patricia Hill Collins, *Black Feminist Thought: Knowledge, Consciousness, and the Politics of Empowerment* (New York: Routledge, 2015).

and empowerment.[26] Applying Collins' framework to women of color librarians, it is particularly important to have them give voice to their own experiences in the library workplace.

Risman's theory on gender as social structure provides another framework that helps to understand the experiences of women of color librarians.[27] Risman suggests that the social structure operates at three levels: individual, interpersonal, and institutional, and interacts with other axes of oppression, such as race, class, and sexuality. While each axis of oppression needs its own analysis, each axis also needs to be understood in relation to other axes of oppression. This "both/and strategy" allows researchers to use a multi-dimensional approach for understanding gender and race, as well as their intersections.[28]

For the purposes of the current study, the empowerment of women of color librarians is of paramount importance. Utilizing Risman's framework, we assumed that each axis of oppression would need to be understood on its own, as well as in relation to other axes of oppression.

The Role of Activism

The general aim of this study is to understand the role of activism, and its costs, for women of color librarians. Political activism may play a significant role for those occupying minority statuses. Schussman & Soule[29] suggest that activism reflects engagement with the political discourse and that women in particular are engaged in political activism (in their study, activism was examined via protest participation). Activism needs to be understood within an intersectional framework,

---

26. Collins, *Black Feminist Thought.*

27. Barbara J. Risman, "Gender as a Social Structure: Theory Wrestling with Activism," *Gender and Society* 18, no. 4 (2004): 429-50, https://doi.org/10.1177/0891243204265349.

28. Risman, "Gender as a Social Structure," 443.

29. A. Schussman, and S. A. Soule, "Process and Protest: Accounting for Individual Protest Participation," *Social Forces* 84, no.2 (2005): 1089, https:/doi:10.1353/sof.2006.0034.

since race and gender affect participation and motivation in nuanced ways.[30] The type of political engagement with which women of color librarians engage would likely depend on other minority statuses (sexual orientation, disability, socio-economic status, etc.), as well as any family or other personal obligations.

Living at the intersections of multiple oppressed identities offers new avenues for understanding activism and empowerment. Alimahomed found that queer women of color utilize an oppositional consciousness to oppression because of their invisibility in multiple movements.[31] The opportunities for creating new kinds of resistance arise out of the experiences of the marginalized, rather than solely in response to oppression. Collins' suggestion that black feminism in the U.S. must "never stop questioning" social injustices due to its participation in larger social movements, supports Alimahomed's viewpoint.[32] Centering the voices and experiences of women of color librarians, then, will help illuminate new possibilities for examining the role of activism.

The Cost of Activism

Another goal of the current study is to better understand what the cost of activism might be for women of color librarians. The "racial battle fatigue" theoretical framework describes the social-psychological responses (including exhaustion, physical avoidance, frustration, and emotional withdrawal) of African American male students on predominantly white campuses.[33] Racial battle fatigue is the cumulative effect

---

30. Eric Swank and Breanne Fahs, "An Intersectional Analysis of Gender and Race for Sexual Minorities Who Engage in Gay and Lesbian Rights Activism," *Sex Roles* 68, no.11-12 (2013): 11, https://doi:10.1007/s11199-012-0168-9.

31. Sabrina Alimahomed, "Thinking Outside the Rainbow: Women of Color Redefining Queer Politics and Identity," *Social Identities* 16, no. 2 (2010):154, https://doi:10.1080/13504631003688849.

32. Collins, Black Feminist Thought, 273.

33. W. A. Smith, W. R. Allen, and L. L. Danley, "'Assume the Position . . . You Fit the Description': Psychosocial Experiences and Racial Battle Fatigue Among African American Male College Students," *American Behavioral Scientist* 51, no. 4 (2007): 552,

of race- and gender-based microaggressions and helps shed light on understanding the costs of being in historically white environments.

Women of color who use active engagement to respond to racism often experience detrimental effects. Liang, Alvarez, Juang, and Liang[34] examined gender differences among Asian Americans responding to perceived racism. Asian American women who used active coping strategies to directly manage the source of race-related stress (rather than manage the emotional impact of the race-related stress), tended to experience higher levels of race-related stress. Liang et al. speculate that increased stress among Asian American women relative to Asian American men might be explained by increased amounts of time, energy, and cognitive resources that are devoted to directly addressing racism.[35] The increased levels of engagement used to confront racism likely take a significant toll on Asian American women, and perhaps on women of color more broadly.

Methodology

We used an interpretivist approach[36] to focus on meaning-making from the perspectives of women of color librarians. We were interested in understanding their beliefs and worldviews about activism and social justice in the profession. This phenomenological qualitative approach focuses on understanding shared experiences and differences among women of color, particularly regarding their activism and self-care. In this approach, we constructed meaning from the participant's responses as they shared how they engage in social justice and activism within the library profession. We looked through interviewees' reported experiences

---

https://doi:10.1177/0002764207307742.

34. Christopher T. H. Liang, Alvin N. Alvarez, Linda P. Juang, and Mandy X. Liang, "The Role of Coping in the Relationship between Perceived Racism and Racism-Related Stress for Asian Americans: Gender Differences," *Asian American Journal of Psychology* S1 (2009): 59, https//:doi:http://dx.doi.org/10.1037/1948-1985.S.1.56.

35. Liang, "The Role of Coping," 65.

36. Janet Salmons, *Doing Qualitative Research Online* (Thousand Oaks: Sage, 2016), 22.

and used inductive content analysis to look for themes and meaning so the phenomenon could be described and understood. Semi-structured interviews were chosen so that participants could share their experiences through pre-determined interview questions with the opportunity for follow up. We also identify as women of color and hope to explore the patterns and interpretations of how women of color librarians make sense of the world and interpret social reality through the lens of our shared experience.

Reflexivity and Positionality of the Authors

Both authors are queer women of color who have spent many years working in academic institutions. The primary author is an academic librarian and the secondary author is a clinical psychologist who previously worked in higher education as a student-affairs professional. As queer women of color in traditionally white professions, we both have backgrounds that influence how we experience the world, and this informs our interest in this research study. Our cultures and multiple identities have influenced how we choose to do research. We strive to build equality, trust, and respect in the interview process and believe we gained authentic responses in return.

We were not impartial in this study. Our positions as interviewers and examiners of data were as partial "insiders"; we drew on our own knowledge to identify research questions and issues. There are characteristics we share with participants and we have experienced the research phenomena being studied, but we did not directly contribute data. We believe that our status as "insiders" enhanced our credibility and assisted us in our interviews.

The literature shows that for "in-group interviews," responses are different if one is not a member of the community being studied. This is especially true for members of underrepresented and marginalized communities. For example, it has been "repeatedly shown that black women are reticent to discuss experiences of racism with white interviewers."[37] A shared identity with the researchers encourages participants to express emotions, such as anger and passion, which helps give meaning to the data and production of knowledge. Personal characteristics influence meaningful partnerships with participants, and thus the success of the research.

The interviews were interactive conversations and dialogues between the researchers and the participants. Our roles as "insiders" made it easier to recruit participants to the study and build rapport, since we understood the culture and existing norms that are relevant for women of color. We also acknowledge that the experiences of women of color are vast and diverse, and we do not lay claim to or understand all the narratives that were shared. We drew on previous scholarship and the data gathered to understand the research problem and explore surfaced themes, while acknowledging the impact our identities may have on the interpretation of the data.

Anti-Oppressive Methodologies

We used elements of anti-racist approaches, feminist research methodologies, and queer theory in this study. We strove to be culturally responsible by building an authentic relationship between the interviewer and the participant. Each party played equal roles in carving out a pathway of mutual respect during the interviews. Anti-racist research challenges and ruptures the very structures within which one is trying to operate, showing that research on "racial domination and social oppression...provides subjects with an opportunity to speak about their experiences within the broader contexts of structural and institutional forces of society."[38] Feminist social scientists encourage research that takes place within a non-hierarchal relationship. For example, instead

37. Amin, "Voices of Minority Immigrant Women," 197.

38. George Jerry Sefa Dei, "Critical Issues in Anti-Racist Research Methodologies," in *Critical Issues in Anti-Racist Research Methodologies*, ed. George Jerry Sefa Dei et al. (New York: Peter Lang, 2005), 11.

of studying the "Other" or holding all knowledge, feminist research supports a shared experience and natural involvement with the content area.[39] Queer researchers continually "foster questioning stances that interrogate the normative and the status quo, as well as the institutions and values of a 'normal' society" or profession.[40]

Participants were viewed as experts, which runs counter to "traditional" methodologies. We placed importance on giving voice to those who are not often heard from within the profession, and increasing the visibility of stories from oppressed and marginalized groups in the discipline of library and information science. Anti-racist, feminist, and queer researchers must not "hide behind objectivity and value neutrality… the research must seek to assist the subjects to tell their stories and narrate their experiences, hopes and fears."[41] Using anti-racist methodologies was integral to the research that we wanted to conduct--as queer women of color, it was a personal and a political choice, and a way to show solidarity with other women of color librarians.

Data Collection

The data collection methodology was that of a semi-structured interview. A set of ten questions was developed in advance, with follow-up questions determined during the interview when more details were needed.[42] A conversational style was adopted to encourage participants to openly discuss personal experiences as women of color activists. This was a deliberate choice—we wished to conduct interviews as a dialogue

39. Nuzhat Amin, "Voices of Minority Immigrant Women," in Critical Issues in *Anti-Racist Research Methodologies*, ed. George Jerry Sefa Dei et al. (New York: Peter Lang, 2005), 197.

40. Fairn Herising, "Interrupting Positions: Critical Thresholds and Queer Pro/Positions," in *Revisiting Critical, Indigenous, and Anti-Oppressive Approaches*, ed. Leslie Allison Brown et al. (Toronto: Canadian Scholars Press, 2015), 141.

41. Andrew C. Okolie, "Towards an Anti-Racist Research Framework: The Case for In-depth Interviewing," in *Critical Issues in Anti-Racist Research Methodologies*, ed. George Jerry Sefa Dei et al. (New York: Peter Lang, 2005), 253.

42. Salmons, *Doing Qualitative Research Online*, 129.

between two people, during which interviewees would be regarded "as co-participants rather than as data collection instruments."[43] A dialogue or conversation would also promote relationship-building, so the research would be done *with*, rather than *on*, the participants.

An opening statement was read prior to the start of the interview that described the research study and informed participants that all responses would be anonymized, with all identifying information obscured. At the beginning of each interview, consent was collected from the participant; they were informed that the interview could be ended at any time. To protect participant anonymity, each participant was accorded a set of randomly assigned initials. Questions were asked in predominantly the same sequence, with similar follow-up questions.

Recruitment of Potential Participants

The search for potential participants took place during the first two weeks of June 2017. Participants were recruited online from responses to a call for participants for "women of color librarians who consider themselves activists." We also indicated that we were "especially interested in hearing the voices of queer women of color" librarians, since the literature shows very little research on this subgroup. We wanted to raise the visibility and voices of queer women of color, since the literature shows that they "utilize an oppositional consciousness to oppression because of their invisibility in multiple movements."[44] We realized that, even when trying to be inclusive to all women of color, language and terminology is still a barrier. For example, we received an email from a potential participant who asked, "Are you interested in interviewing queer *trans* women of color?" Of course, the answer was resoundingly in the affirmative.

---

43. Amin, "Voices of Minority Immigrant Women," 194.

44. Alimahomed, "Thinking Outside the Rainbow," 154.

The call for participants was posted on the listservs for the American Indian Library Association (AILA),[45] Asian/Pacific American Librarians Association (APALA),[46] Black Caucus of the American Library Association (BCALA),[47] and REFORMA: The National Association to Promote Library and Information Services to Latinos and the Spanish Speaking.[48] The call was also posted on social media groups aimed at librarians of color.

Potential participants contacted the primary author who explained the nature of the research and, if the participant was agreeable, scheduled a time to be interviewed. Participants were not asked to identify their activist activities or prompted to explain how they engaged in activism. This was a conscious decision, since women of color are often tasked with justifying their work and identity, and we wished to avoid this. Participants were asked to confirm that they self-identified as women of color and as activists. Twenty-six people responded to the call and the first fifteen were selected for interviews.[49] We did not track where the participants first saw the call for research.

Information and Communication Technology (ICT)

Participant interviews were scheduled from June 12-30, 2017. Participants were given the option to use text or chat software to conduct the interview online or to answer questions via telephone. Over 70% of participants chose to do the interview online, stating that they were "frequent text/chat communicators," and that an online interview was "more convenient." Online interviews used the messaging app Facebook Messenger and Google Hangouts/Google Chat, where the data

45. AILA website, accessed May 1, 2017, http://www.ailanet.org.

46. APALA website, accessed May 1, 2017, http://www.apalaweb.org

47. BCALA website, accessed May 1, 2017, www.bcala.org

48. REFORMA website, accessed May 1, 2017, http://www.reforma.org

49. While fifteen participants are a small number to draw conclusions from, it is a number appropriate for standard qualitative analysis, which seeks to derive detailed insights from a small sample size.

was captured verbatim. For phone interviews, data was collected via transcription. Both online and phone interviews ranged from thirty to eighty minutes, and the data was collected synchronously.

The primary author had not previously conducted interviews via an Information and Communication Technology, and found that with online communication, it was easy to miss non-verbal cues or to misinterpret them. The length of time between posting and responding varied with each participant, which proved difficult at times with pacing and turn-taking in the conversation. Since it was difficult to determine when a participant was done "talking," individuals were asked to indicate when they had completed answering a question by typing "<done>."

Content Analysis of Transcripts

After the interview, the online transcripts were edited to remove extra spacing, images, and names, and phone interviews were transcribed line by line. The style and tone of the responses were kept intact. These transcripts provided the principal source of data for this study. The model of content analysis selected for the transcripts was inductive content analysis, which is described as:

> …A process designed to condense raw data into categories of themes based on valid inference and interpretation. This process uses inductive reasoning, by which themes and categories emerge from the data through the researcher's careful examination…[50]

Through a careful analysis of the transcripts, primary themes were identified in relation to the responses to each question.

50. Yan Zhang and Barbara M. Wildemuth, "Qualitative Analysis of Content," in *Applications of Social Science Research Methods to Questions in Information and Library Science*, ed. Barbara M. Wildemuth (Westport, CT: Libraries Unlimited, 2009), 309.

Findings

Participant Demographics

Data collection yielded fifteen interviews: eleven interviews via online private chat messaging and four interviews via the telephone. They included seven academic librarians, six public librarians, one PhD candidate/research assistant, and one independent publisher/former academic librarian.[51] Years of experience in the library and information science field ranged from two years to twenty years. We were deliberate about stating experience in the terms of the "library and information science field" and not "as a librarian" or a "professional position," since many women of color spend significant years working as staff. For example, there are approximately twice as many women of color library assistants (24.5%) as women of color librarians (12.4%).[52] Participants hailed from the following four regions: eight from the West (CA-7, OR-1); four from the Midwest (IN-1, MI-1, MO-1, OH-1); one from the South (TN-1) and two from the East (NY-2).[53]

Participants were asked to broadly describe their multiple identities, particularly the ones salient for social justice work. We did not provide categories or labels.[54] The terms that participants chose to describe themselves by are listed below, with no demarcation on the chart between

51. The term "librarian" will be used throughout to refer to all the respondents, although not all respondents currently work in a library or hold that job title or position.

52. "Diversity Counts 2009-10 Update," American Library Association, accessed May 20, 2017, http://www.ala.org/aboutala/offices/diversity/diversitycounts/2009-2010update.

53. We used the U.S. census regions to group states and the District of Columbia. The Census Bureau defines four census regions: Northeast, Midwest, South, and West. "Geography," United States Census Bureau, accessed July 1, 2017, https://www.census.gov/geo/reference/webatlas/regions.html

54. Since pre-determined categories were not offered, participants chose to describe their identities based on what they decided was most salient.

race, ethnicity, sexual orientation, and gender identity/assigned sex. Some respondents chose multiple terms to describe themselves, while others did not. The terms were chosen by the participants, and in some cases, we grouped terms together, with the understanding that categories, especially those around race,[55] change over time,[56] and that personal power comes from being able to select your own terminology to describe your identities. For the purposes of reporting data, we will use the terms described by the respondents.[57]

---

55. We acknowledge that race is a social construct.

56. Anna Brown, "The Changing Categories the U.S. Has Used to Measure Race," Pew Research Center, accessed January 3, 2018, http://www.pewresearch.org/fact-tank/2015/06/12/the-changing-categories-the-u-s-has-used-to-measure-race/.

57. Other self-described identities are captured in the forthcoming section "Complexity of Layers."

Of the six participants captured in the category African American or Black, over half described themselves as both, while one stated African American and two used the term black. One participant said she used different terms depending on who she was speaking to. We combined the responses into one category, while acknowledging 1) that the terms are not synonymous or interchangeable, and that race, ethnicity, and nationality influence both terms and 2) that language, while descriptive, is also dynamic and responsive. See Shahida Muhammad, "I'm Not African American…I'm Black," Ebony, accessed January 3, 2018, http://www.ebony.com/news-views/im-not-african-american-im-black#axzz53A6d8AVr; Aisha Harris, "Where I'm From," Slate, accessed January 3, 2018, http://www.slate.com/articles/arts/culturebox/2014/07/black_american_versus_african_american_why_i_prefer_to_be_called_a_black.html; and Joe Pinsker, "The Financial Consequences of Saying 'Black' vs. 'African American,'" The Atlantic, accessed January 3, 2018, https://www.theatlantic.com/business/archive/2014/12/the-financial-consequences-of-saying-black-vs-african-american/383999/.

Three participants described themselves as Asian Pacific Islander or Asian Pacific American or as part of the Asian/Pacific Island community. Since the early 2000 census, the category of Asian has usually been separated from Pacific Islander (which usually includes Native Hawaiian, Samoan, and Guamanian). For the purpose of this study, the category Asian/Pacific American is used to capture how participants described themselves.

We are using the participant chosen term mixed-race, which encompasses people with mixed ancestry of more than one race, and multiracial people.

We are using the gender-inclusive term Latinx to capture participants who described themselves as Latino or Hispanic. We also acknowledge that there are issues with the above terms, based on colonialism, erasure of culture and heritage and the invisibility of Latinx folks with African or indigenous/Native American/American Indian heritage. See "'Latinx' and Gender Inclusivity," *Merriam Webster*, accessed January 3, 2018, https://www.merriam-webster.com/words-at-play/word-history-latinx; Raul A. Reyes, "Are You Latinx? As Usage Grows, Word Draws Approval, Criticism," *NBC News*, accessed January 3, 2018, https://www.nbcnews.com/news/latino/

Terms or Categories Chosen by Participants	No. of Participants
African American or Black	6
Asian/Pacific American	3
Mixed-Race	3
Latinx	3
LGBTQ+/Queer	6
Cis/Cisgender	4

We were disappointed to have no participants who identified as being from the Indigenous/American Indian/Native American/Alaskan Native community and for future studies, will conduct more intensive outreach to ensure that these voices and stories are heard, especially since the number of Indigenous/American Indian/Native American/Alaskan Native people working in libraries is woefully small (approximately 0.004%).[58]

Intersectionality, Multiple Identities as a Woman of Color Librarian

We asked participants to describe how they identified in relation to social justice work. This question was intentionally framed to capture

---

are-you-latinx-usage-grows-word-draws-approval-criticism-n651396; Raquel Reichard, "Why We Say Latinx: Trans and Gender Non-Conforming People Explain," *Latina*, accessed January 3, 2018, http://www.latina.com/lifestyle/our-issues/why-we-say-latinx-trans-gender-non-conforming-people-explain;

Terry Blas, "I'm Latino. I'm Hispanic. And They're Different, So I Drew a Comic to Explain," *Everyday Feminism*, accessed January 3, 2018, https://everydayfeminism.com/2015/10/im-latino-hispanic-difference/; and Paul Taylor et al, "When Labels Don't Fit: Hispanics and Their Views of Identity," *Pew Research Center*, accessed January 3, 2018, http://www.pewhispanic.org/2012/04/04/when-labels-dont-fit-hispanics-and-their-views-of-identity/. Taylor states in the study that the majority of "Latinos" identified themselves by country of origin, such as "Mexican American" or "Cuban."

"LGBTQ+" is a term/acronym used by participants to self-describe the identities of lesbian, gay, bisexual, trans, and queer/questioning. The "+" can also include intersex, asexual, aromantic, pansexual, polysexual, and others.

"Cis" or "cisgender" is used to describe a person who identifies as the sex they were assigned at birth.

58. "Diversity Counts 2009-10 Update,"

the complexity of identities for women librarians of color. Responses fell into two main themes: audience and context, and the complexity of layers.

Audience and Context

A close reading of the responses revealed that participants often *choose* how many of their identities to disclose based on the environment and "who is in the room." A Filipina American participant stated: "I am aware that certain identities become more prominent in specific interactions—the relational and situational aspect of social interactions." A mixed-race woman elaborated: "Mostly it depends on how white I feel I am perceived to be and how important identifying as a person of color is to the conversation. It depends who I am talking to. I will add in that I am a first-generation college graduate or my economic upbringing if I am speaking to an extremely privileged group."

An assistant director from an academic library in the Midwest addressed the concept of *choice* in deciding how much of her identity to reveal, the recognition that some audiences may be more hostile, and that certain aspects of one's identity may be "hidden" by not actively revealing them:

> ...throughout our existence we wear many different hats and layers and it depends how we show up and how safe we feel. I am an African American lesbian. I may share that or not depending on the audience. I allow people to see pieces of my identity.

The emphasis on "unveiling" particular identities based on audience and situation appears to be one process by which women of color librarians navigate their multiple identities in work settings and speaks to how difficult it can be to present oneself as a whole person in an environment that does not support your culture. As one interviewee stated, "Sometimes I wonder how much code switching has to be done in order to survive in these libraries, as a professional."

Complexity of Layers

Three queer-identified interviewees addressed the intersection of race, gender, and sexual orientation through their layered descriptions: "...a Latinx queer cisgender woman," a "mixed heritage Chicana Filipina queer woman of color," and a "biracial, Fil-Mex, working class, queer, first year of transition, non-binary, on hormones, 'she.'" The interviewees expressed how important it was to be able to name themselves, despite how other people may perceive them based on appearance or presentation.

Other identities described for women of color librarians included: first-generation immigrant, mother, person with chronic illness, upper middle class, introvert, Christian, Buddhist, recovering Roman Catholic, fat, straight, raised by a single parent, working class, early-career librarian, and community organizer.

The participants in this study acknowledged that naming the various and complex ways they identify was an important component of owning the intersections of who they are. By providing space for the participants to identify themselves in an open-ended way, we attempted to affirm all of their multiple identities.

Importance of Seeing Women of Color

Intersectionality was named as one of the most pressing issues facing women of color librarians. Many stated that it was a struggle to have their whole selves seen and valued in the profession. A Latinx librarian discussed how, in a profession dominated by white women, when women of color are "lucky enough to get a professional position, that many try to blend in and they often lose their identity in the process." A black academic librarian stated the struggle of intersectionality best by explaining how this can come from external forces and from internal struggles:

> [There is a] lack of understanding and practice of intersectionality in our profession. WOC get treated like a monolith without attention to the many identities we hold. Or we get fractured within ourselves because we struggle to deal with our relative areas of privilege. (e.g., it's like either talk about LGBTQIA or disability or class issues in a white context or talk about issues of being a women of color librarian but never mix in other issues or acknowledge how the intersection of issues plays out for folks). I know it's hard and can get messy, but we hurt ourselves and each other when we fail to engage with that complexity.

Queer and trans women of color spoke about the lack of visibility of their intersecting identities, and how, within the library and information science field, when race and ethnicity are discussed, we often neglect to think about or include people of color who are also members of the lesbian, gay, bisexual, transgender and queer community. Conversely, when sexual orientation and gender identity is deliberated, it is often assumed that the LGBTQ community is white. A Latinx public librarian lamented that it was difficult to find and connect with other queer women of color, since the profession is so white that often "settling" for just being in a people of color space felt like community, and how the LGBTQIA spaces in librarianship were very white. A trans woman talked about solidarity and the importance of "creating our own space." "Our voices are not heard in our organizations; our ideas do not hold as much merit. We need more women of color, more queer women of color in order to affect change in this white, straight profession."

Through the examination of the experiences of women of color librarians we see and acknowledge how their multiple intersecting identities play out within different communities. As Hudson states, "We cannot effectively challenge structures of racial domination within the field without being part of larger conversations and movements addressing such systems in other contexts."[59] The simultaneous experience of some identities being salient, while other identities are invisible, can make it

59. David J. Hudson, "On 'Diversity' as Anti-Racism in Library and Information Studies: A Critique," *Journal of Critical Library and Information Studies*, 1, no. 1 (2017): 27, https://doi.org/10.24242/jclis.v1i1.6.

difficult for women of color to feel acknowledged as whole beings in their various communities.

Motivations for Engaging with Social Justice and Activism

Although engaging in activist work can be difficult, the respondents overwhelmingly said that they were passionate about it. The motivations for doing activist work varied, but overwhelmingly, the main reason that woman of color librarians became activists or do social justice work is due to individual experiences of oppression, followed by a sense of family history and upbringing.

Individual Experiences of Oppression

Activist women of color librarians are motivated by feelings of marginalization. Five participants stated that they engage in social justice and activism because pain they have suffered motivates them to try to effect change and to champion for the welfare of others. An academic librarian from South America talked about the discrimination and harassment she faced as someone who spoke English as a second language: "I have suffered so I know what people are going through and I can fully identify as an immigrant." A trans woman of color stated that her social justice work was related to reclaiming her voice after years of bigotry: "Ever since I came out, at 18, I didn't wanna take shit anymore, I wanted voice and agency and wanted to stop being powerless. That is why I march and organize for others now." An African American librarian, in the profession for 10 years, said: "As a person of color with multiple identities, social justice is a form of survival. We have to educate and inform the people, because lives depend on it."

Finally, an Asian Pacific Islander American librarian talked about how they continue to do activist work even though it can be painful. "I feel compelled to do this work because it's the right thing to do. But I ask myself 'why' a lot too because it hurts so much and it is tiring and the other route [ignoring, not engaging, and trying to pass] seems easier. And if no one else is addressing critical issues of oppression in the workplace, often there is no choice but to stand up."

Family and Upbringing

A consistent theme was the influence of parents and ancestors on participant involvement in social justice and activism. A mixed-race academic librarian simply stated: "Because I can. Because I must. Because I don't know how not to. Because my parents raised me to raise my voice." Participants shared stories of being raised in social justice and activist environments, being involved in their communities, and feeling like they were part of something larger than just themselves. Parents and relatives of some participants were involved in the Chicano Civil Rights movements of the late 1960s and early 1970s, activists in the Japanese American concentration camps, feminist trailblazers, community organizers, union leaders, and involved in community reconciliation efforts after the Los Angeles riots:

> My parents took myself and my brother to Koreatown after the L.A. Riots to help clean up the neighborhood. I remember broken glass and the smells of burnt down buildings. We were young kids. So, it has always been a part of my life. I began to see that the only way to understand who I was, was to be in a place of service, to actually understanding myself to be an activist."

An African American academic librarian talked about how, "It is my duty, birthright, and passed on to me by my ancestors." Another declared, "I feel it is in my DNA [based on family history] to express the unjust and expose hidden powers and structures."

The connection to social change legacies motivates some women of color librarians to continue their activism. For these participants, a commitment to social change is deeply ingrained in them by their families of origin.

Importance of Activism and Social Justice Work in the Profession

Why are activism and social justice work important in the library and information science profession? Participants' main response revolved around the whiteness of the profession. Six participants talked about how it wasn't just important, but crucial and necessary because of the "overwhelming" amount of work necessary to combat institutional racism in libraries and the incredible whiteness of library staff and librarians. One queer Asian Pacific Islander quipped, "If I don't work for justice and equity, who would? My white colleagues?" A Latinx librarian stated: "Yes, social justice work and activism is so relevant, because it [the profession] is so fucking white. We need to move the definition of diversity forward!" All interviewees spoke about the explicit and implicit racism, sexism, homophobia and other forms of discrimination and oppression that they experienced and witnessed, both interpersonally and at systemic levels of their institutions.

All the women of color interviewed were passionate about the need to have open acknowledgment and conversation about racism and other oppressions in the field. An African American librarian used hashtags to express her frustration with the silence around whiteness: "So I say, #oscarssowhite, #LISsowhite, because it is just so damn white and we don't talk about it!" A librarian from the Midwest stated: "We need to fight for what is right, and acknowledge the issues, because black people make up five percent of librarians! After that color don't even matter." Finally, an academic librarian on the East Coast reflected on the past and how things haven't changed much in the profession: "I realize that looking at the history and present of our profession, oppression is all over it. And those of us who fight against that oppression now and those who did so in the past were pushing against the grain."

Interviewees also addressed systemic oppression, as libraries do "a great deal of mimicking of the way power structures are in our western society, with white men in power again and again, and pervasive discrimination, prejudice and exploitation." A black librarian echoed this sentiment, discussing how, as women of color librarians, "we are tasked as professionals with making information free and available to everyone...within power structures that deny marginalized groups and oppress from within with unequal treatment, racism, and sexism." As Hudson states, this silence needs to be addressed, because in librarianship there is "an erasure of the structural character of racism—that is, the entrenchment of white supremacy as a foundational and sustaining element of the discursive and material conditions of our society."[60] One librarian mused that since libraries are very much part of the dominant cultural paradigm, "Sometimes I wonder how radical I can be if our structures perpetuate racism, sexism, homophobia, heteronormativity, fat phobia, ableism etc. Just because we are in library positions doesn't mean we are seen or heard. I am keenly aware that I'm largely operating in a white world." Another commented, "We are hired to do the work, but then we enter spaces that are so fully white, in culture, beliefs and practices, where are we supposed to start?"

Activism and social justice were mentioned by several women as essential practices that can keep people accountable who participate in oppressive behavior. For example, white women were called out by several respondents for being gatekeepers when it came to new opportunities. Three black librarians stated that white women often created barriers for them as well as other women of color, while not acknowledging or perhaps not being consciously aware of doing so. A queer mixed-race librarian talked about how racist and sexist perceptions are often perpetuated by white women in the profession, and how "it is a violence against our being." An African American librarian who had risen to middle management, shared:

> There is a definite hoarding of opportunities and access [by white women]. Some of us are fortunate and have participated in programming that assists with [professional] growth and expands access...but then again the structures need dismantling. You know, like my girl Audre Lorde says—master's tools and all that.[61]

---

60. Hudson, "On Diversity," 10.

61. The interviewee is referencing Audre Lorde's 1984 seminar piece "The Master's

A Latinx librarian reflected that, when white women succeed and become administrators or managers, they often actively work against women of color achieving the same parity, becoming competitive or "threatened":

> They are not willing to help women of color...they are not willing to change their behavior because they are so content, and so comfortable when they 'make it.' They don't realize or they don't care that there are so many more barriers for us. In fact, they often choose to create more hurdles.

A black academic librarian addressed gatekeeping with regard to the lack of opportunity and how difficult it was to secure a permanent full-time position: "We are good enough for interim positions but not to [permanently] move up. When people do get positions, it is because they are 'in the know'—they heard about it at happy hour at the bar with all the other white ladies, and you weren't invited. It is the new version of the 'old boys club.'"

Several interviewees did mention the difference that the Spectrum Scholarship Program[62] has made in recruiting more students of color to the profession. They noted, however, that for twenty years it has not been enough and that the work of diversifying the profession cannot rest on a lone program. An African American librarian strongly stated that, "the profession reflects a [need for activism and social justice], because the whole notion of such small growth of people of color is an abomination." To sum it up, a queer mixed-race librarian explained, "Social justice and activism pushes our profession to an important edge... where we actually need to think about equity, ourselves, our purpose, our vision and how that informs programming and what we communicate to our communities about who we are."

Tools Will Never Dismantle the Master's House" which calls out the racism underlying white feminism.

62. Spectrum Scholarship Program, accessed May 15, 2017, http://www.ala.org/advocacy/spectrum.

Invisible Labor and Activist Work

Do women of color librarians engage in activist and social justice work as part of their paid positions, or do they do the activist work as unpaid labor, in addition to their stated job responsibilities? More than 65% of the women of color interviewed said that it was very challenging to juggle activism and work, and that when it was possible, it was incorporated into their jobs. A Pacific Islander public librarian stated that infusing activism into her paid position eased the burden and pain that can occur when doing social justice work, and also ensured that she "walked the talk." A Filipina academic librarian said it would be "hypocritical to leave that part of me that is an activist at the door." An African American librarian saw her success in doing both as a matter of navigating her role on campus and in the library "by using my position to do what I felt passionate about." Two librarians remarked that their institutions appreciated and valued the work that they do for social justice—because it made the institution "look good"—but stressed that activism and social justice work needed to be a part of every single position, not just the jobs filled by people of color. A mixed-race librarian and a Latinx librarian questioned why they were the only ones at their libraries doing activist and social justice work, wondering "Where are the white people?"

It also became clear that positionality within a library played a role in how comfortable librarians felt doing activist work, and that it was more difficult to incorporate activist and social justice work into paid work as a newer librarian. When interviewing for a recent academic library position, an Asian Pacific Islander academic librarian said: "When I first started out in libraries, they [my unpaid social justice work and my paid position] were separate. I did the former on the weekends and evenings, and was not open about it. Now, I am upfront about the social justice work I do in ALA and that seemed to be why they hired me." A public librarian also had similar sentiments:

> Whenever I interview now I make sure they know these aspects [social justice and activism] come with me and that it is non-negotiable. I'm lucky to work in a place now that values it, even if they don't always understand it and sometimes resist it. This wasn't always the case. When I was a new librarian and just needed to eat, I wasn't as bold.

Whether activism and social justice are incorporated into job responsibilities or not, respondents overwhelmingly agreed that the work is often unacknowledged by colleagues or supervisors, and invisible, except for the moments where it brings the institution positive press and accolades. One woman of color asked "How can we measure the added value that we bring by doing this work? How can we ensure it is seen and visible, considered important and beneficial?"

Barriers to Social Justice and Activist Engagement

Women of color librarians identified two substantial barriers to engaging in social justice and activist work: the lack of allyship, and the current political climate. These barriers wear down their physical and mental resources and consume their energy and time.

Lack of Allyship

Often, women of color librarians are the only person of color at their institution. This puts them in an impossible position of both personally experiencing race-based trauma, while also often serving as the solo voice interrupting racism, sexism, and other forms of oppression and discrimination in the workplace. Speaking up can then lead to more criticism and attacks, and reinforces feelings of isolation and not belonging in the library profession.

Privilege and oppression are not spread equally throughout our profession. Some librarians experience fewer barriers while others—especially women of color and queer women of color—face serious consequences for engaging in activism or social justice work. Three librarians declared their desire to see white colleagues with privilege speak up, interrupt oppression, act as strong allies, and show their commitment to diversity through their actions. An African American librarian stated, "There are so many issues in our society, and more people need to speak out…especially if you are not [directly] impacted. It is incumbent on our survival [as people of color]."

Interviewees were also adamant that it was "not their job" to educate colleagues on oppression, or to work to make colleagues less racist or bigoted, as this is exhausting emotional labor. A queer mixed-race Latinx asked for white colleagues to recognize that "there is a wrong and a correct way to be an ally [to people of color and queers]" and that actions spoke louder than words. A black librarian on the East Coast, stated:

> I don't do "Ally 101" anymore, it's a waste of time. Especially when I do activism with people who have more privilege than me but want me to do the hard work. Don't use my name to get into spaces if you are not ready to fight for the people. I am pushing myself to the breaking point. You need to be fully committed to the activism too.

Another black librarian stated that:

> …one of the things I would like to see is more of my white colleagues, a lot more, advocating for change as it relates to equity and inclusion. I want them to come to the table and talk about concrete ways that they have done the work and how they have pushed forward to open opportunities for people of color in our profession. If I am at a meeting and am the only person of color, I at least want one of my colleagues to talk about 'Why are we so white?' I am tired of being the only one marching. I want to hear them say 'This is ridiculous, we need to have active goals and commitments to bring in people of color who are senior librarians.' To all the white people in positions of power: I want to see you do your work. Give me some solid numbers of your work. Show me. What have you done?

Interviewees pointed out that white colleagues who have power and privilege have a responsibility to stand up and advocate for others and to show real solidarity—not just lip service.

The Current Political Climate

When asked if the current political climate affected their activism, interviewees talked about the need to be even more of an activist and how exhausting, frightening, and mentally taxing the current climate can be. Over 85% of interviewees felt that the current climate is pushing them to be more direct, to interrupt oppression with greater frequency, to be "more vocal (I didn't think it possible)" and "more purposeful in my language." A Latinx librarian stated that "oppressors have taken the current climate as an excuse to pull the gloves off, so to speak, so I've been doing more of the same." A queer mixed-race librarian talked about breaking through complacency: "This year with Trump, it mobilized me, it was the first year I marched—for women, for science, the equality march… it woke me up." A black academic librarian noted that, in this political climate, people who have been marginalized now have a larger "target" on their backs, and they need to be protected. Another followed up by saying that all of the issues feel more urgent now. A mixed-race Asian American librarian said that while it has been humbling, she now realizes that this is not the time to "cower away, as we are change makers but only if we do the work."

Doing so much additional activist and social justice work drained the energy of many women of color. Three librarians mentioned how the current political climate created more work at their institutions, especially in regard to their ability to make patrons feel welcome at the library. Examples included inclusive programming for immigrants, increasing services to vulnerable populations, and bringing Muslim authors to the library to speak.

Several participants brought up issues of anxiety and fear after the election. One participant said: "I recognize how little power I have. If people I care about are in danger, I am in danger. Before [this election] I was more open and free." An immigrant from South America talked about her depression:

> I have been in a lot of pain the past six months. It has changed how I work, because all the [anti-immigration] talk affects my daily life here. It has brought up a lot of the fear that I experienced when I first moved to this country. I will always carry this accent and when people look at me (and not in a good sense), it is scary.

Three black/African American librarians talked about safety. One said that she is more cautious in her daily interactions. Another librarian discussed feeling fear, and the threat of harm or death in the face of rhetoric that is more openly sexist, racist, and homophobic. One African American participant's statement spoke of the real need to plan for safety: "I am so aware of always having to have strategies for what happens. If shit goes down where do I run and who do I call? Women of color don't have the luxury of not planning."

It is clear that there are physical, mental, and emotional costs and personal consequences for engaging in activism and social justice work. The amount of time and energy given up or negatively experienced as depression, pain, and fatigue are real. There are also risks and dangers that may occur because of activism and social justice work—including the very real possibility of job loss and threats to personal safety. An Asian Pacific Islander said that "my direct supervisor is telling me that doing too much [social justice and activist work] will hurt my career." A black librarian who ended up leaving her position discussed how, as a member of the faculty Senate, she fought endlessly for students and the library:

> I damn near broke the administration down with my library chanting. I was the only vocal voice on campus…The only vocal voice in the library, I mean…but it cost me… I had to leave that job and had major health issues after. I don't give a damn though. They will remember my name.

Another mentioned the lack of job security:

> It is difficult…it can put my job at risk to do [activism and social justice] as fully as I would love to. I am lucky to be union. It makes it safer to explore being radical and bringing activism to my branch and system. But there is still a huge cement ceiling that I have to keep in mind. I don't have money, this is not a high-paying career, so I have to pick my

battles. There are little ways to be an activist here at work, but I can only be my full authentic activist self outside of work.

The Practice of Self-Care

With so much trauma, both historical and present day, woven into the fabric of their lives, self-care is crucial for the physical, emotional, and mental well-being of women of color librarians. For activists who are passionate and committed, it can be nearly impossible to prioritize self-care, since working toward a vision of a better society is so compelling and seems more important. For women of color, self-care is an urgent reminder of one's own value and that one's own needs are important too.

The overall consensus regarding self-care was that women of color librarians think it is vital for mental, emotional, and physical health, but do not do enough of it or engage in self-care practices consistently. Almost three-quarters remarked that "just existing" as a woman of color or queer woman of color was exhausting and stressful, since just "holding those identities is so tiring."

With so many external pressures, finding a balance between activism and social justice commitments and self was difficult for women of color librarians. A mixed-race librarian articulated her struggle by saying: "I'm constantly navigating how much to give and how much to pull back for myself." A middle manager who is a longtime activist wryly remarked that, "Friends would tell me you need to figure out where you are going to go to die. Because we give so much of ourselves." A black librarian remarked that women of color librarians constantly take care of others, and "we are so used to putting others' needs before our own, that forcing ourselves to take a step back and assess how we are doing is so important. We can't support and work with others and dismantle oppression if we are on the verge of breaking." Another echoed that sentiment, stating: "Self-care is the core foundation of things that we, as women of color librarians should learn how to implement first and foremost. Without self-care everybody else gets nothing from us. We need to replenish." A Latinx librarian talked about how it "was difficult to practice [self-care] as an activist, since the amount of oppression that keeps coming at us is unyielding. It doesn't stop, so we cannot take a break." An Asian Pacific Islander talked about how self-care is seen as indulgent:

> We are living in the most capitalist country in the world. When you take care of yourself, it is seen as a problem or a weakness. It is so difficult as women of color. We are always giving, take care of everybody. And this is exacerbated by the library. We are not a profession that nurtures our workers, we are not a place of care. It is pivotal to do self-care or you will go fucking crazy. And as a parent, it is even harder—so hard as a working woman of color mother!

The top ways that interviewees performed self-care were: 1) Practicing meditation and mindfulness, 2) Exercising, 3) Spending time with family and friends, and 4) Reading, writing, and making art.

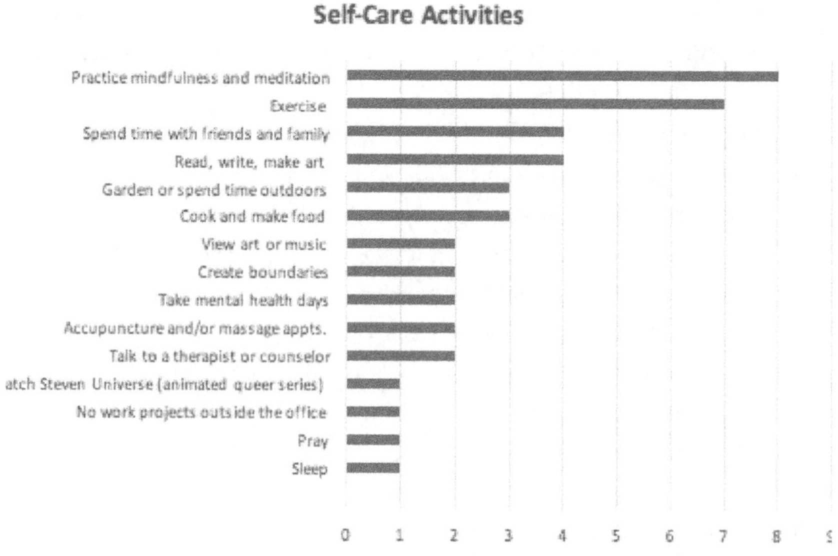

Self-Care Activities

Practice mindfulness and meditation
Exercise
Spend time with friends and family
Read, write, make art
Garden or spend time outdoors
Cook and make food
View art or music
Create boundaries
Take mental health days
Accupuncture and/or massage appts.
Talk to a therapist or counselor
atch Steven Universe (animated queer series)
No work projects outside the office
Pray
Sleep

0 1 2 3 4 5 6 7 8

Meditation and deep breathing are often touted as self-care practices that reduce stress and help to focus the mind. Exercise is also a self-care habit that banishes anxiety and depression and can contribute to better physical health. Creating a supportive community through having "fun and laughter" with family and friends can be healing, especially when surrounded by like-minded people who embrace intersectionality. Reading, writing, and making art allows creativity to flow and time for reflection.

The importance of community, and support systems in the profession was also mentioned. A Latinx academic librarian said that "the strong network of women I have met have helped me," while a mixed-race Asian American librarian said that community was a necessity, because only by supporting each other [women of color] in positive ways "can we stay as sane as possible." An African American academic librarian mentioned that "talking to other sisters affirms that what you are experiencing [racism, sexism, homophobia, etc.] is real, and that you are not crazy, even if all your white colleagues say that you are overreacting." Having community helps women of color navigate whiteness in the profession and is crucial "in knowing we are not alone in feeling uncomfortable." Solidarity for shared experiences was summed up: "We're not here to compete with each other, we're here to build each other up." One participant noted:

> As a trans POC, I needed a support system for self-care, otherwise I couldn't function, especially with the big transition I am going through. I totally believe you need to practice it, as there is only so much we can do as individuals, and a support network you can rely on is key. My Spectrum cohort has been amazing—I met other Queer people in my year who have been amazing.

Another participant said that self-care was also about "believing in my future, and all that is to come. Surrounding myself with greatness, reading works by those who have come before me. Audre Lorde is a great representation of being a writer and librarian. Also, Nella Larsen is my inspiration."[63]

---

63. Nella Larsen was the first black woman to graduate from NYPL Library School.

Additional Findings

In addition to the data gathered in response to questions about identity, social justice and activism, and self-care, another additional finding revolved around the need for women of color librarians to achieve upward mobility. An issue that surfaced multiple times was the lack of professional development and retention strategies for women of color librarians. An African American academic librarian described what she meant by "professional development":

> By that I mean, not just, "Oh hey I am gonna send you to a conference." "Oh hey you can co-author with me." I am talking about supporting us to the point where we do get all the way to the top. Where we are change agents. To the point where we can actually create the change maker gene. And there is representation at all levels. We have not been given the opportunities. We get to a certain point, we are allowed to a certain point and then it's like yeah, it just stops.

With management positions remaining overwhelmingly white, a black librarian who is in management talked about how having a "seat at the table" can change the narrative:

> I can hire and fire, and I am sitting at the table with a different conscience and values in this white profession and I have an insider perspective as to how deep this shit is. When you sit on a search committee as the only person of color and folks are talking about accents and black hair. This is how white people do when they have all the power. I interrupt this and try to educate people on how you "can't say things like that." And we need to get paid for doing this [extra] educational work.

Another librarian talked about the expectation that women of color just assimilate and adapt to the existing culture, "Everyone is happy to hire you, they checked off a box. But no one thinks about retention. There is no effort to understand you, your culture, or how you may react to things differently than other people. You have to just fit in and just do it." In addition, the lack of women of color leaders was mentioned multiple times, as "most management and leads are white females" and how "it has been painfully obvious that the library leadership is not made up of people of color, and yet so many patrons of libraries are. There is such a disconnect." Another librarian said: "All you white folks, you need to hire us more, and pay attention to retention as much recruitment. Stop with diversity fellowships that are only a year or two then, 'Now what?' Don't use us for free labor!"

Conclusion

Women of color are woefully underrepresented in the librarian profession and face multiple forms of marginalization within it. Participants in this qualitative analysis described their intersecting identities and the various functions that activism and social justice serve in their professional and personal lives. For the majority of the participants, activism is a necessary force that sustains them in the library profession and is an important part of their core values, particularly in the current political climate. Activism is a positive coping strategy for the fear, worry, and anxiety that some women of color librarians experience in their work environments and in the larger society. Women of color librarians engage in activism and social justice, whether it is a formal or informal part of their professional responsibilities, and regardless of whether or not their activism is validated or invisible to their peers and supervisors. However, the cost of activism for women of color can be significant. Women of color sometimes receive pushback from peers or supervisors for engaging in activism. They bear the burden of doing activist work, sometimes in addition to (and outside of) their traditional work areas. Finally, women of color librarians adapt multiple coping strategies and self-care habits to help sustain their activism and to help reaffirm their intersecting identities and their whole selves.

Bibliography

Alabi, Jaena. "'This Actually Happened': An Analysis of Librarians' Responses to a Survey about Racial Microaggressions." *Journal of Library Administration* 55, no.3 (2015): 179-191. http://dx.doi.org/10.1080/01930826.2015.1034040.

Alimahomed, Sabrina. "Thinking Outside the Rainbow: Women of Color Redefining Queer Politics and Identity." *Social Identities* 16, no. 2 (2010):151–168. https://doi:10.1080/13504631003688849.

Alvarez, Alvin N., Christopher T. H. Liang, and Helen A. Neville. *The Cost of Racism for People of Color Contextualizing Experiences of Discrimination.* Washington, DC: American Psychological Association, 2016.

American Library Association. "Diversity Counts 2009-2010 Update." Accessed June 09, 2017. http://www.ala.org/aboutala/offices/diversity/diversitycounts/2009-2010update.

Amin, Nuzhat. "Voices of Minority Immigrant Women." In *Critical Issues in Anti-Racist Research Methodologies,* edited by George Jerry Sefa Dei and Gurpreet Singh Johal, 183-204. New York: Peter Lang, 2005.

Barker, Meg, Christina Richards, and Helen Bowes-Catton. "'All the World is Queer Save Thee and Me…': Defining Queer and Bi at a Critical Sexology Seminar." *Journal of Bisexuality* 9, no 3-4: 363-379. http://dx.doi.org/10.1080/15299710903316638.

Blas, Terry. "I'm Latino. I'm Hispanic. And They're Different, So I Drew a Comic to Explain." *Everyday Feminism.* Accessed January 3, 2018. https://everydayfeminism.com/2015/10/im-latino-hispanic-difference/.

Brown, Anna. "The Changing Categories the U.S. Has Used to Measure Race." *Pew Research Center.* Accessed January 3, 2018. http://www.pewresearch.org/fact-tank/2015/06/12/the-changing-categories-the-u-s-has-used-to-measure-race/.

Brown, Leslie Allison, and Susan Strega. *Research as Resistance: Revisiting Critical, Indigenous, and Anti-Oppressive Approaches.* Toronto: Canadian Scholars Press, 2015.

Campbell, Nathanael S., Sara Jansen Perry, Carl P. Maertz, David G. Allen, and Rodger W. Griffeth. "All You Need is … Resources: The Effects of Justice and Support on Burnout and Turnover." *Human Relations* 66, no. 6 (2013): 759-782. http://dx.doi.org/10.1177/0018726712462614.

Collins, Patricia Hill. *Black Feminist Thought: Knowledge, Consciousness, and the Politics of Empowerment.* New York: Routledge, 2015.

Crenshaw, Kimberlé. "Mapping the Margins: Intersectionality, Identity Politics, and Violence against Women of Color." *Stanford Law Review* 43, no. 6 (1991): 1241-1299. https://doi:10.2307/1229039.

Davis, Denise M., Tracie D. Hall. "Diversity Counts." American Library Association. Accessed June 2, 2017. http://www.ala.org/aboutala/sites/ala.org.aboutala/files/content/diversity/diversitycounts/diversitycounts_rev0.pdf.

Dei, George Jerry Sefa, and Gurpreet Singh Johal. *Critical Issues in Anti-Racist Research Methodologies.* New York: Peter Lang, 2005.

Dei, George Jerry Sefa. "Critical Issues in Anti-Racist Research Methodologies." In *Critical Issues in Anti-Racist Research Methodologies,* edited by George Jerry Sefa Dei and Gurpreet Singh Johal, 1-27. New York: Peter Lang, 2005.

DeLong, Kathleen. "Career Advancement and Writing about Women Librarians: A Literature Review." *Evidence Based Library & Information Practice* 8, no.1 (2013): 59-75. https://doi.org/10.18438/b8cs4m

Dreher, G. F., & Cox, and T. H. Cox, Jr. "Race, Gender, and Opportunity: A Study of Compensation Attainment and the Establishment of Mentoring Relationships." *Journal of Applied Psychology,* 81, no. 3 (1996): 297-308. http://dx.doi.org/10.1037/0021-9010.81.3.297.

Galbraith, Quinn, Leanna Fry, and Melissa Garrison. "The Impact of Faculty Status and Gender on Employee Well-being in Academic Libraries." *College & Research Libraries* 77, no.1 (2016): 71-86. https://doi.org/10.5860/crl.77.1.71.

Gómez, Martín J. "Who is Most Qualified to Serve Our Ethnic-minority Communities?" *American Libraries* 31, no. 7, (2000): 39-41.

Harris, Aisha. "Where I'm From." *Slate*. Accessed January 3, 2018. http://www.slate.com/articles/arts/culturebox/2014/07/black_american_versus_african_american_why_i_prefer_to_be_called_a_black.html.

Herising, Fairn. "Interrupting Positions: Critical Thresholds and Queer Pro/Positions." In *Revisiting Critical, Indigenous, and Anti-Oppressive Approaches*, edited by Leslie Allison Brown and Susan Strega, 127-151. Toronto: Canadian Scholars Press, 2015.

Hudson, David J. "On 'Diversity' as Anti-Racism in Library and Information Studies: A Critique." *Journal of Critical Library and Information Studies* 1, no. 1 (2017): 1-36. https://doi.org/10.24242/jclis.v1i1.6.

Johnson, Peggy. "Retaining and Advancing Librarians of Color." *College & Research Libraries* 68, no. 5 (2007): 405-417. https://doi.org/10.5860/crl.68.5.405.

Kim, Kyung-Sun, Ming-Hsin Chiu, Sei-Ching Joanna Sin, and Louise Robbins. "Recruiting a Diverse Workforce for Academic/Research Librarianship: Career Decisions of Subject Specialists and Librarians of Color." *College & Research Libraries* 68, no. 6 (2007): 533-552. https://doi.org/10.5860/crl.68.6.533.

Kumaran, Maha and Heather Cai. "Identifying the Visible Minority Librarians in Canada: A National Survey." *Evidence Based Library & Information Practice* 10, no. 2 (2015): 108-126. https://doi.org/10.18438/b8zc88.

Kyrillidou, Martha and Shaneka Morris. "ARL Annual Salary Survey 2013–2014." Accessed June 16, 2017. http://publications.arl.org/ARL-Annual-Salary-Survey-2013-2014/.

"'Latinx' and Gender Inclusivity." *Merriam Webster*. Accessed January 3, 2018. https://www.merriam-webster.com/words-at-play/word-history-latinx.

Liang, Christopher T. H., Alvin N. Alvarez, Linda P. Juang, and Mandy X. Liang. "The Role of Coping in the Relationship between Perceived Racism and Racism-Related Stress for Asian Americans: Gender Differences." *Asian American Journal of Psychology* S, no.1 (2009): 56-69. http://dx.doi.org/10.1037/1948-1985.S.1.56.

Luna, Zakiya. "'Truly a Women of Color Organization': Negotiating Sameness and Difference in Pursuit of Intersectionality." *Gender & Society* 30, no.5 (2016): 769-790. http://dx.doi.org/10.1177/0891243216649929.

Mellor, Steven, Janet Barnes-Farrell, and Jeffrey M. Stanton. "Unions as Justice-Promoting Organizations: The Interactive Effect of Ethnicity, Gender, and Perceived Union Effectiveness." *Sex Roles* 40, no. 5 (1999): 331. https://doi.org/10.1023/a:1018863308356.

Moraga, Cherrie. "La Güera." In *This Bridge Called My Back: Writings by Radical Women of Color*, ed. Cherrie Moraga and Gloria Anzaldúa, 22-29. Albany: State University of New York, 2015.

Muhammad, Shahida. "I'm Not African American…I'm Black." *Ebony*. Accessed January 3, 2018. http://www.ebony.com/news-views/im-not-african-american-im-black#axzz53A6d8AVr.

Nadal, Kevin L., Katie E. Griffin, Yinglee Wong, Kristin C. Davidoff, and Lindsey S. Davis. "The Injurious Relationship between Racial Microaggressions and Physical Health: Implications for Social Work." *Journal of Ethnic & Cultural Diversity in Social Work: Innovation in Theory, Research & Practice* 26, no. 1-2 (2017): 6-17. http://dx.doi.org/10.1080/15313204.2016.1263813.

Okolie, Andrew C. "Towards an Anti-Racist Research Framework: The Case for In-depth Interviewing." In *Critical Issues in Anti-Racist Research Methodologies,* edited by George Jerry Sefa Dei and Gurpreet Singh Johal, 241-268. New York: Peter Lang, 2005.

Pinsker, Joe. "The Financial Consequences of Saying 'Black' vs. 'African American.'" The Atlantic. Accessed January 3, 2018. https://www.theatlantic.com/business/archive/2014/12/the-financial-consequences-of-saying-black-vs-african-american/383999/.

Reichard, Raquel. "Why We Say Latinx: Trans and Gender Non-Conforming People Explain." *Latina*. Accessed January 3, 2018. http://www.latina.com/lifestyle/our-issues/why-we-say-latinx-trans-gender-non-conforming-people-explain.

Reyes, Raul A. "Are You Latinx? As Usage Grows, Word Draws Approval, Criticism." *NBC News.* Accessed January 3, 2018. https://www.nbcnews.com/news/latino/are-you-latinx-usage-grows-word-draws-approval-criticism-n651396.

Risman, Barbara J. "Gender as a Social Structure: Theory Wrestling with Activism." *Gender and Society* 18, no. 4 (2004): 429-50. https://doi.org/10.1177/0891243204265349.

Rosa, Kathy and Kelsey Henke. "2017 ALA Demographic Survey." *American Library Association.* Accessed June 16, 2017. http://www.ala.org/tools/sites/ala.org.tools/files/content/Draft%20of%20Member%20Demographics%20Survey%2001-11-2017.pdf.

Salmons, Janet. *Doing Qualitative Research Online.* Thousand Oaks: Sage, 2016.

Schussman, A., and S. A. Soule. "Process and Protest: Accounting for Individual Protest Participation." *Social Forces* 84, no. 2 (2005): 1083-108. http://doi:10.1353/sof.2006.0034.

Sharma, Renu. "Researching the Spiritual: Applying Soul to Research Practice." In *Critical Issues in Anti-Racist Research Methodologies,* edited by George Jerry Sefa Dei and Gurpreet Singh Johal, 146-182. New York: Peter Lang, 2005.

Simpson, Ruth. "Masculinity at Work." *Work, Employment and Society* 18, no. 2 (2004): 349-68. http://doi:10.1177/09500172004042773.

Smith, W. A., W. R. Allen, and L. L. Danley. "'Assume the Position . . . You Fit the Description': Psychosocial Experiences and Racial Battle Fatigue Among African American Male College Students." *American Behavioral Scientist* 51, no. 4, (2007): 551-78. http://doi:10.1177/0002764207307742.

Swank, Eric and Breanne Fahs. "An Intersectional Analysis of Gender and Race for Sexual Minorities Who Engage in Gay and Lesbian Rights Activism." *Sex Roles* 68, no. 11-12 (2013): 660-674. http://doi:http://dx.doi.org/10.1007/s11199-012-0168-9.

Taylor, Paul, Mark Hugo Lopez, Jessica Martinez, and Gabriel Velasco. "When Labels Don't Fit: Hispanics and Their Views of Identity." *Pew Research Center*. Accessed January 3, 2018. http://www.pewhispanic.org/2012/04/04/when-labels-dont-fit-hispanics-and-their-views-of-identity/.

United States Census Bureau. "Geography." Accessed July 1, 2017. https://www.census.gov/geo/reference/webatlas/regions.html.

Zhang, Yan and Barbara M. Wildemuth. "Qualitative Analysis of Content." In *Applications of Social Science Research Methods to Questions in Information and Library Science,* edited by Barbara M. Wildemuth, 308-319. Westport, CT: Libraries Unlimited, 2009.

Chapter 14

When Will My Reflection Show? Women of Color in the Kennesaw State University Archives

JoyEllen Freeman

Introduction

I have always seen myself in fiction. Before I could read on my own, I remember seeing representations of myself in *Amazing Grace* by Mary Hoffman and Caroline Binch, in *Jamaica's Find* by Juanita Havill, in *The Invisible Princess* by Faith Ringgold, and in the original Addy book series by Connie Hill Porter. I owe these early literary experiences to my mother. She intentionally filled my personal library with stories about young African American girls who were smart, tenacious, beautiful, and proud of their heritage. Through books of fiction, my mother created a worldview that always celebrated and empowered girls like me.

Life eventually forced me to step out of the safe haven that my mother created through my library. I quickly learned that my books did not represent the world I was living in, and that society does not always celebrate my presence as a black woman. At times, society may even refuse to acknowledge my existence altogether. Although I learned early on to seek representations of myself in works of fiction, exercising this same behavior in archival spaces has rendered a more complicated experience. For example, around the same time I learned to search for representations of black women in fictional worlds, I learned that searching for my family's genealogical records in the real world often led to disappointment. My father—who had taken on the role of the family genealogist—explained to me that his research could not go beyond the mid-nineteenth century because many of our ancestors were slaves, and records of their existence were either unavailable or simply did not exist. Such circumstances are common for people of color because for many years, mainstream[1] archival records under-documented or inaccurately documented minority ethnic groups in the United States. Since the mid-twentieth century, however, scholars have taken an interest in the histories of underrepresented groups, such as "women, people of color, the working class, and other groups whose experiences had previously been underdocumented."[2] During this same time period, archival literature followed suit and "explored many approaches archivists could employ to document society and institutions more holistically."[3] Fewer writings, however, specifically address silences and underrepresentation as they pertain to women of color in archival collections.

Using a combination of oral history interviews, a review of scholarly research, a user study, and personal narratives, this chapter uses the Kennesaw State University (KSU) Archives as a case study to explore the interactions between women of color and a state-funded, public university archives and special collections repository. The KSU Archives is a relatively young archival institution embedded within a university that has doubled in size since 2005 and a region that has experienced highly increasing levels of diversity since the 1980s. Hence, the KSU Archives provides an interesting case where keeping up with university

1. In this chapter, the phrase "mainstream archives" refers to archival repositories that do not specifically collect the records of a traditionally oppressed or under-documented group. Some archivists refer to mainstream archives as the "official record." Examples can include government archival institutions, many university archival collections, corporate archival collections, and the like. While these repositories often contain documentation about underrepresented groups, the documentation may not adequately document underrepresented groups through their own words.

2. Jessica Wagner Webster, "'Filling the Gaps': Oral Histories and Underdocumented Populations in The American Archivist, 1938–2011," *The American Archivist* 79, no. 2 (2016), 255.

3. Wagner Webster, "Filling the Gaps," 255.

and regional growth poses a challenge for archivists trying to match these changes with the appropriate collection development policies. The main goal of this study was to determine factors that affect research experiences of women of color searching for representations of themselves in the KSU Archives. Research findings indicate that women of color have difficulty finding representations of themselves in the KSU archives due to a lack of relevant collections in the repository and the high level of archival illiteracy among patrons. Both factors lead to feelings of disappointment and frustration that produce negative feelings about archival research. Despite these challenges and frustrations, findings also suggest that many women of color desire to further engage with the KSU Archives to help document a more inclusive history.

Literature Review

For many years, historical records silenced the voices and stories of historically marginalized communities. Howard Zinn was one of the most well-known historians to emphasize this point. In his 1970 address to an audience of archivists, which was eventually published as an article entitled "Secrecy, Archives, and the Public Interest," Zinn asserts that history, as a collective, is "biased toward the important and powerful people of society."[4] Zinn accuses history of focusing on "the rich, not the poor, the successful not the failures, the old not the young, men not women, white, not black. . . ."[5] Zinn's statement embodies the general zeitgeist of the 1960s and 1970s—a period of social change in the United States that also created a revolutionary period of awareness among archivists, historians, and cultural heritage professionals. Richard Cox and James O'Toole call this professional awakening, "a new social history," because this era not only challenged archivists to diversify the types of records they were collecting but also to rethink

4. Howard Zinn, "Secrecy, Archives, and the Public Interest," The Midwestern Archivist 2, no. 2 (1977): 21.

5. Ibid.

"how [repositories] decided what records they would keep."[6] Over the next few decades and into the twenty-first century, archivists and historians used scholarship to bring attention to the issue of diversity and inclusion within archival spaces. For example, Deborah Gray White's article "Mining the Forgotten: Manuscript Sources for Black Women's History" was one of the early scholarly writings to reveal the systemic issues that often led to the omission of black women in history. According to White, "interest in doing black women's history [was] minimal" prior to the 1970s.[7] When this interest did increase, historians often ran into challenges because "many indexes were compiled before either blacks or black and white women became important subjects of study," making it difficult to "identify the papers of black women or records that contain significant material about black women."[8] These issues have continued into the twenty-first century, as evinced by Jean Pfaelzar's research on Chinese female immigration into the United States during the late nineteenth and early twentieth centuries. While Pfaelzar had no issues locating archives that document "the ship's logs, newspaper accounts, habeas corpus actions, and immigration files, Chinese female immigrants' own telling seemed to be mostly silenced."[9]

The experiences of these historians prompt questions about the myriad ways in which underrepresented groups suffer omission from archival collections and the historical record. In 2000, Elisabeth Kaplan analyzed this issue by exposing the role that archives play in the construction of identity and perception. Kaplan concludes that archivists must acknowledge the crucial and non-neutral role that they play in shaping the history and perceptions of communities.[10] Rodney Carter's 2006 article

---

6. Richard Cox and James O'Toole, *Understanding Archives & Manuscripts* (Chicago: Society of American Archivists, 2006), 71.

7. Deborah Gray White, "Mining the Forgotten: Manuscript Sources for Black Women's History," *Journal of American History* 74, no.1 (1987): 238.

8. Ibid.

9. Jane Pfaelzar, "Hanging Out: A Research Methodology," *Legacy* 27, no. 1 (2010): 140.

10. Elisabeth Kaplan, "We Are What We Collect, We Collect What We Are: Archives and the Construction of Identity," *The American Archivist* 63, no. 1 (2000): 126-151.

"Of Things Said and Unsaid: Archival Silences, and Power in Silence," also speaks about the myth of neutrality in archives, especially as it relates to power. Archival silences, Carter argues, can "have a potentially disastrous impact on marginalized groups," because a lack of archives compromises both social identity and collective memory.[11] Michelle Caswell speaks of these same implications by repurposing the phrase "symbolic annihilation."[12] A term first used among feminists, Caswell et al. use symbolic annihilation in archives to describe how "marginalized communities feel regarding the absence of or misrepresentation of their communities in archival collection[s]" and spaces.[13] Caswell warns, "If professional archivists remain complicit in the ongoing silencing of minority groups, mainstream archival institutions will cease to be relevant to a majority-minority society."[14]

Increasing diversity awareness in archival spaces in order to provide an authentic view of the past has prompted a new set of goals and challenges for modern-day archivists. Archivists have attempted to identify, preserve, and represent archives of underrepresented groups in various ways. In the late twentieth century, archivists and librarians from Historically Black Colleges and Universities (HBCU) developed a collaborative program to locate and identify primary source material that documents African American educational history. This collaboration, formally known as the Cooperative HBCU Archival Survey Project (CHASP) focused on making descriptions of African American education archives more available to researchers. Another notable and important attempt to embed culturally sensitive practices into archival spaces was the development of the *Protocols for Native American Archival Materials*, a document that served to establish guidelines for preserving

11. Rodney G.S. Carter, "Of Things Said and Unsaid: Power, Archival Silences, and Power in Silence," *Archivaria* 61 (2006): 220.

12. Michelle Caswell, "Seeing Yourself in History: Community Archives and the Fight against Symbolic Annihilation," *The Public Historian* 36, no. 4 (2014).

13. Michelle Caswell, Marika Cifor, and Mario H. Ramirez, "To Suddenly Discover Yourself Existing: Uncovering the Impact of Community Archives," *The American Archivist* 79, no. 1 (2016): 59.

14. Caswell, "Seeing Yourself in History," 36.

and curating Native American historical materials based on the notion of ethnic sovereignty and ownership.[15] The message embedded within the *Protocols* is similar to Joel Wurl's message in his article, "Ethnicity as Provenance: In Search of Values and Principles for Documenting the Immigrant Experience." Wurl encourages archivists to have a greater respect for ethnic communities as owners of material and to view archival repositories as stewards of this material committed to documenting history in a culturally sensitive way.[16] He contends that, while ethnicity is not "foreordained on the basis of bloodlines . . .", it is a "product of complex social interaction" and therefore, should not be discounted as "a form of provenance."[17] More recently, Mary Caldera and Kathryn M. Neal published *Through the Archival Looking Glass: A Reader on Diversity and Inclusion.* Through ten separate essays, this volume presents a widespread understanding of diversity in archival spaces, including collection management, recruitment practices, outreach, and community collaboration.

The meanings of diversity and inclusion are still coming to fruition for archivists because, while both terms are widely used, they are not necessarily interchangeable. At the 2016 Annual Meeting of the Society of American Archivists (SAA), former SAA president Dennis Meissner insisted that archivists must focus on the "behavior of inclusion rather than the fact of diversity" in order to truly "achieve a profession, association, and historical record that more truly embraces the diversity of our society."[18] Hence, many archivists, like myself, are devoting less time discussing the issue of diversity and more time implementing practices that engage underrepresented populations with archival spaces.

---

15. First Archivists Circle, "Protocols for Native American Archival Materials," last modified April 9, 2007, accessed September 11, 2017, http://www2.nau.edu/libnap-p/protocols.html.

16. Joel Wurl, "Ethnicity as Provenance: In Search of Values and Principles for Documenting the Immigrant Experience," *Archival Issues* 29, no. 1 (2005).

17. Ibid., 68.

18. Dennis Meissner, "Society of American Archivists 2016 Presidential Address," YouTube video, 2016, https://www.youtube.com/watch?v=IrDi4T653Ng.

Background

Taking steps toward diversity and inclusion in archives requires an acknowledgement of multiple stories and voices. This section of the chapter will use the KSU Archives as a case study to demonstrate how a university archives is attempting to eradicate the "one-story" mentality that dominated its archival holdings for many years.

Kennesaw State University is a comprehensive[19] public university located in Cobb County, Georgia. With an enrollment of over 35,000 students, KSU is now the third largest university in the state of Georgia. Despite its current size, the university had humble beginnings. KSU opened as Kennesaw Junior College in 1966 with just over 1,000 students and thirty-seven faculty members.[20] The school was not only small in terms of size, but also in terms of ethnic diversity. According to Dr. Thomas Scott, KSU Professor Emeritus of History and Campus Historian, there was little ethnic diversity when he arrived on campus in 1968. "There was one Chinese ethnic faculty member, and that was it."[21] By 1970, the percentage of African American students on campus was only 0.6 percent.[22] "There were always some faculty members that were embarrassed by the lack of diversity," but the minimal diversity at Kennesaw Junior College was not out of the ordinary considering the demographics of Cobb County.[23] According to Dr. Thomas Scott—author of *Cobb County, Georgia and the Origins of the Suburban South*—"in 1960 African Americans constituted only seven percent of

19. Kennesaw State University is a public university that is part of the University System of Georgia (USG). The USG categorizes public universities and colleges into four categories. Kennesaw State University falls within the "comprehensive university" category. See http://www.usg.edu/news/usgfacts for more information.

20. "First Week Brings 1000 Students," *The Sentinel*, October 3, 1966.

21. Thomas A. Scott (KSU Professor Emeritus of History, Campus Historian, and author) in discussion with the author, February 2, 2017.

22. Thomas Allan Scott, *Kennesaw State University: The First Fifty Years, 1963 – 2013* (Kennesaw: Kennesaw State University Press, 2013), 68.

23. Scott, discussion.

Cobb's population" and by the late 1960s, the county was ninety-six percent white.[24] In some areas of the county, "people . . . could go for weeks without seeing anybody who was other than Caucasian."[25] Over the next fifty years, these statistics changed drastically in Cobb County and at KSU as more minorities began settling in various areas of the county, particularly in the city of Marietta.[26] As of 2015, over 40% of Cobb County residents were non-white.[27] During the 2016–2017 academic year at KSU, nearly 45% of the student body was composed of minorities.[28] By establishing the Office of Diversity and Inclusion in 2008 and other diversity-focused initiatives, KSU has directed its diversity efforts into a systematic approach that includes university-wide climate assessments, diversity and inclusion action planning, curricular programming, and presidential commissions for underrepresented groups.[29]

Documenting the rapidly changing culture of diversity at KSU and the northwest Georgia region has become a large undertaking for the university archives and special collections. The KSU Archives is a division of the Department of Museums, Archives and Rare Books (MARB). The Archives was founded in 2004 with Dr. Tamara Livingston serving as its first director. The mission of the KSU Archives is to "identify, collect, and make accessible records of enduring value to preserve institutional and community memory into the future."[30] Specifically,

24. Thomas Allan Scott, *Cobb County, Georgia and the Origins of the Suburban South: A Twentieth-Century History* (Marietta: Cobb Landmarks and Historical Society, Inc., 2003): 348.

25. Scott, discussion.

26. Scott, *Cobb County, Georgia and the Origins of the Suburban South*, 665.

27. United States Census Bureau, "QuickFacts: Cobb County, Georgia," accessed September 11, 2017, https://www.census.gov/quickfacts/fact/table/cobbcountygeorgia/PST045216.

28. Office of Institutional Research, Kennesaw State University, *Kennesaw State University 2016 – 2017 Factbook*, accessed August 15, 2017, http://ir.kennesaw.edu/docs/2016-17_factbook.pdf.

29. Kennesaw State University, "History and Mission," *Office of Diversity and Inclusion*, accessed December 5, 2017, http://diversity.kennesaw.edu/about/mission-statement.php.

30. Kennesaw State University Archives, "Core Values," accessed May 31, 2017, http://archives.kennesaw.edu/about/values.php.

the Archives seeks to develop "an inclusive record of the activities of [Kennesaw State University] and to document the work of individuals and organizations in northwest Georgia."[31] The Archives accomplishes this goal by acquiring university records as well as special collections from members and organizations within northwest Georgia cities and counties. Through these efforts, the KSU Archives has grown from "a small seminal collection [into] a full-fledged archives" containing more than 640 collections.[32] Serving as the backbone of the holdings are a wide variety of university records documenting the growth and development of KSU students, departments, personnel, and administrators. The core of the special collections originally came from Dr. Thomas Scott, who "donated many of his . . . manuscript collections having to do with various aspects of history of northwest Georgia, especially Marietta. . . ."[33] While these collections are crucial to understanding the history of KSU and the northwest Georgia community, many of them only capture stories of prominent white families or well-known African American activists in Cobb County.

I became the Outreach/Special Collections Archivist at the KSU Archives in May 2016. My first task was to gain an understanding of the context and content of the archival collections in the repository. I was impressed by the historical richness of the holdings, which include a variety of materials including local family letters, oral histories, and organizational records from some of the region's most iconic local businesses. After conducting a variety of searches using our collection database, I began to notice that I could not pull up any relevant search results for people of color other than African Americans. Even the information that did come up about African Americans was sparse—especially regarding African American women. Because I am a woman of color, this experience was disheartening for me. It produced familiar feelings of mistrust that I had learned as a child when I was unable to

31. Ibid.

32. Tamara Livingston, interview by Lawrence Walker, 2009, transcript, Kennesaw State University Oral History Project, Kennesaw, GA, 6.

33. Ibid.

find accurate representations of my heritage in mainstream textbooks. I decided to examine the experiences of other women of color as they interacted with the KSU Archives to see if their research experiences produced similar sentiments, and if so, for what reasons. My ultimate goal from these research experiences and follow-up interviews was to gain feedback from these women to determine ways that the KSU Archives could improve its documentation of women of color.

Methodology

The research study involved two components. The first component was a small series of interviews that I conducted with faculty and staff from KSU. I chose to interview faculty and staff members holding leadership positions relating to history, archives, and diversity at KSU. Faculty and staff members from the Department of History and Philosophy, Interdisciplinary Studies Department, and Office of Diversity and Inclusion answered questions about the history of KSU, specifically focusing on diversity initiatives over the years. These interviews provided context for understanding the climate of diversity at KSU since its establishment.

The second component of the research was a user study that analyzed the research experiences of women of color in the KSU Archives. The first call for participants went out among students, faculty, and staff using the KSU campus-wide notification system in January 2017. A second call for participants was dispersed in February 2017. Participants were required to be at least eighteen years of age and identify as a woman of color. Due to the nature of the study, participants were also required to have access to a laptop. About fourteen women responded to the solicitation and eleven agreed to participate in the study. Five participants identified as African American; two participants identified as Asian American; three participants identified as Hispanic/Latina; and one participant identified as multiracial. Participants were allowed to ethnically self-identify to prevent my own ignorance from limiting the scope of the research study. The age range spanned from eighteen to sixty-two (see **Table 1**).

Racial Category	Name	Age
African American	Participant 3 Participant 4 Participant 6 Participant 9 Participant 10	19 19 25 34 37
Asian American	Participant 1 Participant 8	18 20
Hispanic/Latina American	Participant 2 Participant 5 Participant 7	19 24 36
Multiracial	Participant 11	62

Table 1: Participant Profiles

To complete the user study, all participants were required to make one appointment at the KSU Archives. Upon arrival, participants received a brief overview of the KSU Archives and its holdings. Participants also received an overview of the two search tools they would be using—Archon and SOAR. Archon is a content management system that the KSU Archives previously used to create archival finding aids and make them accessible to the public. SOAR is a customized instance of DSpace that makes born-digital and digitized archival material accessible to the public. Once all briefings were complete, participants began the search assignment. Each participant was asked to search for archival collections and/or individual materials that represent women belonging to all ethnic or racial group(s) they identify with. Essentially, participants were searching for representations of themselves within the holdings of the KSU Archives.

As participants conducted searches, they filled out guided notes[34] to document information related to their search experience, including the number of search terms used, the number of relevant materials identified, and the amount of time required to conduct searches.[35] After participants completed the search portion of the study, they filled out a follow-up questionnaire[36] about their perceptions of the research experience.

Findings and Results

Overall research findings confirm that women of color struggle to find representations of themselves within the KSU Archives and are not impressed with the university's current holdings documenting women of color. Although these experiences generally produce feelings of frustration, the research findings also confirm that female patrons of color have a variety of ideas about how to improve the KSU Archives' collection and are willing to collaborate with archivists to improve collection development and outreach methods targeting women of color.

For the majority of women participating in the study, this was their first time visiting an archival repository and conducting archival research. Only three women had previous experience using archives, and of these three, only one had experience using the KSU Archives. Although some may argue that the lack of archival experience among participants could skew research results, this statistic reflects the experience level of most patrons at the KSU Archives. In addition, the novelty of archives introduced a factor into the research findings that I did not anticipate. For example, participants were asked to describe their impressions of the Archon interface. Over seventy percent of participants felt that Archon was user-friendly, describing it as "relatively simple and easy to use."[37]

---

34. See Appendix 1.

35. Participants were not required to conduct searches for a preset amount of time. Search time was left to the discretion of the participant in order to simulate a more genuine and organic research experience.

36. See Appendix 1.

37. Participant two in discussion with the author, January 23, 2017.

Two participants admitted minor difficulties understanding how to conduct research with Archon. Participant four felt that Archon was "kind of confusing, but very interesting,"[38] while participant eleven said, "It was difficult at first."[39]

Despite any initial hurdles of acclimating to archival research, all participants were able to conduct searches in both Archon and SOAR. The success of these searches varied greatly. The average search time was thirty-eight minutes, and participants used an average of seven search terms. After comparing all recorded search terms, I found that participants used a total of sixty different search terms to complete their research.[40] Example search terms included African American woman/women; colored women; women of color; Hispanic woman/women; India; feminist; El Salvador; and Native American.

The type of search terms participants used provides insight into how they identify themselves and how they expect these identifications to appear in archival collections. Some participants, such as participant ten, chose to use plural and singular iterations of racial search terms, assuming this strategy would yield the highest level of results. Participant ten used the following search terms:

> *black female; black women; black woman; African American woman; African American women; Negro women; Negro woman; colored woman; colored women.*

Other participants, such as participant five, chose search terms that closely aligned with her representation of self, both ethnically and academically. Participant five used the following search terms:

> *El Salvador, Spanish women, latin women; Latin America; Hispanic women; Spanish engineers; Latin engineers; Hispanic engineers; Spanish engineer*

38. Participant four in discussion with the author, February 24, 2017.

39. Participant eleven in discussion with the author, January 19, 2017.

40. Search terms such as "African American woman" and "African American women" were counted as two separate search terms. Search terms such as "Latina" and "latina" were not counted as separate search terms.

After speaking with participant five, I learned that her Salvadoran nationality is extremely important to her. She prefers to identify as indigenous or Salvadoran as opposed to merely Latina or Hispanic. This factor posed an additional challenge during her search process. After completing the search, participant five did not find any archival materials representing women of her ethnic group. This outcome contrasts with that of participant ten. Participant ten found five results in Archon documenting the history of African American women. When asked if she was pleased with the amount of results that her Archon search produced, participant ten said, "No, surely there are more than five results that illustrate black women's contributions to the KSU community."[41] Participant ten did, however, find many more results using SOAR—a total of twenty. This was the highest search result of any participant. Aside from participant ten, no other participant found more than seven search results documenting women of her racial or ethnic group (see **Table 2**).[42]

Racial Category	Name	# of WOC Results Identified
African American	Participant 3	3
	Participant 4	4
	Participant 6	7
	Participant 9	2
	Participant 10	25
Asian American	Participant 1	1
	Participant 8	2
Hispanic/Latina American	Participant 2	0
	Participant 5	0
	Participant 7	0
Multiracial	Participant 11	6

Table 2: Search Results

41. Participant ten, discussion.

42. Figure two shows the total number of search results that each participant identified in both Archon and SOAR.

A quantitative analysis of the results shows that African American women are more likely to find representations of themselves in the KSU Archives, while Hispanic/Latina American women, Asian American women, and multiracial women are less likely to find accurate representations of themselves. The qualitative data also confirms this finding, and suggests that personal factors contribute to the discrepancy as well. Quantitatively, there is no doubt that the KSU Archives contains a minimal amount of material documenting women of color, particularly Hispanic/Latina female history and Asian female history. While many collections at the time of the study contained individual series or items representing African American history, the KSU Archives held roughly seven archival collections out of 640 that focused exclusively on documenting the African American experience in the northwest Georgia region. The KSU Archives did not hold any collections exclusively documenting Native Americans, Asian Americans, or Hispanic/Latin Americans. These numbers manifested themselves throughout the research study. Out of the five Hispanic/Latina and Asian American participants, no one found results using the Archon database. Two participants found less than three results using SOAR. Even among African American women, who had the highest success in search results, none of the participants found more than five results using Archon. The multiracial participant, who identified as African American and Native American, expressed that she was unable to find many search results that related to Native American female history—most of her searches only yielded results for black female history.

The underrepresentation of women of color in the KSU Archives affected each participant differently. For example, participant one, who identifies as Indian American, noted that most of her searches did not yield results of any relevance. "Most [results] were regarding Native Americans who were wrongly called Indian/Indian American. . .. I was not surprised. Indian women hardly make an appearance in American culture even though there are plenty of Indian women living in the USA."[43] For participant one, the KSU Archives is playing a role in con-

43. Participant one in discussion with the author, January 23, 2017.

firming her already disillusioned view of mainstream historical records and how they document Indian American women. Likewise, participant seven candidly noted that her inability to identify materials documenting Hispanic/Latina women made her feel "erased and forgotten."[44] Participant nine found an oral history interview conducted by an African American woman, yet all perspectives about race and equality were from the white, British judge that the woman was interviewing. Participant nine admitted, "It was interesting, but I would have preferred to hear from the black woman instead of the white judge."[45] In this instance, the material participant nine identified was relevant, yet it still did not represent women of her ethnic group in a way that she had hoped.

Other participants had more positive experiences. Participant three, who identifies as African American, found three results from her searches including an oral history interview with an African American woman who worked at the Bell Aircraft Corporation in Cobb County during World War II. After analyzing the interview, participant two said that the record made her feel proud to be an African American woman.[46] Participant ten, who also identifies as African American, enjoyed reading an oral history interview conducted with the first African American woman hired by the Cobb County Sheriff's office. After reading the interview, participant ten noted, "It's great to find [this record] but there should be more!"[47]

Challenges

The research findings produced in this study provide a first step towards understanding the issues that women of color face while interacting with the KSU Archives. However, a further study is required to combat two main challenges that appeared during the course of the study.

44. Participant seven in discussion with the author, February 17, 2017.

45. Participant nine in discussion with the author, February 3, 2017.

46. Participant two, discussion.

47. Participant ten, discussion.

The first challenge was user interaction with Archon and SOAR. Both databases allow users to conduct searches using a variety of methods (e.g. searching by record group, subjects, creators/authors), but as to be expected, most participants used keyword searching. The keyword search function is powerful for both databases, but the results produced are very different. Participants could receive hundreds or even thousands of results by doing a keyword search in SOAR, not realizing that the majority of these results have little to do with their research topic. This circumstance occurs because SOAR contains the digital archives of all KSU student newspapers, Southern Polytechnic State University newspapers, and a variety of other university and northwest Georgia-related publications that have been digitized as searchable PDF/A documents. Many of the keyword search results that SOAR produces are from newspaper articles that may or may not have much to do with the topic at hand. Archon, however, is a database that only contains finding aids. Hence, keyword searches in Archon are essentially limited to metadata that archivists have created. Unlike SOAR, Archon is not capturing words from the content itself. Archon produces a very different user experience than SOAR, because it yields fewer results and often requires an archivist's help to access the identified records. Participants noted that they were more likely to find relevant results in Archon. Participant four made note of this difference on her post-search questionnaire: "[Archon results were] few but they were more accurate. SOAR had a lot but less accurate."[48]

When I initially developed this study, I did not anticipate patrons misunderstanding the functions of SOAR and Archon, even after they received a short tutorial prior to engaging in the research study. Most of the participants had never conducted archival research before, so they had trouble grasping the idea of an online finding aid and how this resource differs from a single archival item in a digital repository. Hence, the research study shows that participants' archival experiences were not only affected by a lack of relevant material, but also by inexperience

---

48. Participant four, discussion.

in conducting archival research. The latter problem requires its own research study, as this issue may not be unique to women of color. A follow-up research study should examine the ways patrons navigate finding aids at the KSU Archives and how these experiences affect their confidence in locating and using archival material. This type of study can help inform KSU archivists of additional resources that all patrons may need, such as better finding aid metadata, more user-friendly databases, and increased research assistance.

The second challenge of this study was the size and demographic makeup of the participants. While I was glad to work with eleven dedicated participants, a more accurate research study requires a larger number of participants. In addition, over half of the participants in the study identified as African American. This statistic makes sense considering that African Americans make up more than half of Cobb County's ethnic minority population.[49] However, the intent of this research study was to investigate the experiences of all women of color equally, regardless of an ethnic group's demographic percentage on campus or in the northwest Georgia community. Further research should include a higher number of Asian American, Native American, and Hispanic/Latina American women of color as participants.

Next Steps: Outreach

The archival interactions that participants experienced were by no means homogeneous, yet participant one asked a question that seemed to capture the overall sentiment of the research findings. She asked, "We all attend KSU, why are some of us ignored?"[50] Attempting to answer, let alone resolve, such a heavy question is overwhelming for any archivist. As an outreach archivist, I am choosing to use this question to influence the work of the KSU Archives in a new way. Over the next few years, the path toward archival outreach for women of color will take a new

49. United States Census Bureau, "QuickFacts: Cobb County, Georgia."

50. Participant one, discussion.

direction at KSU. The new direction will focus on relationship building. By investing in new relationships with underrepresented groups, my goal is to improve the KSU Archives in the areas of collections management and user friendliness. This includes increasing our collection of materials that specifically document women of color in our region and also working with patrons to assess needs for topical research guides and other helpful materials that can empower underrepresented communities to increase their use of our collections.

One of the unexpected lessons I learned from conducting this research study was the importance of onversation. Because all participants had to come to the KSU Archives to participate in the study, I had the chance to meet and connect with eleven women of color who might not otherwise have come to the KSU Archives. Many times, I stayed and talked with these women after their appointments were over and learned about their life stories. I learned how and why they identify with a certain ethnic group, how they ended up at KSU, and what kind of career goals they have. The research appointments often morphed into storytelling experiences, during which the women would educate me about their lives and the issues they face in their community being seen, acknowledged, and heard as women of color. For example, participant eleven attended KSU during its early years, before it received university status. She told me about her English classes and how the professors did not see any point in reading books written by African American writers because those books did not belong in an American literature class; they belonged in an African American literature class.[51] Participant five had a fascinating story about her family's experience as Salvadoran refugees and how she wants to pursue a career in politics by way of engineering.[52] These stories, among countless others, make up the fabric of both university and regional history. Figuring out how to capture these stories is a work in progress.

---

51. Participant eleven, discussion.

52. Participant five, discussion.

Although I am still in the early stages of developing relationship-based outreach methods for women of color, I know that I have allies. Many participants suggested specific student groups and other diversity-based organizations that may be candidates for archival outreach and relationship building. Some participants in the study expressed personal interest in collaborating with the KSU Archives to document the history of women of color on campus and in the northwest Georgia region. Participant six suggested the creation of archive projects targeted at women of color. She desires a partnership where women of color like herself learn to "seek the information ourselves and contribute to the archives . . . while also becoming familiar with archiving."[53] Relationships between archival repositories and women of color not only benefit archival programs by diversifying donors, holdings, and users, but more importantly, these relationships lead to bonds of trust and respect. These relationships also come with a responsibility to document properly and to portray women of color as critical agents in history—not as adjuncts or afterthoughts. For the KSU Archives, this research study served as the first step toward progress. Participant seven acknowledges this progress and is grateful for its future implications:

> This study is a step in the right direction; we need to have an archive that reflects the diverse population of KSU. I hope to one day come back and find records about women like me. Latinas, Afro Latinas, and indigenous women from Latin America. We exist, we are here, we matter, and we are part of this school! And we always have been.[54]

Conclusion

A combination of quantitative and qualitative data show that women of color struggle to find accurate representations of themselves within the holdings of the KSU Archives, which leads to feelings of disappointment and frustration. The lack of archival materials relating to women

53. Participant six, discussion.

54. Participant seven, discussion.

of color is a large factor in these struggles, but it is not the only one. Many women of color struggle to navigate the KSU Archives' finding aids and finding aid databases. Improving these issues will require time, intentionality, and fresh outreach methods for underrepresented groups. Of utmost importance are the relationships that the KSU Archives must build in order to foster trustworthy and collaborative partnerships among the many women of color who are ready and eager to tell their stories.

Bibliography

Caswell, Michelle. "Seeing Yourself in History: Community Archives and the Fight against Symbolic Annihilation." *The Public Historian* 36, no. 4 (2014): 26–37.

Caswell, Michelle, Marika Cifor, and Mario H. Ramirez. "To Suddenly Discover Yourself Existing: Uncovering the Impact of Community Archives." *The American Archivist* 79, no. 1 (2016): 56–81.

Carter, Rodney. "Of Things Said and Unsaid: Power, Archival Silences, and Power in Silence." *Archivaria* 61 (2006): 215–233.

Cox, Richard, and James O'Toole. *Understanding Archives & Manuscripts*. Chicago: Society of American Archivists, 2006.

First Archivists Circle. Protocols for Native American Archival Materials. Last modified April 9, 2007. http://www2.nau.edu/libnap-p/protocols.html.

"First Week Brings 1,000 Students." *The Sentinel*, October 3, 1966.

Kaplan, Elisabeth. "We Are What We Collect, We Collect What We Are: Archives and the Construction of Identity." *The American Archivist* 63, no. 1 (2000): 126–151.

Kennesaw State University Office of Institutional Research. *Kennesaw State University 2016–2017 Factbook*. Kennesaw: Kennesaw State University, 2017. Accessed August 15, 2017. http://ir.kennesaw.edu/docs/2016-17_factbook.pdf.

Kennesaw State University Archives. "Core Values." Accessed May 31, 2017. http://archives.kennesaw.edu/about/values.php.

Livingston, Tamara. Interview with Lawrence Walker. By Lawrence Walker. Kennesaw: Kennesaw State University Oral History Project, 2009.

Meissner, Dennis. "Society of American Archivists 2016 Presidential Address." YouTube video. August 5, 2016. https://www.youtube.com/watch?v=IrDi4T653Ng.

Pfaelzar, Jane. "Hanging Out: A Research Methodology." *Legacy* 27, no. 1 (2010): 140–159.

Scott, Thomas Allan. *Cobb County, Georgia and the Origins of the Suburban South: A Twentieth-Century History*. Marietta: Cobb Landmarks and Historical Society, Inc., 2003.

Scott, Thomas Allan. *Kennesaw State University: The First Fifty Years, 1963–2013*. Kennesaw: Kennesaw State University Press, 2013.

United States Census Bureau, "QuickFacts: Cobb County, Georgia." Last modified July 1, 2016. Accessed September 11, 2017. https://www.census.gov/quickfacts/fact/table/cobbcountygeorgia/PST045216.

Webster, Jessica Wagner. "'Filling the Gaps': Oral Histories and Underdocumented Populations in *The American Archivist*, 1938–2011." *The American Archivist* 79, no. 2 (2016): 254–282.

White, Deborah Gray. "Mining the Forgotten: Manuscript Sources for Black Women's History." *The Journal of American History* 74, no. 1 (1987): 237–242.

Wurl, Joel. "Ethnicity as Provenance: In Search of Values and Principles for Documenting the Immigrant Experience. *Archival Issues* 29, no. 1 (2005): 65–76.

Zinn, Howard. "Secrecy, Archives, and the Public Interest." *The Midwestern Archivist* 2, no.2 (1977): 14-26.

Appendix

Profile Questions

Name:
Age:
Racial/Ethnic Identification:
Institutional Affiliation:
Patron type:

- Undergraduate student
- Graduate Student
- Faculty member
- General public/community member

Search Data

Listing of all words/phases used to conduct searches:

Length of time required to conduct searches:

Number of potential collections/materials identified:

Post-Search Questions

1. Have you ever been to an archive before? If yes, have you ever been to the KSU Archives before?
2. Do you have any prior experience using online archival search tools?
3. Do you have any prior experience using online archival search tools provided by the KSU Archives?
4. What were your initial impressions of the Archon interface?

5. Describe your experiences conducting searches in Archon. Did you come across challenges? Explain.
6. Were you pleased with the amount of results that your Archon search produced?
7. Which folder/item from your Archon search did you select for analysis? Why did you select this folder/item?
8. Briefly summarize the information you found in the box/folder/item you selected. Include as much of the following information as possible:
   - Is this a single record, or are there multiple records?
   - Who created the record?
   - Do you think multiple people were involved?
   - Is the creator a woman of color?
   - What is the creation date for the record?
   - Where was this record created?
   - What type of activity produced this record?
   - What kind of information can you glean from this record?
   - How does this information represent or not represent women of color?
   - What are your general interpretations of this record?
   - Did you find what you were looking for?
   - How does this record relate to your life as a woman of color?
   - As a woman of color, how does this record make you feel?
9. Considering your entire search process, how do you feel about the collections held in the KSU Archives?
10. Are there any ways you think the KSU Archives could improve its collections? Explain.

Chapter 15

Selection and Self-Identity

Robin Bradford and Stephanie Sendaula

In the popular imagination, libraries are often synonymous with books; specifically, dreamlike images of neatly-presented, if not stately and imposing bookshelves. But many people are unaware of how these books come to appear on library shelves. Who finds these books? How do they find them? Why do they find them? It is not always common knowledge, but libraries do, in fact, buy the materials in their collections. In our experiences as public librarians, patrons have wondered if materials were donations, or if publishers give complimentary copies of books to libraries. While many public libraries do incorporate donations into their collections, most items are carefully selected and purchased. One's identity is inherently tied into all purchasing decisions within a library: books, DVDs, CDs, databases, and other technologies. Through the lens of our experiences as black women responsible for selecting materials for public libraries, we explore how our identities, especially our race and gender, have impacted these decisions. We also explore the challenge of buying materials for communities different from our own identity, and wonder how women of color view themselves in these roles, either individually or within the library as a whole. How can we increase the number of women of color in these positions? How do they respond when their chosen materials are questioned or challenged—either by staff or patrons?

The Selecting Process

"Collection development is what librarians call the process by which we add materials to library collections, and it's one of those library terms that sounds like it means a lot, but actually tells you very little," says contributor Robin Bradford in the article, *The Power of Our Choices*. She continues, "In the broadest sense, collection development librarians are charged with seeking out and acquiring materials in accordance with the mission of any given library."[1] This mission can be stated in a number of ways, but usually involves the desire to positively enrich the community by providing a welcoming place, along with equal access to a variety of learning resources and programs. Chicago Public Library goes into more detail: "We welcome and support all people in their enjoyment of reading and pursuit of lifelong learning. Working together we strive to provide equal access to information, ideas and knowledge through books, programs and other resources."[2]

Besides reflecting the mission of the library, the selection process can involve several factors. How many other librarians are involved in collection development? Is it a team or solo effort? Is seeking and acquiring materials one's full-time job, or is someone balancing that duty along with other responsibilities such as reference or instruction? For public libraries, is a selector buying for an individual branch within a system or for multiple branches within a city or county? How much funding does the library allocate for materials? Is there a preference for fiction or nonfiction? Does the library participate in standing orders, where vendors automatically send books based on current trends? What constitutes "equality of access" in the collection? Does that involve having unpopular or unpalatable items, regardless of the personal views of the staff? Or is it making sure that materials by and relating to

---

1. Robin Bradford, "Librarians in the 21st Century: The Power of Our Choices," *Literary Hub*, February 9, 2017, http://lithub.com/librarians-in-the-21st-century-the-power-of-our-choices/.

2. Urban Libraries Council, "Mission Statements," last accessed December 15, 2017, https://www.urbanlibraries.org/mission-statements-pages-236.php.

people of various identities are readily available? Many libraries have collection development policies that specifically restrict certain materials—self-published materials, for instance. Libraries may also require pre-publication reviews of books, which further restricts the range of voices being offered to the public. Who are you buying for, or more specifically, who resides in the community you serve? This last question can pose a challenge when serving communities where there are few patrons from your own demographic—in our case, black women.

Aspects of Privilege

The latest figures from the American Library Association state that librarianship is 88% white.[3] Black men and women comprise 5% of credentialed librarians, or 6,160 out of 118,666 individuals. The Bureau of Labor Statistics estimates that these figures shifted to 84% white and 7.5% African American in 2016.[4] Unfortunately, there is no data on the number of people of color who are involved in the selection process, either as their full-time position or as one of their many responsibilities. In our case, we faced a challenge in having the power to select materials for a given community while still being otherwise marginalized, either by race or gender. "Public librarians tended to shape local collections according to standards of taste and appropriateness that changed over time," says Cheryl Knott in *Not Free, Not for All: Public Libraries in the Age of Jim Crow*.[5]

Knott is referring to public libraries historically, although this fact still rings true today. Recognizing the power and privilege involved in the purchasing process, we realized that we could not separate our identities from our roles as selectors. Bias in collection development is not a new

3. American Library Association, "Diversity Counts 2009-2010 Update," last accessed April 16, 2017, http://www.ala.org/offices/diversity/diversitycounts/divcounts.

4. U.S. Bureau of Labor Statistics, "Labor Force Statistics from the Current Population Survey," last accessed April 17, 2017, https://www.bls.gov/cps/cpsaat11.htm.

5. Cheryl Knott, *Not Free, Not for All: Public Libraries in the Age of Jim Crow* (Boston: University of Massachusetts Press, 2015), 169.

concept. "If you find yourself thinking, 'I don't need this title because we don't really have many X readers here,' your privilege is showing," says Amy Koester in her blog post, "Selection is Privilege."[6] We discovered that our identities as black women with different cultural and religious backgrounds influenced how we considered materials, and whether we viewed particular items as controversial. "Each of us has a myriad of identities—our gender, race, class, sexuality, and so much more—that inform our experiences in life and our interactions with the world," says Ijeoma Oluo in *So You Want to Talk about Race*.[7] She goes on to explain that one can be privileged in some areas of life and underprivileged in others, leading to contradictory thoughts about which identity you identify with the most, and whether that changes over time. This is how we felt as black women: an underrepresented demographic in librarianship as well as in our communities, yet still in a position—selecting materials for a community—that holds power. With that in mind, we both found that our approach to collection development was that books, DVDs, and CDs can be a bridge to someone else's cultural discovery; they can teach people about other cultures and in the process teach people about themselves.

The Myth of Neutrality

It is often difficult to be neutral when selecting materials because of our ingrained identities, and because the goal of acquiring materials that serve people of all backgrounds is not a neutral act. Similarly, libraries strive to inform the public, whether through educational databases, information literacy classes, or other services. "Collection development, organizing displays and shelving, labeling materials with stickers... are other common library decisions that may appear neutral but lack objectivity," stated Cory Eckert at the 2017 American Library Association

6. Amy Koester, "Selection is Privilege," *The Show Me Librarian* (blog), February 8, 2015, http://showmelibrarian.blogspot.com/2015/02/selection-is-privilege.html.

7. Ijeoma Oluo, *So You Want to Talk About Race* (Berkeley, CA: Seal Press, 2018), 75.

Annual Conference.[8] Kendra Jones expanded on that thought: "Having Santa come to your library is not a neutral stance...We don't live in an America where it's safe for people to speak out...Even when you think libraries are being neutral, they're not."[9]

Just as white librarians may not think twice about buying books with white characters, librarians of color may not consider fiction or nonfiction books about people of color, disabled people, or the LGBTQ community to be controversial. An example of identity blurring the lines between the personal and professional occurred when one of the authors supported her library's decision to buy a novel about a black woman who falls in love with someone of a different race. When the book failed to circulate, it was considered a failed experiment in providing the community with books different from ones they were accustomed to seeing on library shelves. For selectors, circulation statistics, which include how many times a particular book is checked out during a specific amount of time, are an important factor in determining future purchasing decisions.

As Knott suggests, however, these statistics do not always tell the whole story: "While circulation statistics can indicate how heavily a collection was used and how use changed over time, they cannot tell us who read the borrowed books. For instance, did the original borrower read them, or were they intended for family members or friends? ... Nor can they tell us which books were taken home but never read....[10] In this case, the author worried that the failure of this book to circulate would cause the library to rethink purchasing additional titles with black women as romantic interests, reinforcing the idea that there is no market for these books. These situations can also lead to self-doubt among collection development librarians when making future purchases, for example, second-guessing yourself when buying or displaying books with

---

8. Stephanie Sendaula, "Libraries Are Not Neutral Spaces: Social Justice Advocacy in Librarianship," *Library Journal*, July 7, 2017, http://lj.libraryjournal.com/2017/07/shows-events/ala/libraries-are-not-neutral-spaces-ala-annual-2017/.

9. Ibid.

10. Knott, *Not Free, Not for All: Public Libraries in the Age of Jim Crow*, 203.

disabled characters, and wondering whether colleagues would question your motives or see them as an effort of forced diversity.

When it comes to African American librarians working in selection, one of the baseline hurdles to overcome is the question of competence. Collection development is often considered a "specialist" position, and in a profession where the statistics show that less than 10% of librarians are African American, there is sometimes pushback to the idea that a member of an underrepresented group could be qualified enough to select materials for an entire community. That pushback is usually in the sometimes subtle, sometimes not so subtle, form of the "résumé check." In his book, *Who's Afraid of Post-Blackness*, Touré defines the résumé check as, "…like a descendant of the free papers check that free Blacks dealt with during slavery—a white person basically assumes you do not belong and checks to see if you do."[11] One of the authors was, and still is, constantly asked about credentials when discussing her work as a collection development librarian—even after performing the job for over fifteen years. Questions such as, "What library school did you go to? What year did you graduate? What classes did you take? How many libraries have you worked in? Which libraries? What is your undergraduate degree in?" are all commonly asked, not in the regular "getting to know you" context, but when someone is concerned that a position has been unfairly given to someone undeserving or under-qualified.

In another example, when tasked with buying large-print materials, one author chose titles that dealt with questioning or leaving one's faith, since her personal experiences reflected the same. These purchases were challenged, not by patrons, but by other staff who were unsure if large-print readers would be interested in nonfiction materials, let alone ones focusing on spirituality and religion. This left the author in a position to defend herself and make a case for the necessity of these books in the library's collection. Ultimately, she was successful and patrons were happy to see not only more nonfiction titles in the large-print section, but

11. Touré, *Who's Afraid of Post-Blackness: What It Means to Be Black Now* (New York: Free Press, 2011), 81.

ones that dealt with the subject of faith. However, this incident shows that selectors of varied backgrounds may face unexpected challenges due to selecting books that they may not personally perceive as divisive.

Overcoming Limitations

In *The Meaning of the Library: A Cultural History*, Alice Crawford explains that, "the library as an idea does indeed unify opposites: like rhetoric, it has no immanent ethics, no immanent qualities of virtue or vice, but is a tool that can both liberate and oppress."[12] By suggesting that large-print readers would not be interested in nonfiction, library staff are engaging in a form of oppression, or over-generalization. Passive aggressive resistance to materials or a specific person's expertise can come in many forms from many directions. For example, instead of public services librarians objecting to materials, technical services staff can also raise questions or objections when materials are received in the library. In one instance, after being repeatedly told that the selector in charge of the subject area was qualified to make these decisions, questioning of the author's selections eventually stopped—but the negative impact of the situation was long lasting.

After materials are successfully purchased and processed, a frequent question among library staff is why items that are routinely stolen should be purchased, the presumption being that materials thought to be geared towards African Americans are the most stolen items in the library. The frustrating experience of handling materials presumed to be for an African American audience, and the limitations and stigmas placed on them, has been referenced in relation to everything from hip hop CDs to urban fiction books. This questioning has occurred at multiple libraries, not limited to certain geographic locations or to staff of any particular experience or education level. However, this question was never asked in relation to purchasing CDs by the Beatles or Metallica,

12. Alice Crawford, *The Meaning of the Library: A Cultural History* (Princeton, NJ: Princeton University Press, 2015), 17.

not to mention any genres that are constantly lost or missing in libraries. It was automatically assumed those materials would be replaced as many times as necessary to keep them available for patrons. Yet, an assumption made of urban fiction books is that they are frequently stolen and not deserving of replacement. When looking into books that routinely go missing from libraries on a more national level, urban fiction is rarely mentioned. In a 2016 article on *Open Culture*, blogger Candace Huber lists the top categories of books stolen from libraries as including the Bible, textbooks and reference, and exam prep books.[13]

The awkwardness that some white librarians experience when working with staff whose backgrounds differ from their own isn't limited to materials selection and how they might be informed by racial stereotypes of the materials, or the people using them. It is also the overall dismissal of the knowledge possessed by librarians of color, along with attempts to isolate or silence them. In the article "Perceptions of Discriminatory Practices and Attitudes," Cynthia Preston quotes research conducted by business executive Edward W. Jones Jr. and published in *Harvard Business Review* in which he explains a phenomenon called "running the gauntlet" that is experienced by many African American professionals in majority white workplaces.

> This refers to the fine line African American professionals walk as they try to maintain their ethnic identity and at the same time not offend their white peers and business associates. To quote, *running the gauntlet* means "being smart but not too smart. Being strong, but not too strong. Being confident but not egotistical to the point of alienation. Being the butt of prejudice and not being unpleasant or abrasive. Being intelligent but not arrogant. Being honest but not paranoid. Being confident yet modest…"[14]

---

13. "What Are the Most Stolen Books? Bookstore List Features Works by Murakami, Bukowski, Burroughs, Vonnegut, Kerouac, & Palahniuk," *Open Culture*, July 26, 2016, accessed May 26, 2017, http://www.openculture.com/2016/07/what-are-the-most-stolen-books.html.

14. Cynthia Preston, "Perceptions of Discriminatory Practices and Attitudes: A Survey of African American Librarians," *College & Research Libraries* 59, no. 5 (1998): 434-445.

As an example, one author was discussing collection statistics with colleagues out of the office, and there was a disagreement about content. Once back in the office, she printed out the statistics and brought them to a meeting in an attempt to help clear up the misunderstanding. Instead of admitting the mistake, one of her colleagues employed the shaming and silencing tactic of accusing the librarian of having to "always be right" as a way to end the conversation. The thinking is, if you're labeled as "always right," you'll be ashamed enough to stop displaying intelligence and disagreeing with colleagues who may have an incomplete grasp of information. As a result, you're labeled as "arrogant" or "uppity." The fear of being labeled or considered troublesome is often enough to keep librarians of color silent, because when it comes to disagreeing with white colleagues, the only thing worse for them than being wrong is being right.

Similarly, it is impossible to remain neutral, since wanting an equitable collection where all identities are given fair representation is not a neutral stance. In fact, it is a political one. In her article "It Is Becoming Impossible to Remain Neutral," Stacie Williams says: "We can really see who we're working with and who we're hoping to serve and understand that an approach that asks anyone to be invisible or accept a default status quo that allows others to question their existence has not ever been the way forward."[15] Likewise, we as a profession can't move forward and retain more marginalized people in collection development positions until we ensure that their voices will be heard and their identities will remain unchallenged. In short, people need a safe space to be their true selves. We are both passionate about collection development because we realize the impact that our behind-the-scenes choices have had, such as the spark of eagerness and awareness when a teen or an adult discovers a book or CD or DVD they wouldn't have expected. This indirect connection is what can and should draw more underrepresented people to become selectors, provided that they are also invested in and supported

15. Stacie Williams, "Librarians in the 21st Century: It Is Becoming Impossible to Remain Neutral," *Literary Hub*, May 4, 2017, http://lithub.com/librarians-in-the-21st-century-it-is-becoming-impossible-to-remain-neutral.

at work. In the meantime, we can continue to advocate for change within the library profession and society as a whole, while emphasizing that librarians of color and those from other underserved groups shouldn't carry the burden of change alone.

Bibliography

American Library Association. "Diversity Counts 2009-2010 Update." Accessed April 16, 2017. http://www.ala.org/offices/diversity/diversitycounts/divcounts.

Bradford, Robin. "Librarians in the 21st Century: The Power of Our Choices." *Literary Hub*. February 9, 2017. http://lithub.com/librarians-in-the-21st-century-the-power-of-our-choices/.

Crawford, Alice. *The Meaning of the Library: A Cultural History*. Princeton, NJ: Princeton University Press, 2015.

Knott, Cheryl. *Not Free, Not for All: Public Libraries in the Age of Jim Crow*. Boston: University of Massachusetts Press, 2015.

Koester, Amy. "Selection is Privilege." *The Show Me Librarian* (blog). February 8, 2015. http://showmelibrarian.blogspot.com/2015/02/selection-is-privilege.html.

Oluo, Ijeoma. *So You Want to Talk about Race*. Berkeley, CA: Seal Press, 2018.

Preston, Cynthia. "Perceptions of Discriminatory Practices and Attitudes: A Survey of African American Librarians." *College & Research Libraries* 59, no. 5 (1998): 434-445.

Sendaula, Stephanie. "Libraries Are Not Neutral Spaces: Social Justice Advocacy in Librarianship." *Library Journal*. July 7, 2017. http://lj.libraryjournal.com/2017/07/shows-events/ala/libraries-are-not-neutral-spaces-ala-annual-2017/.

Touré. *Who's Afraid of Post-Blackness: What It Means to Be Black Now*. New York: Atria, 2011.

Urban Libraries Council. "Mission Statements." Accessed December 15, 2017. https://www.urbanlibraries.org/mission-statements-pages-236.php.

U.S. Bureau of Labor Statistics. "Labor Force Statistics from the Current Population Survey." Accessed April 17, 2017. https://www.bls.gov/cps/cpsaat11.htm.

"What Are the Most Stolen Books? Bookstore Lists Feature Works by Murakami, Bukowski, Burroughs, Vonnegut, Kerouac & Palahniuk." *Open Culture*. Accessed May 26, 2017. http://www.openculture.com/2016/07/what-are-the-most-stolen-books.html.

Williams, Stacie. "Librarians in the 21st Century: It Is Becoming Impossible to Remain Neutral." *Literary Hub*. May 4, 2017. http://lithub.com/librarians-in-the-21st-century-it-is-becoming-impossible-to-remain-neutral.

Chapter 16

Reflections on the Intersection of Publishing and Librarianship: The Experiences of Women of Color

Charlotte Roh

In my first year of library school, I went to a networking dinner at a local conference that was organized by Spectrum Scholar[1] alumni. I had invited a classmate of mine, who was the only white, female library student in the group. As we paid our checks, we made small talk with the cashier, who asked why we were in town. "Oh, we're here for a library conference," we said. "A library conference! You don't look like librarians! Except you," he said, nodding at my classmate, the lone white woman in the group. "You look like a librarian."

The Demographics of Publishing and Librarianship

As many people know, the demographics of librarianship are primarily white and female—so much so that the stereotypes about librarianship invariably rebound on many of us—even librarians who are white and female. My white female colleague experienced a rare moment of reversal; she was stereotyped into an identity that "othered" her from the group (who, even in this moment of reversal, found themselves

1. The Spectrum Scholarship program is the American Library Association's major diversity program. More information is at http://www.ala.org/advocacy/spectrum.

denied identity from the profession). The experience of being the lone representative of an ethnic group is not a new one to many professional women of color. This experience is borne out by the numbers— 86.7% of librarians are white (see **Figure 1**), and 81% identify as women.[2]

Similarly, the demographics of publishing are white and female. Scholarly publishing is 63.64% female and 36.3% male.[3] Trade publishing is 78% female, but at the executive level, 40% male.[4] Like librarianship and other feminized professions that are female-dominated in numbers but male-dominated in control and leadership, there are fewer women at the top of the career ladder than there are at the bottom. The two professions have more than a love of books in common; they also share a lack of gender and racial diversity (see **Figure 2**).

Connecting the Demographics to Impacts

Over the past year, I've been asked to write and speak to the library audience on the impact these demographics have on the publishing pipeline, particularly in scholarly communication, where "authoritative" knowledge is constructed.[5] Along with my colleagues Harrison

---

2. Kathy Rosa and Kelsey Henke, "2017 ALA Demographic Study," *ALA Office of Research and Statistics*, January 2017, http://www.ala.org/research/sites/ala.org.research/files/content/Draft%20of%20Member%20Demographics%20Survey%2001-11-2017.pdf.

3. Albert N. Greco, Robert M. Wharton, Amy Brand, "Demographics of Scholarly Publishing and Communication Professionals," *Learned Publishing* 29 (2016): 97-101.

4. Jason T. Low, "Where is the Diversity in Publishing? The 2015 Diversity Baseline Survey Results," *The Open Book*, January 26, 2016, http://blog.leeandlow.com/2016/01/26/where-is-the-diversity-in-publishing-the-2015-diversity-baseline-survey-results/#more-11897.

For those interested in children's literature, Sarah Park Dahlen at St. Catherine's University is doing critical work—both qualitative and quantitative—on diversity representation amongst publishers, authors, and the characters within the books themselves. There are also statistics from the Cooperative Children's Book Center at the University of Wisconsin-Madison.

5. Harrison Inefuku and Charlotte Roh, "Agents of Diversity and Social Justice: Librarians and Scholarly Communication," in *Open Access and the Future of Scholarly Communication: Policy and Infrastructure*, eds. Kevin Smith and Katherine A. Dickson (New York: Rowman and Littlefield 2016), 107.

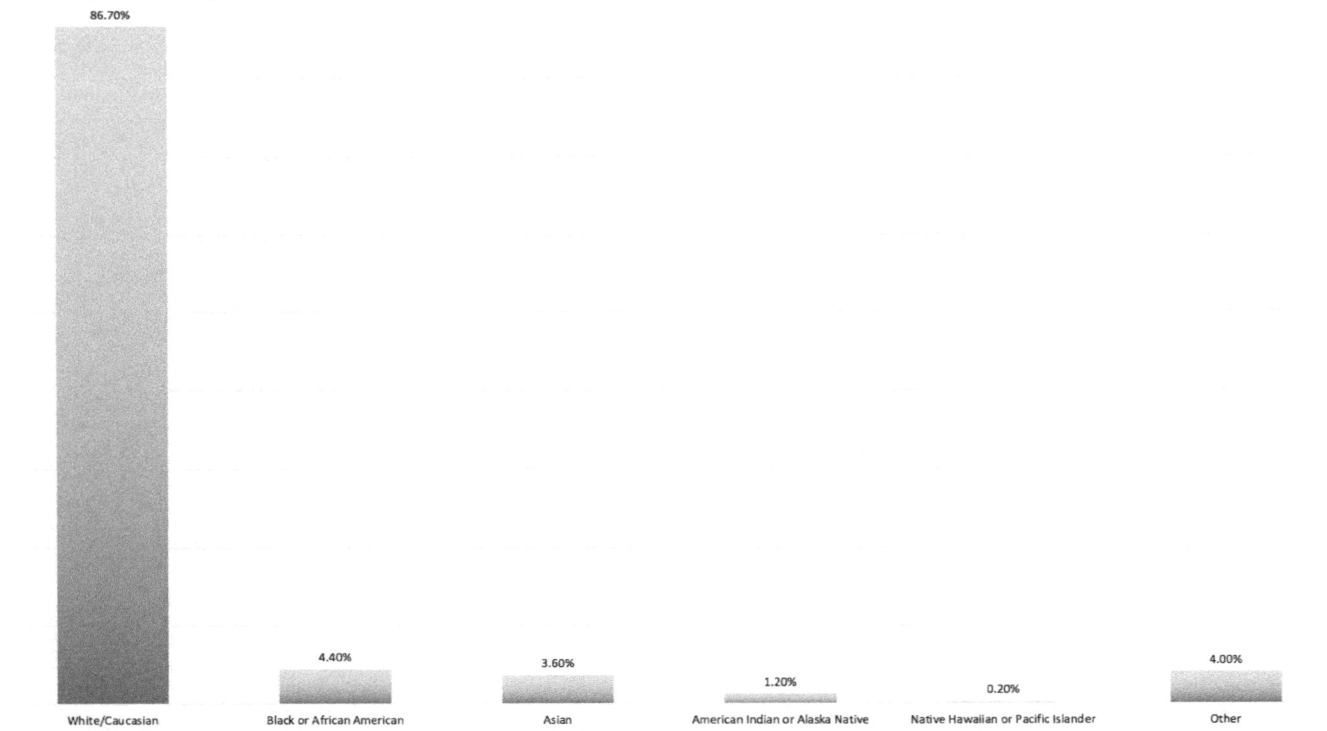

Figure 1. Demographics of librarians. Data from Kathy Rosa and Kelsey Henke, "2017 ALA Demographic Study," ALA Office of Research and Statistics, January 2017, http://www.ala.org/research/sites/ala.org.research/files/content/Draft%20of%20Member%20Demographics%20Survey%2001-11-2017.pdf.

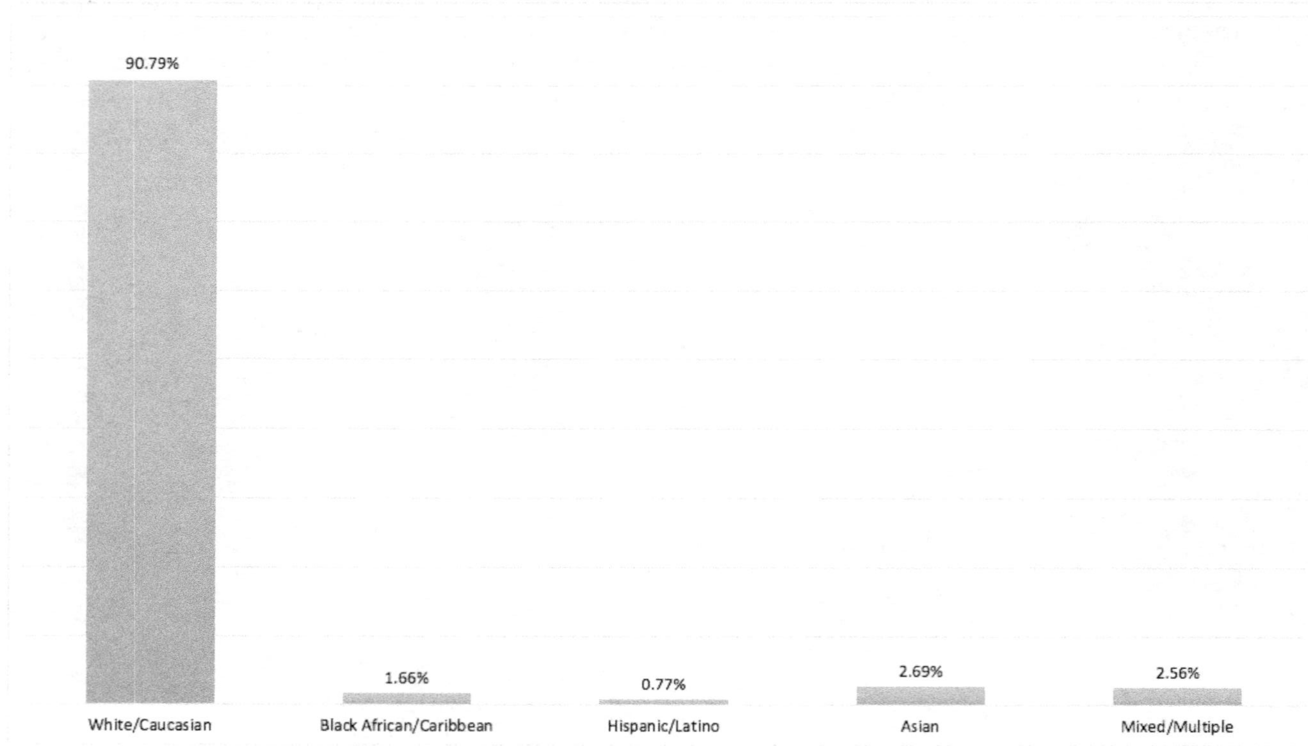

Figure 2. Demographics of publishing. Data from A. Greco, R. Wharton, and A. Brand, "Demographics of scholarly publishing and communication professionals," *Learned Publishing* 29, no. 2 (2016): 97-101 http://onlinelibrary.wiley.com/doi/10.1002/leap.1017/full.

Inefuku and Emily Drabinski, I've made the point that the publishing ecosystem is compromised—that "the traditional scholarly communication system is a closed feedback loop that justifies the decisions of publishers (who might say, 'This won't sell') and librarians (who might say, 'Nobody will read this'). We might well ask just who publishers and librarians are imagining when they think of their readers."[6] This is highly possible when one considers the relationship between librarians and publishers. Publishers are not just vendors of books, databases, and software systems, but also sponsors of conferences, scholarships, and programs. Librarians participate in focus groups, write reviews, consult over comped dinners, and work for publishing companies. The relationship goes beyond the transaction of a book sale, and it is no wonder that the demographics are so similar.

In my presentations, I've attempted to make these demographics transparent by using the charts you see in this chapter, along with a visualization of the basic publishing process (see **Figure 3**), in order to show where power structures can reinforce the white male majority perspective and how the existence of peer review and editorial boards are no guarantee that a diversity of voices will be heard.

This is particularly true if one factors in the demographics of academia (see **Figure 4**), where peer review, editorial board members, and citations are all subject to bias.[7] In my teaching, I point to the section of the graph that says "Your fellow academics" and point out that this reflects back to the larger population of academics. I ask my workshop participants to reflect on the diversity of certain subject fields, of their fields. Peer review, like the old adage about justice, is not really blind. Just in 2017:

- *American Historical Review*, a leading history journal, apologized

6. Ibid., 115.

7. Carole J. Lee, Cassidy R. Sugimoto, Guo Zhang, and Blaise Cronin, "Bias in Peer Review," *Journal of the American Society for Information Science and Technology* 64, no. 1, January 2013, DOI: 10.1002/asi.22784.

for assigning a review to a white supremacist.[8]

- *Hypatia,* a feminist philosophy journal, apologized for, but did not retract, a paper that analogized Rachel Dolezal to transgender people.[9]
- *The Journal of Political Philosophy* apologized for an issue devoted to the Black Lives Matter movement that included zero black authors.[10]
- *Third World Quarterly* published a paper advocating a return to colonialism, leading fifteen members of its editorial board to resign.[11]

Three out of these four journals apologized, and all acknowledged that something had gone wrong in the editorial process. There were a range of reasons: the editors had not fully understood, they had chosen reviewers who were not appropriate, they had chosen authors without considering fully the implications. But all three also apologized in the wake of publicity and outcry—how many blind peer review processes and published articles have there been that were not so transparent, that went unreported in *Inside Higher Ed* or *The Chronicle of Education*?

Personal Experiences from Academic and Mainstream Publishing

Though these efforts may seem positive, they are very little and very late for many women of color who are isolated in their professions. For example, just last year, at the 2016 annual Society for Scholarly Publishing

8. Scott Jaschik, "The Wrong Reviewer," *Inside Higher Ed*, April 18, 2017, https://www.insidehighered.com/news/2017/04/18/history-journal-apologizes-assigning-review-book-urban-education-and-inequality.

9. Elizabeth Anderson, Leslie Francis, Heidi Grasswick, Miriam Solomon, and Lisa Tessman, "Statement by the Board of Hypatia" *Hypatia*, May 18, 2017, http://hypatiaphilosophy.org/Editorial/index.html#boardstatement.

10. Meena Krishnamurthy, "Open Letter from the Editors of the Journal of Political Philosophy," *Philosopher*, May 25, 2017, https://politicalphilosopher.net/2017/05/25/open-letter-from-the-editors-of-the-journal-of-political-philosophy/.

11. Colleen Flaherty, "Resignations at Third World Quarterly," *Inside Higher Ed*, September 20, 2017, https://www.insidehighered.com/news/2017/09/20/much-third-world-quarterlys-editorial-board-resigns-saying-controversial-article.

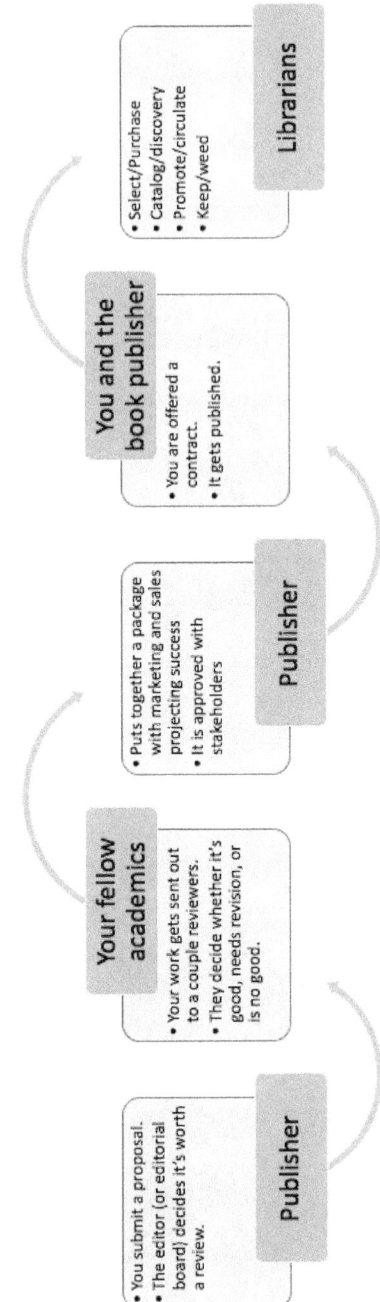

Figure 3. The Basic Publishing Process. CC-BY Charlotte Roh.

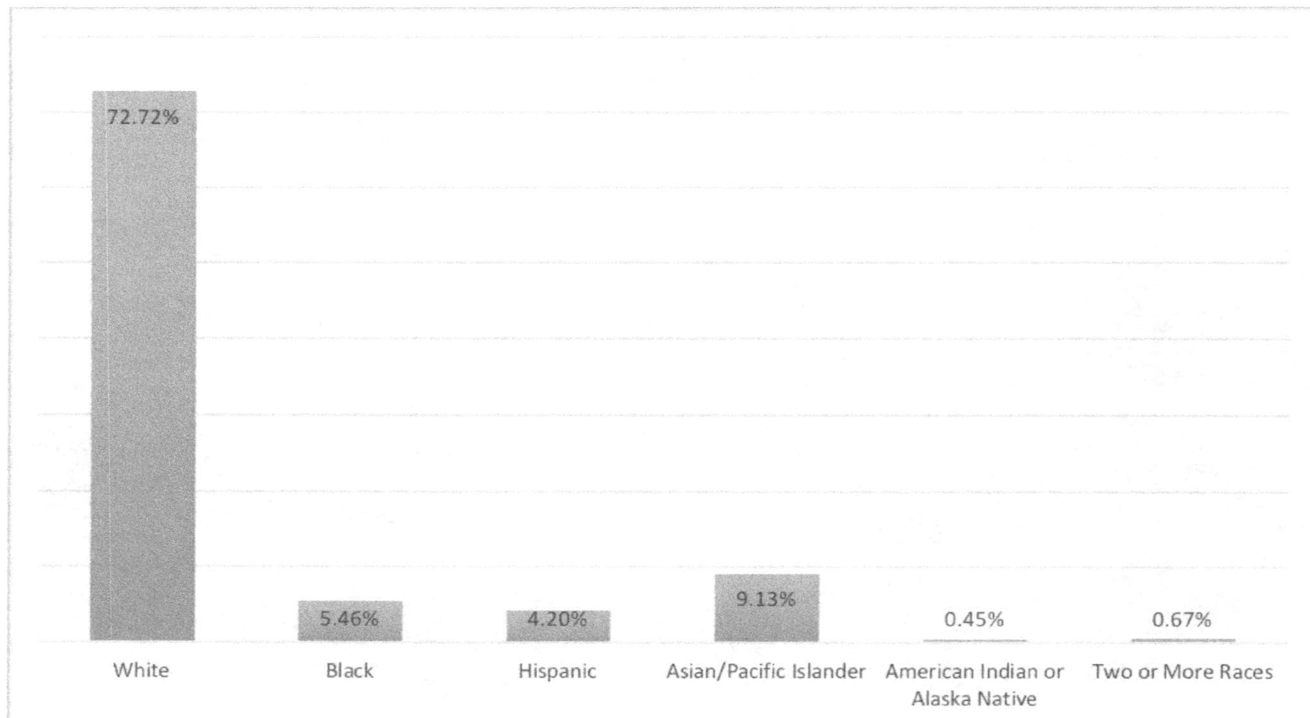

Figure 4. Demographics of faculty. Data from National Center for Education Statistics, "Table 315.20. Full-time faculty in degree-granting postsecondary institutions, by race/ethnicity, sex, and academic rank: Fall 2009, fall 2011, and fall 2013," Digest of Education Statistics 2015, https://nces.ed.gov/programs/digest/d15/tables/dt15_315.20.asp.

(SSP) meeting, a very well-meaning gentleman suggested that perhaps I would benefit from being the only minority in the room. (In fact, I was the only visible minority on the conference planning committee.) I am unable to describe the look that I felt on my face as I informed him that research and personal experience had shown that to be untrue. He walked away disappointed, and I had to question whether I really was benefiting from tokenism. I've since come to realize that my tokenism is not my problem. I am grateful for the opportunities I've been offered, and I work very hard, as do all the women of color in my field that I have had the pleasure and honor to know. That does not mean that I do not feel the impacts of tokenism, however, nor am I the only person who feels this way. For example, Patricia Hswe, who has experience in both publishing and librarianship, commented:

> I haven't gone to school or worked with many people who look like me. For a long time, even while obviously being one of a very few POC, I didn't interpret the absence of more colleagues of color as a reflection of the employer's or organization's oversight or lack of commitment to POC. I wasn't thinking critically about the people and place that hired me, perhaps because I was just so grateful to have a job and be gainfully employed.... More recently, I wonder if some of the recent positive things in my career are partly the result of groups, professional association committees, and organizations deciding—not quite all of a sudden but kind of, like they're riding a wave of "wokeness"—that they need to step up and invite more POC members to join them or lead them. At the same time that I wonder this, I find myself also thinking: But does this mean I'm really good at what I do, or was I invited because I'm not white and I'm not male? Which is it: competence or color? I like to think it's both, but I also detest that this thought appears at all in my consciousness. It amounts to a different strain of imposter syndrome.[12]

In Patricia's case, we can see that even the idea or question of tokenism can have negative impacts, leading to questions and doubt. Even if we are sure of our qualifications, it is difficult not to feel the weight of that representation, because it is most likely that, as Patricia notes, it is

12. Patricia Hswe, email message to author, 2017.

both competence and color that has led to opportunities. This leads to a double bind of debt and doubt, an additional burden to perform not just to prove ourselves, but on behalf of others.

This burden to perform is impossible to ignore for women of color. Harriet Green, who has also worked in both publishing and librarianship, has had a similar experience. She notes that:

> My entire academic and professional careers have been experiences in "colorblind" situations: From grade school through to both graduate degrees, I attended very Predominantly White Institutions where it wasn't unusual for me to be the only POC in class, or I could count the total number of POC in the office on my hands. But while things have been cordial between myself and colleagues the vast, vast majority of the time, I've always known that "color blindness" is a facade: Everyone is always aware of your ethnicity, your culture, your appearance, and/or your background—the context always is there and it always matters as we pursue our professional and personal growth. So to claim "color blindness" in our interactions is to assert that our clearly racialized society built on white privilege is a neutralized playing field, when it's not; and that my context simply doesn't matter, when it very much does.[13]

Harriet's observation that "white privilege is a neutralized playing field" echoes the belief that libraries and librarians are neutral, which is similar to the publishing industry's belief in its ability to discern quality literature or provide for unbiased peer review. We know that in truth, libraries and publishing organizations, like any other public or private sphere, can be sites of white privilege and oppression for people of color. The solution is not a passive claim to color blindness, but active reinforcement of perspectives and people of color for racial justice.

Emily Ruth Hazel, who spent many years in various aspects of the book industry, told me that

> When I worked for Lee & Low Books, an independent publisher of multicultural children's and young adult literature, I felt the importance of our work in creating and promoting high quality books "about everyone, for everyone," including many in which people of color (and girls

13. Harriet Green, email message to author, 2017.

> and women) played starring roles.... For five years, I managed Lee & Low's New Voices contest, an annual award given to encourage writers of color to become first-time children's book authors in a market in which they are still vastly underrepresented. During that time, I was the only person of color on the small editorial staff and thus also felt the importance of cultivating editorial diversity as well as actively seeking out and nurturing authors and illustrators of color to create books that reflect diverse perspectives and that are culturally accurate and nuanced.[14]

This responsibility to seek out, cultivate, and nurture a diversity of voices, particularly in scholarly communication librarianship, is a burden that I feel as well. But it should be everyone's problem that women of color like Patricia, Harriet, Emily, and myself have a shared solitary experience of being the only visibly non-white people in our spaces. It should be everyone's problem that people and forms of knowledge have been—and still are—marginalized.[15] Representational equality is a well-intentioned step in the right direction, but it becomes tokenism, not when the minorities that are included don't effect change, but when the white majority culture passively refuses to gain the cultural competencies that will turn this ship around. No wonder that, when race and ethnicity are even tangentially involved, publishing often founders on the shoals of ignorance.[16]

This ignorance is dangerous because, as well-meaning as an individual may be, racism and sexism are parts of our culture that are internalized

---

14. Emily Ruth Hazel, email message to author, 2017.

15. An example of this behavior is described by April Hathcock in her blog post "Making the Local Global: The Colonialism of Scholarly Communication," where a group of us experienced what it felt like to be marginalized en masse. April Hathcock, "Making the Local Global: The Colonialism of Scholarly Communication," *At the Intersection* (blog), September, 27, 2016, https://aprilhathcock.wordpress.com/2016/09/27/making-the-local-global-the-colonialism-of-scholarly-communication/.

16. Examples in scholarly and mainstream publishing abound, but I want to point to an editorial in *Write Magazine*, the quarterly publication of The Writers' Union of Canada. In an issue about Indigenous writers, editor Hal Niedzviecki espoused cultural appropriation. The journal apologized and he stepped down, but then high-ranking (white) editors across Canada decided to actually create an "appropriation prize." Sarah Hagi, "A Bunch of White Canadian Editors Really Love Cultural Appropriation," *Vice*, May 12, 2017, https://www.vice.com/en_ca/article/a-bunch-of-white-canadian-editors-really-love-cultural-appropriation.

and revealed through our perceptions and values. We default to enabling and promoting the Western white male majority voice. We perpetuate the colonialist infrastructures of the university and police whether someone is plagiarizing (a Western ethical construct) or writing in proper English (a marker of class, privilege, and nationality). I am guilty of this myself, as an editor in academic publishing in my past career, in my present career as a scholarly communication librarian, and in my work as an editorial freelancer and consultant. My own ignorance and racism is deeply rooted—as a student, ethnic minority voices were completely left out of my education. I studied mostly male European and American artists and authors in school and came into publishing with no knowledge of the racist structures in which I resided. It was only when I left university press publishing that I began to realize how my ignorance had hurt me. I was woefully ignorant that, as a Korean American, I was perceived as a privileged model minority. I had no idea how to ask for mentorship, nor did my supervisors realize that I needed guidance since my background as a low-income, first-generation immigrant was invisible. I worked too hard and accepted the words of those who told me that I didn't have leadership potential, because I had no idea that Asians were perceived as workhorses. I believed in the good intentions of my coworkers (and friends) in non-profit publishing and in the myth of meritocracy.

Unfortunately, many of the scholar authors that I work with do believe in this same meritocracy. They are not aware that "meritocracy" is a satirical term, coined as recently as 1958 in a novel about a dystopian United Kingdom.[17] The authors I work with are good students who've been rewarded for doing the right thing in school and have remained in academia as a result. Theoretically, doing all the right things will lead to publication, tenure, and promotion. I enable and inform as best as I can, telling graduate students such things as: "See yourself not just as an author, but as a future editorial board member," and "Don't just ask publishers at booths for free books. Ask them about trends in

17. Michael Dunlop Young, *The Rise of the Meritocracy* (London: Thames and Hudson Publishers, 1958).

publishing." I tell young researchers that, while they might not be on an editorial board, it is appropriate for them to approach an editorial board member with questions about a journal in order to learn more about how to not only be authors but reviewers and editorial board members themselves. These tips are helpful for minority students, particularly first-generation college students whose parents aren't able to advise them. I tell them, because they don't know already, that publishing in prestige outlets is a central requirement for tenure. The publication record has real impact on whether minority scholars are promoted and retained within publishing.

> Who determines which stories become "classics," must-reads carried by libraries and bookstores, part of the canon taught in schools? This is a vital question because the stories and images we find (or don't find) in books and other media profoundly shape our psyche and our expectations of what roles people of color play (as with the development of gender norms). Librarians and publishers are in many ways the shapers and doorkeepers of literary culture. We all have natural biases, areas of greater knowledge, and differing familiarity based on our personal experiences and on what we choose to study. It is therefore essential to cultivate diversity in readership, in authorship, and in leadership—those who consume and create content, and those who fund and advocate for the creation, production, and distribution of that content.—Emily Ruth Hazel[18]

Scholarly Communication is Not Enough

As Emily says, "Librarians and publishers are in many ways the shapers and doorkeepers of literary culture." This is what I tell those in the scholarly communication ecosystem, that we need to look beyond our existing biases to greater knowledge, and for representational diversity in our workplaces, in our work processes, and in the scholarly record, for the sake of our larger culture. The reality is more complex. There is a long record of scholars who have fulfilled all the requirements of tenure,

18. Emily Ruth Hazel, email message to author, 2017.

who have published and still perished. There is the case of Andrea Smith, who in 2008 was denied tenure at the University of Michigan by the women's studies department—a reminder that white women are not always allies. In the words of Jane Chin Davidson and Deepa S. Reddy, who discuss this case in depth, "the rejection of women of color, even if they publish prodigiously and are hailed by their students as excellent teachers…is both a refusal of recognition and the subjection to a fraternal norm (under the definition of fraternal as the long tradition of a *paternal* structure of institutional brotherhood)."[19] This refusal of recognition is the process of making diverse voices invisible, even as the number of white women in academia reaches parity with white men (see **Figure 5**).

Gender	Males	Females
White	316,912	258,579
Black	18,905	24,283
Hispanic	17,198	16,019
Asian/Pacific Islander	43,519	28,727
American Indian/Alaska Native	1,736	1,802
Two or more races	2,547	2,744

Figure 5. Full-time faculty by race and gender. [Data from National Center for Education Statistics, "Table 315.20. Full-time faculty in degree-granting postsecondary institutions, by race/ethnicity, sex, and academic rank: Fall 2009, fall 2011, and fall 2013," *Digest of Education Statistics* 2015, https://nces.ed.gov/programs/digest/d15/tables/dt15_315.20.asp]

More recently, there is the case of Aimee Bahng, an Asian American professor at Dartmouth whose entire English department voted

19. Jane Chin Davidson and Deepa S. Reddy, "Performative Testimony and the Practice of Dismissal"in *Written/Unwritten: Diversity and the Hidden Truths of Tenure*, ed. Patricia A. Matthew (Chapel Hill: The University of North Carolina Press, 2016), 132–134.

unanimously that she be granted tenure but was denied by upper administration. According to the institution's own report, sixteen percent of faculty at Dartmouth are minorities and only eighteen of 209 full professors identified as underrepresented minorities.[20] Aimee Bahng had 1) the support of her colleagues and 2) extraordinary support from the campus community. There were student protests and widespread reporting on the case.[21]

These are just two of many cases where women of color have encountered difficulty obtaining tenure despite their publication records. At times I am disheartened by this truth: that the teaching I do on and against the colonialist power and structures of scholarly communication still resides within these structures. Am I simply complicit by teaching people of color how to employ publishing cultural competencies that reinforce white dominant cultural behavior?[22] Or am I effecting change in the system so that people of color can be truly represented rather than feeling, like so many of the women in this essay, like the only one? The answer is that I don't know, and I won't know, until I see change over time. Until then, I can only count on my community to keep me accountable to the values of justice in my chosen profession, while I continue to learn more about historical and contemporary injustices.

Addressing Injustice in Scholarly Communication

As a scholarly communications librarian at an institution that supports social justice, I feel empowered to speak frankly and clearly about how we can address these problems. My action points are straightforward and vary only slightly depending on the audience. I ask for awareness

---

20. Catherine Morris, "Denied Tenure at Dartmouth, Aimee Bahng Feels Diversity Efforts Ring Hollow," Diverse Issues in Higher Education, May 18, 2016, http://diverseeducation.com/article/84350/.

21. Dr. Bahng is now at Pomona College in California.

22. April Hathcock, "White Librarianship in Blackface: Diversity Initiatives in LIS," *In the Library with the Lead Pipe*, October 7, 2015, http://www.inthelibrarywiththeleadpipe.org/2015/lis-diversity/.

and cultural competencies (e.g., to understand histories and realities in race, gender, sexuality, ability, and culture) in order to subvert our biased systems.

To publishers, I ask that we interrogate our existing structures—editorial boards, reviewers, authors, readers, content, language—to see where we could do better. In the words of Safiya Noble, "The gatekeeping function of publishing is fundamental to issues of social justice. If you are not published, you cannot be classified and catalogued."[23] As publishers seek a broader audience online and consider challenges such as metadata (i.e., classification and cataloging) in order to facilitate discovery and access, I ask that we also think more broadly about what access means to authors and the broader scholarly community to whom our actions matter so much.

For librarians, the understanding that we hold power in cataloging and classification is not a new idea.[24] However, I ask that we interrogate our purchasing decisions, our cataloging and discovery systems, and our own place in the scholarly communication system as we inhabit different roles. We are familiar with evaluating our collection decisions for the sake of budget cuts and rising costs, but we can also wield that power pro-actively for the sake of representational equity.

For faculty and students, I urge that we consider ourselves as empowered members of an ecosystem rather than supplicants at publishers' portals. Frequently this means asking researchers to see themselves, not only as authors, but also as reviewers and editors with power to change representation. We are all community members who can hold authors, reviewers, editors, and fellow librarians accountable for how scholarship is communicated and represented.

23. Safiya Noble, "Social Justice and Library Publishing" (presentation, Library Publishing Forum, Baltimore, MD, March 20-22, 2017).

24. Hope A. Olson, "The Power to Name: Representation in Library Catalogs," *Signs* no. 3: 639 (2001).

Library and Publisher Efforts in Representation

For the most part, the response to my work has been positive, particularly from librarians, which I attribute to the long culture of self-criticism in the library profession. Libraries have had diversity programs in place for decades: conference scholarships, the Spectrum Scholarship Program, and the ARL Diversity and Inclusion Initiatives are examples. It is also encouraging that in 2017, the Library Publishing Coalition (LPC) has initiated a task force on ethics that includes diversity and bias as part of its charge.[25]

Publishing is also trying to change, largely in response to the 2015 Lee and Low Diversity Baseline survey.[26] The Association of American University Presses (AAUP), funded by the Mellon Foundation, established a diversity fellowship program with the goal of increasing minority representation in the profession. Three of the fellows have already been hired full time, and the program has engendered conversations within the presses themselves about the need for diversity in our traditionally white supremacist systems.[27] The Society for Scholarly Publishing (SSP) has recently discussed gender parity, and its first panel on ethnic diversity took place at the 2017 annual meeting, reporting on the efforts of book publishers. After the panel, I spoke briefly with a woman next to me, Ashley Morgan, who told me of her efforts to diversify the editorial board of the *American Journal of Transplantation*. "It creates a false representation in our field if our editorial boards don't reflect the people who are actually doing the research,"[28] she said. Though these may feel like

25. In the interests of full disclosure, I am on this task force as the first Library Publishing Coalition Fellow.

26. Low, "Where is the Diversity in Publishing? The 2015 Diversity Baseline Survey Results."

27. Jesus Hernandez, Charles Brandquist, Helen Atwan, Gita Manaktala, and Rebecca McLeod, "Toward a Diverse Workforce in Scholarly Publishing: Strategies, Tactics and Lessons Learned" (presentation, Society for Scholarly Publishing, Boston, MA, May 30-June 1, 2017).

28. Ashley Morgan, Assistant Managing Editor, *American Journal of Transplantation*, in conversation with the author, June 2017.

small efforts, they are signs of a step-by-step change, what I consider allyship in action, and I am encouraged to see them.

Bibliography

Anderson, Elizabeth, Leslie Francis, Heidi Grasswick, Miriam Solomon, and Lisa Tessman. "Statement by the Board of Hypatia." *Hypatia.* May 18, 2017. http://hypatiaphilosophy.org/Editorial/index.html#boardstatement.

Davidson, Jane Chin and Deepa S. Reddy. "Performative Testimony and the Practice of Dismissal." In *Written/Unwritten: Diversity and the Hidden Truths of Tenure*, edited by Patricia A. Matthew, 132–134. Chapel Hill: University of North Carolina Press, 2016.

Flaherty, Colleen. "Resignations at 'Third World Quarterly'." *Inside Higher Ed.* September 20, 2017. https://www.insidehighered.com/news/2017/09/20/much-third-world-quarterlys-editorial-board-resigns-saying-controversial-article.

Greco, Albert N., Robert M. Wharton, and Amy Brand. "Demographics of Scholarly Publishing and Communication Professionals." *Learned Publishing* 29 (2016):97-101. http://onlinelibrary.wiley.com/doi/10.1002/leap.1017/full.

Hagi, Sarah. "A Bunch of White Canadian Editors Really Love Cultural Appropriation." *Vice.* May 12, 2017. https://www.vice.com/en_ca/article/a-bunch-of-white-canadian-editors-really-love-cultural-appropriation.

Hathcock, April. "Making the Local Global: The Colonialism of Scholarly Communication." *At the Intersection* (blog). September, 27, 2016. https://aprilhathcock.wordpress.com/2016/09/27/making-the-local-global-the-colonialism-of-scholarly-communication/.

Hathcock, April. "White Librarianship in Blackface: Diversity Initiatives in LIS." *In the Library with the Lead Pipe.* October 7, 2015. http://www.inthelibrarywiththeleadpipe.org/2015/lis-diversity/.

Hernandez, Jesus, Charles Brandquist, Helen Atwan, Gita Manaktala, and Rebecca McLeod. "Toward a Diverse Workforce in Scholarly Publishing: Strategies, Tactics and Lessons Learned." Presentation at the Society for Scholarly Publishing, Boston, MA, May 30-June 1, 2017.

Inefuku, Harrison and Charlotte Roh. "Agents of Diversity and Social Justice: Librarians and Scholarly Communication." In *Open Access and the Future of Scholarly Communication: Policy and Infrastructure*, edited by Kevin Smith and Katherine A. Dickson, 107–115. New York: Rowman and Littlefield, 2016

Jaschik, Scott. "The Wrong Reviewer." *Inside Higher Ed*. April 18, 2017. https://www.insidehighered.com/news/2017/04/18/history-journal-apologizes-assigning-review-book-urban-education-and-inequality.

Krishnamurthy, Meena. "Open Letter from the Editors of the Journal of Political Philosophy." *Philosopher*. May 25, 2017. https://politicalphilosopher.net/2017/05/25/open-letter-from-the-editors-of-the-journal-of-political-philosophy/.

Lee, Carole J., Cassidy R. Sugimoto, Guo Zhang, and Blaise Cronin. "Bias in Peer Review." *Journal of the American Society for Information Science and Technology* 64, no. 1 (January 2013). doi: 10.1002/asi.22784.

Low, Jason T., "Where is the Diversity in Publishing? The 2015 Diversity Baseline Survey Results." *The Open Book* (blog). January 26, 2016. http://blog.leeandlow.com/2016/01/26/where-is-the-diversity-in-publishing-the-2015-diversity-baseline-survey-results/#more-11897.

Morgan, Ashley (Assistant Managing Editor, *American Journal of Transplantation*). In conversation with the author, June 1, 2017.

Morris, Catherine. "Denied Tenure at Dartmouth, Aimee Bahng Feels Diversity Efforts Ring Hollow." *Diverse Issues in Higher Education*. May 18, 2016. http://diverseeducation.com/article/84350/

Noble, Safiya Noble. "Social Justice and Library Publishing." Presentation at the Library Publishing Forum, Baltimore, MD, March 20-22, 2017.

Olson, Hope A. "The Power to Name: Representation in Library Catalogs." *Signs* no. 3: 639 (2001).

Rosa, Kathy, and Kelsey Henke. "2017 ALA Demographic Study." *ALA Office of Research and Statistics.* January 2017. http://www.ala.org/research/sites/ala.org.research/files/content/Draft%20of%20Member%20Demographics%20Survey%2001-11-2017.pdf

Young, Michael Dunlop. *The Rise of the Meritocracy.* London: Thames and Hudson Publishers, 1958.

Chapter 17

Positionality, Epistemology, and New Paradigms for LIS: A Critical Dialog with Clara M. Chu

Todd Honma and Clara M. Chu

Introduction

Professor Clara M. Chu has spent her lifetime advocating on behalf of marginalized groups in the field of Library and Information Studies (LIS). In 2002, the American Library Association honored her with the Equality Award for her work in promoting equality in the library profession. She currently serves as the Director of the Mortenson Center for International Library Programs, and Mortenson Distinguished Professor at the University of Illinois Library at Urbana-Champaign. As a multilingual Peruvian-born Chinese Canadian and U.S. resident, Prof. Chu embodies many intersections: woman of color, immigrant, multicultural, transnational, having grown up in a working-class community. These intersectional identities have shaped how she sees the world and the myriad possibilities that libraries represent for those who occupy marginalized spaces, both domestically in the U.S. and within the global south. In particular, her influential scholarship on the topic of information justice and "transformative information services" has set a new standard for how we conceptualize and implement new ideals for twenty-first century librarianship. This chapter features a dialog between

Clara M. Chu and her former student and advisee, Todd Honma, allowing them to reconnect ten years after working together at the University of California, Los Angeles.

Positionality and Perspective in LIS

Todd: Hi Clara! Thank you for sitting down with me to share your insights and experiences. I think anyone who is familiar with you and your work can see the connections between your positionality and the types of efforts that you have been a part of, from the diversity, recruitment, and retention work you do at the institutional level to the various community-based projects you've spearheaded, both locally and internationally. One of the important lessons of feminist standpoint theory is that our positionality affects how we understand the world, and shapes the types of questions we ask and the types of knowledges that we create.[1] With such a unique positionality as your own, can you speak to how a critical understanding of one's positionality in the world can be a productive source for the work we do in LIS? Feel free to bring in examples from your own experiences!

Clara: I think growing up in a working-class community and as a child of immigrant parents in Peru and then Canada influenced how I see the information world. Because my parents weren't highly educated, I was not exposed to what would be called "high culture"—the performing arts, museums, etc. Instead, popular media was my reference, such as US/Hollywood movies or eating fast food—whatever was commonplace culturally in Canadian mainstream society that didn't make you look further. As an Asian immigrant, you're often viewed as a

1. Sandra G. Harding, *The Feminist Standpoint Theory Reader: Intellectual and Political Controversies* (New York: Routledge, 2004); Patricia Hill Collins, *Black Feminist Thought: Knowledge, Consciousness, and the Politics of Empowerment*, [2nd ed.] (New York: Routledge, 2009); Chela Sandoval, *Methodology of the Oppressed* (Minneapolis: University of Minnesota Press, 2000).

perpetual other.[2] In other words, because of your physical appearance, mainstream white society sees you as foreign and different. When you are racialized in such a way, you realize that your everyday experiences aren't the so-called 'norm,' requiring one to make that special effort to get to know what the rest of the world is about and what the rest of the world exactly sees. And when you're young, it's just easy to identify with the mainstream to fit in and hope that they will overlook your skin and the difference of experience that may come with it. I used libraries while growing up in Canada and it exposed me to the stories that my Canadian friends read, which formed the basis to participate in a collective experience and connect culturally with them.

Todd: So it sounds like your early experiences reflect how libraries can function as a tool of assimilation into normative white society…

Clara: In some respects, yes, libraries helped with that acculturation process. But framed another way, the library and information field helped me to understand my particular positionality in society as someone who didn't quite belong to the cultures that I was reading about. Libraries presented the opportunity to access knowledge and information about other cultures, other peoples, other histories and to learn about those who are more privileged, which in turn helped me to gain a critical perspective on how society is structured. In that sense, libraries can function as a space of critical inquiry and consciousness raising. Even if you may not have been born with certain types of privilege, libraries do offer the opportunity to gain knowledge and information, and through that, the ability to critique the systems that may oppress you and the potential to create change. So, I think the opportunity to gain that fuller picture, to know where information comes from, to know that you can access that information, especially through the internet these days, you don't need to settle for what the mass media provides, meaning you don't have to

2. Claire Jean Kim, "The Racial Triangulation of Asian Americans," *Politics & Society* 27, no. 1 (1999): 105–38.

be the recipient of just soundbites…it's important to question and see who is privileged and who is silenced.

Todd: Yes, and acknowledging the types of privileges highlights how information is not exempt from the power dynamics that are found in society at large, which I think the field of LIS hasn't always been keen on identifying or theorizing. But if we are to critically analyze libraries and other information institutions, we have to be able to contextualize them within broader social forces, including how information can be a contested site of privilege and inequality. From there we can begin to innovate the different possibilities and modes of transformation that can allow greater access and transparency for all. What might those types of possibilities look like, do you think?

Clara: I think that libraries offer a myriad of possibilities; in the global south and to some extent in the global north, libraries are their collections and places. I could easily see that from the way that my mother used to view libraries. When I asked her about going to the library, she said, 'Oh no, they are for more educated people.' As far as I know, she never stepped foot in a library. How do we change such preconceptions and outreach to marginalized communities who may not even think about using the library? For example, we can consider what outreach can do; even though my mother didn't go to the library, she did go to a church. She went because she was approached by individuals who would pick her up at the house and drive her to church every week, and so that kind of outreach may be necessary to ensure people have the opportunity to use the library, or even to just find out what a library has to offer. Thus, if libraries are to effectively function as a place that can smooth the path and connect you to information, creating innovative strategies for outreach and accessibility will allow people to connect with these spaces and figure out where they fit in in the world, and obtain more knowledge about what they can do and the opportunities that they have.

Todd: I'm glad you brought in that example because it illustrates how there can be a disconnect between our theoretical understanding of libraries versus the way that they play out on a practical level. In other words, the story about your mother helps us to understand how her particular views of the library—as an exclusionary space for educated people that doesn't include her—asks us to reevaluate how to implement better institutional strategies. Bringing it back to the concept of positionality—and what your mother's unique positionality asks us to think about—is that while we can be mindful of how our own social locations shape our views of the world, we need to also recognize that positionalities different from our own can highlight different sets of questions, concerns, and pathways to explore, in terms of research, practice, theory, etc.,[3] particularly if we start from a position that examines the life of non-library users and the types of obstacles—whether material or ideological—that prevent them from using libraries in the first place. How can we better incorporate these different perspectives into the work we do in LIS?

Clara: I think libraries can fall into the trap of feeling validated for the work that they do without being self-reflexive or critical about what's missing or what can be improved. If people are coming to the library, then it is easy to assume libraries are already addressing their needs. So if libraries are thinking of themselves in that way, then it goes back to what historian Wayne Wiegand has said about library scholars and educators as having blind spots and tunnel vision—we always think of users in the life of the library (oh they're here, they're using our resources, look at what we do for them) and that perspective shapes the research mindset of how we can do it better: we conduct a user study, we ask how can we provide more to solve their individual problems, and how can the library become a place to address their needs. What Wiegand has argued is that we need to look at the other side of the coin and ask the question: how are libraries a part of the life of

3. Harding, *The Feminist Standpoint Theory Reader.*

the user, how are libraries part of American life, American existence, and individual existence?[4] I think we need to look at things from both sides of the coin, not only to see libraries as the center, but also to see the center as the individual or society and how do libraries play a part. Libraries are being put in a position to see themselves more and more in this light. We are seeing a trend where libraries are being defunded; in the United Kingdom, public libraries are being closed. More of our politicians are questioning: with the availability of the internet, why do we need libraries? Libraries are seeing themselves as having to defend their position. Apart from statistics, we need to share stories about the meaning of libraries in the lives of people. By listening to these stories and expanding the scope of how we understand the role of libraries, we are able to connect to either individual or collective experiences and the meaning of libraries.

Todd: That's an important point, because the meaning of libraries can be different for different people and different communities, for example marginalized communities, working class communities, communities of color, etc. The more voices we are able to hear, the more questions and visions that we can consider. This is particularly true for voices that have been marginalized, suppressed, or delegitimized within the institution. For me, the opportunity to bring in new perspectives and expand the discursive field is one of the crucial aspects of efforts to "diversify." It's not just about serving an additive function of creating a more diverse pool or workforce, but it's about what those different experiences help us to understand that we would ordinarily overlook or take for granted. In that sense, diversity is an epistemological necessity in order to push the field and profession in new and exciting directions.[5]

---

4. Wayne A. Wiegand, "Tunnel Vision and Blind Spots: What the Past Tells Us about the Present; Reflections on the Twentieth-Century History of American Librarianship," *Library Quarterly* 69, no. 1 (1999): 1–32.

5. Laura Hyun Yi Kang, "Epistemologies," in *A Companion to Gender Studies*, ed. Philomena Essed, David Theo. Goldberg, and Audrey Lynn Kobayashi (Oxford: Wiley-Blackwell, 2009).

Clara: Since we are sharing stories and how understanding our position shapes our epistemology and new ways of doing, I want to ask you about you growing up and especially studying during a time when you were exposed to ethnic studies and how that has shaped your views. I find that fascinating, because I'm of the generation that was sort of in the middle, because the generation before me focused on practice, meaning that enhancing and addressing equal opportunities and diversity was about action—that is, providing services. But I think your generation started to question what information is out there and understanding that there are systems of power. Can you talk about whether exposure to ethnic studies has shaped the way you think about libraries and information, and in which ways?

Todd: I was of a generation that had exposure to ethnic studies, but I was also part of a generation that was pre-Internet. On one hand, I inherited a critical framework for understanding race and its intersections with other systems of oppression, but I was also growing up at a time when information wasn't as easily available as it is today. I took my first ethnic studies course in high school, and that gave me the language and tools to critique society through the lens of race and racial oppression, but at the same time I had to navigate the specific infrastructures of a non-digital library at the time. Even though I was equipped with these critical tools, I still had to figure out where to get information because it wasn't as easy as it is today when you can use Google or go online and find a lot of different sources. So part of my formative experience was with navigating the high school library and encountering the limitations of the library and realizing that such a library has a very specific type of collection development, which I felt didn't meet the needs of who I was as a student back then. For example, when I was looking for literature by queer people of color, I didn't find anything in the library—it was all white male authors. And so I turned to the public libraries in the city (San Francisco) and realized that those collections were limited as well.

Growing up, I was also involved in subcultural spaces, like the Bay Area music scene that had different sources of information, like zines, that weren't found in the space of the library at that time. All of these institutions combined—high school libraries, city libraries, and alternative libraries like info shops and zine spaces—helped me understand on an informal level how information is structured. I wouldn't have phrased it that way back then, but it gave me a sense of how there are different types of knowledges that are validated or not in different institutional settings. And when I say that, I think it's implicit that these forms of knowledges are racialized, gendered, classed, etc., in particular ways. I think that's really how ethnic studies helped me to not just conceptualize the world, but also navigate the world, understanding how certain types of information are not validated, that it's not just coincidental or individual, but part of an overall system that legitimizes certain people and their knowledge and marginalizes others.

Epistemology and Systems of Domination

Todd: We've been discussing the need for an epistemological expansion in how we think about LIS. I'm hoping we can turn to how this plays out structurally. When invoking the concept of intersectionality, there tends to be an emphasis on how the individual occupies intersectional identities, or what Kimberlé Crenshaw calls "multiple grounds of identity."[6] However, it is important to point out that Crenshaw's theorization of intersectionality underscores the interconnectedness of systems of oppression that shape the structural, political, and representational dimensions of identity. In the field of LIS, there tends to be an emphasis on the individual in lieu of the systemic, particularly when addressing topics related to race and racism, often euphemistically coded within the term "diversity." Can you elaborate on how you see this discourse of diversity functioning—or even impeding—critical conversations and why you think a structural approach is important to understanding intersectionality?

---

6. Kimberlé Crenshaw, "Mapping the Margins: Intersectionality, Identity Politics, and Violence against Women of Color," *Stanford Law Review* 43, no. 6 (1991): 1241–1299.

Clara: I think we can begin with the word diversity, which is commonly focused on our discreteness. These days, if we look at how diversity is understood, we talk about inherent diversity, which involves the traits that one is born with, versus acquired diversity, which are traits that one gains from experience. I think, regardless, people tend to look at diversity within the framework of how we can come together, to focus on the positive. But to focus on the positive brings up what you brought up in your article,[7] an emphasis on the celebratory aspect of diversity, which leads us to monthly celebrations of ethnicity or sexual orientation, etc. But simply recognizing difference doesn't move us forward, because we are still not seeing the interconnectedness of systems of oppression. The challenge in relying on a term such as "diversity" is that we are not confronting the systems of oppression that establish and exploit the various forms of group differentiation that institutionalize unequal distributions of wealth and privilege. For example, we might address particular issues that, say, Asian Americans need to work on or African Americans need to work on, rather than come up with an overall plan to tackle the system of racial discrimination that causes these issues in the first place. So, in terms of what we need to do in our field, I would say that it's a call to action where diversity needs to be an act not just of celebration, but of social justice, one that frames our need to teach information as power. Thus, whether it's in practice, research, or teaching one to become an LIS professional, we need to see information as power.

Todd: Can you elaborate on what you mean by "information as power," as opposed to "information is power"?

Clara: "Information is power" tends to be regarded as a statement, often a statement of some type of universal truth—if one possesses information, one possesses power. Implicit within that formulation

7. Todd Honma, "Trippin' Over the Color Line: The Invisibility of Race in Library and Information Studies," *InterActions: UCLA Journal of Education and Information Studies* 1, no. 2 (2005).

is, again, the emphasis on the individual, as the individual is the one who can possess information and thereby possess power. But such a statement doesn't ask you to rethink the overall system within which information functions, a system (as we've been discussing) that is steeped in privilege and oppression. "Information as power" asks that we take a more active and critical approach to how we understand information and its dynamic role in society.

Todd: I appreciate how you are conceptualizing information within a framework of a capacity for action. The recognition of information as power is important as a way to actively uncover and dismantle the systems of power and privilege that function within LIS. Yet, I am also cautious about operating at solely the level of the theoretical, so I was hoping you could give us some examples of how such power structures play out at the professional/practical level.

Clara: It plays out in a lot of different facets of the LIS field. For instance, in terms of recognizing information as power within information literacy, we can see this addressed in the last ACRL framework of information literacy (adopted in 2016), noting that information can be privileged, biased or invisible.[8] If we can teach people to be able to see these different elements, then we equip them with a critical understanding of how information is constructed within various fields of power. For example, that certain cultures or experiences or histories are privileged over others; or they may be stereotyped or simplified so that we only see certain things, which can serve particular political interests or agendas; or that they just don't exist, that we haven't documented them, so they are invisible. If we can teach that through information literacy, then we are enabling the ability to critique information systems as well as instilling agency, in order to uncover that which they haven't been able to learn yet, with the possibility for further action. Other aspects of the LIS

8. ACRL, "Framework for Information Literacy for Higher Education," *Association of College & Research Libraries (ACRL)*, January 11, 2016, http://www.ala.org/acrl/standards/ilframework.

field can take a similar approach. In terms of collection development, we need to see what is in our collections, what may be missing in our collections, or what are just stereotypical representations of experiences, communities, and cultures. We must be able to critically assess our programs and policies, and then reflect on how such reassessments provide opportunities to deepen our collective goals of social justice.

The polarization we are experiencing in our country and worldwide compel us to see how we are interconnected, the acts and experiences of those with privilege with those without, that communities are in a symbiotic relationship. This involves recognizing what you mentioned earlier about the interconnectedness of systems of oppression. If we can't get to a place where we can learn about the interconnectedness of systems of oppression, then I think it's up to our institutions, whether they're libraries or educational institutions, to initiate what may be uncomfortable conversations to get us to a place where we can have critical discussions. I think institutions such as libraries need to become that space of questioning what we don't know and experience what we don't know. And only through that particular questioning and dialogue can we come to a better place as a society, where libraries can be places where information is a potential for opportunity.

One of the things I really appreciated about the film *Hidden Figures* was the lesson the viewer learns from the scene where one of the African American women scientists isn't allowed to borrow a library book on Fortran programming as a result of practices of segregation of the time, so she takes it without permission. By learning to program on her own, she was promoted and helped advance the work of NASA. Without access to the information contained in the book, the loss would have been not just to the individual, but for society. This is a clear example how in popular media we are being exposed to what libraries can be and that which they are not, and also illustrates how systemic forms of discrimination can deny equitable access to information which, in turn, impacts one's ability to learn and to act on the world.

Todd: When you said you want libraries to be spaces to have critical conversations, do you think those critical conversations are currently going on? Or is that an aspirational model that libraries need to strive towards? And is simply having those types of conversations enough?

Clara: There are examples of celebrating the other or communication to learn about community information needs, which can lead us to knowing different histories, experiences, and cultures; but the kinds of conversations that I am referring to, which are to discuss our intersectionality in terms of understanding systems of oppression, that's more aspirational. I don't see those particular kinds of conversations happening. I see the ways that libraries have helped create opportunities: information about citizenship, information about getting access to health care, teaching people how to fill out job applications, and providing access to technology. While this is all good, if we don't have the conversations that open people's eyes to systems of oppression, then each of us are not conscious of our own culpability in allowing those systems to exist (including the role of libraries in perpetuating some of these very systems). I think that until we do what Paulo Freire talks about, which is to have a sense of *conscientization*, which means to become literate and be able to read the world around us so that we can act on it, act to help each other, then libraries have not fulfilled all that they can.[9] Of course, engaging in such conversations is just a first step within a much larger project of social transformation, but hopefully a step that will lead to further action. And while I applaud libraries for all the work that they do, I think we can go a lot further in uncovering those systems of oppression and allowing people to use information to change systems, especially to ensure that we do our civic duty and inform our politicians and administrators of things that need to be changed and things that continue to divide communities, privileging some and not others.

---

9. Paulo Freire and Donaldo P. Macedo, *Literacy: Reading the Word & the World* (South Hadley, Mass.: Bergin & Garvey Publishers, 1987).

Collaboration, Social Justice, and New Paradigms for LIS

Todd: You've opened up many conversations about issues of social justice in LIS, publishing work on "transformative information services" and furthering concepts such as "information justice," which I feel really challenges us to rethink the dominant paradigms in the field of LIS.[10] First, I must thank you for all your really important and influential work in linking LIS to social justice. Personally speaking, your reconceptualization of LIS to centralize the importance of social justice has been so instrumental—as well as inspiring—for my own work. You've written that one of your goals is to "eradicate the culture of silence created when individuals are oppressed by information practices/systems that deny them access and representation." In eradicating such a culture, what type of culture would you like to see take its place?

Clara: In terms of eradicating the culture of silence, I mean that in many different ways. For example, going beyond that which is not there, recognizing something that has not been published, or if there's biased information, doing something about it. Libraries have more opportunities with information and communication technologies to be a part of efforts where communities can create new information and knowledge that is authentic, where communities have agency in representing themselves, in ensuring that their histories are not forgotten, and that which represents their culture and their heritage is available for future generations to see themselves in and to learn from. Both agency as well as voice are critical parts of what libraries can support in offering collections of information. This can include providing tools to document silenced voices and publish alternative experiences to complement current collections, developing programs where this type of information can be shared, and creating digital repositories where all of this information can be housed. There's something called BiblioBoard where libraries are

10. Clara M. Chu, "Transformative Information Services: Uprooting Race Politics," in *Proceedings of the Black Caucus of the American Library Association Conference*, 19th-22nd July 1999, Las Vegas, 1999.

coming together and using technology where they can host information that is being published by their local communities and also highlight local information or specific types of information that may not readily be searchable on the Internet (e.g., materials that exist within library catalogs or on the "deep web").

These are just some examples, but I think what is more critical is a strategy that I have been embracing in my work, which is to not only to talk about social justice but to act to address social justice in the library and information field—whether as practitioner, educator, or scholar. This entails conceptualizing social justice as contributive justice, which Paul Gomberg describes in his book *How to Make Opportunity Equal: Race and Contributive Justice.*[11] Contributive justice is the process whereby each of us has the opportunity to contribute. By everyone contributing, then there will be the opportunity to ensure that all of our stories, all that we can offer, will be accessible to others. With all contributing, there is greater possibility of accessibility of a broader range of information. This is slightly different from distributive justice, which focuses on equitable distribution. One of the challenges of distributive justice is how do we ensure equitable distribution – a challenging formula to devise. If we embrace contributive justice, where everyone has the ethic of contributing, we all have a role to play, and everyone takes ownership in doing their part. Those who can contribute more will do so, while others may contribute less, but all contribute to the shared labor. I've been a proponent of such a framework for the library and information field.[12]

For example, for those scholars who are interested in doing work on racial issues and social justice, that they do so is of import, regardless of their particular racial or ethnic background. If all of us contribute to enhancing research in this field while recognizing our positionalities,

---

11. Paul. Gomberg, *How to Make Opportunity Equal: Race and Contributive Justice* (Malden, MA: Blackwell Pub., 2007).MA: Blackwell Pub., 2007

12. José Antonio Merlo-Vega and Clara M. Chu, "Out of Necessity Comes Unbridled Imagination for Survival: Contributive Justice in Spanish Libraries during Economic Crisis," *Library Trends* 64, no. 2 (2015): 299–328.

then there will be more voices to expand the discourse and to tackle the issues.

Todd: What specific role do you see women of color in the profession/field playing in creating new paradigms and advancing different or alternative ways of conceptualizing LIS?

Clara: I think that each of us, whether it's women of color or whatever perspective you come from, if we use a contributive justice lens, then you bring valuable contributions to the table, you bring those particular perspectives. As a woman of color, I would be able to tell you: these are my experiences, this is what doesn't work, this is what would help me to understand better, or learn better, or do something and contribute. So, somebody else, who might have more privilege and not have that information, would be able to then be part of that conversation and say, "I didn't realize this and I didn't know that by creating a system that does this, it reduced certain possibilities."

For example, what do libraries know about and offer on parenting for mothers of different cultures? What do we know about expectations for daughters raised in homes with different cultures? And whose frame of reference do we use in providing services to mothers and daughters in diverse communities? In many first-generation immigrant homes, different practices are exercised, but the needs of such immigrant mothers and daughters have not necessarily been accommodated in libraries. Libraries need to hear from different experiences, and when people such as women of color are able to have agency and voice their needs and perspectives—and not just voice them but work towards them—we can bring different concerns and different solutions to the table. If daughters of immigrants spoke, would libraries learn of potential feelings of cultural isolation and maybe even bullying because they practice their cultural heritage? This is a potential area where women of color in LIS can draw attention to unmet needs.

By voicing what works and what doesn't, we have the opportunity to ensure that we create systems that are more relevant, that might work better and create more opportunity and more access. Unless we can open up and allow more people to be at the table to share what those concerns are and what those needs are, we just end up working from limited knowledge and assume we have the answers based on that perspective. I think those are the blind spots and tunnel vision, as we talked about earlier—where we assume we've asked the right questions and gained the right responses, when actually we haven't given the opportunity for people to speak for themselves.

Todd: I appreciate how you are linking experiential knowledge to how that can then potentially create change at the systemic level and how we all need to contribute to that process. I think the examples also highlight how essential a praxis-oriented approach is for LIS—meaning, embracing the inter-connected components of critical reflection, dialogue, and collaborative action—a model of LIS that allows for us to constantly be re-evaluating the work that we do within an overall context of trying to create a more just, egalitarian, and sustainable world.

Clara: I'd like to get your insights about the shifting paradigms in LIS. Having worked in a library, having studied library and information science, and now as a faculty member in Asian American Studies, do you see new paradigms for LIS and if so, what are they, and what does it mean for where we should go from here?

Todd: I agree with what you discussed earlier about the necessity of bringing critical conversations to LIS that are sensitive to issues of power, privilege, and forms of structural disenfranchisement. Certainly, Library Juice Press comes to mind, since they are publishing a lot of cutting edge work, making connections between libraries and questions of oppression (along the lines of class, race, gender, sexuality, etc.). I also appreciate the discussions that are taking place in the open access journal *In the Library with the Lead Pipe*. I think it's hard to say whether these critical approaches will be actual paradigms that will shift the field, but we can say they are *emerging* paradigms. We'll have to wait and see how much traction they can gain in a field that is still resistant to embracing new paradigms. This is why I always try to be critical about asking: what are the systems you are inheriting and how much do you agree with them, and if you don't, how can you actively transform them rather than simply continuing to reproduce them? I think there's a certain level of complacency in how we have inherited problematic legacies of talking about oppression in very convoluted terms—for example, in how we talk about race in LIS, using terms like diversity or multiculturalism, that don't get us to address structures of oppression. With this new movement of critical research, we are actually naming forms of oppression, and the next step is to figure out what actions can be implemented. The strategies you mentioned earlier in terms of forms of action predicated on the ethos of praxis and collaboration and contribution, those aspects are so important because they get us to rethink the forms of engagement that are possible, to rethink the more stagnant model of libraries that we've inherited but that we know in practice has the potential to be so much more. There are a lot of dynamic things that need to be done. To quote Ruth Wilson Gilmore, infiltrate what's there and innovate what's not![13]

It is going to take a while, and it's not going to be instantaneous, but I hope the work that we do—the collective "we" as in all the scholars currently doing this critical research on intersectional politics in LIS, the practitioners who are doing the necessary work of implementing innovative library programs, as well as the work that the journals and publishers are doing in putting these voices out there—is laying the foundation for things to change.

Clara: It's been over ten years since you published your "Trippin' Over the Color Line" article.[14] How do you see the state that we're at?

---

13. Ruth Wilson Gilmore, "What Is to Be Done?," *American Quarterly* 63, no. 2 (2011): 245–265.

14. Honma, "Trippin' Over the Color Line."

Todd: Well, I wrote that article to bring in a critical language to LIS that I felt was absent, and I think it has definitely opened up conversations, judging by the way that it has been received—it seems to be a lot more popular now than when it was published ten years ago! I would leave it up to this next generation to continue this work…

Clara: Thank you, I've had the opportunity to learn since we last were able to work together as faculty and student, not necessarily with clear answers but in continuing to open up the conversation. If we don't move in that direction, then the lost opportunities will just send us spiraling into a deeper abyss.

Todd: And we certainly can't have that!

Bibliography

ACRL. "Framework for Information Literacy for Higher Education." *Association of College & Research Libraries (ACRL).* January 11, 2016. http://www.ala.org/acrl/standards/ilframework.

Chu, Clara M. "Transformative Information Services: Uprooting Race Politics." In *Proceedings of the Black Caucus of the American Library Association Conference, 19th-22nd July 1999, Las Vegas*, 1999.

Collins, Patricia Hill. *Black Feminist Thought: Knowledge, Consciousness, and the Politics of Empowerment.* [2nd ed.]. New York: Routledge, 2009.

Crenshaw, Kimberlé. "Mapping the Margins: Intersectionality, Identity Politics, and Violence against Women of Color." *Stanford Law Review* 43, no. 6 (1991): 1241–1299.

Freire, Paulo, and Donaldo P. Macedo. *Literacy: Reading the Word & the World.* South Hadley, Mass.: Bergin & Garvey Publishers, 1987.

Gilmore, Ruth Wilson. "What Is to Be Done?" *American Quarterly* 63, no. 2 (2011): 245–265.

Gomberg, Paul. *How to Make Opportunity Equal: Race and Contributive Justice.* Malden, MA: Blackwell Pub., 2007.

Harding, Sandra G. *The Feminist Standpoint Theory Reader: Intellectual and Political Controversies.* New York: Routledge, 2004.

Honma, Todd. "Trippin' Over the Color Line: The Invisibility of Race in Library and Information Studies." *InterActions: UCLA Journal of Education and Information Studies* 1, no. 2 (2005).

Kang, Laura Hyun Yi. "Epistemologies." In *A Companion to Gender Studies*, edited by Philomena Essed, David Theo. Goldberg, and Audrey Lynn Kobayashi. Oxford: Wiley-Blackwell, 2009.

Kim, Claire Jean. "The Racial Triangulation of Asian Americans." *Politics & Society* 27, no. 1 (1999): 105–138.

Merlo-Vega, José Antonio, and Clara M. Chu. "Out of Necessity Comes Unbridled Imagination for Survival: Contributive Justice in Spanish Libraries during Economic Crisis." *Library Trends* 64, no. 2 (2015): 299–328.

Sandoval, Chela. *Methodology of the Oppressed.* Minneapolis: University of Minnesota Press, 2000.

Wiegand, Wayne A. "Tunnel Vision and Blind Spots: What the Past Tells Us about the Present; Reflections on the Twentieth-Century History of American Librarianship." *Library Quarterly* 69, no. 1 (1999): 1–32.

About the Contributors

Negeen Aghassibake is a student at the University of Texas at Austin School of Information (M.S. 2018). She is currently an Assessment Graduate Research Assistant at the University of Texas Libraries, a Collections Intern at the Texas State Historical Association, and a volunteer at the Dell Children's Medical Center Library and Family Resource Center.

Tarida Anantachai is an Outreach Librarian at the Syracuse University Libraries. She received her MS in Library and Information Science from the University of Illinois at Urbana-Champaign and her BA in English and American Literature from Brandeis University. Her research interests include diversity and inclusion, early career development and mentoring, and outreach programming. Prior to her stint in librarianship, Tarida also worked for several years in the academic publishing industry.

Robin Bradford is Collection Development Librarian at Timberland Regional Library in Tumwater, WA, and a regular contributor for *Library Journal*, *Booklist's* Corner Shelf, and various online blogs specializing in genre fiction and publishing. She received her B.A. in English from Monmouth College, M.A. in English from Indiana State University, M.S. in library science and information studies from University of Illinois at Urbana-Champaign, and her J.D. from Indiana University School of Law–Indianapolis. In 2016, she was named the Cathie Linz Librarian of the Year by the Romance Writers of America. She's dedicated to increasing the diversity of library collections to reflect the diversity of every community.

Kawanna Bright is a PhD candidate in the University of Denver's Morgridge College of Education Research Methods & Statistics Program, focusing on assessment in libraries. Prior to returning to school full-time, Ms. Bright was an academic librarian who, over the span of twelve years, held positions as the Head of Information & Research Services at the Florida International University, Green Library; Head of Information Services & Student Engagement at the University of Texas at San Antonio; Instructional Services Librarian at NCSU; and Instructional Services Librarian and Minority Resident Librarian at the University of Tennessee, Knoxville. She is a 2003 graduate of the University of Washington, iSchool. One of Ms. Bright's main research areas is diversity in libraries, a topic she engaged with throughout her career. Ms. Bright has both served on and chaired diversity committees within two academic libraries, participated in diversity-based professional development programs—including serving as a keynote speaker, engaged in diversity-related research, and served as a diversity consultant. Most recently, Ms. Bright and her co-researcher were awarded the Beta Phi Mu/LRRT Research Round Table Research Paper Award for their paper titled *Including the Voices of Librarians of Color in Reference and Information Services Work*. Ms. Bright will be applying the quantitative and qualitative research skills from her PhD program training directly to her library assessment work, including her work on assessing diversity in libraries.

Jennifer Brown is the Emerging Technologies Coordinator in Columbia University Libraries' Digital Scholarship division; her role involves researching and acquiring novel technologies, and coordinating the division's instructional efforts at large. She also teaches information literacy sessions for Columbia's first-year undergraduate writing classes, serves as Vice Chair / Chair Elect of LITA's Diversity and Inclusion Committee, and sits on a university-wide Race, Ethnicity, and Inclusion Task Force. She holds an M.S. in Information (LIS specialization) from the University of Michigan's School of Information and a B.A. in Media Studies from the University of California, Berkeley.

Genevia M. Chamblee-Smith has five years of experience working in academic and special libraries. She currently works as a Contract Librarian for the International Food Policy Research Institute (IFPRI) in Washington, DC Her research interests include promoting diverse and inclusive work environments in libraries, peer mentoring, and critical pedagogy within librarianship. She is an avid football fan and enjoys knitting socks.

Camille Chesley is a Reference Librarian and Subject Librarian for Journalism at the University at Albany Libraries. She received her MS in Library and Information Science from the University of Illinois at Urbana-Champaign and her BA in East Asian Studies from Oberlin College. Her research interests include gaming and gamification in library instruction, information literacy assessment, critical librarianship, and diversity and inclusion in LIS.

Clara M. Chu is the Director of the Mortenson Center for International Library Programs and Mortenson Distinguished Professor at the University of Illinois at Urbana-Champaign. She specializes in the social construction of library and information use, practices, and systems that impact access and collective memory in multicultural communities. Her graduate degrees are from Western University (Canada). She serves on the editorial boards of *Libri* and *Library Trends*, and co-edits the International Insights Column of *College & Research Libraries News*.

Sojourna Cunningham is the Social Sciences and Assessment Librarian at the University of Richmond. Her research interests include studying the user experience within the academic library, specifically relating to improving patron interactions with the library as a physical and digital space. Her other interests include innovative library assessment, librarian education, and inclusion efforts for librarians of color within the profession. Sojourna is a 2014 American Library Association Emerging Leader and is an alumnus of the Minnesota Institute for Early Career Librarians from Traditionally Underrepresented Groups. Sojourna will complete a Masters in Liberal Arts with a concentration in Public History from the University of Richmond in 2018. She also holds a Masters in Library Science from the University of North Carolina at Chapel Hill and a BA from the University of Pittsburgh.

Jan E. Estrellado, PhD, is a licensed psychologist whose research focuses on the intersections of race, ethnicity, and trauma in therapy settings. She is specifically interested in examining clinicians' competencies treating people of color who are also trauma survivors. She is the Associate Director of Clinical Training for Psychology at Sharp Mesa Vista Hospital. Jan's clinical work focuses on issues related to sexual orientation, gender identity, race and ethnicity, as well as with anxiety disorders, depression, and trauma recovery. Jan is a lecturer at San Diego State University teaching classes on multicultural counseling, trauma, and stress management, and she also maintains a small private practice.

Fobazi M. Ettarh is a Student Success Librarian at California State, Dominguez Hills. A school librarian by training, she specializes in information literacy instruction, K-12 educational pedagogy, and co-curricular outreach. Her research interests include critical pedagogy; equity, diversity, and inclusion within librarianship; and the intersections of organizational structures, power, and labor. Recently, she coined and defined the concept of *vocational awe*, as seen in the article "Vocational Awe and Librarianship: The Lies We Tell Ourselves." Fobazi was recognized as a 2017 ALA Emerging Leader.

JoyEllen Freeman is the Outreach and Special Collections Archivist in the Department of Museums, Archives and Rare Books at Kennesaw State University. She holds a bachelor's degree in English from the University of Georgia and a master's degree in Archival Studies from Clayton State University. JoyEllen is certified as an archivist by the Academy of Certified Archivists. Before arriving at Kennesaw State University, JoyEllen worked as an intern for various archival repositories, including the Archives Research Center at the Atlanta University Center Robert W. Woodruff Library, the Internet Archive, the National Archives at Atlanta, the Roswell Historical Society, and the Fulton County Teaching Museum. JoyEllen is co-chair of the Teaching with Primary Sources Committee within the Society of American Archivists and serves as Mentoring Program Assistant Manager for the Society of Georgia Archivists. She has published articles and chapters in various professional publications, including *Archival Issues* (2016) and *Participatory Heritage* (2017).

LaVerne Gray, MSEd, MLIS, a native of Chicago, Illinois, is a PhD Candidate at the College of Communication and Information at the University of Tennessee-Knoxville with a concentration in Information Sciences. LaVerne is an American Library Association Spectrum Doctoral Fellow, which provides financial support and mentorship for students of color pursuing a Doctorate in LIS. She was a librarian for eight years at three different universities (Texas A&M, University of Illinois at Chicago, and the University of Tennessee Knoxville). LaVerne was inspired to become a librarian through her work in the Peace Corps, during which she spent over two years in the Ivory Coast and Togo, West Africa. She enjoys researching the role of women of color in information/library access in socioeconomically disadvantaged communities.

Shelley P. Haley received her doctorate in Classical Studies from the University of Michigan. She is one of a very small group of women of African descent who are professional classicists. Her research includes the role of a classical education in the lives and activism of nineteenth century Black women who earned college degrees in the United States, including Fannie Jackson Coppin, Anna Julia Cooper, and Mary Church Terrell. Currently she is a professor of Africana Studies and Classics at Hamilton College where she teaches courses on black feminist thought, critical race feminism, Cleopatra, and Cicero.

Todd Honma is currently an assistant professor of Asian American Studies at Pitzer College. He holds masters degrees in Information Studies and Asian American Studies from UCLA and a PhD in American Studies and Ethnicity from USC.

Sofia Leung (she/hers), a first generation Chinese American and a native New Yorker, is the Teaching and Learning Program Manager and liaison to the department of Comparative Media Studies/Writing at the Massachusetts Institute of Technology. She believes that social justice work is library work and that we should all be collectively engaged in our liberation. Sofia is focused on building community among people of color in libraries and beyond.

Rosalinda Hernandez Linares is the Information Literacy and Special Initiatives Librarian at Oberlin College, where she coordinates the development and evaluation of information literacy initiatives and is a liaison to the Politics, Anthropology, French, Italian, and Hispanic Studies departments. She was previously the Diversity Residency Librarian at the University of Louisville. Rosalinda holds a Master of Information and Library Science degree from the University of Pittsburgh and a BA in Classical Civilizations from Wellesley College. She co-authors an annual, comprehensive bibliography in *Reference Services Review* on library instruction and information literacy in school, academic, and special libraries.

Alyse Minter is a Research and Instruction Librarian for Education at Towson University, where she supports graduate students studying instructional technology, reading education, and educational leadership. Her research interests include education and multiliteracies, critical race theory, gender studies, African American studies, and organization and leadership development. Alyse is a first-year doctoral student in the Language, Literacy, and Culture program at the University of Maryland, Baltimore County (UMBC).

Alexsandra Mitchell is a Brooklyn-based international research scholar whose work explores the African Diaspora, spirituality, and the arts. She presently serves as a reference librarian and an archivist at the Schomburg Center for Research in Black Culture, New York Public Library. Prior to joining the staff in the Manuscripts, Archives, and Rare Books Division, Alexsandra was a lecturer at New York University's Gallatin School for Individualized Study and worked with institutions such as National Geographic Television, the Library of Congress, the West African Research Center in Dakar, Senegal, the New York Historical Society, and the Weeksville Heritage Center in Brooklyn, New York. Her many fellowships and awards include a National Diversity in Libraries Conference travel award, the Academy Awards Documenting Cinema Film Librarians Conference travel award, and two scholarships from the Rare Book School at the University of Virginia. Alexsandra is curator of the Schomburg Center's "Live from the Reading Room: Correspondence" podcast series, "Live from the Archive" programming series, and the Schomburg Center's community archives program, "Everyday Archives." She is also a first-year doctoral student in Cornell University's Africana Studies program and the co-author of *Research Techniques and Strategies for the Study of Black Writings*, forthcoming from Rowman & Littlefield.

Nisha Mody is a Health & Life Sciences Librarian at UCLA and a recent graduate from the Library and Information Science program at the University of Illinois at Urbana-Champaign. Before entering the library world, she worked as a speech therapist and in IT consulting. She is interested in critical librarianship and social justice, especially as it relates to reference and instruction within the health sciences. She is a First Year Academic Librarian Experience blogger for ACRLog, was Consulting Editor and Contributing Writer for *Hack Library School*, and enjoys writing creative non-fiction in her spare time.

Alanna Aiko Moore is the Ethnic Studies, Gender Studies and Sociology Librarian at the University of California, San Diego (UCSD) Library. She joined the library in 2006 and is also the Liaison Librarian to UCSD's Campus Community Centers. Alanna completed her MLIS at Dominican University and her undergraduate studies at Lewis and Clark College. Prior to entering the library profession, Alanna was a community organizer and trainer at non-profits in the Pacific Northwest and Chicago, working on racial and gender justice, queer youth empowerment, and criminal justice reform. Her research interests include mentoring for librarians of color, the lived experiences of women of color and queer women of color librarians, intersectionality, and critical information literacy. Alanna has collaborated with librarian-activists on national and local presentations, book chapters, articles, and webinars. Alanna is a Spectrum Scholar, a past fellow of the ARL Leadership and Career Development Program, and has received the ACRL University Libraries Section Outstanding Professional Development Award. She has served on the Joint Conference of Librarians of Color Steering Committee, the Asian Pacific American Librarians Association Executive Board, and the UCSD Lesbian Gay Bisexual and Transgender Resource Center's Advisory Board. She is also active in the Spectrum Advisory Committee, the Gay Lesbian Bisexual Transgender Roundtable of ALA and in ACRL.

Lalitha Nataraj is an Instruction and Reference Librarian at California State University, San Marcos University Library and an adjunct librarian at MiraCosta College. Before serving in her current role, Lalitha spent several years as a public librarian championing adult and early literacy resources and programs, as well as advocating for the inclusion of diverse materials in children's and teen library collections. Her professional interests include: feminist pedagogy, critical information literacy, and scholarly inquiry and the research cycle.

Teresa Y. Neely is professor of librarianship and assessment librarian in the College of the University Libraries & Learning Sciences, University of New Mexico, Albuquerque, NM. Dr. Neely has worked in academic research libraries for more than twenty years and is the author or co-author/editor of six books and conference proceedings. She has authored/co-authored numerous scholarly peer-reviewed articles, book chapters, conference papers, and a white paper for ACRL. Her current research agenda includes African American and Native American rap and hip-hop lyrics as activist narrative; women and the economic enterprise in the nineteenth-century southwest, and text and sentiment analysis in social media data.

Caitlin M. J. Pollock is the Digital Humanities and Africana Studies librarian for the Center for Digital Scholarship at Indiana University-Purdue University Indianapolis's University Library. She holds a Master's degree in Library and Information Science from Pratt Institute and an M.A. in Digital Humanities from Loyola University Chicago. Her research interests include the role of librarians in digital humanities research and pedagogy, library history, Black digital humanities, and nineteenth-century African American female activists.

Alyssa Jocson Porter is a Filipina-American, tenure-track librarian at Seattle Central College where she is the liaison to STEM and creative arts programs. She was named an American Library Association Emerging Leader in 2016, and is an active member of the Asian/Pacific American Librarians Association, having served on the Communications & Media Committee, Literature Awards Committee, and Executive Board. When she doesn't have her librarian hat on, Alyssa likes to spend her time relaxing with her husband and their dog, Astro.

Charlotte Roh is the Scholarly Communications Librarian at the University of San Francisco, a Jesuit University with a social justice mission. Her background is in academic publishing and she discovered she was allergic to cats in library school at Urbana-Champaign.

Stephanie Sendaula is an Associate Editor at *Library Journal*, where she edits reviews of nonfiction titles and contributes to feature articles, among other responsibilities. She received her M.L.I.S. from Drexel University and her B.A. in journalism from Temple University. She was previously a public librarian in New Jersey handling reference, instruction, and collection development. As a public librarian, she became an advocate for comics and graphic novels as well as diversity in all forms of literature, all of which she is still passionate about today.

Gayatri Singh is the Reference & Information Services Coordinator, and Librarian for Communication at the University of California, San Diego. She received her Master's degree in Library Science at the University of North Carolina, Chapel Hill. The first librarian in her life, Eleanor Peterson, introduced her to reading and coffee, which eventually led her down the path to librarianship. Her professional interests include: critical librarianship, research services, instruction, and outreach.

Sharon Spence-Wilcox is a Black Jamaican immigrant who credits her family for her love of learning and questioning. She is a tenured librarian at Seattle Central College and liaison to Humanities, ESL, and ABE programs. In 2014 she received the Excellence in Teaching, Learning, and Service Award from her peers. Her interests include the integration of contemplative practices with anti-oppression pedagogies and social justice education. Music nourishes Sharon's soul and she balances work and home life with an eclectic soundtrack.

Kimberly Tate-Malone is an African-American recently tenured librarian at Seattle Central College. She is currently the liaison to the Allied Health B.A.S. programs, but has previously liaised with the Science and Math Division. Kimberly's research interests include: the intersections of race and gender in librarianship, critical and anti-bias pedagogy, open access, and patient-centered care. In her spare time, Kimberly enjoys reading, cooking, eating, and pretending to be both athletic and handy.

Aditi Worcester is the Processing Archivist at California State University at San Marcos. Prior to this, she has worked in special collections (UCSD), helped manage and develop community archives (Escondido

Public Library), and preserve state government records (Texas State Library and Archives Commission). She received her Master's degree in Library and Information Studies at the University of Texas at Austin. Her research interests include usability, access, and outreach.

INDEX

A

academic librarian(s), 125, 352, 367, 369-82; *see also* **librarian(s)**
of color, 7, 175, 207-10, 228, 255, 269, 303
as care workers, 301, 306, 307
academic librarianship, 35, 38, 206, 334; *see also* **librarianship**
and multiculturalism, 253-57, 269
and women of color librarians, 304, 329, 330
activism, 16, 23, 35, 204, 354
library, 17, 23-36, 44, 54, 371-78
and women of color librarians, 349, 354-56, 361, 369, 374-79, 383
Andrews, Regina Anderson, 18, 23-30, 32-38, 47-53

B

Belpré, Pura Teresa, 18, 30-35, 38, 43, 51
Beyoncé, 121-3, 126, 135, 137
bias(es), 207, 209, 351, 417, 431, 439, 443, *see also* **implicit bias**
gender, 352-3
in hiring, 288, 339
racial, 52, 305, 353
Black bourgeoisie, 19, 24, 25
Black librarian(s), 37, 52, 61-2, 64, 182, 185, 379, 382; *see also* **librarian(s)**
dearth of, 123, 131, 137
expectations for, 53, 54, 376
and systemic oppression, 371-2
bodily misrecognition, 262, 264

C

collection development, 166, 310, 402, 420
appropriate policies for, 393, 416-19, 457
balance in, 110, 111
bias in, 34, 417, 453
neutrality in, 418-23
colonialism, 3, 97, 432
colorism, 42, 47-49, 51
community(ies), 2, 10-1, 18, 21, 83, 106, 222, 235, 261, 266, 268
and archivists, 394, 395
Asian American, 205
Black, 32, 153, 158
of color, 48, 152, 200-1, 206, 219, 228-9, 238, 309, 320, 452
and collection development, 415-20, 457
diverse, 186, 235, 337-42, 351, 461, 468
ethnic, 254, 396
Indigenous, 365
Latina, 203-4
LGBTQ, 368, 419
of librarians, 156, 158, 198, 240, 259-61, 309
marginalized, 88, 201, 212, 305, 357, 393, 395, 450, 452
minority, 111, 186

Muslim, 78-89, 98
Puerto Rican, 30, 32
role of libraries in, 27-32, 80
South Asian, 93, 98-103, 108-15
and support networks, 10, 381
underrepresented, 106, 114, 205, 235, 409
community colleges, 274, 288
Crenshaw, Kimberlé Williams, 3, 198, 454
critical race theory, 3, 6, 18, 241, 471, 473
cultural taxation, 288, 301-05, 308, 313, 320
culture, 31, 84, 126, 168, 200, 203, 439, 448, 459
of academia, 281, 285
American, 34, 405
dominant, 97, 200, 306
majority, 238, 304, 306, 307, 437
performance, 331, 332
popular, 85, 97
South Asian, 107, 112-15
workplace, 209, 210, 255

D

data, 53, 99, 114, 178, 189, 240-1, 275, 308, 358, 382, 413, 417,
analysis of, 176-78, 189, 190, 309
qualitative secondary, 176, 189
qualitative, 213, 405, 410
quantitative, 213, 405, 410
collection methodology, 177, 189, 190, 255, 322, 357-64
on gender makeup of faculty/tenured faculty in higher ed., 302, 304, 310
meta-, 408, 442
on tenure and promotion, 310-1, 320
database(s), 407, 418
deep acting, *see also* **emotional labor, surface acting**
and emotional labor, 168-9, 178
and librarians, 172, 183, 188, 277
and women of color librarians, 282, 290-1
demographic(s), 81, 163, 166, 206, 215-6, 431
of LIS, 2, 64, 205, 333, 418, 427
participant, 275-6, 308-10, 321, 363, 408
of publishing, 428-31
of South Asians in U.S., 95, 99
diversity, 53, 173, 207, 398, 400
and inclusion, 228, 231, 257, 329, 443
diversity work, 210, 227, 230, 311-15, 330-45
Du Bois, W.E.B., 27, 28, 38, 49

E

emotional burden, 337, 342, 345
emotional labor, 6, 10, 52, 106, 168-9, 172, 178, 274, 278-9, 302, *see also* **invisible labor; deep acting; surface acting**
concept of, 166, 168, 277, 279
and intersectionality in librarianship, 167, 330

in library work, 10, 170-72, 283, 287, 294-96
and public services work in LIS, 163, 169, 170, 175-8
and stereotypes of gendered professions, 164, 165
of women of color librarians, 163, 175, 228, 273-75, 282, 288-90
emotive dissonance, 169, 171, 178, 183

F

feminism, 5, 12, 201, 203-4, 235, 256
Black, 52, 202, 355
indigenous, 201-04
white, 4, 155
feminist theory, 6, 18, 46, 201, 241, 255, 448

G

Great Migration, 51-2
gender identity, 11, 39, 174, 240, 319-20, 364, 368
and burden of care, 308, 313-4
and cultural taxation, 308, 313

H

Harlem Renaissance, 18, 25-27, 47, 52
hate crime(s), 77-8, 89, 98, 110
heritage, 103, 236, 367, 400, 459
Black girls, 137, 391
cultural, 31, 105, 393, 461
ethnic, 213-15
racial, 214, 215
homophobia, 39, 255, 371-2, 381
hooks, bell, 3, 147-8, 157
Hughes, Langston, 26, 30, 47
Hurston, Zora Neale, 29, 30, 47
Hutson, Jean Blackwell, 61, 70

I

identity(ies), 4-5, 39-40, 82, 84, 96-7, 213-15, 238, 257, 260, 264, 340, 394, 415, *see also* **intersectional identity; gender identity; social identity**
American, 106, 286
Black women, 150, 418
cultural, 96, 99, 188
ethnic, 213-15, 247, 422
formation of, 255, 259, 260
issues of, 253, 262, 349
of librarians, 46, 260, 261, 264, 304, 367
marginalized, 4, 22, 199, 330
multidimensional, 85, 261, 262
multiple, 87, 152, 257, 357, 363-69
Muslim, 77, 85, 88
negotiating, 319-21
oppressed, 238, 355
personal, 214, 250
professional, 115, 158, 213, 216, 250, 340
racial, 115, 213-15, 247, 313
South Asian, 99, 109
and women of color, 197-200, 205-11, 261, 262
and women of color librarians, 279, 303-06, 349, 367

immigrant(s), 99, 108, 377, 447-8
European, 19, 51, 52
first or second-generation, 205, 281, 367, 438, 461
South Asian, 102, 107, 109
Immigration Acts, 95, 107
implicit bias
of the Dewey Decimal system, 34
and leadership among WOC librarians, 239, 283, 284
in the library workplace, 318, 439
imposter syndrome, 316, 435
Information and Communication Technology (ICT), 361-2, 459
institutionalized racism, 108, 130, 132, 278, 288, 293, 371
intersectional identity(ies), 22, 77, 86-8, 157, 189, 263, 330, 368, 383, 447, 454
and diversity work for librarians, 342-3
and WOC, 166, 198, 216, 275, 303
intersectionality(ies), 198, 204, 254, 290, 155, 353, 367, 381, 454, 458
and Black female librarianship, 16, 148
concept/theory of, 4-7, 18, 155, 165, 454
and LIS, 6, 7, 165, 167, 263
of race/ethnicity, gender, culture, and sexual orientation, 163-68, 178, 190, 277, 287
in reference and information work, 163, 190, 285
and women of color librarians, 155, 365-68
invisible labor, 173-5, 190, 374,
concept of, 166, 172
and the intersection of race/ethnicity and gender, 163-67
and mentoring, 184, 188
and RIS, 163, 167, 175-78, 187, 191
and tokenism, 184, 188
and women of color librarians, 178, 187-91
Islamophobia, 77-83, 89, 97-8

J

justice, 203, 460-1, *see also* **social justice**

L

labor, 107, 202, 221, 302, 314, 374, 383, 460, see also emotional labor, invisible labor
feminized, 7, 263
racialized, 202, 279
traditional, 283, 292
Larsen, Nella, 18-24, 29-34, 38, 41, 50, 381
librarian(s), *see also* **academic librarian(s); women of color librarian(s); Black librarian(s); public librarian(s**
Asian, 180, 184-5
collection development, 416, 419, 420
and emotional labor, 182-3, 188

first wave, 35, 47, 49-51
and invisible labor, 184, 187
Latina, 181, 183, 186-7
Muslim women, 78-82, 85
school, 180
South Asian American, 93, 97, 99, 107, 109, 115
librarianship, 64, 103, 427, *see also* **academic librarianship**
Black female, 16, 18
critical, 6, 7, 35, 219, 334
public, 35, 81, 84
whiteness of, 53, 257
Lorde, Audrey, 3, 18, 35, 39, 41-46, 52, 147, 291, 381

M

mentorship, 212, 267, 294
microaggression(s), 2, 3, 10, 78, 106, 130, 214
gender-based, 280, 356
and librarianship, 254, 285, 286, 318-23
racial, 208, 280, 351, 356
and self-care, 291-93
systemic, 125, 307
and women of color librarians, 207, 225, 226, 282, 287
in the workplace, 338, 342, 343
model minority, 107-09, 204, 438
movement(s), 25, 353, 355
Black Arts, 18, 52
Black Lives Matter, 432
Black Power, 37, 52
Civil Rights, 44, 370
feminist, 9, 18, 203, 204, 353
literacy, 15, 16
mujerista, 204, 235, 239
multiculturalism, 253, 255-57, 268, 463
Muslim Journeys Bookshelf, 86-7

N

network(s), 291, 323 *see also* **support network(s)**
information, 208-9
social, 97, 127-8, 157, 199, 213
neutrality, 89, 340, 359, 418
norm(s), 53, 136, 170, 226, 236, 278-9, 307, 358, 439-40

O

Obama, Michelle, 121-23, 135
oppression, 155, 203-4, 237, 330, 354, 358, 453, 462-3, *see also* **systems of oppression**
multiplicities of, 154, 353
systemic, 8, 157, 337, 371
in the workplace, 370, 375
outreach, 102
archival, 408, 410
community, 82, 85, 450
methods of, 402, 410, 411
power structure(s), 4, 152, 155, 431
in the library, 371-2, 456
white, 17, 51-2
in the workplace, 158-9, 210

P

predominantly white institution (PWI), 36, 122, 314, 317, 330, 436

privilege, 204, 368, 417, 455

systems of, 6, 337, 456

white, 320, 436

public librarian(s), 78-81, 89, 102-3, 106, 108, 112, 368, 374

publishing

academic, 432, 438

demographics of, 427-8

and librarianship, 427-8

and scholarly communication, 428, 431, 437-9, 441-2

Q

queer theory, 6, 241, 358

R

racial battle fatigue, 279, 282, 288, 355

racialization, 83, 98

racism, 27, 34, 54, 81, 83, 109, 125-6, 200, 255, 305, 356, *see also* **institutionalized racism**

and Black women, 147, 207

implicit, 53, 371

in the library profession, 131, 132, 351, 454

structural, 136, 372

systemic, 201, 207, 342

and white people, 133, 293

recruitment, 174, 264, 323

diversity, 106, 114, 153, 154

of librarians of color, 2, 6, 81, 174, 205, 206, 266

retention, 230-1, 205-7, 209-10, 213, 230-1, 255-6

of faculty of color, 295, 323

of/for librarians of color, 154, 174, 238, 266, 383

programs, 153-4

of women of color librarians, 240, 295, 382

Ranganathan, S.R., 17, 115

S

self-care, 16, 213, 241, 251, 291, 294, 336, 381

practice of, 292-3, 379, 380

and women of color librarians, 349, 356, 379-83

sexism, 18, 38, 104, 203, 207, 305, 338, 437

in LIS, 52, 371, 372, 381

and women of color librarians, 255, 375

Shockley, Ann Allen, 18, 35-41, 52

social identity(ies), 11, 240, 340, 395

multiple, 4, 99

intersectionality of, 198-9, 330

social justice, 54, 101, 224, 227, 236, 239, 333, 375-6, 382, 441, 457, 460, 474

definition/meaning of, 331, 335

diversity and, 294, 455

issues of, 349, 442, 459

in LIS, 220, 236, 329, 459, 460

motivations for engaging with, 369-70, 374
and women of color librarians, 356, 383
work of, 330, 349, 363-78, 472
social justice activism, 369-70, 372, 378-9, 382-3
and Black women, 15, 23
in LIS, 371, 373, 375
and WOC librarians, 349, 356, 369, 370, 374-76, 383
special collections, 35, 93, 392, 398, 399
African American, 36, 37, 52
stereotype(s), 43, 101, 164, 167, 200, 204, 263
cultural, 263, 307, 456
librarian, 82, 100, 316
about librarianship, 103, 114, 164, 427
Muslim, 77, 83, 85, 89
racial and gendered, 52, 164, 226, 262, 306
racist, 129, 200, 209, 422
and women of color, 237, 283
support network(s)
and librarianship, 310-1, 344, 381
and women of color, 148, 199
surface acting, 178, 182-3, 277
system(s) of oppression, 4-5, 54, 165, 453, 458
institutional, 333, 334, 342
interconnectedness of, 454-5, 457

T

talented tenth, 49, 50
technology(ies), 100, 104, 113-4, 225, 458, *see also* **Information and Communication Technology (ICT)**
tokenism, 124-5, 184, 188, 210, 435, 437

V

voice(s), 150-2, 201, 360, 438,
Black feminist, 147-8
of Black women, 55, 152, 153, 159
communities of, 337, 341-2
diversity of, 431, 437, 440
of librarians of color, 253, 258, 350
marginalized, 205, 393, 452
metaphor of, 148, 151
of/for Muslim women, 78, 84
silencing and external suppression of, 148, 459
strategic use of, 152, 156
suppression of, 156-59
of/for women of color, 6, 152, 201, 203, 237, 350-55, 375

W

Wells, Ida B., 23
white supremacy, 6, 47-8, 95, 254, 372, 443
whiteness, 53, 340, 344
of librarianship, 6, 34, 45, 53, 257, 334, 371
of librarians, 54, 334, 340-42, 371, 381

of libraries, 46, 52
Williams, Serena, 126-7
women of color (WOC) librarians, 11-2, 30, 93, 148, 158, 255, 259, 280, 283, 307, 322-4,350, 382
and bodily misrecognition, 262, 264
cost of activism for, 355, 383
empowerment of, 354-59
gendered and racialized experience of, 353-4, 360
and identity, 260-1, 303
intersectional experiences of, 269, 303, 320
and self-care, 349, 379
on the tenure/promotion track, 304, 307, 310
womanhood, 16, 54, 201, 204
womanism, 202-04, 235

X

Xicanisma, 203

Z

Zinn, Howard, 393

CPSIA information can be obtained
at www.ICGtesting.com
Printed in the USA
BVHW040535050220
571439BV00003B/6

9 781634 000529